Ius Gentium: Comparative Perspectives on Law and Justice

Volume 57

More information about this series at http://www.springer.com/series/7888

Carlos Iván Fuentes

Normative Plurality in International Law

A Theory of the Determination of Applicable Rules

Springer

Carlos Iván Fuentes
Office of Legal Affairs, United Nations
New York, NY
USA

The views expressed herein are those of the author and do not necessarily reflect the views of the United Nations.

ISSN 1534-6781 ISSN 2214-9902 (electronic)
Ius Gentium: Comparative Perspectives on Law and Justice
ISBN 978-3-319-43927-3 ISBN 978-3-319-43929-7 (eBook)
DOI 10.1007/978-3-319-43929-7

Library of Congress Control Number: 2016947755

Printed on acid-free paper

This Springer imprint is published by Springer Nature
The registered company is Springer International Publishing AG Switzerland

A un tal Lucas

Foreword

This book by Carlos Iván Fuentes—like so many scholarly studies—is the chronicle of a journey. It invites us to accompany the author from the initial intuition that motivated the decision to inquire further, through the tribulations he faced in his path, to the final destination in the form of a theory that provides a suitable explanation of the initial concerns. Very much like Dante, who midway in his life's journey found that the path which led aright was lost, Carlos Iván Fuentes recounts in this book how he came to the realization that the classical theory of sources did not provide him with a suitable framework to understand how the international judge determines the rules applicable to the settlement of a dispute. And very much like Dante, he tells us the story of how, in the vast emptiness in which he found himself, Alf Ross and his Scandinavian form of legal realism would become the Virgil who would guide his way towards a theory of normative plurality.

As the starting point of this journey, Carlos Iván Fuentes chooses two contrasting decisions of the International Court of Justice: one (the advisory opinion on the *Legality of the Threat or Use of Nuclear Weapons*) in which a comprehensive survey of relevant normative instruments still led the Court to the conclusion that ultimately there was no international law applicable to the matter at stake; the other (the judgment on the merits of the *Ahmadou Sadio Diallo* case) in which the Court did not hesitate to seek systemic support for its interpretation of the law applicable to the case in the jurisprudence of various human rights bodies and regional courts. A strict reliance on the traditional theory of sources of international law as taught in our law schools—he finds—does not suffice to explain the divergence in the approaches that the Court adopted in each of these cases. And his intuition, inspired by the jurisprudence of the international law of human rights, is that our attention should be shifted from the sources themselves to the decision-maker. Different normative instruments—he tells us—coexist in an unordered space, so that meaning can be produced by the free interaction of those instruments around a given problem. Decision-makers, therefore, cannot base their activity on a doctrine that limits the possible sources of law, pre-establishing their relative weight and relationship to each other. Instead (and this is where Alf Ross comes for the first time to the rescue), our focus should be on the not objectified factors that precondition the decision-makers' understanding of what constitutes international law in a given case.

Thus Carlos Iván Fuentes invites us to engage in the journey with a deconstruction of the theory of sources from a historical perspective. In his first Chapter, he shows how, from the emergence of international law in the 1600s until the present, scholars have always had recourse to an irreducible non-objectified element to complement their attempts to classify the rules of international law. From divine or natural law in the classics of our discipline to the general principles of law, principles of justice, *jus cogens* or soft law in more recent constructions of the law of nations, there has always been a variable in the equation, an external element which did not fit an objective and ordered set of sources.

He then turns, in his second Chapter, to Article 38 of the Statute of the International Court of Justice, which is nowadays often elevated as a paradigm of the theory of sources in international law. He shows that this Article only provides a general frame of reference, which fails to encompass the normative phenomenon as a whole. Through the detailed review of how the International Court of Justice identified the applicable law in three decisions, Carlos Iván Fuentes shows that the international judge has had resort to a "jurisprudence of incorporation" to frame recent developments of international law into the rigid parameters of the list of sources found in Article 38.

This is when the initial intuition returns with the idea that the jurisprudence of human rights bodies may provide a new paradigm to understand the phenomenon of normativity in international law. In his third chapter, Carlos Iván Fuentes shows how these human rights' bodies have exercised larger freedom in their recourse to a vast array of instruments (resolutions, general comments, recommendations, guidelines, etc.) to complement the meaning of international human rights conventions, which allowed them to develop a set of interpretative tools that was better suited to advancing the protection of human rights in the face of changing circumstances of the international community. As such, they encourage us to liberate ourselves from the strictures of the classical theory of sources to appreciate the determination of the applicable rules of law in its whole dimension.

The theory of normative plurality that ensues is based on Alf Ross's idea that judicial decisions are at least partially determined by a set of free, not formulated, not objectified factors spontaneously arising in the judge as the mouthpiece of the community. In his final Chapter, Carlos Iván Fuentes adjusts the theory to take into account certain recent phenomena of international law: from the original focus on the judicial function, he extends the idea to a broader range of institutions performing advisory or quasi-judicial functions. Then, he further develops the theory, identifying three guiding notions that assist decision-makers in determining the norms that are relevant in a given case, namely: (1) specificity, i.e. the particular tradition that guides decision-makers in determining what constitutes normative information; (2) completeness, or the idea that every international situation is capable of being determined as a matter of law; and (3) purpose, that is the decision-makers' understanding of their role in the international community. These notions allow him to shed light on the socio-psychological process by which decision-makers arrive to their decision, thus bringing out the creative dimension of the judicial or quasi-judicial function in the determination of the rules of law.

This brief personal log of ideas gathered in my own journey through this volume does not render justice to the pages that follow. The true appeal of reading this book lies in letting the author lead our way through the twists and turns of the theory and practice of international law. While our path is generally guided by the compass of normative plurality, this study is actually an exploration of the international judicial function as a whole. Carlos Iván Fuentes has a unique talent in describing with simplicity and rich background knowledge the case-law of judicial bodies as diverse as the International Court of Justice, the International Tribunal for the Law of the Sea, the Inter-American and European Courts of Human Rights or the United Nations Administrative Tribunal. He displays the same ease in dissecting the classics of our discipline (Grotius, Zouche) and the latest theories of realism or critical legal studies, complemented with references to other social sciences. He makes ample use of what I would call "artisanal footnotes", i.e. references that are not automatically generated by legal research software, but rather reveal that what made it to the final text is the result of months of purposeful inquiry and inquisitive flânerie in libraries and texts. Most of all, his realist theory of the determination of applicable rules is built on a solid command of the traditional techniques of international scholarship, such as the study of the preparatory works of a legal text (as shown in his examination of Article 38 of the Statute of the International Court of Justice) or the exegesis of the case-law (as demonstrated in his description of the jurisprudence of incorporation in the second Chapter or of human rights decisions in his third Chapter). At a time when too many authors in the legal literature want to deconstruct without understanding how things are built or try to be Picassos without studying Michelangelo, it is refreshing to read an author who masters both the traditional and modern expressions of our legal language.

But what should we, as international lawyers, take from normative plurality? For the spectators of the judicial (or advisory or quasi-judicial) function, this theory is an invitation to change our perspective in the reading of the case-law of international institutions, freeing ourselves from the strictures of the classical theory of sources to try to assess the full creative power that decision-makers exercise in the determination of the law applicable to a given case. The focus on the notions of specificity, completeness and purpose, in other words, provides us with an opportunity for a different reading of well-known precedents of international law to reveal the socio-psychological factors that influenced them. For those who are in the position of decision-makers (judges, experts, etc.) or are called to participate in the formation of those decisions (counsel of parties, secretariat officials, etc.), the theory is a call to understand our own subjectivity. In his general course at The Hague Academy, Georges Abi-Saab (who was my own Virgil when I engaged in this same exercise of crafting a thesis) claims, citing Gunnar Myrdal, that in legal studies, as in other social sciences, the highest degree of objectivity that scholars may reach is the awareness of their own subjectivities. The theory of normative plurality developed by Carlos Iván Fuentes in this book is a key contribution to this quest.

March 2016 Santiago Villalpando[1]

---

[1]The views expressed in the present contribution are solely those of the author and do not necessarily reflect those of the United Nations.

Acknowledgements

It is hard for me to imagine myself writing anything remotely close to this book if I had not had the support of the exceptional group of people that have directed, have formed part of, or have been associated to the McGill Centre for Human Rights and Legal Pluralism.

The Centre's O'Brien Fellowship on Human Rights and Legal Pluralism provided by the *crucial* financial support to pursue doctoral studies and conduct the research that eventually produced this book. The O'Brien Fellows and other students associated to the Centre provided the collegiality and mutual support needed to endure Montreal's harsh winters and enjoy its glorious summers.

I will be eternally grateful to the members of the Center for the intellectual debts I know I owe them, and for those I suspect I do. Special thanks go to Prof. Evan Fox-Decent, for agreeing—again—to supervise my research and believing in me; and to the Centre's Founding Director, Professor René Provost, who throughout my time at McGill gave me many pieces of advice I will always regret I did not follow.

Throughout my education, the good advice of a number of professors was instrumental for me to get to the point in my life where I believed I could finalize a project of this magnitude: Salvador Sanchez, Alfredo Castillero Hoyos, Isaac Chang Vega, Ingrid Chang Valdez, Jaime Franco, Frédéric Mégret and Richard Janda.

I also wish to thank my colleagues at the United Nations who did not let me forget how important this project was for me: Hafida Lahiouel, Julio A. Baez, Arancha Hinojal, and Fanny Schaus.

Special thanks to my friends and colleagues, Tomoko Iwata, Andrea Truppin, Shawn Stanley, and Victoria Colamarco, who patiently went over drafts of my doctoral dissertation and/or this book, and provided valuable advice along the way.

I must also thank the members of my doctoral committee, the external examiner of my dissertation, and the members oral defence committee for their comments and suggestions.

The semi-final draft of this book was read—virtually at the same time—by my friend and colleague, Santiago Villapando, who had graciously agreed to write the foreword, and by the external reviewer engaged by Springer to evaluate the manuscript. When their comments reach me in December 2015 and January 2016, respectively, I was surprised to see that they were substantially similar. Subsequent lunches and coffees with Santiago made me better understand his and the external reviewer's comments and suggestions and to find a way to address them.

Their comments made me realize—paraphrasing Julio Cortazar—*that this book is many books, but mostly it is two books*. One is about the journey into the realization that modern international legal theory cannot explain the practice of international courts and tribunals, and the other is about a new theory on the application of binding and non-binding instruments by international courts and tribunals. It was panful to move some parts, and even more so to completely cut others; but this has helped to improve the flow of the book. For this reason, I am grateful to Santiago and the external reviewer.

As always, I must thank my parents, Miguel Ángel and Elsie Magaly, for preparing the path that brought me here. I also wish to thank my brothers, Miguel Ángel and Luis Carlos, and my sister, Rosita, who have provided me with emotional support, regardless of the distance.

Finally, I wish to thank again my wife, Tomoko, for the constant encouragement I have received from her since the moment we met.

The views expressed in this book are my own and do not necessarily reflect the views of the United Nations.

Contents

Abbreviations

CBP	Convention of *Belém do Pará*, also known as the Inter-American Convention on the Prevention, Punishment, and Eradication of Violence against Women
CEDAW	Convention on the Elimination of All Forms of Discrimination against Women
CFD	Inter-American Convention on Forced Disappearance of Persons
CRC	Convention of the Rights of the Child
ECHR	European Court of Human Rights
GM	Global Mechanism of the United Nations Convention to Combat Desertification
HRC	Human Rights Committee
IACHR	Inter-American Court of Human Rights
ICCPR	International Covenant on Civil and Political Rights
ICJ	International Court of Justice
ICTR	International Criminal Tribunal for Rwanda
IFAD	International Fund for Agricultural Development
ILC	International Law Commission
ILOAT	International Labour Organization Administrative Tribunal
ITCY	International Criminal Tribunal for the former Yugoslavia
MERCOSUR	Southern Common Market
OAS	Organization of American States
PCIJ	Permanent Court of International Justice
UN	United Nations
UNAT	United Nations Administrative Tribunal (abolished)
UNCCD	United Nations Convention to Combat Desertification
UNCLOS	United Nations Convention on the Law of the Sea
UNESCO	United Nations Educational, Scientific and Cultural Organization
VCLT	Vienna Convention on the Law of Treaties

Table of Cases

International Court of Justice

Permanent Court of International Justice

Inter-American Court of Human Rights

European Court of Human Rights

International and Hybrid Criminal Tribunals

Arbitral Awards

International Administrative Tribunals

Other

Chapter 1
Introduction

Abstract In the introductory chapter, I set the stage by discussing the choices made by the International Court of Justice as to what constituted the law applicable in the Advisory Opinion on the *Legality of the Threat or Use of Nuclear Weapons* and in the case concerning *Ahmadou Sadio Diallo*. I propose that the Court's understanding of what constitutes International Law is preconditioned by the legal tradition in which it operates, the rules that define the scope of its functions, and its own understanding of its role. Then, I explain the content of the following chapters, leading to the normative plurality hypothesis: the practice of international human rights law recognises that different normative instruments coexist in an un-ordered space, and that meaning can be produced by the free interaction of those instruments around a given problem.

1.1 "We Had Nothing Before Us"[1]

On 8 July 1996, the International Court of Justice (hereinafter, ICJ or the Court) delivered its Advisory Opinion on the *Legality of the Threat or Use of Nuclear Weapons*[2] (hereinafter, *Nuclear Weapons*). This Advisory Opinion is rightfully considered both historical and controversial because of the events leading to it and its outcome.[3] It is widely acknowledged that the opinion was the result of intense lobbying by non-governmental organizations at the World Health Organization and the General Assembly of the United Nations (hereinafter, UN).[4] The Advisory Opinion itself was a half-victory for both nuclear and non-nuclear States, and can be

[1]Charles Dickens, A Tale of Two Cities (Cambridge: Chadwyck-Healey, 2000) at 1, online: Literature Online <http://lion.chadwyck.com>.
[2]*Legality of the Threat or Use of Nuclear Weapons*, Advisory Opinion, [1996] ICJ Rep 226 (reprinted in 35 ILM 809) [*Nuclear Weapons*].
[3]See e.g., Richard A. Falk, "Nuclear Weapons, International Law and the World Court: A Historic Encounter" (1997) 91:1 AJIL 64.
[4]Martti Koskenniemi, "Case Analysis: Faith, Identity, and the Killing of the Innocent: International Lawyers and Nuclear Weapons" (1997) 10:01 Leiden J Int'l L 137 [Koskenniemi, "Killing of the Innocent"].

C.I. Fuentes, *Normative Plurality in International Law*,
Ius Gentium: Comparative Perspectives on Law and Justice 57,
DOI 10.1007/978-3-319-43929-7_1

seen as either "hopelessly misguided or brilliantly politic."[5] At the very least, it remains the only Advisory Opinion in the history of the ICJ in which every sitting judge delivered a declaration, a separate opinion or a dissenting opinion.

The General Assembly asked a straightforward question—"Is the threat or use of nuclear weapons in any circumstance permitted under international law?"[6]—which required the Court to conduct a thorough review of the existing international law at the time. Instead of giving a straightforward answer, the Court's reply to the question was presented in six operative paragraphs. In the first two paragraphs, the Court found that there was neither—A—a specific authorization nor—B—a comprehensive and universal prohibition of the threat or use of nuclear weapons in customary or conventional international law. The Judges' votes reflect the prevailing opinion at the time: the Court decided unanimously with regards to the lack of specific authorization, but only by majority with regards to the absence of comprehensive and universal prohibition.

Not having found a rule explicitly created to deal with the use or threat of use of nuclear weapons, the Court went on to explore the relevant rules in the context of war. That is, the Court addressed the issue of whether such use is compatible with *jus ad bellum* and *jus in bello*. In so doing, the Court rejected several arguments based on international human rights law and environmental law,[7] which were raised by some States during the public hearings.

The next two operative paragraphs of the opinion set the basis for analysis of the use or threat of use of nuclear weapons in the context of war. In paragraph C, the Court stated that any nuclear attack in violation of the UN Charter's prohibition of aggression or which failed to meet the requirements for self-defence was unlawful. Then, in paragraph D, the Court found that the use of nuclear weapons should be compatible with the laws applicable to armed conflict, giving special attention to international humanitarian law. Both paragraphs were unanimously adopted, as they simply stated the terms of the discussion for the decision of the Court. However, the dissenting opinions show that this paragraph was the minimum common denominator.

Under the premises set forth in the previous paragraphs, the Court stated in paragraph E that, while the threat or use of nuclear weapons would generally violate

---

[5]Burns H. Weston, "Nuclear weapons and the World Court: ambiguity's consensus" (1997) 7:2 Transnat'l L & Contemp Probs 371 at 372.

[6]Request for an advisory opinion from the International Court of Justice on the legality of the threat or use of nuclear weapons, GA Res. 49/75[K], UN GAOR, 49th Sess., Supp. No. 49, UN Doc. A/RES/49/75[K] (1994) 71.

[7]For example, Australia argued the illegality of the use of nuclear weapons on the basis of, *inter alia*, international environmental law, *Legality of the Threat or Use of Nuclear Weapons Case*, "Verbatim Record of the Public sitting" (30 October 1995) at 46–48, online: International Court of Justice <http://www.icj-cij.org/docket/files/95/5925.pdf>; while Malaysia made use of international human rights instruments to develop the same argument *Legality of the Threat or Use of Nuclear Weapons Case*, "Verbatim Record of the Public sitting" (7 November 1995) at p 55–56, online: International Court of Justice <http://www.icj-cij.org/docket/files/95/5935.pdf>.

the principles and rules of international humanitarian law, it "cannot conclude definitively whether the threat or use of nuclear weapons would be lawful or unlawful in an extreme circumstance of self-defence, in which the very survival of the State would be at stake."[8] The Court split seven-seven on this point, and, for the second time in its history, the Court had to decide a point in an Advisory Opinion by the President's casting vote.[9]

What paragraph E means in legal terms is unclear. Judge Vladlen S. Vereshchetin and the then President of the Court, Judge Mohammed Bedjaoui, stated in their respective declarations that paragraph E cannot be read as a "finding either in favour of or against the legality of the threat or use of nuclear weapons".[10] However, as Judge Mohamed Shahabuddeen stated in his dissenting opinion, "[i]f the Court is in a position in which it cannot definitively say whether or not a prohibitory rule exists, the argument can be made that, on the basis of that case, the presumption is in favour of the right of States to act unrestrained by any such rule."[11]

1.2 "We Had Everything Before Us"[12]

On 30 November 2010, the ICJ delivered its judgment on the merits in the case concerning *Ahmadou Sadio Diallo* (hereinafter, *Diallo*).[13] The case, which had been in litigation before the Court for over a decade, attracted the attention of academics as a case of diplomatic protection of foreign investors,[14] and in some respects as an opportunity to further clarify certain aspects of the customary law of diplomatic protection[15] as presented by the Court in the *Barcelona Traction* case[16] as well as in the International Law Commission's (hereinafter, ILC) Draft Articles on Diplomatic

[8]*Nuclear Weapons, supra* note 2 at para 105.2.E.

[9]The only other case was: *South West Africa (Ethiopia v. South Africa; Liberia v. South Africa)*, Second Phase, [1966] ICJ Rep 6 (reprinted in 5 ILM 932).

[10]*Nuclear Weapons, supra* note 2 at p 272 (Declaration of President Bedjaoui).

[11]Ibid at 426 (Dissenting Opinion of Judge Shahabuddeen).

[12]Dickens, supra note 1 at 1.

[13]*Ahmadou Sadio Diallo (Republic of Guinea v. Democratic Republic of the Congo)*, Merits, Judgment, [2010] ICJ Rep 639 (reprinted in 50 ILM 40) [*Ahmadou Sadio Diallo*, Merits].

[14]See, e.g. S.J. Knight and A.J. O'Brien, "Ahmadou Sadio Diallo-Republic of Guinea v. Democratic Republic of The Congo-Clarifying the Scope of Diplomatic Protection of Corporate and Shareholder Rights" (2008) 9 Melb J Int'l L 151.

[15]Annemarieke Vermeer-Künzli, "Diallo and the Draft Articles: The Application of the Draft Articles on Diplomatic Protection in the Ahmadou Sadio Diallo Case" (2007) 20:04 Leiden J Int'l L 941.

[16]*Case Concerning the Barcelona Traction, Light and Power Company, Limited, (Belgium v. Spain)*, (Second Phase), [1970] ICJ Rep 3 [*Barcelona Traction*].

Protection.[17] However, "the case became transformed in substance into a human rights protection case instead of one involving the diplomatic protection of a national under the law of state responsibility for the treatment of aliens."[18]

According to the Application of the Republic of Guinea to the Court, Mr. Ahmadou Sadio Diallo, a businessman of Guinean nationality who had been a resident in the Democratic Republic of the Congo for over three decades, was unjustly imprisoned, despoiled of his investments, businesses, property and bank accounts, and then expelled from the Democratic Republic of the Congo by the authorities of that country.[19] Allegedly, these acts occurred because Mr. Ahmadou Sadio Diallo was pursuing recovery of "substantial debts owed to his businesses [specifically, two limited liability companies: Africom-Zaire and Africacontainers-Zaire] by the State and by the oil companies established on its territory and of which the State is a shareholder."[20]

In its memorial, the Republic of Guinea claimed to be Mr. Diallo's diplomatic "protector, and also the protector of the companies which he founded and owns",[21] and requested reparations for the damages caused to Mr. Diallo himself and to Africom-Zaire and Africacontainers-Zaire. The few references to Mr. Diallo's human rights in the Republic of Guinea's application instituting proceedings pale in contrast to the assertions of his financial losses as a result of his expulsion from the Democratic Republic of the Congo.[22]

In the Preliminary Objections' judgment, the Court had already decided that Guinea had no standing to offer diplomatic protection to Africom-Zaire or to Africacontainers-Zaire,[23] and therefore found the case admissible only "in so far as

---

[17] *Report of the International Law Commission*: *Fifty-eight session*, UNGAOR, 61st Sess, Supp. No. 10, UN Doc A/61/10 (2006) at para 49 (reference is made to the text of the Draft Articles on Diplomatic Protection and Commentaries, adopted by the ILC on Second Reading) [*Report of the ILC, 58th session*].

[18] Sandy Ghandhi, "Human Rights and the International Court of Justice The Ahmadou Sadio Diallo Case" (2011) 11:3 Hum Rights Law Rev 527 at 528.

[19] *Ahmadou Sadio Diallo* (*Republic of Guinea v. Democratic Republic of the Congo*), "Application instituting proceedings", at p 3, online: International Court of Justice <http://www.icj-cij.org/docket/files/103/7175.pdf>.

[20] Ibid.

[21] Ibid, at p 33.

[22] Bruno Simma "Human Rights before the International Court of Justice: Community Interest Coming to Life?" in Holger Hestermeyer et al., *Coexistence, cooperation and solidarity*: *Liber Amicorum Rüdiger Wolfrum* (Leiden: Martinus Nijhoff Publishers, 2012) 577 at 593 [Simma, "Community Interest"].

[23] According to the ILC Draft Articles in: "[a] State of nationality of shareholders in a corporation shall not be entitled to exercise diplomatic protection in respect of such shareholders in the case of an injury to the corporation unless: [...] (*b*) The corporation had, at the date of injury, the nationality of the State alleged to be responsible for causing the injury, and incorporation in that State was required by it as a precondition for doing business there" *Report of the ILC, 58th session*, *supra* note 17 at para 49 (art 11); the Court found no evidence that such requirement existed in the Democratic Republic of the Congo at the time, *Ahmadou Sadio Diallo* (*Republic of Guinea v. Democratic Republic of the Congo*), Preliminary Objections, Judgment, [2007] ICJ Rep 582 at paras 86–94 [*Ahmadou Sadio Diallo*, Preliminary Objections].

it concerns protection of Mr. Diallo's rights as an individual [...and...] Mr. Diallo's direct rights as *associé* in Africom-Zaire and Africontainers-Zaire"[24] The Court would eventually rule that Democratic Republic of the Congo did not violate Mr. Diallo's direct rights as *associé* in the aforementioned companies.[25] However, the Court discussed at length the possible violation of Mr. Diallo's individual rights, in the light of the International Covenant on Civil and Political Rights (hereinafter, ICCPR),[26] the African Charter on Human and Peoples' Rights, (hereinafter, the Banjul Charter)[27] and the Vienna Convention on Consular Relations.[28]

In the course of the analysis of the possible violation to Mr. Diallo's right not to be illegally or arbitrarily expelled from the Democratic Republic of the Congo under ICCPR[29] and the African Charter,[30] the Court stated that its interpretation of the aforementioned instruments "is fully corroborated by the jurisprudence of the Human Rights Committee"[31] (hereinafter, HRC) and "consonant with the case law of the African Commission on Human and Peoples' Rights".[32]

The point has been made that although the ICJ is not a human rights tribunal,[33] the *Diallo* case is unique because it dealt with the violation of the individual rights of a person under both universal and a regional human rights conventions, as well as a UN codification convention.[34] Above and beyond that, "the extent to which the Court took human rights protection on board in the judgment marks a sea

---

[24]*Ahmadou Sadio Diallo*, Preliminary Objections, ibid at p 617 and 618.

[25]*Ahmadou Sadio Diallo*, Merits, *supra* note 13 at p 693.

[26]*International Covenant on Civil and Political Rights*, 16 December 1966, 999 UNTS 171, (1967) 6 ILM 368 [*ICCPR*].

[27]African Charter on Human and Peoples' Rights, 27 June 1981, 1520 UNTS 271, (1982) 21 ILM 58 [*African Charter*].

[28]*Vienna Convention on Consular Relations*, 24 April 1963, 596 UNTS 261 [*VCCR*].

[29]"An alien lawfully in the territory of a State Party to the present Covenant may be expelled therefrom only in pursuance of a decision reached in accordance with law and shall, except where compelling reasons of national security otherwise require, be allowed to submit the reasons against his expulsion and to have his case reviewed by, and be represented for the purpose before, the competent authority or a person or persons especially designated by the competent authority", *ICCPR*, *supra* note 26 at art 13.

[30]"A non-national legally admitted in a territory of a State Party to the present Charter, may only be expelled from it by virtue of a decision taken in accordance with the law", *African Charter*, *supra* note 27 at art 12.4.

[31]*Ahmadou Sadio Diallo*, Merits, *supra* note 13 at para 66.

[32]Ibid at para 67.

[33]See Ghandhi, *supra* note 18 at 528.

[34]*Ahmadou Sadio Diallo*, Merits, *supra* note 13 at p 730–732 (Separate Opinion of Judge Cançado Trindade); however, Judge Simma has noted that "the *Congo v. Uganda* Judgment of 2005 [is] the first judgment in the Court's history in which a finding of human rights violations, combined with findings of violations of international humanitarian law, was included in the *dispositif*", Simma, "Community Interest", *supra* note 22 at 591; indeed the Court found that "the Republic of Uganda, by the conduct of its armed forces [...]; as well as by its failure, as an occupying Power, to take measures to respect and ensure respect for human rights and international humanitarian law in Ituri district, violated its obligations under international human rights law and international

change."[35] One of the judges sitting in the *Diallo* case has recently noted that the Court:

> [E]ngages in straightforward assessments of breaches of human rights treaty provisions and in so doing expressly refers to, and follows, the jurisprudence of UN and regional monitoring bodies, without engaging in any of the exercises in coyness that had marked the Court's relationship with other international courts and tribunals before[36]

In fact, throughout the judgment, the Court made reference—surprisingly, without quoting their text or analysing their content[37]—to two decisions of the African Commission, a recommendation of the HRC on a petition, and two of its General Comments as well as the interpretation by the European Court of Human Rights (hereinafter, ECHR or the European Court) and the Inter-American Court of Human Rights (hereinafter, IACHR or the Inter-American Court) of the instruments of their respective systems containing analogous rights.[38]

This is not, however, without a caveat. The Court apparently saw the need to explain and justify the use of the precedent by the HRC:

> Although the Court is in no way obliged, in the exercise of its judicial functions, to model its own interpretation of the Covenant on that of the Committee, it believes that it should ascribe great weight to the interpretation adopted by this independent body that was established specifically to supervise the application of that treaty. The point here is to achieve the necessary clarity and the essential consistency of international law, as well as legal security, to which both the individuals with guaranteed rights and the States obliged to comply with treaty obligations are entitled.[39]

As it appears that the Court is concerned with the possibility of fragmentation in the interpretation of international human rights instruments, it has been noted by many authors that a dialogue between the Court and other Human Rights bodies and tribunals seems to have started and that "the question [of] how the Court will deal with the jurisprudence of specialised human rights courts and treaty bodies will pose itself with greater frequency".[40]

(Footnote 34 continued)

humanitarian law", *Armed Activities on the Territory of the Congo* (*Democratic Republic of the Congo v. Uganda*), [2005] ICJ Rep 168 at p 280.

[35]Eirik Bjorge, *Ahmadou Sadio Diallo* (*Republic of Guinea v. Democratic Republic of The Congo*), 105 AJIL 534 at 539.

[36]Bruno Simma, "Mainstreaming Human Rights: The Contribution of the International Court of Justice" (2012) 3:1 J Int. Disp. Settlement 7 at 20–21 [Simma, "Mainstreaming"].

[37]See Ghandhi, *supra* note 18 at 533 ("What is surprising is that no analysis is made of either the Maroufidou case or assessment of the parameters of General Comment No. 15 [on 'The position of aliens under the Covenant']").

[38]*American Convention on Human Rights*, 22 November 1969, 36 OASTS 1, 1144 UNTS 123; *ICCPR*, *supra* note 26; *European Convention for the Protection of Human Rights and Fundamental Freedoms*, Europ TS No 5, 213 UNTS 211.

[39]*Ahmadou Sadio Diallo*, Merits, *supra* note 13 at para 68.

[40]Simma, "Mainstreaming", *supra* note 36 at 25.

1.3 Normative Plurality in International Law

It is not my intention to discuss whether nuclear weapons are legal under current international law or whether the ICJ's interpretation of Article 13 of the ICCPR expanded its scope beyond the intentions of the drafters of the Covenant. Instead, I wish to focus on the process followed by the Court to find the relevant law to apply in reaching its findings. The opinion of the ICJ in the *Nuclear Weapons* advisory opinion is an interesting example for illustrating this inquiry because the question was open enough for the Court to make a complete survey of the international law on disarmament as well as branches of international law which could potentially deal with the possible consequences of the use of nuclear weapons. Indeed, in its analysis, the Court referred directly or indirectly to thirty-six treaties on diverse topics, extensively discussed customary international humanitarian law and the customary law of self-defence, explored the possibility of a customary law of nuclear disarmament, reviewed the general principles of neutrality and proportionality, and quoted three Security Council resolutions, six General Assembly resolutions, and six declarations of various specialised conferences. However, the ICJ not only failed to fully answer the question asked by the General Assembly, but, in so doing, implied that there is no international law applicable to the use of nuclear weapons in an extreme circumstance of self-defence. As Prosper Weil has put it, "[n]o lawyer would readily accept the idea that on whatever matter—and even more so on a matter of such an importance—international law has nothing to say, and the I.C.J. nothing to conclude."[41]

While the ICJ may have determined that there was no clear answer to the problem within the numerous rules and principles that they quoted in their decision, lawyers specializing in international humanitarian law would not necessarily agree.[42] Arguably, international humanitarian law has sufficient principles and customary norms which would make the use of nuclear weapons illegal.[43] A similar claim could be made by environmental and human rights lawyers regarding their respective areas of expertise. The minority of the Court did consider that "there was

---

[41]Prosper Weil, "'The Court cannot conclude definitively…' *non liquet* revisited" (1997) 36 Colum J Transnat'l L 109 [Weil, "*Non liquet* revisited"].

[42]In its study on Customary International Humanitarian Law, which was mandated in 1995 and concluded in 2004, the International Committee of the Red Cross "had to take due note of the Court's Opinion [on *Nuclear Weapons*] and deemed it not appropriate to engage in a similar exercise at virtually the same time." The same study found that "although the existence [of] the rule prohibiting indiscriminate weapons is not contested, there are differing views on whether the rule itself renders a weapon illegal or whether a weapon is illegal if a specific treaty or customary rules prohibits its use." Jean-Marie Henckaerts and Louise Doswald-Beck, eds., *Customary international humanitarian law* (Cambridge: Cambridge University Press, 2005) at 248 and 255.

[43]Commenting briefly about the Advisory Opinion on the occasion of the general debate on all disarmament and international security agenda items at the First Committee of the General Assembly of the United Nations on its 51st session, the ICRC found it "difficult to envisage how a use of nuclear weapons could be compatible with the rules of international law", UN C1OR, 51st Sess., 8th Mtg., UN Doc. A/C.1/51/PV.8 (1996) at p 10.

sufficient legal and factual basis on which the Court could have proceeded to answer the General Assembly's question—one way or another."[44] However, such considerations were based on the content of the instruments, customary rules—or lack of thereof—, and general principles that the Court relied on. Little has been said about the norms and principles that were not used.[45] In this sense, the material outcome of this Advisory Opinion, or of any decision of the ICJ for that matter, was dependent on the factors that preconditioned the choice as to what constitutes international law and where to find it.

As simple as this conclusion might seem, it raises a plethora of scenarios in which the opinion of the Court might have been different. What if the General Assembly resolutions are enough to prove the existence of a customary rule, in the absence of the conditions necessary for meaningful practice to develop?[46] What if the Non-Proliferation regime could be taken as State practice? What if International Humanitarian Law were part of *jus cogens*? Lawyers are taught that the answers to these and many other questions are to be found in the doctrine of sources of international law, or in the diverse theories that attempt to justify it.[47] Interestingly, the ICJ has never spoken about a 'doctrine of sources' or a 'theory of sources.' In fact, the ICJ has referred to the sources of international law in a handful of cases,[48] while ICJ's predecessor, the Permanent Court of International Justice (hereinafter, PCIJ or the Permanent Court) used the phrase 'sources of law' only in the advisory

---

[44]*Nuclear Weapons*, *supra* note 2 at p 428 (Dissenting Opinion of Judge Shahabuddeen).

[45]Louise Doswald-Beck, "International humanitarian law and the Advisory Opinion of the International Court of Justice on the legality of the threat or use of nuclear weapons" (1997) 316 Int'l Rev. Red Cross 35 (indicating that the Court should have used the principle of prohibition of indiscriminate weapons instead of the one that prohibits weapons that cause excessive suffering).

[46]It is noted that the International Law Commission, on its recent work on the identification of customary international law, has proposed draft conclusion on the significance of resolutions of international organizations and intergovernmental conferences for the identification of a customary norm: *Report of the International Law Commission*: *Sixty-seventh session*, UNGAOR, 70th Sess, Supp. No. 10, UN Doc A/70/10 (2015) at para 83 and 84 (The draft conclusions provisionally adopted by the Drafting Committee for the topic of Identification of customary international law are available under symbol A/CN.4/L.869) [*Report of the ILC*, *67th session*].

[47]Oscar Schachter, "Towards a Theory of International Obligation" in Stephen M. Schwebel, ed., *The Effectiveness of international decisions*; *papers of a conference of the American Society of International Law and the proceedings of the conference* (Leiden: Sijthoff, 1971) 9 at 9–10 [Schachter, "International Obligation"].

[48]"Sources of law" in *North Sea Continental Shelf*, (*Federal Republic of Germany v. Denmark*; *Federal Republic of Germany v. Netherlands*), [1969] ICJ Rep 3 at para 36; "legal sources" in *Continental Shelf* (*Tunisia v. Libyan Arab Jamahiriya*), [1982] ICJ Rep 18 at para 22; "sources of international law" in *Military and Paramilitary Activities in and against Nicaragua* (*Nicaragua v. United States of America*), Merits, [1986] ICJ Rep 14 at para 56 and 178 (reprinted in 25 ILM 1023) [*Nicaragua*, Merits]; "source of the rule of law" in *Application for Review of Judgment No. 333 of the United Nations Administrative Tribunal*, Advisory Opinion, [1987] ICJ Rep 18 at para 72; "source of applicable law" in *Maritime Delimitation in the Area between Greenland and Jan Mayen*, Judgment, [1993] ICJ Rep 38 at para 44; and "source of law" in *Nuclear Weapons*, *supra* note 2 at para 64.

opinion on the *Treatment of Polish Nationals and Other Persons of Polish Origin or Speech in the Danzig Territory*.[49]

The judgment of the ICJ in the *Diallo* case is illustrative of a developing trend in the Court, specifically in international human rights law, since for most of its history it had relied only on its own precedent or that of arbitral tribunals.[50] Although before *Diallo* the ICJ had cited the International Criminal Tribunals for the former Yugoslavia (hereinafter, ICTY) and Rwanda (hereinafter, ICTR) in matters of law and fact, it was to state that the Court "found itself unable to subscribe to the [ICTY Appeals] Chamber's view" in matters of general international law.[51] Specifically, the Court could not agree with the characterization of armed conflicts and the imputability of acts under the law of State responsibility expressed in the Appeals Chamber's Decision on the Defense Motion for Interlocutory Appeal on Jurisdiction in the case against *Duško Tadić* (hereinafter, *Tadić*).[52]

A decade and half after *Nuclear Weapons*, the Court found that when it has been asked to determine whether there was a violation to a regional human rights instrument "it must take due account of the interpretation of that instrument adopted by the independent bodies which have been specifically created [...] to monitor the sound application of the treaty in question"[53] The Court, however, went beyond that and applied the precedent of other independent regional bodies, namely the ECHR, IACHR, to instruments adopted in their respective systems. This is remarkable considering that an argument could be made for the need to restrict the use of the interpretation of regional tribunals to regional treaties in cases outside their territorial

---

[49] *Treatment of Polish Nationals and Other Persons of Polish Origin or Speech in the Danzig Territory* (1932), Advisory Opinion, PCIJ (Ser. A/B) No. 44 at p 19.

[50] See Gilbert Guillaume, *The Use of Precedent by International Judges and Arbitrators*, (2011) 2:1 at J Int Disp Settlement 5 at 19 [Although not entirely true at the moment of the publication of the lecture, which was delivered five months before the *Diallo* judgment was handed down, Judge Guillaume stated that "[i]n fact, the Court's policy of precedent essentially aims to assure a constructive dialogue with arbitration tribunals dealing with interstate disputes, primarily in border disputes"]; its is noted that in 2012, in a case concerning maritime borders, the Court cited a judgment of the International Tribunal for the Law of the sea: *Territorial and Maritime Dispute (Nicaragua v. Colombia)*, Merits, [2012] ICJ Rep 624 at paras. 178 and 241, citing *Delimitation of the maritime boundary in the Bay of Bengal (Bangladesh/Myanmar)*, Judgment, [2012] ITLOS Rep 4 at paras 169 and 499.

[51] *Application of the Convention on the Prevention and Punishment of the Crime of Genocide (Bosnia and Herzegovina v. Serbia and Montenegro)*, Merits, Judgment, [2007] ICJ Rep 43 at para 403 (reprinted in 46 ILM 188).

[52] *The Prosecutor v. Duško Tadić (Prijedor Case)*, IT-94-1, Decision on the Defense Motion for Interlocutory Appeal on Jurisdiction (2 October 1995) (International Tribunal for the Former Yugoslavia, Appeals Chamber).

[53] *Ahmadou Sadio Diallo*, Merits, *supra* note 13 at para 67.

jurisdiction.[54] Judge Gilbert Guillaume, speaking shortly before the judgment in the *Diallo* case was rendered, stated that the Court "always abstained itself from the smallest reference to the rationales employed by the regional jurisdictions."[55] In contrast, the view expressed by Judge Antônio A. Cançado Trindade, in his separate opinion in *Diallo*, identifies the Court's use of the precedent of the regional human rights systems as a turning point in its jurisprudence, as the Court "has gone much further, beyond the United Nations system, in acknowledging the contribution of the jurisprudential construction of two other international tribunals, the [IACHR] and the [ECHR]."[56]

*

As Weil has put it:

> Le problème des sources est au carrefour de toutes les grandes controverses du droit international, quintessence et révélateur des pensées et des arrière-pensées. Tous les chemins du droit international partent de là, tous y mènent.[57]

The substantive issues raised both in *Nuclear Weapons* and *Diallo* are immensely important in international law. Arguably, the subject matter of *Nuclear Weapons* is crucial for the collective existence, as we currently know it, of the human race. In *Nuclear Weapons*, there were clear attempts to frame the consequences of the use of nuclear weapons as a matter governed by international human rights law or international humanitarian law. In the end, the opinion of the Court framed the issues therein through the optic of the freedom of States.

Diallo, on the other hand, while seemingly pedestrian in some aspects, opened the question of what States can do to protect their nationals from the actions of other States. Although it did not begin as a case on the protection of an individual's human rights, by the end, all claims related to the rights of Mr. Diallo concerning the financial loses of his companies were dismissed,[58] and the focus had shifted

---

[54]See Mads Andenas, "International Court of Justice, Case Concerning Ahmadou Sadio Diallo (Republic Of Guinea v. Democratic Republic Of The Congo) Judgment of 30 November 2010" (2011) 60 ICLQ 810 at 817; see also Gentian Zyberi, *The Humanitarian Face of the International Court of Justice: Its Contribution to Interpreting and Developing International Human Rights and Humanitarian Law Rules and Principles* (Antwerpen: Intersentia, 2008) at 406 ("Besides other factors related to these courts different jurisdictions and the different ways cases are argued before them, the ICJ might also want to avoid any possible criticism of regional bias").

[55]Guillaume, *supra* note 50 at 19–20; *contra* Zyberi, ibid at 395 (suggesting that the first reference to the ECHR was made in para 91 of *Barcelona Traction*).

[56]*Ahmadou Sadio Diallo*, Merits, *supra* note 13 at p 811; "in this regard the Diallo Judgment is a positive example to follow", Simma, "Mainstreaming", *supra* note 36 at 25.

[57]Prosper Weil, "Le droit international en quête de son identité: cours général de droit international public" (1992) 237 Rec des Cours 11 at 133 [Weil, "Cours général"].

[58]In this regard, Judge Simma has noted that "the human rights aspects rose like a phoenix from the ashes of the case, if I am allowed this rather unflattering metaphor, and enjoyed equal rank if not priority both in the Parties pleadings and in the final Judgment of the Court", Simma, "Community Interest", *supra* note 22 at 593.

almost entirely to his rights as a legally admitted alien in the Democratic Republic of the Congo.[59]

Leaving substantive issues aside, both *Nuclear Weapons* and *Diallo* raise interesting questions from the point of view of international adjudication. My particular interest in both lies in the Court's use of what I perceive to be a different measure of legal authority for different types of disputes. Although *Nuclear Weapons* was based on an open question about the legality—or lack thereof—of a certain State activity, it is my view that the set of sources used to arrive at the conclusions was a rather restricted one. I argue that this is due to the fact that the Court ultimately viewed the opinion as one that turns on issues dealing with the freedom of States. In *Diallo*, the Court not only saw fit to support its own interpretation of the ICCPR and the African Charter with that of the HRC and the African Commission, but also confirmed that other regional human rights tribunals subscribed to such an interpretation when applying similar international instruments. This fairly comprehensive interpretative procedure followed by the Court contrasts with the relatively narrow legal question before it: whether the actions of the Democratic Republic of the Congo were in line with the ICCPR and the African Charter.

* *

For the time being, *Diallo* has exhausted its illustrative purpose, as I will argue later that it presents discrete but interesting advances in the issue of sources applicable to international human rights law. This is not necessarily because it is a novel way to construct meaning in international human rights law, but because it is the first time that the ICJ has itself gone through such a process in a contentious case. For the remainder of this introduction, I will focus on the understanding of the sources of international law within the framework of and from the point of view of the judicial function of the ICJ, as seen through the lens of the *Nuclear Weapons* Advisory Opinion. For this, I will use law in its past, present, and future phases—in the form of legal traditions, regulations, and the role of law—to analyse *Nuclear Weapons* and the decisions made therein as to what constitutes law.

In my opinion, the ICJ's understanding of what constitutes International Law is preconditioned by the following interdependent aspects:

- the legal tradition in which it operates;
- the rules that define the scope of its functions; and
- its own understanding of its role.

---

[59] Although, a recent trend on international investment law argues that "certain material standards of [international investment law] can be conceptualized to be human rights-like guarantees of a minimum standard of protection", see e.g. Nicolas Klein, "Human Rights and International Investment Law: Investment Protection as Human Right" (2012) 4 Gottingen J Int'l L 179 at 181; see also, Bruno Simma, "Foreign Investment Arbitration: A Place for Human Rights?" (2011) 60:3 ICLQ 573 at 576 ("After all, the ultimate concern at the basis of both areas of international law is one and the same: the protection of the individual against the power of the State"); Human Rights, Trade and Investment, Report of the High Commissioner for Human Rights, UN Doc No. E/CN.4/Sub.2/2003/9 (2 July 2003) at para 24.

The ICJ is one of the main organs of the UN. It was preceded by the PCIJ, which was established pursuant to the Covenant of the League of Nations.[60] Much of the Statute of the ICJ is taken from the PCIJ's, which was drafted in the early 1920s.[61] In this sense, the ICJ is the most prominent form of a tradition of international adjudication that started with the PCIJ, as opposed to a tradition of arbitration embodied by the still existing Permanent Court of Arbitration.[62]

In its relatively short history, the PCIJ expressed its opinion about the rules of international law applicable to its judicial function, specifically in the merits decision on *The Case of the S.S. "Lotus"*. In the view of the Permanent Court, the very nature of international law is to regulate the interactions between States as independent entities; "[t]he rules of law binding upon States therefore emanate from their own free will..."[63] That is, international law arises exclusively from the consent of the State. The ICJ has not expressly adopted the cited dictum of the *Lotus* case in its jurisprudence, but the Court has not expressly rejected it either. In fact, there are very few cases in which the Court used sources not emanating from express or tacit consent of the States,[64] and when States have agreed on the status and nature of an instrument, the Court has accepted it as proposed without further analysis.[65]

Needless to say, the tradition of international adjudication in which the ICJ operates is framed in a larger tradition of international law. It has been argued that

[60] "The intention in 1946 was that there should be continuity between the new Court and the old Court." Robert Y. Jennings, "General Introduction" in Andreas Zimmermann, Christian Tomuschat and Karin Oellers-Frahm, eds., *The Statute of the International Court of Justice: A Commentary* (Oxford: Oxford University Press, 2006) 1 at 4.

[61] "[T]he Statute of the International Court of Justice was firmly based upon the final version of the Statute of its predecessor; the arrangement and even the numbering of the Articles being largely parallel in both versions." Ibid; for the specific changes see Ole Spiermann, "Historical Introduction" in Zimmermann, Tomuschat and Oellers-Frahm, ibid, 39 at 61–62.

[62] "The distinction between arbitration and adjudication related to national law: adjudication implemented ideals of a court taken from national legal systems, whereas, from the perspective of those systems, arbitration was exceptional, consensual and ad hoc." Spiermann, ibid at 41–44; See also Ole Spiermann, *International legal argument in the Permanent Court of International Justice: the rise of the international judiciary* (Cambridge: Cambridge University Press, 2005) at 3–14.

[63] *The Case of the S.S. "Lotus" (France v. Turkey)* (1927), PCIJ (Ser. A) No. 10 at 18.

[64] See e.g., *Reparations for Injuries Suffered in the Service of the United Nations*, Advisory Opinion, [1949] ICJ Rep 174 at 182 ("The Court is here faced with a new situation. The question to which it gives rise can only be solved by realizing that the situation is dominated by the provisions of the Charter considered in the light of the principles of international law"); *Fisheries (United Kingdom v. Norway)*, [1951] ICJ Rep 116 at 132 ("It does not at all follow that, in the absence of rules having the technically precise character alleged by the United Kingdom Government, the delimitation undertaken by the Norwegian Government in 1935 is not subject to certain principles which make it possible to judge as to its validity under international law").

[65] *Maritime Dispute (Peru v. Chile)*, [2014] ICJ Rep 3 at paras 48 and 57 (in para. 48, the Court observed that "it is no longer contested that the 1952 Santiago Declaration is an international treaty", and then, in para. 57 it was of the view that it "is required to analyse the terms of the 1952 Santiago Declaration in accordance with the customary international law of treaty interpretation").

statements such as those found in the *Lotus* case reveal the deep entanglement between international legal thinking and a 'liberal theory of politics', by which the sovereignty of the State is understood as analogous to liberty in the liberal discourse.[66] A legal order which is ultimately defined by and in reference to the individual and equal liberty of its members will necessarily be ruled by a law of coordination.[67]

Undeniably, consent has played an essential role in the making of international law since long before the existence of the PCIJ.[68] However, it would be naïve to say that no other factors have had relevance in the making of international law throughout history, especially since current times are witness to "a dynamic process in which sovereignty is being complemented, and eventually replaced, by a new normative foundation of international law."[69] However, this speaks to the dynamic aspect of the tradition. There is something to be said about the rules that govern the function of the Court and how they interact with the tradition of international law. In particular, I refer to the Statute of the ICJ. The rules found therein represent the state of the tradition of international law at a certain point of time, either by stating the settled doctrine or by incorporating recent developments.[70] By virtue of their crystallization in an authoritative document and their intended normative effect, the rules defining the function of the Court shape the content of its decisions[71] and,

---

[66]Martti Koskenniemi, *From apology to Utopia: the structure of international legal argument* (Cambridge: Cambridge University Press, 2005) at 300 [Koskenniemi, *From apology*].

[67]"Essentially, international law is a law of co-ordination, not, as is most national law, a law of subordination. The expression law of co-ordination means that its own actors have created and apply it between themselves, and are responsible for enforcing it"; Shabtai Rosenne, *The perplexities of modern international law* (Leiden: Martinus Nijhoff, 2004) at 15 [Rosenne, *The perplexities*].

[68]"The Westphalia conception of international order rest upon the essential role of consent in the process of forming international obligations. The [United Nations'] Charter conception superficially respects, or at least contains nothing to contradict, this traditional mode of law-creation"; Richard A. Falk, "The Interplay of Westphalia and Charter Conceptions of the International Legal Order" in Cyril Edwin Black and Richard A. Falk, eds., *The Future of the international legal order* (Princeton: Princeton University Press, 1969) at 55. See also, Hans Kelsen, "Les rapports de système entre le droit interne et le droit international public" (1926) 14 Rec des Cours 227. ("toute cette théorie des « sources » n'est qu'une paraphrase de la théorie bien connue de l'auto-limitation de l'État, suivant laquelle l'État ne pourrait être obligé que par sa propre volonté") [Kelsen, "Droit interne et le droit international public"].

[69]Anne Peters, "Humanity as the A and {Omega} of Sovereignty" (2009) 20:3 EJIL 513 at 514.

[70]Reference is made to the wording of the: *Statute of the International Law Commission*, GA Res. 174 (II), UN GAOR, 2nd Sess., UN Doc. A/RES/174 (II) at art 15.

[71]"The judicial function in the international sphere has emerged as a third party alongside states and derives its power from the act that created the organ. It can function only within this framework", Hélène Ruiz Fabri, "Enhancing the Rhetoric of Jus Cogens" (2012) 23:4 EJIL 1049 at 1056.

therefore, the tradition of the Court.[72] Due to the iconic place of the ICJ in the international legal system, its decisions indubitably affect the larger tradition of international law.[73]

The advisory function of international courts is different from the adversarial proceedings which constitute their primary function. In the ICJ both functions are, *mutatis mutandi*, governed by the same rules.[74] A chamber of the ICJ has recognised that in its reasoning on a case it "must obviously begin by referring to Article 38, paragraph 1, of the Statute of the Court",[75] which states:

> The Court, whose function is to decide in accordance with international law such disputes as are submitted to it, shall apply:
>
> a. international conventions, whether general or particular, establishing rules expressly recognised by the contesting states;
> b. international custom, as evidence of a general practice accepted as law;
> c. the general principles of law recognised by civilized nations;
> d. subject to the provisions of Article 59, judicial decisions and the teachings of the most highly qualified publicists of the various nations, as subsidiary means for the determination of rules of law.[76]

This Article, taken almost entirely from the Statute of the PCIJ,[77] defined the applicable law for international conflicts under the Court's jurisdiction as treaties,

---

[72]"The experience of organs such as the General Assembly and the Security Council shows what a close influence the solution of the procedural debate has on the rights of the parties rather than on than on the organization and internal administration of the organ. Matters of 'procedure'; in the International Court should be regarded in the same light (…) These remarks are relevant to all the law applied by the Court, both as the reasons for the decision and the law applied to govern the method by which the Court reaches its decision." Shabtai Rosenne, *The law and practice of the International Court, 1920–2005*, vol. III, 4th ed. (Leiden: Martinus Nijhoff, 2006) at 1027–1028 [Rosenne, *The law and practice*].

[73]See e.g. Mahasen M. Aljaghoub, *The advisory function of the International Court of Justice 1946–2005* (Berlin: Springer, 2006) at 155; Alain Pellet, "Article 38" in Zimmermann, Tomuschat and Oellers-Frahm, *supra* note 60, 677 at 789 [Pellet, "Article 38"].

[74]*Charter of the United Nations*, 26 June 1945, Can TS 1945 No.7, at Annex, Art. 68 [when referring to the Annex: *Statute of the ICJ*]; see also Hersch Lauterpacht, "Some Observations on the Prohibition of 'Non Liquet' and the Completeness of the Law", in Frederick Mari van Asbek, ed, *Symbolae Verzijl, présentées au professeur J.H.W. Verzijl à l'occasion de son LXX-ième anniversaire* (The Hague: Martinus Nijhoff, 1958) 196 at 199 ("every question forming the subject matter of the request for an Opinion may be couched in the form of a claim, for instance, in proceedings for a declaratory judgement") [H. Lauterpacht, "Non liquet and Completeness"].

[75]*Delimitation of the Maritime Boundary in the Gulf of Maine Area* (*Canada v. United States of America*), [1984] ICJ Rep 246 at para 83 (reprinted in 23 ILM 1197).

[76]*Statute of the ICJ*, *supra* note 74 at art 38.1.

[77]Protocol of Signature Relating to the Statute for the Permanent Court of International Justice Provided for by Article 14 of the Covenant of the League of Nations, 16 December 1920, [1921] 6 LNTS 379, (1923) 17 AJIL Supp 55, online: United Nations Treaty Collection <http://treaties.un.org/doc/Publication/UNTS/LON/Volume%206/v6.pdf> (being the only difference the inclusion of the phrase: "whose function is to decide in accordance with international law such disputes as are submitted to it").

custom, and general principles of law. Subsidiary means to find the existence of a rule are "judicial decisions and the teachings of the most highly qualified publicists of the various nations",[78] However, it must be remembered that there is no *stare decisis* for the purposes of the International Court of Justice[79] or any other international court. Article 38 has a double function. In addition to establishing the sources of international law that the Court shall apply,[80] it also states that the general function of the Court with regard to the body of law it is bound to apply is to resolve international disputes using international law.[81]

There are other legal institutions that affect the function of the Court, such as the prohibitions upon international tribunals to decide a case in *non liquet* and to create international law. While they certainly are part of the tradition of international law,[82] and arguably are part of the unwritten rules that regulate the functions of the Court,[83] I treat them as different aspects because of their contested and mutually contradictory nature, at least in cases where the law appears to be silent.[84] As was the case in the *Nuclear Weapons* Advisory Opinion, when confronted with this dilemma, Judges choose one option as the lesser evil. In this sense, the application of one prohibition or the other in a particular case depends mostly on the

[78] *Statute of the ICJ*, *supra* note 74 at art 38.

[79] Ibid at art 59; *Interpretation of Peace Treaties with Bulgaria, Hungary and Romania (second phase)*, Advisory Opinion (second phase), [1950] ICJ Rep 221 at p 233 (Dissenting Opinion of Judge Read); M. Shahabuddeen, *Precedent in the world court* (Cambridge; New York: Cambridge University Press, 1996) at 97–102.; see also Rosenne, *supra* note 67 at 147–148; contra Gerald G. Fitzmaurice, "Some Problems Regarding the Formal Sources of International Law" in Frederick Mari van Asbek, ed, *Symbolae Verzijl, présentées au professeur J. H. W. Verzijl à l'occasion de son LXX-ième anniversaire* (The Hague: Martinus Nijhoff, 1958) 124 at 154. ("[I]t will be suggested that the decisions of international tribunals, while not operating directly as judicial precedent, and while not therefore technically a formal source of law, have a status different from that of a merely material source, and could be characterised as quasi-formal in character").

[80] *Nicaragua*, Merits, *supra* note 48 at para 56 ("the sources of international law which Article 38 of the Statute requires the Court to apply,"); see also Joost Pauwelyn, *Conflict of Norms in Public International Law: How WTO Law Relates to other Rules of International Law* (Cambridge: Cambridge University Press, 2003) at 90 ("Article 38 is, of course, but a treaty provision focusing on one given, although crucially important, court. It is in that sense part of international law and does not define international law.").

[81] Pellet, "Article 38", *supra* note 73 at 693.

[82] "*Report of the International Law Commission covering the work of its tenth session, 28 April–4 July 1958*" (UN Doc A/3859) in *Yearbook of the International Law Commission 1958*, vol 2 (New York: UN, 1958) at 83 (A/CN.4/SER.A/1958/Add.1) (the reference corresponds to the Model Rules on Arbitral Procedure).

[83] The issue of *non-liquet* was raised throughout the discussion of the PCIJ Statute, Ole Spiermann, "'Who Attempts Too Much Does Nothing Well': The 1920 Advisory Committee of Jurists and the Statute of the Permanent Court of International Justice" (2002) 73 Brit YB Int'l L 187 at 212–218 [Spiermann, "Who Attempts Too Much"].

[84] As for their mutually contradictory nature, Stone stated "to prohibit *non liquet* entails the imposition upon the court of a duty to develop new rules", Julius Stone, "Non Liquet and the Function of Law in the International Community" (1959) 35 Brit YB Int'l L 124 at 132.

understanding of the members of the Court (or the majority, at least) about the role the international judicial institution plays at that moment in time.

The prohibition of *non liquet* comes from the assumption that "every international situation is capable of being determined as a matter of law."[85] While most lawyers would be comfortable accepting this assumption, the assumption also implies that international law is to some extent complete. Evidently, in a complete juridical order, Courts would limit themselves to applying the law, and would never have to transgress their juridical function in order to legislate. The ICJ itself has insisted that "as a court of law, [it] cannot render judgment *sub specie legis ferendae* or anticipate the law before the legislator has laid it down".[86]

In the discussions that led to the adoption of Article 38 of the Statute of the PCIJ, some of the members of the Advisory Committee mandated to draft the rules expressed concerns about creating a closed list of possible sources.[87] To ensure that the Court would not be faced with the possibility of finding that no international law was applicable in a particular case, the Advisory Committee members included the third source: general principles of law.[88] In 1920, it was thought that "by making available without limitation the resources of substantive law embodied in the legal experience of civilized mankind [...] it made certain that there would always be at hand, if necessary, a legal rule or principle for the legal solution of any controversy involving sovereign States."[89] The provision proved itself useful to the PCIJ in two cases.[90] Judge Hersch Lauterpacht argues that such an inclusion reinforced the existence of the prohibition of *non liquet* by noting that since "the principle of completeness of the legal order is in itself a general principle of law, it became on that account part of the law henceforth to be applied by the Court."[91] It is worth quoting the *Andronov* case of the now abolished UN Administrative Tribunal (hereinafter, UNAT), in which the Tribunal reacted to a possible gap in completeness by stating that the international law applicable to the disputes between staff members of the United Nations and the Organization "must be interpreted as a

[85]Lassa Oppenheim, Robert Y. Jennings and C.A.H. Watts, *Oppenheim's international law*, 9th ed (London: Longmans, 1993) at 13.

[86]*Fisheries Jurisdiction (United Kingdom v. Iceland)*, Merits [1974] ICJ Rep 3 at para 53; *Fisheries Jurisdiction (Federal Republic of Germany v. Iceland)*, Merits [1974] ICJ Rep 175 at para 45 (with identical text).

[87]Spiermann, "Who Attempts Too Much", *supra* note 83 at 214–215.

[88]Rosenne, *The law and practice*, *supra* note 72 at 1546; see also Michael Akehurst and Peter Malanczuk, *Modern Introduction to International Law*, 7th ed (New York: Rutledge, 2007) at 48.

[89]H. Lauterpacht, "Non liquet and Completeness", *supra* note 74 at 205.

[90]*Case of the Mavrommatis Palestine Concessions (Greece v. United Kingdom)* (1924), PCIJ (Ser. A) No. 2 at p 16 and 28; *Case Concerning the Factory at Chorzów (Germany v. Poland)* (1927), PCIJ (Ser. A) No. 9 at 21 and 31.

[91]H. Lauterpacht, "Non liquet and Completeness", *supra* note 74 at 205.

comprehensive system, without *lacunae* and failures."[92] The message is that there are real *lacunae* international law.[93] For the ICJ, there is apparently an obligation to overcome those *lacunae*[94] either by applying equitable principles as a rule of law,[95] shaping the required rule,[96] applying the general principles of law,[97] or having recourse to other sources not listed in Article 38 of its Statute.[98]

* * *

In sum, the *Nuclear Weapons* Advisory Opinion presents us with some of the most pressing problems in modern international legal theory. The evolution of international humanitarian law and international human rights law has started to produce significant changes in international law.[99] Evidence of this is that both disciplines, together with international environmental law, played a significant role in the Court's decision. Twenty years before, the topic of nuclear weapons use would have been jurisprudentially regarded as within the realm of the liberty of the

---

[92]*Andronov v. Secretary-General of the United Nations*, Judgment of 20 November 2003, UNAT Judgment No. 1157, [2003] U.N. Jur. Yb. 497, UN Doc. AT/DEC/1157 at p 9 (emphasis is from the original); see also *Desgranges v. Director-General of the International Labor Organization*, Judgment of 12 August 1953, ILOAT Judgment No. 11 (one of the fundamental tenets of all legal systems is that no court may refrain from giving judgment on the grounds that the law is silent or obscure).

[93]Weil, "Cours général", *supra* note 57 at 212; see also Hersch Lauterpacht, *The Function of Law in the International Community* (Oxford: Clarendon Press, 1933) at 86 ("The view that there are gaps in law is theoretically false, and practically dangerous only if it is understood as meaning that the legal order as a whole may break down in cases of supposed insufficiency of law for the reason that the judge is in such cases entitled or obliged to abdicate his judicial function by refusing to give a legal decision. But if it is false to assume that there exists a gap in the sense that the legal order contains no solution at all, it is equally false to assume that there exist no gaps in any sense whatsoever, and that the necessary consequence of the presumed silence of the law is a rigidly negative attitude towards interests claiming legal protection").

[94]Pellet, "Article 38", *supra* note 73 at 705.

[95]*North Sea Continental Shelf, supra* note 48 at para 88.

[96]*Pulp Mills on the River Uruguay (Argentina v. Uruguay)*, [2010] ICJ Rep 14 at para 205.

[97]*Application for Review of Judgment No. 158 of the United Nations Administrative Tribunal*, Advisory Opinion, [1973] ICJ Rep 166 at para 36.

[98]*Nuclear Tests (Australia v. France)*, [1974] ICJ Rep 253 at para 43; *Nuclear Tests (New Zealand v. France)*, [1974] ICJ Rep 457 at para 46.

[99]International Law Association, Committee on International Human Rights Law and Practice, "Final Report on the Impact of International Human Rights Law on General International Law" (2008) 73 Int'l L Ass'n Rep Conf 663; also found in: Menno T. Kamminga, "Final Report on the Impact of International Human Rights Law on General International Law", in Menno T. Kamminga and Martin Scheinin, eds, *The Impact of Human Rights Law on General International Law* (Oxford: Oxford University Press, 2009); see also, Antônio Augusto Cançado Trindade, "International law for humankind: towards a new jus gentium (I). General course on public international law" (2005) 316 Rec des Cours 9; Theodor Meron, *The humanization of international law* (Leiden: Martinus Nijhoff, 2006).

State.[100] However, modern legal theory regards disciplines such as international human rights law, international humanitarian law, and environmental law as 'self-contained' regimes,[101] which disconnects a large part of their evolution and innovation from the general discipline. While arguably the disconnection between the self-contained regimes and general international law has allowed for innovations to take place within the regimes,[102] it also limits the extent to which information can be exchanged between different regimes. For instance, the value given to international humanitarian law in *Nuclear Weapons* contrasts with the fact that it was discussed in a different operative paragraph than the rest of international law.[103] As a consequence, international humanitarian law was effectively subordinated to the general international law regime.

The several resolutions of the UN General Assembly calling for an absolute ban on nuclear weapons, and even suggesting that it was the desire of the international community to forbid the use of nuclear weapons, were taken into account in the Advisory Opinion—not as law per se, but as evidence of the opinion of member States on the content of their legal obligations in the international arena. It is the nature and current state of legal tradition to seek its basis in the sovereignty of the State, especially when dealing with the freedoms of States. Therefore the opinions of a collective international body—undeniably political—cannot override the expressed will—or lack thereof—of the State, but only contribute to building legal meaning out of practice and only under certain conditions. That is, the Court has recognised that in certain circumstances such resolutions can provide evidence of the *opinio juris* necessary to identify a customary norm of international law,[104] effectively framing a relatively recent development of international law within the framework of Article 38 of its Statute.[105] I call this the jurisprudence of incorporation.

Ultimately, the international instruments that framed the Court's Advisory Opinion in *Nuclear Weapons* complied with the mandate of Article 38. Specifically, the Court reviewed the content of international conventions and looked for evidence of general practices accepted as law in order to render its Advisory Opinion. In the absence of clearly relevant and applicable treaties in force and customary law on the

[100] *Nicaragua*, Merits, *supra* note 48 at para 269 ("in international law there are no rules, other than such rules as may be accepted by the State concerned, by treaty or otherwise, whereby the level or armaments of a sovereign State can be limited, and this principle is valid for all States without exception").

[101] *Report of the ILC, 58th Session, supra* note 17 at para 251 (the reference corresponds to conclusion 11).

[102] For instance, it is because the American Convention on Human Rights created a regime of responsibility different from the customary law of State responsibility that the Inter-American Court has the ability to innovate in their conception of State responsibility, *Case of the Mapiripán Massacre (Colombia)* (2005), Inter-Am Cr HR (Ser C) No. 134, at paras 101–112.

[103] *Nuclear Weapons, supra* note 2 at 266 (see paragraph D of the operative).

[104] *Nuclear Weapons, supra* note 2 at para 70.

[105] The ongoing work of the ILC on the identification of customary international law seems to confirm this approach; see *Report of the ILC, 67th session, supra* note 46.

topic of nuclear weapons, the ICJ looked for general legal principles that would be applicable to the question posed to the Court by the General Assembly. There was no discussion of factors which, according to Article 38, would be extra-legal. For instance, the Edinburgh resolution of the *Institut de Droit International* on "The Distinction between Military Objectives and Non-Military Objects in General and Particularly the Problems Associated with Weapons of Mass Destruction"[106] was not even mentioned by the Court. Neither was the HRC's General Comment No. 14 to the ICCPR on "Nuclear weapons and the right to life".[107] This, of course, has not been the case in subsequent cases dealing with human rights, in which the Court made use of diverse documents produced by the HRC and other UN treaty-based bodies.[108]

At the very end of the Advisory Opinion, the Court was confronted with the ultimate question: are the rules and principles of international humanitarian law above the customary law and UN Charter right of self-defence? Although the International Law Commission agreed on the propriety of leaving decisions as to what forms part of *jus cogens* to "State practice and jurisprudence of international tribunals,"[109] the Court declined to apply this concept. The Judges' understanding of the legal role and place of the Court came into play here and, confronted with the possibility of changing the face of international law by deciding either way, the Court for the first time in its history decided to sacrifice the prohibition of *non liquet*.

Ultimately, making a finding on the superiority of either international humanitarian law or the law of self-defence would have amounted to recognizing that international law remained a law of coordination among States or had shifted to supporting a construct of law that validates humanity and humanitarian law concerns. The Court's Advisory Opinion confirms that, as legal scholars, we live in

[106] Institut de Droit International, "The Distinction Between Military Objectives and Non-Military Objects in General and Particularly the Problems Associated with Weapons of Mass Destruction", Session of Edinburgh—1969, online: Institut de Droit international <http://www.idi-iil.org/idiE/resolutionsE/1969_edi_01_en.pdf>.

[107] CCPR, *General Comment No. 14: Nuclear weapons and the right to life (Art. 6)*, (9 November 1984) in *Compilation Of General Comments and General Recommendations adopted by Human Rights Treaty Bodies*, UN Doc HRI/GEN/1/Rev.9 (Vol. I) (2008) at 188.

[108] *Legal Consequences of the Construction of a Wall in the Occupied Palestinian Territory*, Advisory Opinion, [2004] ICJ Rep 136 at paras 109–112; *Ahmadou Sadio Diallo*, Merits, *supra* note 13 at para 66; *Judgment No. 2867 of the Administrative Tribunal of the International Labour Organization upon a Complaint Filed against the International Fund for Agricultural Development*, Advisory Opinion, [2012] ICJ Rep 10 at para 39; *Questions relating to the Obligation to Prosecute or Extradite (Belgium v. Senegal)*, [2012] ICJ Rep 422 at para 39.

[109] "*Report of the International Law Commission covering the work of its fifteenth session, 6 May–12 July 1963*" (UN Doc A/5509) in Yearbook of the International Law Commission 1963, vol 2 (New York: UN, 1964) at 198 (The referenced text corresponds to the provisional Draft Articles on the Law of Treaties, specifically para 3 of the commentary to art 37).

times of jurisprudential transition at the international law level.[110] But it also reminds us that the Court's role in the international community is a relatively conservative one.[111] It has been suggested that:

> [T]he main role of the ICJ with regard to the development of international law is arguably not that of a ground-breaking body but rather that of a stock-taking institution or, to put it in somewhat more colorful terms, that of being the gate-keeper and guardian of general international law.[112]

As for the principle of completeness of international law, the Court's opinion speaks for itself: based on the assumptions as to what constitutes law under which the Court operates, the international legal order finds itself plagued with unsolvable *lacunae* in the most controversial topics.

****

The factors that conditioned the choice of what constitutes law in the *Nuclear Weapons* Advisory Opinion are pervasive to all of international law. Until relatively recently, there has been little theoretical work on the sources of international law. Putting together international judicial decisions and State practice, and labelling it as 'the doctrine of sources of international law' has never been enough to explain how documents, practices, principles and standards should be applied or interpreted. Even as human rights law is having a significant impact on general international law and producing a change in some of its structures, the theoretical work about this process—and its possible outcomes—is fairly limited.

Although Article 38 of the ICJ Statute was conceived to apply exclusively to the Court,[113] it is considered as "a de facto authoritative statement of points of reference for formally competent statements of the law."[114] That is, the dominant approach to the theory of sources is eroded in an article that was not meant to sustain such a large part of international legal theory. "Ignoring the realities of

---

[110]Speaking about the lack of *locus standi in judicio* at the ICJ by virtue of the Statute of the Court, Cançado Trindade was of the view that: "[l]egal instruments, whichever their hierarchy, are a product of their time, and I am sure that we all agree as to the need to work for the realization of justice at the level of the challenges of our time, so as to respond properly to them", *Judgment No. 2867 of the Administrative Tribunal of the International Labour Organization upon a Complaint Filed against the International Fund for Agricultural Development*, Dissenting Opinion of Judge Cançado Trindade, [2012] ICJ Rep 10 at para 118.

[111]Jonas Grimheden, "The International Court of Justice—Monitoring Human Rights", in Gudmundur Alfredsson, Jonas Grimheden and Bertrand G. Ramcharan, eds, *International Human Rights Monitoring Mechanisms: Essays in Honour of Jakob Th. Möller*, 2nd ed (Leiden: Martinus Nijhoff Publishers, 2009) 249 at 249–250.

[112]Jorge E. Viñuales, "The Contribution of the International Court of Justice to the Development of International Environmental Law: A Contemporary Assessment" (2008–2009) 32 Fordham Int'l LJ 232 at 258.

[113]Pellet, "Article 38", *supra* note 73 at 700; Alf Ross, *A textbook of international law: general part* (London: Longmans & Green, 1947) at 83.

[114]Malcolm N. Shaw, *International law*, 5th ed. (Cambridge: Cambridge University Press, 2003) at 66.

contemporary transnational prescription, this emphasis has tremendously exaggerated the image and importance of the autonomous nation-state, often confining law creation to the activity of state officials and stipulating the consent of every affected state to the making of law."[115] As a corollary, the contemporary understanding of the identification and application of the sources of international law is dependent on two treaties on treaty law, on the customary law on customary law[116] and on a general principle of completeness of international law that forces Courts to use general principles of law to avoid *non liquet*.[117] It does not get more self-referential than this.[118]

As discussed above, the *Nuclear Weapons* Advisory Opinion can be analysed and explained by showing how legal tradition, rules, and self-understanding played a role in defining what constitutes international law. In the same manner, I argue that a serious analysis of how human rights theory is transforming the mainstream understanding of the sources of international law cannot start with the doctrine of sources itself. On the contrary, by discussing the interdependent notions that play a role in international decision-making, I show the pluralist nature of normativity in international law. However, the doctrine of sources cannot be completely ignored, as it remains one of the notions that influence the decision-making process.

*****

Leaving the substantive aspects aside, the road taken by the Court in the *Nuclear Weapons* Advisory Opinion was definitively the most appropriate if its final objective was preservation of the system in which the Court operates. An opinion finding the use or threat of use of nuclear weapons illegal would have been, to put it

[115]Myres Smith McDougal and W. Michael Reisman, "The Prescribing Function in World Constitutive Process: How International Law Is Made" (1979) 6 Yale Stud World Pub Ord 249 at 258.

[116]H. Meijers, "How is International Law Made?—The Stages of Growth of International Law and the Use of its Customary Rules" (1978) 9 Neth YB Int'l L 3 at 3; see also, Stephen Hall, "The Persistent Spectre: Natural Law, International Order and the Limits of Legal Positivism", [2001] 12 EJIL 269 at 284 ("According to Article 38(1)(b) of the Statute of the International Court of Justice, the Court is to apply to such disputes as are submitted to it 'international custom, as evidence of a general practice accepted as law'. This formulation is universally, or almost universally, regarded as reflecting the customary law requirements for the existence of a custom.").

[117]H. Lauterpacht, "Non liquet and Completeness", *supra* note 74 at 205; see also H. Lauterpacht, "International Law—The General Part", in E. Lauterpacht, *International Law: Being the Collected Papers of Hersch Lauterpacht*, vol 1 (London: Caledonian Graphics Ltd, 1978) 1 at 96; *Eastern Extension, Australasia and China Telegraph Company, Ltd. (Great Britain) v. United States (1923)*, VI RIAA 112 at 114.

[118]Ross has stated that "the doctrine of the sources can never in principle rest on precepts contained in one among the legal sources the existence of which the doctrine itself was meant to prove", Ross, *supra* note 113 at 83; Conklin notes another irony in the structural framework of the international legal system: "The identity of a peremptory norm is all the more problematic when one appreciates the ironic twist that it is a treaty, the VCLT [*infra* note 134], which is invariably offered as the authority for the existence and the identity of peremptory norms", William E. Conklin, "The Peremptory Norms of the International Community" (2012) 23:3 EJIL 837 at 843.

lightly, too political for a court and extremely difficult to enforce. The Court itself has recognised that it has a "duty to safeguard the judicial function."[119] Ultimately, "self-preservation of the system is just a tipping device which comes into play when both sides mount equally persuasive arguments based on existing international rules."[120]

In the context of the Advisory Opinion concerning the *Accordance with international law of the unilateral declaration of independence in respect of Kosovo*[121] (hereinafter, *Kosovo*), an author has explored the proposition that "by rendering an advisory opinion, the Court seeks to, and needs to, maintain its authority vis-à-vis multiple constituencies that have a stake in its decisions, and on which the Court to some extent is dependent."[122] He adds: "In substance, the overriding conclusion is that the response provided by the Court may not have satisfactorily catered to the interests formally expressed by the main constituencies of the Court—the General Assembly and the Security Council—, but the result may well have served to protect the stature of the Court in relation to its key constituencies."[123]

It seems that while the prohibition of *non liquet* by the ICJ is theoretically absolute, it is somehow less sinful when broken in Advisory Opinions.[124] In any case, the Court's "response appropriately may reflect the state of the law and the specific role the Court plays in such matters. Whether the Court should respond in that way to a specific request is, of course, quite another question."[125]

* * * * * *

This book is about the necessity of conceptualizing the most basic elements of international legal theory in a moment of change from a perspective that seeks theoretical integration. My principal concern is the sources of international law, but because of the nature of the discussion, I will invariably discuss the interpretation of international norms.[126] As stated above, rather than start with the doctrine of

---

[119] *Case concerning the Northern Cameroons* (*Cameroon v. United Kingdom*), [1963] ICJ Rep 15 at 38.

[120] Anthony D'Amato, "Softness in International Law: A Self-Serving Quest for New Legal Materials: A Reply to Jean d'Aspremont" (2009) 20:3 EJIL 897 at 909.

[121] *Accordance with International Law of the Unilateral Declaration of Independence in Respect of Kosovo*, Advisory Opinion, [2010] ICJ Rep 403.

[122] André Nollkaemper, "The Court and its Multiple Constituencies: Three Perspectives on the Kosovo Advisory Opinion", in Marko Milanovic and Michael Wood, *The Law and Politics of the Kosovo Advisory Opinion* (Cambridge: CUP, 2015) 219 at 219.

[123] Ibid at 239.

[124] Weil, "*Non liquet* revisited", *supra* note 41 at 119.

[125] Ibid.

[126] See Duncan French, "Treaty Interpretation and the Incorporation of Extraneous Legal Rules" (2006) 55 ICLQ 281 at 282 (In discussing treaty interpretation and how it related to other topics such as "hierarchy of sources, jus cogens, the relationship between treaty law and customary international law, and other matters of treaty application", French found that "these issues are clearly not altogether separable as they all relate to the broader topic of how two or more rules of international law co-exist").

sources as it has existed since the early 20th century, I will engage in a threefold analysis of the topic: legal tradition, current regulation, and self-understanding of relevant actors about their role.

My hypothesis, which I call 'normative plurality in international law', is that the practice of international human rights law recognises that different normative instruments coexist in an un-ordered space, and that meaning can be produced by the free interaction of those instruments around a given problem. I will argue that decision-makers cannot base their activity on a doctrine that limits the possible sources of law,[127] pre-establishes their relative weight in an abstract manner[128] or pre-defines the way in which they relate to each other.[129] Having said that, I do not envisage 'normative plurality' as a normative theory of sources, but as a descriptive hypothesis of how decision-makers understand and apply international law in a specific case.[130]

In other words, I propose that when faced with a case, decision-makers must survey the *acquis* of international law in order to identify all the instruments containing relevant normative information for a particular situation. The *acquis* of international law is formed by all norms which have been expressively or tacitly agreed by members of the international community, or subsets thereof. The instruments containing relevant normative information then come to complement the set of rules of law directly applicable to the situation, resulting in a complete system of norms advancing a common purpose.

In Chap. 2, I argue that since the emergence of international law in the sixteen hundreds until the present, every account of the sources applicable to international law has relied on a normative form that challenges the theoretical objectivity and internal logic of the doctrine itself at a given time. That is, at least one of the elements taken into consideration by the diverse authors cannot be precisely described as an objective source. Therefore, as precise as the doctrine attempts to be, there has always existed an element that ultimately allows for a free interpretation of what constitutes law. Alf Ross stated that, along with the *lex lata* and the partially objectified rules of the international legal order, are "the free, not formulated, not objectified factors."[131] I argue that these 'not objectified factors' have

---

[127]"A useful theory about law must avoid the temptation, so common in conventional legal method, to drastically reduce the universe of variables to a text or a few purportedly key social factors. You cannot get far with any of the problems we started with if you limit yourself to a few texts", W. Michael Reisman, "The View from the New Haven School of International Law" (1992) 86 Am Soc Int'l L Proc 118 at 121.

[128]Prosper Weil, "Towards relative normativity in international law?" (1983) 77 AJIL 413.

[129]"In practice the free factors will after all become more or less masked as an 'interpretation' of the objectivated sources", Ross, *supra* note 113 at 81.

[130]The manner in which Kooijmans used the term "acquis of international law" reflects the meaning I which to express here: the "accepted common standard[s]" in international law, Pieter H. Kooijmans, "Human Rights, Universal Values?", Dies Natalis Address, Institute of Social Studies, 12 October 1993, p. 7 online: Erasmus Universiteit Rotterdam <http://lcms.eur.nl/iss/diesnatalis1993OCR.pdf>.

[131]Ibid.

always been present in international legal theory. Therefore, I engage in an analysis of how scholars have spoken about legal sources from the 16th century until now. The main focus will be to identify relevant trends by virtue of the not-objectified factor that was predominant. As they either are dismissed or pass to a higher stage of objectification, new factors come into play, such as divine law, natural law, general principles of law, principles of justice, *jus cogens*, and soft law.[132] The contribution of this chapter to the main argument is to show that international law has never solely relied on formal sources to arrive to solutions. As in the early stages of the discipline, the development of international law was in the hand of scholars, the object of study is the most relevant writers at a given time. Having said that, this chapter must not be read as a historical analysis but rather as a trend analysis of the extra-legal elements that became relevant at different times.

In Chap. 3, I review the practice of different actors of the international legal order, by looking both at the sources recognised by Article 38 and those that have been generally accepted over time. I engage in a deep analysis of Article 38 of the ICJ Statute, understanding that it "deserves neither over-praise nor harsh indignity."[133] By focusing on Article 38 for what it does and does not say, I argue that, even in general international law, Article 38 constitutes only a frame of reference and, therefore, it must be displaced from its paradigmatic position. I review the sources mentioned in Article 38 of the ICJ Statute, including the establishment of subsidiary means to find rules, as well as other sources that have been recognised by the jurisprudence of the ICJ even though they are not listed in Article 38. I will also discuss the issue of abstract hierarchy among sources of international law. Finally, I will review three cases in which the ICJ, when confronted with normative forms which do not conform to the requirements of the doctrine of sources as elaborated by its own jurisprudence, treated them as belonging to one of the categories mentioned in Article 38, which I have called the 'jurisprudence of incorporation'.

The purpose of the chapter is to show that, with the arrival of international organizations and the establishment of the permanent international judiciary, the international community has increasingly being engaged in the constant elaboration of norms, standards and guidelines, while international judicial entities advanced a restricted interpretation of what constitutes international law. In particular, the jurisprudence of incorporation will show that when faced with instruments that do not perfectly fit the categories in Article 38 of the Statute, mostly due to multilateralism and informal methods to reach agreement among States, the rigidness of the ICJ's approach has led to the reinforcement of it by means of re-drawing the boundaries of the categories.

In Chap. 4, I discuss certain relevant cases of international human rights courts that challenge the way in which the doctrine of sources is understood. The common

[132]As Ross put it in the framework of his theory: "all of them fictions meant to conceal the absence of objectivity and serving to give to one's own subjective evaluation of the relevant considerations a false colouring of objective learning", Ross, *supra* note 113 at 82.

[133]Pellet, "Article 38", *supra* note 73 at 680.

element in the cases to be discussed is the use of both binding and non-binding instruments which are external to the jurisdiction of the respective court in order to re-frame the obligations of States. International human rights courts have justified such use by invoking the customary rules of treaty interpretation, as reflected in the Vienna Convention on the Law of Treaties (hereinafter, VCLT), and specifically the principle of systemic integration.[134] In this chapter I engage in a substantive analysis of how actions taken by human rights bodies in the creation of standards through resolutions, general comments, recommendations, and guidelines have been used by human rights courts to complement the meaning of international human rights conventions. I argue that the advances brought by international human rights courts and bodies portrays a broader understanding of normativity which has been present in other self-contained regimes and might eventually be present in general international law.

In Chap. 5, I argue that while the practice of human rights courts promotes coherence among the regional and the universal human rights regimes, the principle of systemic integration is not meant to expand the normative content of the interpreted treaty on the basis of external instruments, especially non-binding instruments. Therefore, such practice cannot be conceptualised as interpretation, but as the application of external instruments. To defend this argument, I rely in the theory of Alf Ross concerning the sources of international law. Then, after adjusting Ross's theory to the specific problems of the 21st century, and proposing three mutually reinforcing notions (specificity, completeness and purpose) that assist the judge in determining the applicable law to a case, I develop the content of the normative plurality hypothesis.

It has always fascinated me how, despite the thousands of pages dedicated to the *Tadić* Decision on the Defense Motion for Interlocutory Appeal,[135] it is never mentioned that of the five judges siting on the bench for that case, two of them were renown scholars deeply engaged in international human rights issues, and another one was a professional judge with extensive experience in domestic and international human rights. Part of the normative plurality hypothesis is that socio-psychological aspects influence the decision of judges as to what constitutes law. The three guiding notions constitute the incursion of the hypothesis into those socio-psychological aspects and its weight on decision making. I argue that these notions despite not being considered central to the definition of law, they play a quintessential role on the decision-making process and therefore influence the personal decision of the judge as to what constitutes international law.

The three guiding notions operate as a result of the decision-maker's awareness that the evolution of the international legal system has led to the constant

[134] *Vienna Convention on the Law of Treaties*, 23 May 1969, 1155 UNTS 331 at art 31, (1969) 8 ILM 679 (A treaty shall be interpreted in good faith in accordance with the ordinary meaning to be given to the terms of the treaty in their context and in the light of its object and purpose. (…) 3. There shall be taken into account, together with the context: (…) (c) *any relevant rules of international law applicable in the relations between the parties*).

[135] *Tadić*, *supra* note 52.

production of instruments, many of which are non-binding, containing specific targets, aspirations, commitments and norms on an ever increasing number of issues. The awareness of this specificity on a particular issue, along with the need to understand the system of international law as materially complete, and the decision-maker's understanding of what is its role in the international community, result on the understanding of which materials have a direct influence on the case at hand, regardless of their abidingness.

The structure of the book is also meant to present the tradition of international law at different stages and the ever present need to rely on non-formal sources. For this reason, rather than presenting my hypothesis and subsequently defend it, I have opted to highlight the tradition, the challenges international lawyers face with the doctrine of sources, and the solutions found in international human rights law, before developing the three guiding notions and presenting the central statement of the hypothesis. I acknowledge that at times the central argument of the individual chapters may seem unrelated to the central hypothesis and the ultimate argument of the book, and for that, I beg the reader for patience. As the chapters reach their individual conclusion, their contribution to the overall argument becomes evident.

International law is in a process of evolution. The effect of human rights in areas of general international law, such as treaty reservations, state immunity, and consular rights, among others, is undeniable. However, most of the studies on this topic focus on the doctrinal aspects of this effect. That is, these studies seek to explain how international law regulated these topics in the past, and how it currently regulates them. As public international law is in constant change, our theoretical understanding of the most basic elements of international law should evolve with it.

A topic as important as the sources of international law should be revisited periodically. The process of change makes such revisiting even more urgent. Because of its own nature, the doctrine of sources of international law is capable of defining the scope of international action and the rights and obligations of all actors involved. "The relationship between general international law and international human rights law is obviously a two-way process."[136] For this reason I propose an approach that takes into account both the development of the tradition of international law since its beginnings, and the evolving practice of international human rights courts.

[136]Kamminga, *supra* note 99 at 2; See also Simma, "Community Interest" *supra* note 22 at 603 ("What we can observe already is that the Court has become a major player in a process in which human rights and general international law mutually impact upon one another: human rights "modernize" international law, while international law "mainstreams", or "domesticates" human rights.").

Chapter 2
Talking About Sources: The Constant Reliance on a Non-objectified Element

Abstract In this chapter, I argue that since the emergence of international law in the sixteen hundreds until the present, every account of the sources applicable to international law has relied on a normative form that challenges the theoretical objectivity and internal logic of the doctrine itself at a given time. That is, at least one of the elements taken into consideration by the diverse authors cannot be precisely described as an objective source. Therefore, as precise as the doctrine attempts to be, there has always existed an element that ultimately allows for a free interpretation of what constitutes law. I argue that these 'not objectified factors'—bowring from the terminology used by Alf Ross—have always been present in international legal theory. In this chapter, I engage in a historical analysis of how scholars have spoken about legal sources from the 16th century until now. The main focus will be to identify relevant trends by virtue of the not-objectified factor that was predominant.

2.1 Introduction

"*[L]e débat sur les sources du droit international, cet « evergreen » de la doctrine internationaliste, continue, génération après génération, à fasciner les juristes et à figurer au premier rang de leurs préoccupations.*"[1] The amount of pages devoted to describing, explaining, and conceptualising the sources of international law is not small. It seems that most international law scholars have wondered about this topic at some point in their careers. For practitioners, the sources of law are not so much a point of reflection and study as they are for scholars. However, they constitute the foundations of the profession. Because the most basic piece of knowledge that a lawyer must have is that which allows him or her to identify legal norms, all modern manuals on international law deal with this issue.

In this chapter I will argue that since the emergence of International Law until the present, the doctrine of sources applicable to this branch of the law has relied on—at the very least—a normative form that challenges the theoretical objectivity

[1]Prosper Weil, "Le droit international en quête de son identité: cours général de droit international public" (1992) 237 Rec des Cours 11 at 133.

C.I. Fuentes, *Normative Plurality in International Law*,
Ius Gentium: Comparative Perspectives on Law and Justice 57,
DOI 10.1007/978-3-319-43929-7_2

and internal logic of the doctrine itself at a given time. That is, at least one of the elements taken into consideration by the diverse authors cannot precisely be described as an objective source. Therefore, as precise as the doctrine attempts to be, there has always existed an element that ultimately allows for an open interpretation of what constitutes law.

This chapter will review three trends that have appeared since the publication of Alberico Gentili's *De Iure Belli Libri Tres* in 1589 up until the adoption of the Charter of the UN in 1945. The trends are distinguished by changes to the elements included as sources of international law, and, particularly, the element that seems to break with the internal logic of the doctrine at a particular moment. Needless to say, these trends do not necessarily succeed each other in time. Some of them are extremely long, some are extremely short, and some even overlap. Since they are not mutually exclusive, I do not consider that this lack of symmetry invalidates the point I wish to make. For the purposes of determining duration, and since the plausibility of the idea is my only measure, I will consider each trend alive and on-going for as long as an actor in the international legal order is willing to make an argument on its bases.

In Sect. 2.2, I identify the use of God or divine law as a trend, covering the classic doctrine as stated by Grotius[2] and some of his predecessors,[3] who divided law into that which emanated from God, from nature, and from consent.[4] While arguably, it is possible to trace the origins of modern international law to the writings of Rev. Francisco de Vitoria in the 16th century, Hugo Grotius takes precedence over his contemporaries because of the fact that he was the first to actually present and justify a system of sources as we understand it today. By the very nature of this trend, most of the law is actually not objectified. However, the reliance on God and the Bible as evidence of a divine law differentiates it from subsequent trends.

Section 2.3 is devoted to the decline of divine law and the rise of a secular conception of natural law in legal theory and, subsequently, legal sources. Vattel,[5] Pufendorf,[6] and

[2]See Hugo Grotius, *De Jure Belli ac Pacis*, vol. 2, trans. by Francis W. Kelsey (Oxford: Clarendon Press, 1925) at 38 [Grotius, *De Jure Belli ac Pacis*].

[3]See also Alberico Gentili, *De Iure Belli Libri Tres*, vol. 2, trans. by John C. Rolfe (Oxford: Clarendon Press, 1933) at 7 (although he did not discuss agreements in international law, he declared that "international law is a portion of the divine law").

[4]To be absolutely fair, such division is present since ancient Greece, Le Fur affirms that "l'antiquité a connu un droit naturel international", Louis Le Fur, "La Théorie du Droit Naturel" (1927) 18 Rec des Cours 260 at 272; See also Serge A. Korff, "Introduction à l'histoire du droit international" (1923) 1 Rec des Cours 1.

[5]See Emmerich de Vattel, The Law of Nations or The Principles of Natural Law Applied to the Conduct and to the Affairs of Nations and of Sovereigns, trans. by Charles G. Fenwick (Washington D.C.: The Carnegie Institution, 1926) at 3–8.

[6]See Samuel Pufendorf, *De Jure Naturae et Gentium*, vol. 2, trans. by C.H. Oldfather and W.A. Oldfather (Oxford: Clarendon Press, 1934) at 112.

other writers contemporary to them,[7] postulated the existence of a natural law that comes from the rational thinking of the human being. The characteristic of this period is a more or less open concept of a natural law which does not respond to God.

Section 2.4 begins with the decline of natural law at the beginning of the 20th century and the inclusion of the general principles of international law in the Statute of the PCIJ. Here, I will review the initial understanding of the general principles of international law that was held by the drafters of the Statute. Originally devised as an open-ended concept which would allow the Judges to avoid situations of *non liquet*, the general principles of international law have evolved into rigid elements that rely more and more on the consent of States.

To conclude, I review the codification efforts in the period between World Wars I and II and the beginnings of the UN. Particular attention is paid to the draft code of public international law for the American Republics, prepared by Alejandro Alvarez. This draft code created a complex system of sources which ultimately relied on the principles of international justice, if no positive rule or general principle was available. However, Alvarez's idea of justice was not absolutely abstract. Evidence of those principles of international justice was to be found in the "*voeux* of international conferences, resolutions of recognised scientific institutions or opinions of contemporary publicists of authority."[8] The theory of this period still contributes to the increasing value given to the resolutions of international organizations.

One can say, with little fear of generalization, that two normative forms have enjoyed universal recognition of their relevancy since the emergence of international law: treaties and custom. Expositions of the doctrines of sources of international law diverge on the issues of whether there are other relevant forms, and if so, what their respective normative values are.

The initial premise of this chapter is that treaties and custom have in common their relative objectivity as sources. That is, it is relatively easy to identify by objective standards whether an instrument or a repeated practice constitutes law. Treaties are concluded between States and more recently between States and International Organizations. While the way in which consent is expressed by a State has changed through the years, the requisite of the expression of will remains a necessary element for the validity of a treaty. To make things easier, the rules that establish the required expression of will for a treaty to be valid have been codified in a treaty: the VCLT. The situation of custom is slightly different. The current doctrine establishes that a customary norm exists when State practice is

[7]Wolff, for example, follows the Grotius in its classification; Christian Wolff, *Jus Gentium Methodo Scoentifica Pertractatum*, vol. 2, trans. by Joseph H. Drake (Oxford: Clarendon Press, 1934) at 9, 10 and 18; while sustaining the existence of the Law of Nature, Rachel sustained that the Law of Nations was only formed by what Grotius called voluntary law; contra Samuel Rachel, *De Jure Naturae et Gentium Dissertationes*, vol. 2, trans. by John Pawley Bate (Washington D.C.: The Carnegie Institution, 1916) at 163–165.

[8]International Commission of Jurists, "Public International Law: Projects to be Submitted for the Consideration of the Sixth International Conference of American States" (1928) 22 AJIL Supp 234 at 239.

accompanied by *opinio juris*, that is, that States' acceptance that such practice is law.[9] While the requirement of *opinio juris* is a rather recent development,[10] the practice of Sovereigns—whether kings or States—has always been an element of the formula.

In sum, the will of the State, whether tacit or expressed, remains central to the mainstream understanding about the formation of international law.[11] Therefore, in order to discover what constitutes law under the classification of treaties and custom, the legal professional needs only to identify the expressions of the will of the State that have traditionally been associated with those normative forms.

Custom and treaties are not the only sources of international law.[12] To borrow an expression coined by Alf Ross, customs and treaties are complemented by "free, not formulated, not objectified factors".[13] For the purposes of this chapter I will define 'not objectified factors' as any possible source of law that is presented as an a priori indiscernible category that requires a process of concretization for its practical application. I will argue that 'not objectified factors' have been present throughout the whole history of international law, and that they operated as sources, which were in some form relevant to the legal actors at a given time. While by nature those free factors are relatively easy to conceptualise, it is difficult to authoritatively state their normative content and value. In a sense, they can be called 'informal'. For instance, while it is common for international lawyers to use the concept of the 'general principles of law' in their daily work, it is impossible to authoritatively

---

[9] Or, as put by Judge Negulesco, "the mutual conviction that the recurrence is the result of a compulsory rule"; *Jurisdiction of the European Commission of the Danube (1927)*, Dissenting Opinion by M. Negulesco, PCIJ (Ser. B) No. 14 at 105.

[10] Paul Guggenheim, "Contribution à l'histoire des sources du droit des gens" (1958) 94 Rec des Cours 5 at 52–53.

[11] See Volker Röben, "What About Hobbes? Legitimacy as a Matter of Inclusion in the Functional and Rational Exercise of International Public Power" in Rüdiger Wolfrum and Volker Röben, eds., *Legitimacy in international law* (Berlin; New York: Springer, 2008) at 356 ("[w]hether states can be expected to obey international law depends in essence on their being included in the exercise of this [public] power"); such a view is also shared by those who have separated sources of law from sources of obligations, having as a consequence that treaties are obligations while the source of the law is the will of states; see e.g., *Reservations to the Convention on the Prevention and Punishment of the Crime of Genocide*, Advisory Opinion, [1951] ICJ Rep 14 at 32 (Dissenting Opinion of Judges Guerrero, Sir Arnold McNair, Read, Hsu Mo) ("The fact that in so many of the multilateral conventions […] the parties have agreed to create new rules of law or to declare existing rules of law, with the result that this activity is often described as 'legislative' or 'quasi-legislative', must not obscure the fact that the legal basis of these conventions, and the essential thing that brings them into force, is the common consent of the parties"); See also Gerald G. Fitzmaurice, "Some Problems Regarding the Formal Sources of International Law" in Frederick Mari van Asbek, ed, *Symbolae Verzijl, présentées au professeur J.H.W. Verzijl à l'occasion de son LXX-ième anniversaire* (The Hague: Martinus Nijhoff, 1958) 124 at 155–160.

[12] See, Malcolm N. Shaw, *International law*, 5th ed. (Cambridge: Cambridge University Press, 2003) at 92–119.

[13] Alf Ross, *A textbook of international law: general part* (London: Longmans & Green, 1947) at 80–91.

state all the general principles of law, and extremely risky to formulate one in the absence of previous, perhaps even judicial, recognition of its status.

The given definition of a 'not-objectified factor' requires explaining what is meant by a 'source of law'. This is particularly difficult to determine, considering that throughout the history of international law the concept has been extensively used with diverse meanings, to the point where it is practically empty.[14] While generally speaking, Kelsen is right in that it is preferable to "introduce an expression that clearly and directly describes the phenomenon [I have] in mind",[15] the nature of this particular historical revision requires us to understand the term 'sources of law' for what it has meant at various times, for there is no change in the content of a concept without the concept changing in itself.

In the following pages the term 'sources' will be used to refer either to our current understanding of material source[16] or to a formal source.[17] When a clear distinction between these is required because of changes in language, it will be so indicated. In any case, the term 'source' will not be used to mean 'evidence'. For example, while 'divine will' is a source, the Bible will be evidence of it.

While contemporary theorists/historians of international law have argued that the doctrine of sources has gone through different periods in which its internal logic allowed it to embrace different normative elements,[18] the doctrine of sources has justified the use of normative forms that challenge the purpose of the doctrine. As discussed below, the presence of such normative forms constitutes a tacit recognition of the inherent incompleteness of the international legal system, and of the impossibility of confining the legal method to strictly legal elements.

Sources are, ultimately, the justification for a legal solution as expressed by a relevant actor in the system. The immediate contribution of this chapter to the general argument of the book is to show that the doctrine of sources of international law has never been a rigid construction in the mind of scholars. By reviewing the diverse trends that have proposed and sustained the existence of free factors in

---

[14]Kelsen stated: "[t]he ambiguity of the term 'source' of law seems to render the term rather useless", Hans Kelsen, *Principles of international law* (New York: Rinehart, 1952) at 304 [Kelsen, *Principles*]; he was obviously uncomfortable with the terminology of the time, since in his opinion, by calling custom and treaties 'sources', "*on se sert d'une abréviation, qui risque facilement d'induire en erreur*", Hans Kelsen, "Les rapports de système entre le droit interne et le droit international public" (1926) 14 Rec des Cours 227 at 265.

[15]Kelsen, *Principles*, ibid.

[16]"[T]he material sources might better be described as the 'origins' of law[, … m]aterial historical, indirect sources represent, so to speak, the stuff out of which the law is made", Fitzmaurice, "Some Problems", *supra* note 11 at 153.

[17]"[T]hose provisions operating within the legal system on a technical level", Shaw, *supra* note 12 at 66.

[18]See e.g. Martti Koskenniemi, *From apology to Utopia: the structure of international legal argument* (Cambridge: Cambridge University Press, 2005) at 307 ["A period of naturalism is contrasted with a period of positivism and these again with some 'eclectic' period. Yet, the contrasts re-emerge within modernism as it understands different sources…"].

international law, I will demonstrate that the determination of what constitutes international law has never been an exact science.

The period of time chosen for this chapter requires further explanation. In order to do justice to the argument and also to mark a fundamental change of paradigm that occurred in the first half of the 20th century, I chose the adoption of the Statute of the ICJ as the final point for the purposes of this chapter. The constant production of resolutions and declarations by UN organs and bodies, and the permanent fora that were created for the codification and progressive development of international law, are just a few examples of the transformations that have followed the creation and evolution of international organizations. The trends established by the reaction of the international judiciary to these changes will be the subject of subsequent chapters.

2.2 God as the Law

As it has been the case with most law, it is especially true for international law that "[i]n the beginning was the Word, and the Word was with God, and the Word was God."[19] For most of the earliest Europeans writing about the law of nations or *jus gentium*, all law emanates from a divine will.[20] In the words of Hugo Grotius, "let us give first place and pre-eminent authority to the following rule: What God has shown to be His Will, that is law."[21]

There is a particular difficulty with this section: While all other trends discussed in this chapter—and also those that are not—appeared within a more or less established discipline of international law, the idea that divine law was a relevant aspect of the law predates the origins of modern international law. In fact, it can be rightfully argued that there was no trend at all since international law, as all other law of the time, was, at conception, dependant on divine will. However, "historical rationality is something that can only be known retrospectively",[22] and from today's perspective, there are more or less identifiable points where the influence of religion upon international law started and ended. The fact that the moment when

[19]*The Gospel of John* at 1:1 (please note that as the Gospel was originally written in Greek, the phrase "the Word" is a translation of the Greek word "*Logos*"); while John was clearly using *logos* to speak of Jesus, it is interesting to compare it with the legal connotations that some Greek philosophical schools have given to the term: "[i]n Stoicism the logos is the divine order and in Neoplatonism the intelligible regulating forces displayed in the sensible world. The term came thus to refer, in Christianity, to the Word of God, to the instantiation of his agency in creation, and, in the New Testament, to the person of Christ", *The Cambridge Dictionary of Philosophy*, 1999, *s.v.* "logos".

[20]See Francisco Suarez, *Selections from Three Works*, vol. II (Oxford: Clarendon Press, 1944) at 172; Gentili, *supra* note 3 at 7–8.

[21]Hugo Grotius, *De Jure Praedae Commentarius*, vol. 1, trans. by Gwladys L. Williams and Walter H. Zeydel (Oxford: Clarendon Press, 1950) at 8 [Grotius, *De Jure Praedae*].

[22]Judith N. Shklar, "Comment On Avineri" [1973]:1 Political Theory 399 at 402.

the modern tradition of international law started coincides with the moment when religion effected great influence over society and law, does not invalidate the argument.

It is worth noting that the emergence of modern international law was a long process that can be identified through the progressive disappearance of the Roman conception of *jus gentium*.[23] In the Roman system enunciated by Ulpian, natural law was the law applicable to all living beings, *jus gentium* was applicable to the whole of humanity, and *jus civile* was the human-made law of a city.[24] *Jus gentium* was the divine order of things applicable to human beings; above it was natural law, applicable to beasts and humans equally.

In this section, I will discuss how the earliest scholars spoke about the sources of international law, particularly Grotius. However, the issue of the sources of law rarely appears as such in the writings of the time. Instead, it appears in the relationship among natural law, the law of nations and divine law. By organizing these different laws into a system, the scholars of the time defined the hierarchy among human and divine sources of law and their respective evidences. This trend is characteristic for the presence of God or divine law as the superior mandate which shapes both the law of nations and natural law, and for the extensive use of the Bible and other religious texts as evidence of their content.

Some of the writers of the time did not consider that divine law was intelligible to human beings. However, it still remained essential to the task of the lawyer to discern God's design of nature in order to find rules applicable to international relations. The point to make in this section is that the scholars of the time saw actual positive law only as subsidiary to either a divine law[25] or a natural law dictated by God and understood in reference to His will.[26] In this sense, the determinacy and preciseness found in the writers of the time in relation to custom and agreements stands in contrast to the reference to the natural state of things created by God.

As stated above, Grotius was the first to elaborate a system of sources as we understand it today. This was a transitional moment in which God was both above the law and within the sources of the law. While many of Grotius' contemporaries dealt with important issues which today would be considered within the realm of international law (such as war, embassies, law of the sea, etc.), their treatment was rather topical and did not elaborate on methodological issues.[27] However, an influence of divine law on issues that would today be attributed to international law

[23]See Gordon E. Sherman, "Jus Gentium and International Law", [1918] 12:1 AJIL 56 at 60–61.

[24]Dig. 1.2.1–2 (Ulpian).

[25]Grotius, *De Jure Belli ac Pacis*, *supra* note 2.

[26]"From the foregoing, then, I conclude and state as my third proposition that the natural law is truly and properly divine law, of which God is the Author", Suarez, *supra* note 20 at 198.

[27]See e.g., Balthazar Ayala, *De Jure et Officiis Bellicis et Disciplina Militari Libri III*, vol. II (Washington, D.C.: Carnegie Institution, 1912); Pierino Belli, *De Re Militari et Bello Tractatus*, vol. II, trans. by Herbert C. Nutting (Oxford: Clarendon Press, 1936); Francisci de Victoria, *De Indis et de Ivre Belli Relectiones*, trans. by Franciscus de Victoria (Washington D.C.: Carnegie Institution, 1917).

was present centuries before Grotius. For instance, in discussing the origins of war, Giovani de Legnano acknowledged it was based on divine law and the law of nations.[28] In making such a statement, Legnano made reference to books of the Old Testament as evidence of the former, and to old Latin texts (such as the *Codex Hermogenianus* and Saint Isidore's *Etymologiae*) as evidence of the latter. Whether Legnano meant to speak of the law of nations in the sense that the Romans spoke about *jus gentium*, or in the slightly more modern conception of Saint Isidore,[29] is outside the scope of this analysis. However, it suffices to note that, in his view, neither the Bible nor Roman law could wholly explain the recognition of war. As he expanded on the regulation of war in the law of nations, he used natural law to explain the human inclination to war and therefore, its origins.

Before entering into Grotius' system, it is worth reviewing how the relationship between God and the laws of nations, as presented by his predecessors, became an issue of sources. According to Alberico Gentili, the law of nations was natural law: "That which is in use by all nations of men, which native reason has established among all human beings, and which is equally observed by all mankind."[30] However, he acknowledged that these are unwritten laws given by God.[31] Evidently, as God was the creator of nature, whatever laws were understood by men were ultimately linked to His will. Whether stated by the Romans, Greeks or by the Bible, what was true for many and resisted the test of time was assumed to be law. In this sense, human reason as directed by God is the source of law: "We have not received them through instruction, but have acquired them at birth; we have gained them, not by training, but by instinct."[32]

As for the evidence of this God-given reason, Gentili used the authority of "philosophers and other wise men [who] are regarded as honourable and of good repute", "persuasive arguments", "the civil law of Justinian", and "the Sacred Books of God".[33] Gentili gave special weight to the Bible as evidence of this law, and for this he quoted the *Codex Agobardinus* of Tertullian: "[t]hese testimonies are forthwith divine; they do not need the successive steps which the rest require."[34]

Hugo Grotius did not only start a transition but also experienced it himself in his writings. His first book, *De Iure Praedae*, was written between 1604 and 1605,[35] and it presents a system of international law different from in his later writings. However, only its twelfth chapter was published during Grotius' life, under the title *Mare*

---

[28]Giovani de Legnano, *Tractatus De Bello, De Represaliis et De Duello* (Oxford: Oxford University Press, 1917) at 224.

[29]See James Brown Scott, *Law, the state, and the international community* (New York: Columbia University Press, 1939) at 202.

[30]Gentili, *supra* note 3 at 8.

[31]Ibid at 9–10.

[32]Ibid at 10.

[33]Ibid at 11.

[34]Ibid at 11.

[35]Grotius, *De Iure Praedae*, *supra* note 21 at xiv.

liberum sive de jure quod Batavis competit ad Indicana commercia dissertati, and the world would not come to discover *De Iure Praedae* until 1864.[36] Since the existence of this book did not influence the thinking of its time and, after discovery, was appreciated more for its historical value than for the currency of its argument, it will not be discussed at length here. It suffices to say that *De Jure Praedae* presents a system in which the natural law common to all men, as imprinted by God himself in man, constitutes the primary law of nations.[37] Grotius also recognised that a secondary law of nations exists by the will between nations, its main institution being the international pact with custom in second place because "not everything customary among the majority of people will forthwith constitute law".[38] Grotius later published a book that had great influence during his time, and is today recognised as one of the foundational texts of international law: *De Jure Belli ac Pacis*.

While acknowledging the superiority of an eternal natural law over man-made precepts, *De Jure Belli ac Pacis* presents a slight difference in its sources than *De Jure Praedae*. Grotius enunciates and explains that the law "concerned with the mutual relations among states or rulers of states"[39] was formed by the rules, "derived from nature, or established by divine ordinances, or having its origin in custom and tacit agreement".[40] A note of caution: Grotius' *De Jure Belli ac Pacis* was published in 1625, that is, two decades after *De Jure Praedae* was written. The time did not pass in vain as he "abandoned the scholastic concept of natural law as a basic element of his argument."[41] No mistake should be made, for although God remained the source of all law,[42] precedence was given to the law of nature.

As understood by Grotius in *De Jure Belli ac Pacis*, the collective sense of humanity was central to the law of nature. The rational capacity of human beings and their preference for social life made them capable of expediently understanding nature's design and the laws that governed it. Thus, natural law was viewed as being discernible through the exercise of good human judgement, free from passions and undisturbed by external pressure.

Grotius did not enter into much detail when explaining the nature of divine law, as in his opinion the existence, benevolence and superiority of God were verifiable facts. However, he did devote some sections to the differentiation of divine and natural law with respect to the Bible and other religious books. By the same token, Grotius did not discuss the nature of custom and agreement, beyond enunciating the basics of social contract theory.

---

[36] Ibid at xvi; Karl Zemanek, "Was Hugo Grotius Really in Favour of the Freedom of the Seas?" (1999) 1 J Hist Int'l L48 at 50–51 and fn 8.

[37] Grotius, *De Iure Praedae*, ibid at 13.

[38] Ibid at 26–27.

[39] Grotius, *De Jure Belli ac Pacis*, *supra* note 2 at 9.

[40] Ibid.

[41] Ibid at xxi.

[42] See David Kennedy, "Primitive Legal Scholarship" (1986) 27 Harv Int'l LJ 1 at 79 and 82.

It is remarkable, though, that according to Grotius' system in *De Jure Belli ac Pacis* all sources are interdependent yet not hierarchical. That is, custom and agreements are justified under the natural law obligation to abide by pacts, while natural law is recognizable thanks to the "essential traits implanted in man"[43] by God himself. In *De Jure Praedae* custom was not law in the same sense as expressed will was, and therefore hierarchically inferior to treaties.

But even if the system of *De Jure Belli ac Pacis* constitutes a departure from Grotius' previous views on the relationship between natural and divine law, this book is no less religious than *De Jure Praedae*.[44] Grotius' use of the Bible as evidence of the law is extensive in both texts.[45] Therefore, it would be wrong to see *De Jure Belli ac Pacis* as the start of secular iusnaturalism.[46]

Over one hundred years after Grotius' books appeared, his opinions would be tested by Jean-Jacques Burlamaqui's 1747 *Principles du droit naturel*. It must be

---

[43]Ibid at 14.

[44]Somos, who has done an impressive analysis of Grotious and his contemporaries' writings is of the view that Grotius "presented an unbroken string of forced interpretations that had shocking implications for just war theory, and he did so in order to show that the Bible should not be used in international law at all", however, he also states: "Grotius was clearly no atheist, and I doubt that he set out to write [*De Jure Praedae*], and later [*De Jure Belli ac Pacis*], to construct a secu-lartheory of international relations", Mark Somos, "Secularization in *De Iure Praedae*: from Bible Criticism to International Law" (2005–2007) 26:1 Grotiana 147 at 157 and 190.

[45]The 1738 edition of *De Jure Belli ac Pacis* translated by Jean Barbeyrac—which is not my preferred edition—contains a very useful index of "Passages of Scripture, Illustrated examined or corrected in this Treatise", which illustrates the point here made, Hugo Grotius, *The Rights of War and Peace*, trans. by Jean Barbeyrac (Clark: Lawbook Exchange, 2004); see also David J. Bederman, "Reception of the Classical Tradition in International Law: Grotius' *De Jure Belli ac Pacis*" (1996) 10 Emory Int'l L Rev 3 at 5 (although Bederman discusses Grotius use of Greek and Latin sources, he noted that "Almost the entirety of this textual authority (at least for the 1625 edition of the book) came from antiquity. Those sources can, in turn, be equally divided between biblical quotes and the writings of classical authors.").

[46]Mark W. Janis, "Religion and the Literature of International Law: Some Standard Texts" in Mark W. Janis, Carolyn Maree Evan, eds, *Religion and International Law* (The Hague: Martinus Nijhoff, 1999) at 123 ("His theory of a law of nations based on the consent of sovereigns was meant to be more or less religiously neutral. However, from a reading of his text, it is doubtful that Grotius meant to be or was irreligious or secular"); William P. George, "Grotius, Theology, and International Law: Overcoming Textbook Bias" (1999–2000) 14:2 J L & Religion 605 (arguing that English-language international law textbooks "present Grotius as the one who finally liberated international law from theology when, in fact, his approach to international law was unabashedly theological"); *contra*, Benedict Kingsbury and Adam Roberts, "Introduction: Grotian Thought in International Relations", in Hedley Bull, Benedict Kingsbury and Adam Roberts, eds, Hugo Grotius A\and International Relations (Oxford: Clarendon Press, 1990) 1 at 3–4 (in their view, Grotius presented a "systematic reassembling of practice and authorities on the traditional but fundamental subject of the *jus belli* [laws of war], organized for the first time around a body of principles rooted in the law of nature"); Somos, *supra* note 44 at 190 ("Te fact remains that his use of biblical references in [*De Jure Praedae*] indicate that he was already thinking in terms of the essentially secular, new system of laws that we find in *De iure belli ac pacis*"); Mark Somos, *Secularization and the Leiden Circle* (Leiden: Koninklijke Brill, 2011) at 384 ("If one has to date the birth of secular international law, one cannot find a better year than 1625").

noted that, by that time, the influence of Suarez in the separation of natural law and the *jus gentium* had disappeared. Burlamaqui resembles secular iusnaturalists, such as Christian Wolf and Emmerich de Vattel, who came after him and believed that "the Law of Nations was, in its origin, merely the Law of Nature applied to Nations."[47] However, like Johann Gottlieb Heineccius,[48] he recognised the superiority of God over the latter.

Burlamaqui's critique to Grotius would depart from the latter's reduction of the law of nations to a human law. That is, Burlamaqui rejected the importance that Grotius gave to treaties and custom. Burlamaqui viewed God as the only origin of any common law among nations, and thus denied the existence of a universal and obligatory custom.[49] While Burlamaqui did not construct a system of sources or present the evidence upon which he relied, he drew the principles of a system of law, the validity of which, ultimately resides in God. He divided the law of nations into those that are necessary and those that are arbitrary, the former being natural law and the latter understood as express or tacit convention. However, as with Grotius, even his arbitrary law ultimately depended on the natural law obligation to abide by pacts.[50]

In the writings of scholars belonging to this trend, the content of the law of nations remains, for the most part, a matter of natural law. However, this natural law is handed down in accordance with God's will to all men by way of reasoning. As "things which are well known ought to be stated, but not demonstrated",[51] the content of the law was mostly stated in absolute and universal terms. Evidently, using accepted religious text and God-given reason as irrefutable evidence of the law, elevates the argument to dogma.

A corollary to my argument is that trends re-appear every once in a while, not necessarily because their influence is still important to the body of knowledge they belong to, but rather because a particular scholar felt the need to bring back an argument. A clear example of this is Sir Robert Phillimore's "Commentaries upon international law". Although its first volume was published in 1854, supposedly more secular times, Phillimore's work restates the Grotian model and gives primacy to divine law:

> States are therefore governed, in their mutual relations, partly by Divine, and partly by positive law. Divine Law is either (1) that which is written by the finger of God on the heart of man, when it is called Natural Law; or (2) that which has been miraculously made known to him, when it is called revealed, or Christian law[52]

---

[47]Vattel, *supra* note 5 at 4.

[48]Johann Gottlieb Heineccius, *Elementa Juris Naturae et Gentium* (Indianapolis: Libery Fund, 2008) at 323.

[49]Jean-Jacques Burlamaqui, *The Principles of Natural Law and Politic Law* (Indianapolis: Liberty Fund, 2006) at 176.

[50]Ibid at 177.

[51]Gentili, *supra* note 3 at 10.

[52]Robert Phillimore, *Commentaries upon international law*, vol. 1 (London: W.G. Benning, 1854) at 56.

2.3 Natural Law

While "God's in his Heaven—All's right with the world!"[53]

For international law, this meant leaving the divine law to the clergy and putting the Bible away. The change that came along was dramatic yet not total. That is, scholars started to omit references to God, divine law or religious texts, while keeping most of the general structure of the system created by Grotius. In simpler words, natural law became secular.

This section deals with the trend of natural law, but a different kind of natural law. Among Grotius and his contemporaries, natural law was a product of human reason as directed by God. In their view, since God created all nature, and especially the mind of men, any rule deduced by the mind of men from nature was a direct consequence of God's will. The natural law that emerged in the middle of the 17th century, and was present until the beginning of the 20th, was a law that came directly from human reason. No divine will and no master design came into play.

However, with the decline of God and the religious text that was evidence of His will, all other sources gained relevance. That is, in this trend, valid law could come as "the dictate of right reason"[54] or the treaties and other agreements entered into by states. This comes from the need to order the loosely regulated public international realm (which, judging from the writers of the time, was reduced to the laws of war, the law of the sea, and diplomatic relations) at a time when modern multilateral treaty-making was not yet possible.

The disappearance of God and the Bible from international legal texts was a gradual process, which arguably started in 1650 with Richard Zouche's *Iuris et Iudicii Fecialis, sive, Iuris Inter Gentes*. Zouche's book was a systematic exposition of questions of law that might rise between sovereigns and individuals in times of war and peace. In defining the law that deals with these questions, Zouche stated: "That which natural reason has established among all men is respected by all alike, and is called the Law of Nations, as being a law which all nations recognise."[55] Zouche separated the law of nations and the law of nature, for the former comes from "some general agreement" expressed either by "common customs" or by "compacts, conventions and treaties".[56] However, such separation is rather deceiving as the agreement of nations must be in harmony with reason.[57] Still, there is no mention of a divine will behind either type of law. As for the evidence of this law, Zouche still made use of the Bible along with Roman law and the usual Greek,

---

[53]Robert Browning, *Pippa passes* (Cambridge: Chadwyck-Healey, 1994) at 25, online: Literature Online <http://lion.chadwyck.com>.

[54]Rachel, *supra* note 7 at 8.

[55]Richard Zouche, *Iuris et Iudicii Fecialis, sive, Iuris Inter Gentes, et Quaestionum de Eodem Explicatio*, vol. 2, trans. by J.L. Brierly (Washington D.C.: Carnegie Institution, 1911).

[56]Ibid at 2.

[57]Rachel, who wrote after Zouche, denounced his reliance on reason as confusing the law of nations and the law of nature, Rachel, *supra* note 7 at 179.

Latin and other writings, but "because when many persons at different times and places lay down the same principle, that principle must be referred to a universal cause."[58] The authority of the Bible did not come as a divine mandate but as evidence to "establish what has been received [...] in accordance with natural reason by the custom of nations",[59] and in fact it was quoted only a few times throughout the text.[60]

The importance of reason and usage became more evident with Johann Wolfgag Textor's *Synopsis Juris Gentium*. In opposition to Zouche, Textor did see a common ground between natural law and the law of nations: both come from natural reason. However, while the law of nature comes directly from that reason, "the Law of Nations issues through the medium of international usage."[61] Textor postulates what can arguably be the earliest express separation between material and formal sources of international law:

> [T]wo sources of the Law of Nations are indicated: (1) Reason, which, as the proximate efficient cause, dictates to the various nations that this or that is to be observed as Law among the human race; (2) the Usage of nations, or what has been in practice accepted as law by the nations.[62]

It is, therefore, up to experts to give evidence of the reason behind the practice of States, which itself constitutes the law; "and these two are what I named as the authentic sources of the Law of Nations."[63] So necessary is the interplay of both elements for Textor that, in his opinion, the new law of nations must be allowed to displace what he referred to as an old law of nations, a law strictly based on custom.

Cornelius van Bynkershoek, in his *Questionum Juris Publici Libri Duo* agreed with Zouche and Textor: "It is only from reason and custom that we can learn the general law of nations in this matter."[64] The relevance of reason as a source points to the idea of an action of discovery by men. The objects to be discovered are the laws of a natural society of nations.[65]

Before the end of the first half of the 18th century there was a return to the conception of the laws of nations as the laws of nature applied to nations, first in the

---

[58]Zouche, *supra* note 55 at 2.

[59]Ibid.

[60]Ibid at 2 (Psalms), 4 (Exodus), 8 (Genesis and Kings), 61 (Daniel) and 70 (Ezekiel).

[61]Johann Wolfgang Textor, *Synopsis Juris Gentium*, vol. 2, trans. by John Pawley Bate (Washington, D.C.: Carnegie Institution, 1916) at 4.

[62]Ibid at 1.

[63]Ibid at 2.

[64]Cornelius van Bynkershoek, *Questionum Juris Publici Libri Duo*, vol. 2, trans. by Tenney Frank (Oxford: Clarendon Press, 1930).

[65]Vattel, *supra* note 5 at 8.

religious sense with Heineccius[66] and Burlamaqui,[67] but more decidedly and in the secular sense with Christian Wolf[68] and Emmerich de Vattel.[69]

In Wolf's *Jus Gentium Methodo Scientifica Pertractatum*, this natural law applied to nations was only one part of the laws of nations and is called, following the Grotian tradition, the necessary laws of nature.[70] In opposition to this necessary law, there is a positive law of nations, which is subdivided as voluntary, 'stipulative' or customary depending on the type of will that generates them. "[T]he voluntary law of nature rests on the presumed consent of nations, the stipulative upon the express consent, [and] the customary upon the tacit consent."[71] Under this system, the voluntary law of nature is one "to have been laid down by its fictitious ruler and so to have proceeded from the will of nations."[72] That is, under this highly organised system, Wolf recognised a set of universal rules or principles that come from a supposed consensus of nations that is binding upon them.

In *Le Droit des Gens*, Vattel follows the same classification as Wolf and expands on the possible confusion between the voluntary law and the natural or necessary law of nations.[73] According to Vattel, the voluntary law of nations should develop and complement the necessary law of nations:

> [A]fter having established on each point what the necessary law prescribes, we shall then explain how and why these precepts must be modified by the voluntary law; or, to put it in another way, we shall show how, by reason of the liberty of nations and the rules of their natural society the external law which they must observe towards one another differs on certain points from the principles of the internal law, which, however, are always binding upon the conscience.[74]

The principal change that came with the secularization of natural law was in the places where international law was to be found. While Textor, Zouche and van Bynkershoek integrated natural law with the objective sources, Vattel and Wolf treated them separately but placed natural law above treaty and custom. The result is similar: The practice of States could not produce law unless it was somehow in accord with the rules and principles derived from nature. Vattel is clear in stating that "all treaties and customs contrary to the dictates of the necessary Law of Nations are unlawful."[75]

---

[66]Heineccius, *supra* note 48 at 323.

[67]Burlamaqui, *supra* note 49 at 174.

[68]Wolff, *supra* note 7 at 9.

[69]Vattel, *supra* note 5 at 4.

[70]Wolff, *supra* note 7 at 10.

[71]Ibid at 19.

[72]Ibid at 18.

[73]Vattel, *supra* note 5 at 9.

[74]Ibid.

[75]Ibid at 5.

As for the evidence of that reason, scholars of this trend rely on their own arguments and in the writings of their predecessors.[76] Baldus' dictum seems appropriate to explain their method: "What the world approves, I do not venture to disapprove."[77] This however, makes the content of 'natural' as elusive and unpredictable as dependence on God's will. Even as natural law started to decay and became neglected in modern international law manuals, the writings of celebrated authors continued to appear as evidence of law. In the first edition of Henry Weaton's Elements of International Law (1836), the writings of renowned authors were listed as the first source of international law, above treaties and custom.[78]

2.4 General Principles of Law

The first years of the 20th century were characterised by a constant debate between the rising positivists and the declining iusnaturalists.[79] It eventually became evident that natural law had lost its hegemonic place:

> The law of Nature may have been helpful, some three centuries ago, to build up a new law of nations, and the conception of inalienable rights of men and nations may have exercised a salutary influence, some one hundred and fifty years ago, on the development of modern democracy on both sides of the ocean; but they have failed as a durable foundation of either municipal or international law and cannot be used in the present day as substitutes for positive international law, as recognised by nations and governments through their acts and statements.[80]

That being said, scholars quickly realised that positivism was incapable of delivering all the answers to the problems of the inter-war period.[81] There was a need to look for another non-objectified element. The trend identified in this section is the recognition of the general principles of law as a source of international law.

It is difficult to establish when the general principles of law started to appear as a source of international law. Verdross traces them back to the 'principles of objective law' applied by arbitral tribunals in the Middle Ages[82] and cites arbitral

[76]Zouche, for instance, bases his chapter on "the law of nations" on Iustinianus's Digest, Jean Bodin's fifth book of the Commonwealth, Hobbe's Leviathan and Grotious's *De Jure Belli et Pacis*, Zouche, *supra* note 55 at 3.

[77]Baldus de Ubaldi, *Consilia IV* at ccccxcvi, as quoted by Gentili, *supra* note 3 at 11.

[78]Henry Wheaton, *Elements of international law: with a sketch of the history of the science* (London,: B. Fellowes, 1836).

[79]Le Fur, *supra* note 4 at 325.

[80]*North American Dredging Company of Texas (U.S.A.) v. United Mexican States* (1926), IV RIAA 26 at 29 (para 12).

[81]On this point, see Hans J. Morgenthau, "Positivism, Functionalism, and International Law" (1940) 34:2 AJIL 260 at 261–273.

[82]Alfred Verdross, "Les principes généraux du droit dans la jurisprudence internationale" (1935) 52 Rec des Cours 191 at 207 [Verdross, "Les principes généraux"].

decisions as early as 1861 which use a principle in order to overcome the absence of specific rules of international law.[83] This demonstrates only that the applicability of principles of law was a practice among arbitral tribunals,[84] or at its best that international customary law allowed for the application of principles in certain cases.[85] It was their inclusion in the Statute of the Permanent Court of International Justice that "cemented their role as a source of international law."[86]

The inclusion of the general principles of law in the Statute of the PCIJ was rather controversial. The task of producing a draft-scheme for the PCIJ was entrusted to an Advisory Committee of Jurists, which met in June and July 1920. Baron Edouard Descamps, president of the Advisory Committee, prepared a draft article defining the sources of international law to be applied by the Court. Those were: treaties, custom, "the rules of international law as recognised by the legal conscience of civilized nations" and "international jurisprudence as a means for the application and development of law."[87] Elihu Root immediately rejected the draft article, as he believed that States would submit only to positive rules.[88] Åke Hammarskjöld, deputy secretary of the Committee, described the debate in the following terms:

> The President had, according to his custom, presented four points representing his point of view, and as usual he expressed his opinion that they would be adopted as they stood. Mr. Root, however, in a long and, for once, vehement speech, criticised the points, their basis, their logic, their everything, so that when he had finished nothing was left but a very queer impression.[89]

As the debate continued, Professor Francis Hagerup argued that, if Root's views were adopted, the Court might encounter cases in which no conventional or

[83]Ibid at 210; Raimondo explains five arbitral cases where general principles were used as subsidiary sources of international law, Fabián Raimondo, *General principles of law in the decisions of international criminal courts and tribunals* (Leiden; Boston: M. Nijhoff Pub., 2008) at 10–15.

[84]See e.g. *Eastern Extension, Australasia and China Telegraph Company, Ltd. (Great Britain) v. United States (1923)*, VI RIAA 112 at 114 ("International law, as well as domestic law, may not contain, and generally does not contain, express rules decisive of particular cases; but the function of jurisprudence is to resolve the conflict of opposing rights and interests by applying, in default of any specific provision of law, the corollaries of general principles, and so to find—exactly as in the mathematical sciences—the solution of the problem").

[85]Karl Wolff, "Les principles généraux du droit applicables dans les rapports internationaux" (1931) 36 Rec des Cours 479 at 483.

[86]Raimondo, *supra* note 83 at 16.

[87]Permanent Court of International Justice—Advisory Committee of Jurists, *Procès-Verbaux of the Proceedings of the Committee* (The Hague: Van Langenhuysen Frères, 1920) at 306 (13th Mtg., 1 July 1920, annex No. 3) [*Procès-Verbaux*].

[88]Ibid at 293–294 (13th Mtg., 1 July 1920).

[89]Ole Spiermann, "'Who Attempts Too Much Does Nothing Well': The 1920 Advisory Committee of Jurists and the Statute of the Permanent Court of International Justice" (2002) 73 Brit YB Int'l L 187 at 213 [Spiermann, "Who Attempts Too Much"].

customary rule could be applied.[90] Upon the willingness of most members of the Court to contemplate the possibility of *non liquet*, Lord Walter G.C. Phillimore and Root proposed a new draft which included 'the general principles of law recognised by civilised nations'[91] as a third source. This wording was provisionally adopted and would eventually form part of the draft-scheme that was submitted to the League of Nations[92] and of the Statute of the Permanent Court as Article 38(c).[93]

Evidently, the broad acceptance that Article 38 enjoys today[94] and the recognition of the general principles of law as a source of international law was not automatic. For many years after the entry into force of the Statute of the PCIJ, scholars considered that the only formal sources of international law were custom and treaties.[95] This, however, was a correct appreciation according to the language of the times. For the scholar of the 1920s, 'formal sources' were the methods of creating positive law,[96] while the general principles of law were legal maxims recognised in the internal law of all States.[97] Since principles are not created but rather a product of deductive logic, they did not constitute formal sources of international law. "Only two of the three sources—treaty and custom—are clearly positive in character; i.e. they specify obligations and entitlements pursuant to acts of human will. The character of the general principles is, as we shall see, more ambiguous."[98]

In the 1927 *Lotus* case, the PCIJ was asked to interpret the meaning of the phrase 'principles of international law' in the Treaty of Peace between the Allied Powers

---

[90] *Procès-Verbaux*, *supra* note 87 at 296 (13th Mtg., 1 July 1920) and 308–309 (14th Mtg., 2 July 1920).

[91] Ibid at 344 (15th Mtg., 3 July 1920, annex No. 1).

[92] James Brown Scott, "The Draft Scheme of the Permanent Court of International Justice" (1920) 7 International Conciliation 507 at 525.

[93] Protocol of Signature Relating to the Statute for the Permanent Court of International Justice Provided for by Article 14 of the Covenant of the League of Nations, 16 December 1920, [1921] 6 LNTS 379, at art. 38, (1923) 17 AJIL Supp 55, online: United Nations Treaty Collection <http://treaties.un.org/doc/Publication/UNTS/LON/Volume%206/v6.pdf>.

[94] Shaw, *supra* note 12 at 66.

[95] Charles De Visscher, "La codification du droit international" (1925) 6 Rec des Cours 325 at 339; Paul Heilborn, "Les sources du droit international" (1926) 11 Rec des Cours 1 at 20.

[96] Example of this is Lassa Oppenheim's famous analogy to a stream of water, which has appeared in every subsequent edition of his book: "Just as we see streams of water running over the surface of the earth, so we see, as it were, streams of rules running over the area of law. And if we want to know whence there rules come, we have to follow the streams upward until we come to their beginning. Where we find that such rules rise into existence, there is the source of them", Lassa Oppenheim, *International Law: A Treatise*, vol. I (London: Longmans, Green & co., 1905) at para 15, p 21; see also, De Visscher, ibid at 345 ("Ni la coutume, ni la convention ne sont, à proprement parler, les bases ou les fondements du droit international: elles ne constituent que les sources formelles du droit positif"); Heliborn, *supra* note 88 at 20 ("[c]omme sources du droit international, c'est-à-dire comme modes de sa formation…").

[97] *Procès-Verbaux*, *supra* note 87 at 335 (15th Mtg., 3 July 1920).

[98] See, Stephen Hall, "The Persistent Spectre: Natural Law, International Order and the Limits of Legal Positivism", [2001] 12 EJIL 269 at 284.

and Turkey.[99] The Court stated that "as ordinarily used, [it] can only mean international law as it is applied between all nations belonging to the community of States";[100] and then added "it is impossible (…) to construe the expression 'principles of international law' otherwise than as meaning the principles which are in force between all independent nations and which therefore apply equally to all the contracting Parties."[101] While the interpretation of the expression was adequate for the case *sub judice*, it did little to clarify the meaning of Article 38(c) of the Statute. Many scholars of the time used the *Lotus* judgment to argue that the general principles of law had no independent content.[102]

Another modest contribution to the recognition of general principles of law as a source of international law would occur in 1930. Three years before, the Assembly of the League of Nations had decided to call the First Conference for the Codification of International Law, and to submit three topics for its examinations: nationality, territorial waters and responsibility of States for damage done in their territory to the person or property of foreigners.[103] The Conference took place in The Hague from 13 March to 12 April 1930. The Committee discussing the third topic, responsibility of States, was soon faced with the need to define the sources of 'international obligations' for the purposes of the draft convention.[104] After several meetings a draft article was adopted by a majority vote of 27 to 3, with the following text:

> The expression 'international obligations' in the present convention means obligations resulting from treaty, as well as those based upon custom or the general principles of law, which are designed to assure to foreigners in respect of their persons and property a treatment in conformity with the rules accepted by the community of nations.[105]

The Committee would eventually inform the Conference that it "was unable to complete its study of the question of the responsibility of States (…), and accordingly was unable to make any report to the Conference."[106]

In 1929 Professor Alfred Verdross was invited to co-chair with Professor Albert de Lapradelle the twenty-first Commission of the *Institut de Droit International* on *sources du droit des gens*. By suggestion of the Bureau of the *Institut*, the work was

---

[99]*Treaty of Peace with Turkey Signed at Lausanne*, 24 July 1923, 28 LNTS 11, (1924) 18 AJIL Supp. 4.

[100]*The Case of the S.S. "Lotus"* (*France v. Turkey*) (1927), PCIJ (Ser. A) No. 10 at 16.

[101]Ibid at 17.

[102]Antoine Favre, "Les principes généraux du droit, fonds commun du droit des gens" in Faculté de Droit de L'Université de Genève, ed., *Recueil d'études de droit international*: *en hommage à Paul Guggenheim* (Genève: La tribune de Genève, 1968) 366 at 372.

[103]*Resolution adopted by the Assembly of the League of Nations*, 19 September 1927, 53 OJ Spec Supp 9, (1947) 41 AJIL Supp 106 at 106–107.

[104]Edwin M. Borchard, "'Responsibility of States,' at The Hague Codification Conference" (1930) 24 AJIL 517 at 520–522.

[105]Ibid at 530.

[106]*United Nations Documents on the Development and Codification of International Law*, U.N. Doc. A/AC.10/5 (29 April 1947), (1947) 41:4 AJIL Supp 29 at 82.

divided between the co-chairs: de Lapradelle was in charge of studying treaties and custom, while Verdross was to study whether the general principles of law existed as a different source of international law. Verdross completed a preliminary paper and a draft resolution in November 1930, in which he concluded that "*[l]es rapports internationaux ne sont pas seulement régis par les conventions et la coutume, mais aussi par les principes généraux de droit reconnus par les Nations civilisées…*"[107] As a corollary, arbitral tribunals must apply Article 38 of the Statute of the PCIJ whenever the arbitration treaties or the *compromis* were silent about the sources to apply.[108] The committee submitted a final resolution confirming those findings to the 1932 session of the *Institut* in Oslo, but it was not adopted by the plenary. However, Professor Verdross' work was not in vain. Not long after the Oslo session, he would be invited to teach a course at The Hague Academy of International Law and would choose the topic: *Les principes généraux du droit dans la jurisprudence internationale*. The course would eventually be published in volume 52 of the Academy's course collection.[109] It must be noted that Professor Maurice Bourquin had already recognised that the general principles of law were a source of international law in his course at The Hague Academy. However, this also entailed a change in the concept of sources itself:

> Au regard du droit des gens, elles ne sont pas des sources créatrices. Mais leur coïncidence est tenue pour le signe révélateur d'une norme et constitue ainsi une source du droit des gens, si par source on entend simplement un moyen de constatation.[110]

With the negotiations that gave birth to the UN, the allied powers formed a committee of experts to study the situation of the PCIJ and its future. In 1944, the committee delivered the Dumbarton Oaks Proposals, which established the guiding principles for the creation of the International Court of Justice.[111] The proposals departed from the belief that the statute of the ICJ should be either "(a) the Statute of the [PCIJ], continued in force with such modifications as may seem desirable, or (b) a new Statute in the preparation of which the Statute of the [PCIJ] should be used as a basis".[112] Regarding the sources of law to be applied by the new Court, the Committee found that, regardless of the criticism of Article 38 of the Statute of the PCIJ, "any attempt to alter it would cause more difficulties than it would solve".[113] As a result, Article 38 was slightly modified in the Statute of the ICJ, but

---

[107]Vingt et Unième Commission, *Les principes généraux de droit comme source du droit des gens* (1932) 37 Ann Inst Droit Int'l 283 at 297.

[108]Ibid.

[109]Verdross, "Les principes généraux", *supra* note 82.

[110]Maurice Bourquin, "Règles générales du droit de la paix" (1931) 35 Rec des Cours 1 at 73.

[111]Manley O. Hudson, "The Succession of the International Court of Justice to the Permanent Court of International Justice" (1957) 51:3 AJIL 569 at 570.

[112]"Report of the Informal Inter-Allied Committee on the Future of the Permanent Court of International Justice: February 10, 1944" (1945) 39:1 AJIL Supp. 1 at 1.

[113]Ibid at 20.

maintained the general principles of law as a source of international law applicable to the Court.[114]

Arguably the discussion was put to an end by the Secretary-General of the UN[115] when, in the preparatory work for the first session of the International Law Commission, he stated regarding the sources of international law that:

> The codification of this aspect of international law has been successfully accomplished by the definition of the sources of international law as given in article 38 of the Statute of the International Court of Justice. That definition has been repeatedly treated as authoritative by international arbitral tribunals.[116]

An interesting change that confirmed the relevance of the general principles of law as a source can still be found in the writings of a particular set of authors. The original edition of Lassa Oppenheim's Treatise in International Law establishes that there are only two sources of international law: treaties and custom, as they represent, respectively, express and tacit consent of the States.[117] This formula was maintained through the various editions by the author himself,[118] by Ronald Roxburgh[119] and by Lord Arnold D. McNair.[120] However, the 1948 edition by Sir Hersch Lauterpacht recognises that "although they [treaties and custom] are the principal sources of the Law of Nations, they cannot be regarded as its only sources."[121] A section is devoted to discussing the general principles of law as a source of international law. Their adoption, in Lauterpacht's opinion, is a rejection of both the positivistic and naturalistic approaches to international law.[122]

As controversial as the inclusion of the general principles of law in the draft-scheme of the PCIJ was, their content remains the object of much debate to this day.[123] Lord Phillimore, one of the drafters of the provision, explained during the debates of the Advisory Committee that he interpreted them as those "accepted by all

---

[114]*Charter of the United Nations*, 26 June 1945, Can TS 1945 No. 7, at Annex, Art. 38.

[115]It is widely known that the *Memorandum submitted by the Secretary-General* (*infra* note 116) discussed in this paragraph was actually drafted by Sir Hersch Lauterpacht.

[116]*International Law Commission, Survey of International Law in Relation to the Work of Codification of the International Law Commission* (*Memorandum submitted by the Secretary-General*), 10 February 1949, UN. Doc A/CN.4/1/Rev/1 at 22.

[117]Oppenheim, *supra* note 96 at 22; for an interesting comparison of Oppenheim's editions, including the issue of sources, see Mark W. Janis, "The New *Oppenheim* and Its Theory of International Law Oppenheim's International Law" (1996) 16:2 Oxford J Leg Stud 329.

[118]Lassa Oppenheim, *International Law: A Treatise*, vol I, 2nd ed (London: Longmans, 1912).

[119]Lassa Oppenheim, *International Law: A Treatise*, vol I, 3rd ed by Ronald Roxburgh, (London: Longmans Green, 1920).

[120]Lassa Oppenheim, *International Law: A Treatise*, vol I, 4th ed by Arnold Duncan McNair, (London: Longmans Green, 1928).

[121]Lassa Oppenheim, *International Law: A Treatise*, vol I, 7th ed by Hersch Lauterpacht, (London: Longmans, 1948) at 27.

[122]Ibid at 29.

[123]Bin Cheng, "General principles of law as a subject for international codification" (1951) 4 Curr Legal Probs 35 at 37.

nations in *foro domestico*",[124] which has reinforced the idea that it refers exclusively to the principles of national law which enjoy general—if not universal—recognition.[125] This view does not deny that international law has principles of its own, but it implies an absolute separation between national and international law. Favouring this view, Herczegh argues that "[t]he general principles international law should therefore be traced in the subject-matter of international treaties and in international customary law."[126] The opposing view considers that Article 38.1.c states that the applicable principles are those 'recognised by civilized nations', which does not limit such recognition to strict legislative recognition.[127] But as early as 1934, Frede Castberg pointed out that: "*Il serait par trop irrationnel de permettre à la Cour de rechercher les normes à appliquer dans ses décisions parmi les principes généraux de n'importe quel domaine du droit interne, sans qu'elle pût statuer selon les principes généraux du droit international.*"[128]

My point is that the general principles of law were another normative category which specific content cannot be known a priori, and that allows legal actors to use their creativity in order to construct its specific content. As Cheng has pointed out, an integral analysis of the *procès-verbaux* of the PCIJ Statute shows that the members of the Committee "were only giving a name to that part of international law which is not covered by conventions and customs sensu stricto",[129] a part that has existed under several names to this days.

2.5 Conclusion

"*[Il] a déjà été signalé que le droit international souffre sur bien des points d'un manque d' «objectivation» par rapport à d'autres normativités concurrentes.*"[130] It has been recognised that comparing the international legal order by analogy to

[124] *Procès-Verbaux*, *supra* note 87 at 335 (15th Mtg., 3 July 1920).

[125] Alfred Verdross, "Les principes généraux du droit dans le système des sources du droit international public" in Faculté de Droit de L'Université de Genève, ed., *supra* note 102, 521 at 524.

[126] See e.g., Géza Herczegh, *General principles of law and the international legal order* (Budapest: Akadémiai Kiadó, 1969) at 42–44.

[127] Michel Virally, "Le rôle des "principes" dans le développement du droit international" in Faculté de Droit de L'Université de Genève, ed., *supra* note 102, 531 at 542–543.

[128] Frede Castberg, "La méthodologie du droit international public" (1933) 43 Rec des Cours 309 at 370.

[129] Bin Cheng, *General principles of law as applied by international courts and tribunals* (Cambridge: Grotius Publications Ltd., 1987) at 19.

[130] Joe Verhoeven, "Considérations sur ce qui est commun: Cours général de droit international public" (2008) 334 Rec des Cours 9 at 110.

national legal systems is not helpful to better understand the former.[131] However, the modern international lawyer still seeks for the level of 'objectification' only found in national legal systems when it comes to sources.

In the period between the two world wars, the Pan American Union called for several meetings whose main objective was the codification of American international law. One of the results of such attempts is well known: the American Code of Private International Law; also known as the Bustamante Code, in recognition of its main author, Antonio Sánchez de Bustamante. It is less known that in the meeting held in La Habana, when Bustamante submitted his draft on behalf of the American Institute of International Law, Alejandro Álvarez did the same with a draft code on public international law. Álvarez' draft comprised 30 projects which were meant to be approved as individual treaties. Project number four of the draft code states in its preamble: "Whereas it is proper to determine clearly for the future the fundamental bases of international law, and an end should be put to the uncertainty and the diversity of doctrines existing on this subject…"[132] The project created a complex system on sources which were to be applied in this order: American treaties, American custom, more or less general practices of the American Republics, the manifestation of the legal consciousness of the New World (understood as un-ratified American treaties), rules of universal international law (both customary and conventional), general principles of international law (drawn from rules in force, especially when recognised by arbitral awards) and the precepts of international justice (understood as *voeux* of international conferences, resolution of recognised scientific institutions or opinions of contemporary publicists of authority).[133]

Álvarez' project number four—which, after failing to be adopted in La Habana, was re-submitted to the Rio de Janeiro Meeting in 1927 by the American Institute of International Law as project number one—was never adopted as a treaty. While arguably nobody has gone as far as Álvarez in designing such a comprehensive system, it exemplifies that search for a finite catalogue containing all possible sources of international law. However, it is unavoidable to wonder if the constitutionalisation of international law *à la* Álvarez is possible, useful or even desirable.

As I have demonstrated in the previous pages, the designation of the sources of international law has never been an exact science. As much as scholars try to base international law on an objective and ordered set of sources, the realities of

---

[131] *Report of the International Law Commission: Fifty-eight session*, UNGAOR, 61st Sess, Supp. No. 10, UN Doc A/61/10 (2006) at p 419 (it must be noted that the ILC was speaking specifically about hierarchy in national legal systems).

[132] "Collaboration of the American Institute of International Law with the Pan American Union" (1926) 20 AJIL Supp. 300 at 304.

[133] Ibid at. 304–306; International Commission of Jurists, *supra* note 8 at 238–239.

international relations have always imposed a need for a non-objectified element,[134] a variable in the equation. This exercise of legal history shows, at the very least, that the uncertainty on the topic of sources and the anxieties it raises is anything but recent. The constant reliance on the external, the free, the non-objective is part of the very nature of the international legal system. It always has been. The message is that maybe international legal theory should embrace that uncertainty and work with it. Theory is, after all, the abstract explanation of a complex reality.

As ordered as Alvarez' draft seems to be, it is not free from non-objectified factors. Un-ratified conventions, *voeux* of international conferences and declarations of scientific institutions such as the International Law Association and the *Institut de Droit International*, hardly pass as law by modern standards.[135] Also, they do not necessarily reflect the views of the State and international organizations.

In any case, the point of this chapter was to recognise the multiplicity of legal manifestations that, throughout the history of international law, had enjoyed recognition as sources while being, by definition, non-objectified. General principles of law, natural law, divine law, soft law, "[w]hatever the current terminology, [they remain] a justification for answers produced by international law, rather than a source for those answers."[136] In the following chapters, I will deal with the subsequent period, that is, from 1945 to today, making a clear distinction, however, between the treatment of sources in general international law and in international human rights law. Chapter 3 will deal with the former, by analysing the influence that the decisions of the ICJ, restricted as it is by Article 38 of its Statute, have had in the study of the sources of international law.

---

[134]I am, again, borrowing terms from Alf Ross, who divided the factors that constitute a judicial decision "based on the degree of their objectivity. This is greatest for the formulated rules, least for the spontaneous factors", Ross, *supra* note 13 at 82; as Spiermann explains. "In Ross' view, there were three kinds of sources: (1) 'objective', written sources (treaties); (2) 'partly objective' sources derived from previous practice, whether in courts or among subjects of law (precedent and custom); and (3) '[t]he free, not formulated, not objectified factors spontaneously arising in the judge as the mouthpiece of the community to which he belongs and which he serves", Ole Spiermann, "A National Lawyer Takes Stock: Professor Ross' Textbook and Other Forays into International Law" (2003) 14:4 EJIL 675 at 677–678.

[135]Goldmann notes that among the earliest examples of 'soft law' are the '*voeux*' contained in the Final Acts of the 1899 and 1907 Hague Peace Conferences, Matthias Goldmann, "We Need to Cut Off the Head of the King: Past, Present, and Future Approaches to International Soft Law" (2012) 25:2 Leiden J I L 335 at fn 5.

[136]Spiermann, "Who Attempts Too Much", *supra* note 89.

Chapter 3
The Imperfect Paradigm: Article 38 of the Statute of the International Court of Justice

Abstract In this chapter, I review the practice of different actors of the international legal order, by looking both at the sources recognised by Article 38 of the Statute of the ICJ and those that have been generally accepted over time. By focusing on Article 38 for what it does and does not say, I argue that, even in general international law, Article 38 constitutes only a frame of reference and, therefore, it must be displaced from its paradigmatic position. First, I review the sources mentioned in Article 38 of the ICJ Statute, including the establishment of subsidiary means to find rules, as well as other sources that have been recognised by the jurisprudence of the ICJ even though they are not listed in Article 38. Then, I will discuss three cases in which the ICJ, when confronted with normative forms which do not conform to the requirements of the doctrine of sources as elaborated by its own jurisprudence, treated them as belonging to one of the categories mentioned in Article 38.

3.1 Introduction

The ILC has stated that "international law is not a random collection of norms",[1] in plain and simple terms, it "is a legal system".[2] Although such a statement was made in the context of the diversification and expansion of international law in specialised fields, it does demonstrate that the mainstream understanding of the sources of law goes beyond a simple order in which norms operate at a single level. Having said that, it must be recognised that in the whole body of international law there is no

[1]*Report of the International Law Commission: Fifty-eight session*, UNGAOR, 61st Sess, Supp. No. 10, UN Doc A/61/10 (2006) at para 251 (conclusion 1) [*Report of the ILC, 58th session*]; compare, Alain Pellet, "Complementarity of International Treaty Law, Customary Law, and Non-Contractual Law-Making" in Rüdiger Wolfrum and Volker Röben, eds., *Developments of international law in treaty making* (Berlin; New York: Springer, 2005) at 410. ("from my point of view, the [International Legal System] does not create legal rules, it just permits to determine wheatear a rule has acquired a legal status") [Pellet, "Complementarity"].
[2]*Report of the ILC, 58th Session, ibid.*

C.I. Fuentes, *Normative Plurality in International Law*,
Ius Gentium: Comparative Perspectives on Law and Justice 57,
DOI 10.1007/978-3-319-43929-7_3

rule that authoritatively states the sources applicable to general international law.[3] A body of knowledge that claims to describe such sources has been constructed by the writings of academics and the opinion of international courts, international organizations and States themselves. In parochial terms, there has never been a 'constitutional norm' that would define the sources of international law, explain their authority or dictate the manner in which they interact amongst themselves. In its absence, the actors of the system and its commentators have developed a doctrine which attempts to identify such sources. The heart of the matter is, with no final word on what constitutes a relevant normative form for the purposes of international law, that there are as many enumerations of sources as there are theoretical assumptions about the nature and purpose of this discipline.[4]

The previous chapter discussed the existence of non-objectified elements as sources of international law up until 1945. This is not to say that during the said period there were no trends towards formalism, seeking to separate the 'pure' legal norm, the *lege lata*, from would-be norms. However, since 1945, the discussion about the sources of general international law has consolidated in diverse positivistic theories,[5] while voices to the contrary always seem to be talking of an international legal system that is not here yet. I will leave aside for the moment, to the extent possible, the treatment of sources in international human rights law theory and the practice of international human rights courts; I will argue in subsequent chapters that a parallel trend has developed in that self-contained regime.

[3]Enumerations of sources such as the ones found in the Statute of the International Court of Justice, the Rome Statute of the International Criminal Court and the Treaty on the Functioning of the European Union only apply within the sphere of competencies of the respective institutions; *Charter of the United Nations*, 26 June 1945, Can TS 1945 No. 7, at Annex, Art. 38 [when referring to the Annex: *Statute of the ICJ*]; *Rome Statute of the International Criminal Court*, 17 July 1998, 2187 UNTS 90, (1998) 37 ILM 1002 at art 21 [*Rome Statute*]; *Consolidated Version of the Treaty on the Functioning of the European Union*, [2012] O.J. C 326/47 at art 288 [*Functioning of the European Union*].

[4]Oscar Schachter, "Towards a Theory of International Obligation" in Stephen M. Schwebel, ed., *The Effectiveness of international decisions; papers of a conference of the American Society of International Law and the proceedings of the conference* (Leiden: Sijthoff, 1971) 9 at 9.

[5]See e.g. Hans Kelsen, *Principles of international law* (New York: Rinehart, 1952); Hans Kelsen, Law and Peace in International Relations: The Oliver Wendell Holmes Lectures, 1940–41 (Cambridge: Haravard University Press, 1942); more recently, 'Neo-Kelsenian' approaches such as: Jörg Kammerhofer, "The Benefits of the Pure Theory of Law for International Lawyers, Or: What Use Is Kelsenian Theory" (2006) 12 Int'l L Theory 5; Jörg Kammerhofer, "Uncertainty in the Formal Sources of International Law: Customary International Law and Some of Its Problems" (2004) 15:3 EJIL 523 at 524; Jörg Kammerhofer, *Unearthing structural uncertainty through neo-Kelsenian consistency: Conflicts of norms in international law*, online: SSRN http://ssrn.com/abstract=1535942; there are also revivals of H.L.A. Hart's theories applied to international law in: Jean d'Aspremont, "Wording in International Law" (2012) 25 Leiden J Int'l L 1; Jean d'Aspremont, "Herbert Hart in Post-Modern International Legal Scholarship" in Jean d'Aspremont and Jörg Kammerhofer, eds, *International Legal Positivism in a Post-Modern World* (Cambridge: Cambridge University Press, 2014); Jean d'Aspremont, *Formalism and the Sources of International Law: A theory of the Ascertainment of Legal Rules* (Oxford: Oxford University Press, 2011) [d'Aspremont, *Formalism and the Sources*].

While the absence of a 'constitutional norm' is still evident, there has been an inclination by legal actors to initiate the study of the sources of international law from the Statute of the ICJ. For example, Mendelson has stated that "[i]n international society, the closest we can get to that is the UN Charter; and the Statute of the International Court of Justice, including Article 38(1), is an integral part of the Charter."[6] Indeed, in its Article 38, the Statute defines both the function of the Court and the type of rules it has to apply in the exercise of the judicial function:

> 1. The Court, whose function is to decide in accordance with international law such disputes as are submitted to it, shall apply:
>
> a. international conventions, whether general or particular, establishing rules expressly recognised by the contesting states;
>
> b. international custom, as evidence of a general practice accepted as law;
>
> c. the general principles of law recognised by civilized nations;
>
> d. subject to the provisions of article 59, judicial decisions and the teachings of the most highly qualified publicists of the various nations, as subsidiary means for the determination of rules of law.
>
> 2. This provision shall not prejudice the power of the Court to decide a case *ex aequo et bono*, if the parties agree thereto.[7]

It must be recalled that "[t]he traditional doctrine of the sources of law is based on the view that all law derives its specific validity from coming into existence in certain forms",[8] and not in the fact that the generic terminology describing a particular instrument is enumerated in Article 38 of the Statute. That being said, Article 38 of the ICJ Statute is still considered to be the most authoritative statement of the sources of International Law,[9] although it is widely accepted that it cannot be understood as the embodiment of the doctrine of sources.[10] As d'Aspremont has put it:

> because it offers a handy toolbox for international lawyers in need of a list of sources of international law endowed with some elementary authority, and because of the sophisticated source doctrines that have accompanied it, this provision—although it has not been the only conventional provision to list the sources of international law—has been the lens through which law-identification in international law has been—almost exclusively—construed, and on the basis of which several generations of international lawyers have been trained.[11]

---

[6]Maurice H. Mendelson, "The formation of customary international law" (1998) 272 Rec des Cours 155 at 180.

[7]*Statute of the ICJ*, *supra* note 3 at Art. 38.

[8]Alf Ross, *A textbook of international law: general part* (London: Longmans and Green, 1947) at 79.

[9]Malcolm N. Shaw, *International law*, 5th ed. (Cambridge: Cambridge University Press, 2003) at 66.

[10]See e.g. Alain Pellet, "Article 38" in Andreas Zimmermann, Christian Tomuschat and Karin Oellers-Frahm, eds., *The Statute of the International Court of Justice: A Commentary* (Oxford: Oxford University Press, 2006) 677 at 700 [Pellet, "Article 38"]; for a similar point on the basis of Article 38 of the Statute of the PCIJ, see Ross, *supra* note 8 at 83.

[11]d'Aspremont, *Formalism and the Sources*, *supra* note 5 at 149.

In this chapter I will argue that the contemporary debate on the sources of international law has been excessively influenced by the jurisprudence of the PCIJ and ICJ in the interpretation of Article 38 of each of their respective Statutes.[12] The strict adherence of both international tribunals to the list provided in the Article, along with the jurisprudential elaboration on the meaning of each of its components, has become the cornerstone of the modern doctrine of sources. The conclusion being, that while the Court's function is naturally bound by the letter of the law,[13] the legal imagination needs not be confined to the elements listed in Article 38; and as the trends described in the previous chapter was to rely on external elements, the modern doctrine tends to incorporate distinct forms of normativity within the elements already listed in Article 38 of the ICJ Statute. Such incorporation is not fortuitous; it follows the jurisprudence of the ICJ.[14] However, Klabbers has noted that "[t]here is increasing recognition of the difficulties of shoehorning all international instruments in the recognized sources of Article 38".[15]

In sum, the broad acceptance of Article 38 of the ICJ Statute[16] and the lack of creativity on the part of international law scholars has left this area of international legal theory virtually untouched since the adoption of the Statute of the PCIJ.[17] Even though the intention of the drafters of such an article was never to address the lack of a 'constitutional norm' in public international law.[18]

In order to make this point, I initially discuss the real function of Article 38 within the framework established by the Statute of the Court.[19] I compare and contrast the wording of Article 38 to similar provisions concerning both the scope of the function of other judicial entities, and the description of the rules they are called to apply. In order to develop the argument, it will be necessary to review the definition of each of the elements in Article 38 and the jurisprudence of the Court in further elaborating their content. I recognise that such an approach does not seem original or even interesting. Although much has been written on the sources of international law, most of what has been said plainly repeats and explains Article 38

---

[12]I do not share the enthusiasm of Pellet when he states that the Court has "greatly advanced" the theory of sources of international law, Pellet, "Article 38", *supra* note 10 at 700.

[13]Pellet states "the Court has taken advantage of Art. 38 to clarify the frontiers of the sources of international law, beyond which it does not venture", ibid at 700.

[14]As Pellet has put it, "the case law of the Court has been a powerful tool of consolidation and of evolution of international law", ibid at 789.

[15]See Jan Klabbers, "Law-making and Constitutionalism" in Jan Klabbers, Anne Peters, and Geir Ulfstein, eds, *The Constitutionalization of International Law* (Oxford: Oxford University Press, 2009) 81 at 89 [Klabbers, "Law-making"].

[16]See e.g. Ian Brownlie, *Principles of public international law*, 6th ed. (Oxford: Oxford University Press, 2003) at 5.

[17]Oscar Schachter, "International law in theory and practice: general course in public international law" (1982) 178 Rec des Cours 9 at 35.

[18]Klabbers, "Law-making", *supra* note 15 at 99.

[19]Robert Y. Jennings, "General course on principles of international law" [1967] 121 Rec des Cours 323 at 330 ("it should be borne in mind that Article 38 does not in fact mention the term 'source'; and that it deals strictly with 'court law'") [Jennings, "General course"].

of the Statute.[20] While this methodological choice seems to fall into the logical fallacy described above, it will be necessary to show how the Court contradicts its own interpretation of the norms that control its function in order to incorporate other normative forms in its content.

3.2 Nature and Function of Article 38

As discussed above, the Statute of the ICJ is based on the Statute of its predecessor, the PCIJ. Article 38 in both instruments is almost identical, as it was the expressed intention of the Inter-Allied Committee entrusted to consider the question of the future of the PCIJ not to alter the formula already found in its Statute as the general structure for the future Court.[21] The Inter-Allied Committee specifically pointed out that any change to Article 38 would create more problems than it solved.[22]

In the words of Pellet, "[t]he scope of Art. 38, in its 1945 wording, is twofold: in addition to setting out different sources of law, it summarizes the function of the Court in relation to the law it must apply."[23] I will start by discussing the second of the functions enumerated by Pellet, as it is, in fact the only difference between Article 38 in the Statutes of the ICJ and of the PCIJ.

Indeed, Article 38 of the PCIJ Statute makes no reference to that Court's function nor frames its judicial activity. Its introductory paragraph simply states "The Court shall apply..."[24] Having said that, it must be acknowledged that when the Advisory Committee started to consider the rules applicable to the Court, Professor de Lapradelle did consider that the issue was linked to the question of "[w]hat is the subject-matter of the competence of the Court".[25] However, it was decided that this question had already been settled in previous articles.[26]

[20]Ian Brownlie, *supra* note 16 at 4–5; David L. Kennedy, *International legal structures* (Baden-Baden: Nomos, 1987) at 12; Jonathan I. Charney, "International Lawmaking—Article 38 of the ICJ Statute Reconsidered" in Jost Delbrück and Ursula E. Heinz, eds., *New trends in international lawmaking: international "legislation" in the public interest* (Berlin: Duncker and Humblot, 1997) at 174.

[21]"Report of the Informal Inter-Allied Committee on the Future of the Permanent Court of International Justice: February 10, 1944" (1945) 39:1 AJIL Supp. 1 at 26 and 40 [Inter-Allied Committee].

[22]Ibid at 20.

[23]Pellet, "Article 38", *supra* note 10 at 691.

[24]*Statute of the ICJ*, *supra* note 3 at Art. 38.

[25]Permanent Court of International Justice—Advisory Committee of Jurists, *Procès-Verbaux of the Proceedings of the Committee* (The Hague: Van Langenhuysen Frères, 1920) at 293 [*Procès-Verbaux*].

[26]Ibid.

The insertion of a phrase in the first paragraph of Article 38 was, in fact, the only material change to the article for the ICJ Statute.[27] This change was intended "to give a clearer definition of the Court's mission as an international judicial organ…"[28] The first paragraph of the ICJ Statute reads: "The Court, whose function is to decide in accordance with international law such disputes as are submitted to it, shall apply…"[29] While it could be argued that the insertion to the article was unnecessary,[30] such wording defines the Court's contentious—and by extension advisory[31]—jurisdiction as operating in the realm of international law. This element is not unique to the ICJ; other international entities existing both before and after the adoption of its Statute have featured such a definition of its realm of action. Hudson, writing just before the adoption of the ICJ Statute, stated that "[a]ny international tribunal meriting characterization as such must function within established judicial limitations and must apply international law."[32]

At the time that the Statute of the PCIJ was adopted, an entity of public international law with a general jurisdiction was already operating. By virtue of the Conventions on the Pacific Settlement of Disputes,[33] concluded during The Hague Peace Conferences of 1899 and 1907, the Permanent Court of Arbitration had become a general forum for the settlement of international disputes. However, the aforementioned Conventions provided no indication as to the sources of law the Permanent Court would use.[34] Having said that, the 1899 Convention provides that an arbitral tribunal constituted under its provisions is authorised to declare its competence in interpreting and applying principles of international law.[35] It must be noted that the Permanent Court of Arbitration belonged to a different legal tradition from that which the drafters of the PCIJ Statute desired to create[36]: that of international arbitration.[37] In such a tradition, it is the role of the parties to the dispute to define the legal sources, unless part of the dispute itself is the normative framework

---

[27]There were changes in the form of the Article, as the PCIJ's was a single paragraph with four items, and the ICJ has two paragraphs, with the items being subparagraphs of paragraph 1, and the text of paragraph 2 is the final part of item number four in the old format.

[28]Pellet, "Article 38", *supra* note 10 at 744.

[29]*Statute of the ICJ*, *supra* note 3 at Art. 38.1.

[30]If the ICJ is to apply the sources listed in the enumerated paragraphs, it is obvious that the Court would be "deciding in accordance with international law".

[31]*Statute of the ICJ*, *supra* note 3 at Art. 68.

[32]Manley O. Hudson, *International Tribunals: Past and Future* (Washington D.C.: Brookings Institution, 1944) at 99 [Hudson, *International Tribunals*].

[33]*Convention for the Pacific Settlement of International Disputes*, 29 July 1899, 187 Cons TS 410 [*1899 Convention*]; *Convention for the Pacific Settlement of International Disputes*, 18 October 1907, 205 Cons TS 277.

[34]Ibid.

[35]*1899 Convention*, ibid at art 48.

[36]*Procès-Verbaux*, *supra* note 25 at 8 (reference is made to the speech of Leon Burgeois, member of the Council of the League of Nations, at the first public meeting of the Advisory Committee).

[37]See *supra* p 12 and fn. 62.

of the dispute. The clearest and earliest example of how this tradition presented the judicial function as operating within the rules of international law can be found in the *Institut de Droit International*'s Resolution I of 1895 on a *Projet de règlement pour la procédure arbitrale internationale*:

> Le tribunal arbitral juge selon les principes du droit international, à moins que le compromis ne lui impose des règles différentes ou ne remette la décision à la libre appréciation des arbitres.[38]

Within that same tradition of arbitration, subsequent permanent judicial arrangements have, more or less, maintained the same idea. Such is the case of the Convention on the Settlement of Investment Disputes between States and Nationals of Other States, which provides that:

> The Tribunal shall decide a dispute in accordance with such rules of law as may be agreed by the parties. In the absence of such agreement, the Tribunal shall apply the law of the Contracting State party to the dispute (including its rules on the conflict of laws) and such rules of international law as may be applicable.[39]

This is to say that, as delimitation of the subject matter upon which the Court has an obligation to decide, there is nothing particularly unique about Article 38 of the ICJ Statute. Many other instruments creating international courts and tribunals have indicated—as obvious as it may sound—that their respective functions are to judge on the basis of international law; that is, applicable international law. For instance, the former Central American Court of Justice[40] operated under the following mandate: "in deciding points of fact that may be raised before it, the Central American Court of Justice shall be governed by its free judgment, and with respect to points of law, by the principles of international law."[41]

There are also several examples posterior to the adoption of the ICJ Statute. The Agreement establishing the Caribbean Court of Justice states that: "The Court, in exercising its original jurisdiction under Article XII (b) and (c), shall apply such rules of international law as may be applicable."[42] Also, the United Nations Convention on the Law of the Sea (hereinafter, UNCLOS) established a more narrow approach in proceedings at the International Tribunal for the Law of the Sea by stating that it shall "apply this Convention and other rules of international law

---

[38]Institut de Droit International, "Projet de règlement pour la procédure arbitrale internationale, online: Institut de Droit international", Session of The Hague—1875, http://www.idi-iil.org/idiF/resolutionsF/1875_haye_01_fr.pdf.

[39]*Convention on the Settlement of Investment Disputes between States and Nationals of Other States*, 18 March 1965, 575 UNTS 159, (1965) 4 ILM 532 at art 42.

[40]As opposed to the existing Court, which operates in the framework of the Central American Integration System, see *Convention on the Statute of the Central American Court of Justice*, 10 December 1992, 1821 UNTS 291, 34 ILM 921.

[41]*Convention for the Establishment of a Central American Court of Justice*. 20 December 1907, (1908) 2 AJIL Supp. 231 at art XXI.

[42]*Agreement Establishing the Caribbean Court of Justice*, 14 February 2001, 2255 UNTS 319 at art XVII.

not incompatible with this Convention."[43] It is worth noting that the provision also applies to the ICJ or an arbitral tribunal, in disputes brought to them pursuant to the dispute settlement provisions of UNCLOS.[44]

In sum, the delimitation of the judicial function of the ICJ to international law in Article 38 of its Statute is an interesting feature only in comparison with the analogous provision in the Statute of its predecessor. While it seems from the *travaux préparatoires* that members of the Committee of Jurists entrusted to prepare a draft Statute saw a need in delimiting that function, our current understanding of the international judiciary and its role makes such wording seem obvious. This is especially true when we realise that in the tradition of both international arbitration and adjudication there were already precedents in place delimiting the jurisdictions of international courts and tribunals to international law. In the view of Hudson, "[t]he duty of a tribunal to apply international law will exist in the absence of any stipulation to that effect in the organic instrument under which it is created".[45] Whether the following sub-paragraphs in Article 38 reflect the whole of international law at a given time is another matter. At this point it suffices to say that the function of the first paragraph is, as stated above, to define the function of the Court and to instruct their members to rely on international law in the performance of the judicial activities—this, of course, without prejudice to the Court's being requested to rule *ex aequo et bono*.[46]

The delimitation of the functional jurisdiction of the Court has been the object of much exaggeration, as it has been argued that:

> these words strongly suggest that, in applying treaties and other items in the list which follows, the Court would be complying with international law; in other words, they are recognised processes for the creation or, as the case may be, determination of rules of law.[47]

As stated above, Article 38 has a second function which is "to stress that [the Court] was bound to resort to the sources enumerated in para. 1 of the said provision."[48] Indeed, the plain and simple reading of Article 38 confirms that the intention of the drafters of the PCIJ Statute was to answer the question "What rules are to be applied by the Court of Justice within the limits of this competence?"[49] The point was raised, very early in the discussions of the Advisory Committee, that "The Covenant intended to establish the Permanent Court of International Justice to apply international law; it was the duty of the Committee to point out to the Court how it should carry it out its task."[50]

---

[43] *United Nations Convention on the Law of the Sea*, 10 December 1982, 1833 UNTS 3 at art 293 [*UNCLOS*].

[44] Ibid at art 287.1.

[45] Hudson, *International Tribunals, supra* note 32 at 100.

[46] *Statute of the ICJ, supra* note 3 at art 38.2.

[47] Mendelson, *supra* note 6 at 180.

[48] Pellet, "Article 38", *supra* note 10 at 696.

[49] *Procès-Verbaux, supra* note 25 at 729.

[50] Ibid at 294.

That is, at the most basic level of analysis, Article 38 of the ICJ Statute is a list, and not a particularly original one. There is a lesser-known precedent to the PCIJ that greatly influenced the discussions surrounding Article 38 of its Statute during the meetings of the Advisory Committee of Jurists entrusted with its drafting: the Convention relative to the Creation of an International Prize Court. Another product of the Second Hague Peace Conference of 1907, the Prize Court never came into existence, as the Convention never entered into force. However, it is worth noting that its Article 7 provided that:

> If a question of law to be decided is covered by a treaty in force between the belligerent captor and a Power which is itself or whose subject or citizen is a party to the proceedings, the Court is governed by the provisions in the said treaty. In the absence of such provisions, the Court shall apply the rules of international law. If no generally recognised rule exists, the Court shall give judgment in accordance with the general principles of justice and equity.[51]

The list of sources found in the International Prize Court Convention is, however, different in the fact that it is hierarchical. Tribunals of more recent creation have also contained some indications of the sources that it should apply in a carefully elaborated order. Such is the case of Article 21 of the Rome Statute of the International Criminal Court (hereinafter, Rome Statute), which contains a list of sources to be applied by the International Criminal Court in its decisions, which, as in the case of the Prize Court, is also hierarchical[52]:

> 1. The Court shall apply:
>
> (a) In the first place, this Statute, Elements of Crimes and its Rules of Procedure and Evidence;
>
> (b) In the second place, where appropriate, applicable treaties and the principles and rules of international law, including the established principles of the international law of armed conflict;
>
> (c) Failing that, general principles of law derived by the Court from national laws of legal systems of the world including, as appropriate, the national laws of States that would normally exercise jurisdiction over the crime, provided that those principles are not inconsistent with this Statute and with international law and internationally recognised norms and standards.

[51] *Convention relative to the Creation of an International Prize Court*, 18 October 1907, 205 Cons TS 381 at art 7 [*Convention on a Prize Court*].

[52] This Court has confirmed this notion by stating that when a matter is exhaustive exhaustively dealt with in the Rome Statute or Rules of Procedure and Evidence "no room is left for recourse to the second or third source of law to determine the presence or absence of a rule governing a given subject", *Prosecutor v. Thomas Lubanga Dyilo*, Judgment on the appeal of Mr Thomas Lubanga Dyilo against the decision on the defence challenge to the jurisdiction of the court pursuant to Article 19(2)(a) of the Statute of 3 October 2006, Case No ICC-01/04-01/06-772, 14th December 2006 (International Criminal Court, Appeals Chamber) at para 34 online: International Criminal Court http://www.icc-cpi.int/iccdocs/doc/doc243774.PDF.

2. The Court may apply principles and rules of law as interpreted in its previous decisions.[53]

Lists of such nature are not exclusive to jurisdictional bodies. In fact, such lists have also been established in substantive provisions of international instruments in order to clarify the scope of a particular regime, define the hierarchy of norms within a subsystem or simply state the obligations of States in relation to non-binding instruments adopted in the framework of a regime.

The failed Treaty for a Constitution of the European Union contained a list detailing the hierarchy of legal acts to be taken by the authorities of the Union, which was established as: "European laws, European framework laws, European regulations, European decisions, recommendations and opinions."[54] After the latest amendments adopted through the Treaty of Lisbon,[55] the Treaty on the Functioning of the European Union currently states that "the institutions [of the Union] shall adopt regulations, directives, decisions, recommendations and opinions."[56]

In a similar fashion, the States parties to the Southern Common Market (hereinafter, MERCOSUR) have an established order of substantive norms applicable to the common market:

The legal sources of MERCOSUR are:

I. The Treaty of Asunción, its protocols and the additional or supplementary instruments;

II. The agreements concluded within the framework of the Treaty of Asunción and its protocols;

III. The Decisions of the Council of the Common Market, the Resolutions of the Common Market Group and the Directives of the Mercosur Trade Commission adopted since the entry into force of the Treaty of Asunción.[57]

Despite all of the above, it must also be recognised that other international agreements have either directly referenced the wording used in Article 38 of the ICJ Statute, or simply borrowed the list contained therein for either substantive or jurisdictional purposes. For instance, the *Protocol on the Community Court of Justice*[58] to the *Treaty of the Economic Community of West African States*[59] provides that the Community Court of Justice "shall examine the dispute before it in accordance with the provisions of the Treaty and its Rules of Procedure. It shall also

[53]*Rome Statute*, *supra* note 3 at art 21.

[54]*Treaty establishing a Constitution for Europe*, 29 October 2004, [2004] O.J. C 310/1 at art I-33.

[55]*Treaty of Lisbon amending the Treaty on European Union and the Treaty establishing the European Community*, 13 December 2007, [2007] O.J. C 306/1 at art 2, para 235.

[56]*Functioning of the European Union*, *supra* note 3 at art 288.

[57]*Additional Protocol to the Asunción Treaty on the institutional structure of Mercosur* (*Ouro Preto Protocol*), Argentina, Brazil, Paraguay and Uruguay, 17 December 1994, 2145 UNTS 298 at art 41 [*Ouro Preto Protocol*].

[58]*Protocol on the Community Court of Justice*, 6 July 1991, 2375 UNTS 178.

[59]*Treaty of the Economic Community of West African States*, 28 May 1975, 1976 UNTS 17.

apply, as necessary, the body of laws as contained in Article 38 of the Statutes of the International Court of Justice."[60]

UNCLOS makes reference to the list contained in the Statute of the ICJ as a possible means of agreement between States concerning the delimitation of specific maritime zones:

> The delimitation of the exclusive economic zone between States with opposite or adjacent coasts shall be effected by agreement on the basis of international law, as referred to in Article 38 of the Statute of the International Court of Justice, in order to achieve an equitable solution.[61]

It is also worth mentioning that the Model Rules on Arbitral Procedure prepared by the International Law Commission in 1953 contained a direct reference to the ICJ Statue stating that "[i]n the absence of any agreement between the parties concerning the law to be applied, the tribunal shall be guided by Article 38, paragraph 1, of the Statute of the International Court of Justice."[62] However, upon a revision of the Model Rules requested by the General Assembly,[63] and internal debates at the Commission concerning the draft article in 1958,[64] it was decided that since the cited formula "was considered to be unsatisfactory, and no other general phrase referring to that provision seemed free from drafting difficulties, it was decided to set out the actual terms of Article 38, paragraph 1."[65] The rules as adopted simply replicate the four elements reflected in Article 38, paragraph 1.[66]

Since then, other international instruments have chosen not to refer directly to the Statute of the ICJ, but replicate its formula. Such is the case of Article 33 of the Permanent Court of Arbitration Optional Rules for Arbitrating Disputes between Two States, which copies in its entirety Article 38 of the ICJ Statute.[67] Another

---

[60] *Protocol on the Community Court of Justice*, supra note 58 at art. 19(1).

[61] *UNCLOS*, *supra* note 43 at art 74 and 83.

[62] "*Report of the International Law Commission covering the work of its fifth session 1 June-14 August 1953*" (UN Doc A/2456) in *Yearbook of the International Law Commission 1953*, vol 2 (New York: UN, 1959) at 210 (A/CN.4/SER.A/1953/Add.1).

[63] *Arbitral procedure*, GA Res. 989(X), UN GAOR, 10th Sess., Supp. No. 9, UN Doc. A/RES/989 (X) (1955) at operative paragraph 2.

[64] The actual sources were never an issue at the ILC. The Commissioners were mostly debating whether the arbitral tribunal should 'apply' (drafting committee), 'conform to' (Roberto Ago), 'proceed in conformity with' (Ricardo J. Alfaro), or 'apply the rules contained in' (Secretariat) Article 38 of the ICJ Statute. It was upon a suggestion from Faris Bey El-Khouri that the Commission decided to circumvent the problem by simply stating that the arbitral tribunal 'shall apply', and then reproduce the content of Article 38, paragraph 1. UN CN4OR, 10th Sess., 473th Mtg., UN Doc. A/CN.4/SR473 (1958) in *Yearbook of the International Law Commission 1958*, vol 1, *supra* note 82.

[65] "*Report of the International Law Commission covering the work of its tenth session, 28 April–4July 1958*" (UN Doc A/3859) in *Yearbook of the International Law Commission 1958*, vol 2 (New York: UN, 1958) at p 84 (A/CN.4/SER.A/1958/Add.1).

[66] Ibid at p 87, para 32.

[67] *Permanent Court of Arbitration: Optional Rules for Arbitrating Disputes between Two States*, 2o October 1992, (1993) 32 ILM 572 at art 33.

document based on the former, the Rules of Procedure of the Eritrea-Ethiopia Claims Commission, takes the same approach and copies Article 38 of the ICJ Statute in its Article 19.[68]

As shown in this section, the nature and purpose of Article 38, as evidenced by the intention of the drafters and both previous and subsequent practice, is confined to the limits of the ICJ judicial function. Moreover, it has been shown that States have defined the scope of international law applicable to international tribunals or other institutions, and even attached lists of sources on different occasions.

Lists of sources are important and can be useful in legal discourse, especially when the intention of the drafters was to establish a restrictive catalogue. The debate following the temporary suspension of Paraguay in MERCOSUR is evidence of their function in defining legality within a regime: On 29 June 2012, the Presidents of Argentina, Brazil and Uruguay, after considering events that occurred in Paraguay on 23 June of that same year,[69] issued a declaration suspending the latter from participating in the work and deliberations of the organs of MERCOSUR.[70] Soon after, Paraguay challenged the legality of the resolution before the Permanent Tribunal of Revision of MERCOSUR arguing, among other things, that its "suspension was not effected [...] in application of the sources of law enumerated in art 41 of the"[71] Ouro Preto Protocol[72] to the Asunción Treaty.[73] While the case was unsuccessful, Paraguay continued to state that the measures were adopted through an instrument that does not have legal value within the framework established by the member States of MERCOSUR.[74]

---

[68]Eritrea-Ethiopia Claims Commission, "Rules of Procedure" at art 19, online: Permanent Court of Arbitration http://www.pcacases.com; The Commission confirms that "Article 19 of the Commission's Rules of Procedure is modeled on the familiar language of Article 38, paragraph 1, of the Statute of the International Court of Justice", *Prisoners of War—Ethiopia's Claim 4* (*Ethiopia v. Eritrea*), Partial Award, 1st July 2003 (Eritrea-Ethiopia Claims Commission) at para 22, online: Permanent Court of Arbitration http://www.pcacases.com.

[69]"Paraguay's impeachment: Lugo out in the cold" *The Economist* (30 June 2012) online: The Economist http://www.economist.com/node/21557802.

[70]"Cumbre del MERCOSUR Mendoza 2012: decisión sobre la suspensión del Paraguay en el MERCOSUR en aplicación del protocolo de Ushuaia sobre compromiso democrático", online: Ministerio de Relaciones Exteriores y Culto, Republica Argentina http://www.mrecic.gov.ar/es/cumbre-del-mercosur-mendoza-2012-decisión-sobre-la-suspensión-del-paraguay-en-el-mercosur-en.

[71]*Procedimiento Excepcional de Urgencia solicitado por la República del Paraguay en relación con la suspensión de su participación en los Órganos del Mercado Común del Sur* (*MERCOSUR*) *y la incorporación de Venezuela como Miembro Pleno* (2012), Award No. 01/2012, online: Tribunal Permanente de Revisión http://www.tprmercosur.org/es/docum/laudos/Laudo_01_2012_es.pdf.

[72]*Ouro Preto Protocol*, *supra* note 57 at art 41.

[73]*Treaty for the establishment of a Common Market* (*Asunción Treaty*), Argentina, Brazil, Paraguay and Uruguay, 26 March 1991, 2140 UNTS 257, (1991) 30 ILM 1041.

[74]"Comunicado de Prensa", 7 December 2012, online: Ministerio de Relaciones Exteriores de Paraguay http://www.mre.gov.py/v1/Adjuntos/defensadelosprincipiosDIP/Comunicado-sobre-Reunion-del-Mercosur.pdf.

Of course, not all lists of norms are meant to establish a closed and self-contained legal system. But one of the general points of this chapter is that no authoritative list intending to establish a general international legal system has ever been established. Still, Article 38 of the ICJ Statute has been used as a procedural example and for other substantive purposes on a number of occasions. This enforces the idea that: "this enumeration must be taken as an authoritative formulation of the sources of international law in general, inside or outside the International Court of Justice."[75] However, the fact remains that Article 38 of the ICJ Statute was never intended to establish the sources of international law.[76]

I will now discuss the Court's actual understanding of Article 38 of its Statute, and the ways in which the Court has developed the definition and conceptual scope of the sources listed in paragraph one of the said article.

3.3 The Sources in Article 38

As explained above, this section deals with the sources found in Article 38 of the Statute of the Court, namely treaties, international custom, and general principles of international law. The doctrine of the sources of international law recognises two basic and uncontested methods of law creation: custom and treaties.[77] It has been argued that of the different sources enumerated in Article 38, custom and treaties (along with judicial decisions) "are reasonably well defined [and] are in fact the three principal sources of legal authority in the international community."[78] Both treaties and custom are strictly dependent on actions, decisions, and expressions of conviction from the

[75]Wolfgang Friedmann, "The Uses of General Principles in the Development of International Law" (1963) 57 AJIL 279 at 279.

[76]Kammerhofer, reviewing Pellet ("Article 38", *supra* note 66) stated: "Pellet here correctly distinguishes between the two roles of Article 38. On the one hand, Article 38 is 'only' the applicable law clause (qua lex arbitri) of the International Court of Justice; on the other hand, Article 38 is cited simply too often by scholarship as (at least) the epistemological 'fount' of the formal sources of international law as a whole to be ignored by a commentary. Because traditional scholarship has this (falsely) heightened expectation of Article 38, Pellet has had to consider customary international law (at 748–764), for example, as such rather than as lex arbitri", Jörg Kammerhofer and André de Hoogh, "All Things to All People? The International Court of Justice and its Commentators" (2008) 18 EJIL 971 at 978; see also, Stephen Hall, "The Persistent Spectre: Natural Law, International Order and the Limits of Legal Positivism", [2001] 12 EJIL 269 at 284 ("Although Article 38 strictly applies only to the work of the International Court, it is nevertheless generally accepted as setting out the sources of international law at large.").

[77]"Comme sources du droit international, c'est-à-dire comme modes de sa formation, nous n'envisagerons que la coutume et l'accord", Paul Heilborn, "Les sources du droit international" (1926) 11 Rec des Cours 1 at 20; see also, Shabtai Rosenne, *The World Court: what it is and how it works*, 5th completely rev. ed. (Dordrecht; London: M. Nijhoff, 1995) at 147.(When writing about article 38 of the ICJ Statute, Rosenne specifies that heads (a) and (b) of the article—treaties and custom—"refer to the rules of law itself") [Rosenne, *The World Court*].

[78]Friedmann, *supra* note 75 at 279.

State, which is the essential actor in the system. Even after the creation of international organizations, "States are still the major addressees of rules of international law, and they retain virtual monopoly over the law-making process".[79] The third source to be discussed in this section, general principles of law, is a result of the emergence of the international judiciary of general jurisdiction. While its recognition as a source of international law is not contested anymore, it is still not clear today whether these principles are norms or statements about norms, and whether their origin is the domestic fora of States or if they emanate from international law itself. In any case, their origin can be traced to a theory which seeks to explain the legal order as a meaningful whole. That is, they were intended as a last recourse to avoid *non liquet* if no treaty or custom would provide a clear solution. In the following subsections I will address the meaning given to each of the items founds in Article 38, as per the recorded intention of its drafters and the jurisprudence of the PCIJ and the ICJ.

3.3.1 Treaties

The first of the rules to be applied by the ICJ, as enumerated in Article 38 of its Statute, is "international conventions, whether general or particular, establishing rules expressly recognised by the contesting states".[80] Pellet has stated that "[n]othing in particular can be inferred from the use, in Art. 38, para. 1(a), of the word 'conventions' rather than 'treaties', usually seen as the generic term."[81] In fact, the jurisprudence of the ICJ has recognised that the name of a particular instrument has a limited value in the process of defining its legal nature.[82]

It must be recalled again that the text of Article 38 of the ICJ Statute was copied from the Statute of the PCIJ. A brief look at the *Proces Verbaux* of the Advisory Committee of Jurists shows that there was a general agreement about the place of treaties as a source of obligations between contesting parties. In fact, already at the 14th meeting of the Advisory Committee of Jurists, its President, Baron Descamps, declared that "[a]ll agree that when rules are expressly laid down by a general or special treaty between the parties, it is the first duty of a judge to apply them."[83]

The draft prepared by the President of the Advisory Committee of Jurists was based on the Convention of 18 October 1907 relative to the Creation of an International Prize Court, which already established the duty of the judge to give

[79]O.A. Elias and C.L. Lim, *The paradox of consensualism in international law* (The Hague; Boston: Kluwer Law International, 1998) at 193.

[80]*Statute of the ICJ*, *supra* note 3 at art 38.1(a).

[81]Pellet, "Article 38", *supra* note 10 at 737.

[82]*Maritime Delimitation and Territorial Questions between Qatar and Bahrain (Qatar v. Bahrain), Jurisdiction and Admissibility*, [1994] ICJ Rep 112 at para 23 [*Qatar v. Bahrain, Jurisdiction and Admissibility* (1 July 1994)]; see also *Aegean Sea Continental Shelf (Greece v. Turkey)*, [1978] ICJ Rep 3 at para 96 [*Aegean Sea Continental Shelf*].

[83]*Procès-Verbaux*, *supra* note 25 at 323.

prevalence to treaty rules in force over other sources.[84] At the 15th meeting of the Advisory Committee of Jurists—which took place on 3 July 1920—none of the members of the Committee questioned the content or wording of the President's Draft, which constituted the basis of the discussion.

As discussed above, treaties have been considered an uncontested mode of law creation in international law. However, it has been implied by Pellet that the formula used in Article 38 of the ICJ Statute is embryonic and "less complete" than the definition found in the VCLT.[85] In fact, it must be noted that the ICJ itself has had recourse to the definition of treaties given in the VCLT[86]: "[T]reaty' means an international agreement concluded between States in written form and governed by international law, whether embodied in a single instrument or in two or more related instruments and whatever its particular designation."[87]

However, regardless of the use that the ICJ has given to the above definition, neither the ILC nor the UN Conference on the Law of Treaties envisaged that such a definition would have had any value beyond the articles adopted or the VCLT. The Commentary to the draft articles adopted by the ILC is clear in that "[t]his article, as its title and the introductory words of paragraph 1 indicate, is intended only to state the meanings with which terms are used in the draft articles."[88]

It has been argued that the designation of agreements as 'general or particular' in subparagraph a of Article 38 does not seem to add much to the definition,[89] and that such differentiation serves more theoretical than practical needs.[90] However, it must be recalled that there is a historical reason for such differentiation. "*Pendant longtemps, lorsque le nombre des contractants était supérieur à deux, on n'a pas cru pouvoir se contenir d'un acte unique (...) on établissait donc une série de traites bilatéraux entre lesquels il n'y avait pas de lien juridique*".[91] Guggenheim

---

[84]*Convention on a Prize Court*, *supra* note 51 at art 7 (The said Convention provided that: "If a question of law to be decided is covered by a treaty in force between the belligerent captor and a Power which is itself or whose subject or citizen is a party to the proceedings, the Court is governed by the provisions in the said treaty.").

[85]Pellet, "Article 38", *supra* note 10 at 737.

[86]*Qatar v. Bahrain*, Jurisdiction and Admissibility (1 July 1994), *supra* note 82 at para 23; *Land and Maritime Boundary between Cameroon and Nigeria (Cameroon v. Nigeria: Equatorial Guinea intervening)*, Merits, [2002] ICJ Rep 303 at para 263 [*Cameroon v. Nigeria*, Merits].

[87]*Vienna Convention on the Law of Treaties*, 23 May 1969, 1155 UNTS 331 at art 2.1(a), (1969) 8 ILM 679 [*VCLT*].

[88]*Report of the International Law Commission on the work of its eighteenth session Ganeve, 4 May-19 July 1966* (UN Doc A/5309/Rev.1) in *Yearbook of the International Law Commission 1966*, vol 2 (New York: UN, 1967) at 188 (A/CN.4/SER.A/1966/Add.1) [*Report of the ILC, 18th Session*; except when referring to the commentaries to the draft articles on the law of treaties, with page references to the Yearbook of the ILC: *Commentaries*].

[89]Manley O. Hudson, *The Permanent court of international justice 1920–1942: A Treatise* (New York: The Macmillan Company) at 608.

[90]Pellet, "Article 38", *supra* note 10 at 746.

[91]Paul Guggenheim, "Contribution à l'histoire des sources du droit des gens" (1958) 94 Rec des Cours 5 at 70.

gives the example of the Treaty of Paris of 30 May 1814, which was actually composed of seven separate yet identical treaties between France and each of its allies. He also states that the first collective treaty was the Treaty of Paris of 30 March 1856, which was open to third parties without conditions of accession.[92]

If anything can be extracted from the discussions of the Advisory Committee of Jurists and the subsequent jurisprudence of the ICJ defining the meaning of sub-paragraph (a), it is that identifying a treaty does not seem to be a problematic endeavour. The fact that the ICJ has made use of the VCLT in this and other regards seems to point out that the criteria governing the identification of all international agreements are regulated exclusively by the provisions of the VCLT, whether applying them as conventional or customary law. However, the main rule of identification of the nature of a instrument use by the ICJ in practice has been defined in the *Aegean Sea Continental Shelf* case, in the following terms: "the Court must have regard above all to its actual terms and to the particular circumstances in which it was drawn up".[93] This is in the assumption that the parties to a dispute do not agree on the nature of the instrument, since the Court has not applied the criteria in the opposite case.[94]

3.3.2 Custom

At the beginning of the 14th meeting of the Advisory Committee of Jurists for the PCIJ, Baron Descamps made a speech on the Rules of Law to be applied by the then nascent Court. He said: "[n]ot to recognise international custom as a principle which must be followed by the judge in the absence of expressed conventional law, would be to misconstrue the true character and whole history of the law of nations."[95] Custom has indeed played an immense role in the history of international law. As repeated several times already, and as explained in the previous chapter, custom is regarded as one of two uncontested modes of law creation in international law, even by legal positivists[96]—this despite the fact that "[t]he characteristic of this kind of law is that it is not just unwritten, it is informal…"[97]

---

[92]Ibid at 71.

[93]*Aegean Sea Continental Shelf, supra* note 82 at para 96.

[94]*Maritime Dispute* (*Peru v. Chile*), [2014] ICJ Rep 3 at para 48.

[95]*Procès-Verbaux, supra* note 25 at 322.

[96]See e.g. Hall, *supra* note 76 at 286 and ss.

[97]Mendelson, *supra* note 6 at 172; see also, International Law Association, Committee on Formation of Customary (General) International Law, "Final Report of the Committee: Statement of Principles Applicable to the Formation of General Customary International Law" (2000) 69 Int'l L Ass'n Rep Conf 712 at 713 ("customary law is by its very nature the result of an informal process of rule-creation, so that the degree of precision found in more formal processes of law-making is not to be expected here.").

Just as in the case of treaties, there seemed to be a general agreement about the importance of custom in the discussions leading to the adoption of the PCIJ Statute.[98] There was, in fact, almost no discussion about the wording used to describe customary law,[99] which would eventually become Article 38.1.b of the ICJ Statute: "international custom, as evidence of a general practice accepted as law".[100] Leaving aside the debate on whether such wording is a definition or a description, what has become clear is that the Court has interpreted Article 38.1.b as the methodological guide for the ascertainment of a particular rule. For instance, in one of its early cases, the Court stated that:

> [T]he rule invoked by it is in accordance with a constant and uniform usage practised by the States in question, and that this usage is the expression of a right appertaining to the State granting asylum and a duty incumbent on the territorial State. This follows from Article 38 of the Statute of the Court, which refers to international custom 'as evidence of a general practice accepted as law'.[101]

The Court has further elaborated this view, in what has become the go-to piece of jurisprudence used by other tribunals[102] and the ICJ itself[103] to explain the criterion for identifying a rule of customary international law, the *North Sea Continental Shelf* case:

> Not only must the acts concerned amount to a settled practice, but they must also be such, or be carried out in such a way, as to be evidence of a belief that this practice is rendered obligatory by the existence of a rule of law requiring it. The need for such a belief, i.e., the existence of a subjective element, is implicit in the very notion of the *opinio juris sive*

---

[98]On the 13th meeting of the Committee, the only sceptic voice was that of Mr. Root, *Procès-Verbaux*, *supra* note 25 at 293.

[99]Ibid at 322 (reference is made to the speech by Baron Descamps at the beginning of the 14th meeting, explaining the points in which the Advisory Committee seemed to agree upon).

[100]*Statute of the ICJ*, *supra* note 3 at art 38.1.b.

[101]*Asylum Case* (*Colombia v. Peru*), [1950] ICJ Rep 266 at p 276–277; this is already an elaboration of the PCIJ's view that "The rules of law binding upon States therefore emanate from their own free will as expressed in conventions or by usages generally accepted as expressing principles of law", *The Case of the S.S. "Lotus"* (*France v. Turkey*) (1927), PCIJ (Ser. A) No. 10 at 18 [*Lotus*].

[102]See, e.g. *Arbitration between the Government of the State of Kuwait and the American Independent Oil Company* (*AMINOIL*), *Final Award* (1982), 21 ILM 976 at para 157 (Arbitrators: Paul Reuter, Hamed Sultan, Sir Gerald Fitzmaurice); *Van Anraat v. Netherlands* (dec.), no. 65389/09[*Lotus*], (2010) 49 ILM 127 at para 35 (European Court of Human Rights); *Prosecutor v. Ieng Sary, Ieng Thirith, Khieu Samphan*, 002/19-09-2007-ECCC/OCIJ (PTC38), Decision on the appeals against the Co-Investigative Judges Order on joint criminal enterprise (JCE) (20 May 2010) at para 53 (Extraordinary Chambers in the Courts of Cambodia) (49 ILM 1345).

[103]Very recently the Court has used the *North Sea Continental Shelf* (*infra* note 104) dictum to explain that "...the Court must determine, in accordance with Article 38 (1)(b) of its Statute, the existence of 'international custom, as evidence of a general practice accepted as law' [... t]o do so, it must apply the criteria which it has repeatedly laid down for identifying a rule of customary international law. In particular, as the Court made clear in the *North Sea Continental Shelf* cases, the existence of a rule of customary international law requires that there be "a settled practice" together with *opinio juris*", *Jurisdictional Immunities of the State* (*Germany v. Italy: Greece intervening*), [2012] ICJ Rep 99 at para 55 [*Jurisdictional Immunities*].

> *necessitatis*. The States concerned must therefore feel that they are conforming to what amounts to a legal obligation. The frequency, or even habitual character of the acts is not in itself enough.[104]

The ICJ added later that such a criterion "is of course axiomatic."[105]

All of the above has to be contrasted with other dicta of the Court that seemed to find *opinio juris* in the lack of negative behaviour, rather than in the field of evidence of positive conviction. In the *Fisheries case*, the Court concluded that the straight lines method used by Norway to draw its baselines "had been consolidated by a constant and sufficiently long practice, in the face of which the attitude of governments bears witness to the fact that they did not consider it to be contrary to international law."[106]

This is, of course, merely the description of the process. Since the adoption of the *North Sea Continental Shelf* dictum, there has been a long academic discussion on the relative weight of each element in the identifying process,[107] on the distinction between *opinio juris* and consent,[108] and on the relationship between customary law and other sources,[109] among other issues. I am, however, more interested in the specific manifestations that the Court has used as evidence of *opinio juris* and practice.

Sohn has raised the point that the "rules contained in Article 38 of the Statute of the International Court of Justice were appropriate at the time of their adoption, and they are flexible enough to allow new ways of ascertainment of the existence of a rule of customary international law."[110] I am conscious that current scholarship on the impact of human rights in international law focuses on the notion that the jurisprudence of the ICJ has adopted a more flexible approach with regard to the elements of customary international law.[111] However, I do not necessarily see as useful—either for the development of human rights or for the theory of customary law—the view that tries to push the limits of the definition of customary law and expand the catalogue of normative forms that demonstrate the practice or *opinio juris* of States.[112]

---

[104] *North Sea Continental Shelf, Judgment (Federal Republic of Germany v. Denmark; Federal Republic of Germany v. Netherlands)*, [1969] ICJ Rep 3 at para 77.

[105] *Continental Shelf (Libyan Arab Jamahiriya v. Malta)*, [1985] ICJ Rep 13 para 27 [*Libya v. Malta*].

[106] *Fisheries (United Kingdom v. Norway)*, [1951] ICJ Rep 116 at 128.

[107] See e.g. Frederic L. Kirgis, Jr., "Custom on a Sliding Scale" (1987) 81 AJIL 146.

[108] See, e.g. Olufemi Elias, "The Nature of the Subjective Element in Customary International Law" [1995] 44:3 ICLQ 501.

[109] See e.g. Theodor Meron, "The Geneva Conventions as Customary Law" (1987) 81 AJIL 348 at 351–355; Leila Nadya Sadat, "Custom, Codification and Some Thoughts about the Relationship between the Two: Article 10 of the ICC Statute" (1999–2000) 49 DePaul L Rev 909 at 910.

[110] Louis B. Sohn, Generally Accepted International Rules (1986) 61 Wash L Rev 1073 at 1079.

[111] See e.g. Roozbeh B. Baker, "Customary International Law in the 21st century: Old Challenges and New Debates" [2010] 21:1 EJIL 173.

[112] See also Theodor Meron, *The humanization of international law* (Leiden: Martinus Nijhoff, 2006) at 360–370 (for example, he states that "[a]n expansive approach views the Universal Declaration of Human Rights either as customary per se…").

It must be noted that since 2014 the ILC has been considering the topic of 'identification of customary international law'; and while at the moment this book was concluded only draft conclusions had been provisionaly adopted, at that early stage such conclusions did not depart from the jurisprudence of the Court on the matter.[113]

3.3.3 General Principles of Law

It was stated in 1963 that:

> Although the "general principles of law" were officially recognised as one of the sources of international law over forty years ago (in the Statute of the Permanent Court of International Justice), the practical use made of this source in the decisions of the International Court and of international tribunals has been rather limited.[114]

The circumstances of the adoption of the general principles law, in both the PCIJ and ICJ Statutes, have been discussed extensively in the previous chapter. As they remain a source of law recognised by the jurisprudence of the Court and the writings of academics, they will briefly be discussed here.

While scholars have attempted to classify and qualify the general principles of law as used by international courts and tribunals,[115] the ICJ has rarely defined how it ascertained the existence of a principle.[116] This still makes them, to some extent, an un-objectified source. Moreover, Raimondo has argued that "general principles of law have played a marginal role in the practice of the PCIJ and the ICJ, in that neither has based any ruling exclusively on these principles."[117]

It has been pointed out that customary international law can be understood to include all that is un-written in international law, therefore encompassing the general principles of law.[118] However, such a view does not take into account the fact that when the Court is called to invoke general principles in the Statute, there is

---

[113] *Report of the International Law Commission: Sixty-seventh session*, UNGAOR, 70th Sess, Supp. No. 10, UN Doc A/70/10 (2015) at Chapter VI [*Report of the ILC, 67th session*].

[114] Friedmann, *supra* note 75 at 280.

[115] See e.g., Joost Pauwelyn, *Conflict of Norms in Public International Law: How WTO Law Relates to other Rules of International Law* (Cambridge: Cambridge University Press, 2003) at 125–126; Friedmann, ibid at 286.

[116] See Jonathan I. Charney, "Is international law threatened by multiple international tribunals?" (1998) 271 Rec des Cours 101 at 190 [Charnery, "Multiple Tribunals"].

[117] Raimondo, *supra* note 83 at 22.

[118] Lord Phillimore himself raised this point during the discussions of the Advisory Committee of Jurists, *Procès-Verbaux*, *supra* note 25 at 311; see also Bin Cheng, *General principles of law as applied by international courts and tribunals* (Cambridge: Grotius Publications Ltd., 1987) at 23 [Cheng, *General principles*].

no linkage between their content and the actual practice of States.[119] Moreover, the treatment general principles receive in the jurisprudence of the Court is, in fact, that of self-evident legal truths or legal common sense.[120]

As for the method for their ascertainment, the scholarly view is that "[t]he recognition of its legal character by civilised peoples supplies the necessary element of determination."[121] Such a view is justified in the terms used by the Court in the cases concerning *South West Africa* (*Liberia v. South Africa and Ethiopia v. South Africa*) to deny the existence of *actio popularis* as a general principle under the ICJ Statute:

> But although a right of this kind may be known to certain municipal systems of law, it is not known to international law as it stands at present: nor is the Court able to regard it as imported by the "general principles of law" referred to in Article 38, paragraph 1 (c), of its Statute.[122]

According to Professor Ellis, scholars generally describe the method as having three stages: (1) identification of a principle common to the main legal systems of the world, (2) distillation of its essence, and (3) its modification to international law's particularities.[123] She notes that the third stage appears less often in the doctrine. Although very insightful, her critiques to the method (especially those relating to the identification stage) necessarily have to address its theoretical deficiencies[124] due to the fact that the Court "does not expressly report on a survey of the principal legal systems of the world when it makes these pronouncements."[125]

---

[119]Cheng, ibid, at 24 ("In the definition of the third source of international law, there is also the element of recognition on the part of civilized peoples but the requirement of a general practice is absent").

[120]See e.g., Shabtai Rosenne, *The law and practice of the International Court, 1920–2005*, vol. III, 4th ed. (Leiden: Martinus Nijhoff, 2006) at 1549 [Rosenne, *The law and practice*]; see also, Hersch Lauterpacht, *The Development of International Law by the International Court* (New York: Cambridge University Press, 1982) at 166–167.

[121]Cheng, *General principles*, *supra* note 118 at 24; contra, Grigory I. Tunkin, "Co-existence and international law", [1958] 95 Rec des Cours 1 at 26 ("There is the alternative view that "there may be common legal notions reflecting general features of legal phenomena, but not common legal norms"; as a consequence it has been interpreted that the Statute refers exclusively to principles native to public international law.").

[122]*South West Africa* (*Ethiopia v. South Africa; Liberia v. South Africa*), [1966] ICJ Rep 6 at para 88 (reprinted in 5 ILM 932) [*South West Africa*].

[123]Jaye Ellis, "General Principles and Comparative Law" (2011) 22:4 EJIL 949 at 954.

[124]It is noted that in the article, the only references that Professor Ellis makes to ICJ cases is of three separate or dissenting opinions, in none of them discussing the Court's method or lack of thereof, Ellis, ibid, at fn. 5, 9 and 21.

[125]Charney, "Multiple tribunals", *supra* note 116 at 190–191; see also Theodor Meron, "International law in the age of human rights: general course on public international law" (2003) 301 Rec des Cours 9 at 404–405 [Meron, "General Course"]; Villalpando also notes that "[t]he fact is that, when they have recourse to international customary law, the judgments of the Court do not often engage in detailed investigations searching for 'evidence of a general practice accepted as law'", then he statates that the long elaborations in *North Sea Continental Shelf* and *Nicaragua* remain rather exceptional, Santiago Villalpando, "Editorial: On the International Court of Justice and the Determination of Rules of Law" (2013) 26:3 Leiden J Int'l L 1 at 2.

That is the case of the *Corfu Channel* (United Kingdom v. Albania), in which the Court stated that "indirect evidence is admitted in all systems of law, and its use is recognised by international decisions."[126] However, no examples of presence in systems of law were given, and no international awards or judgments were quoted.

Contemporary scholarship acknowledges that alongside principles recognised by nations, the Court can also apply general principles native to public international law.[127] While it is still debated whether they apply by virtue of Article 38 (c)[128] or because of the fundamental nature of the international legal system,[129] the fact remains that general principles of international law are a source of international law.

Having said that, general principles of international law present a different problem when it comes to the method of identification. As it is more or less accepted that these principles have a customary character,[130] it could be argued that general principles of international law are subject to the same identification applicable to customary law. Waldock has suggested that "a Court will take judicial notice of it without requiring argument."[131] Weil, however, is of the view that they can be found:

> énoncés dans des instruments conventionnels, par exemple à l'article 2 de la Charte; d'autres ont trouvé expression dans des résolutions de l'Assemblée générale (par exemple dans la Déclaration relative aux principes du droit international touchant aux relations amicales entre États); d'autres encore sont tout simplement énoncés par la jurisprudence elle-même.[132]

However, the jurisprudence of the ICJ, specifically its Advisory Opinion on the *Legal Consequences for States of the Continued Presence of South Africa in Namibia* (hereinafter, *Presence of South Africa in Namibia*), does not favour the views of Judge Waldock or Weil. In the said opinion, the ICJ stated that "[i]n

---

[126]*Corfu Channel (United Kingdom of Great Britain and Northern Ireland v. Albania)*, Merits, [1949] ICJ Rep 4 at p 18.

[127]There is evidence of such difference in the jurisprudence of the PCIJ: in the case of the *Factory at Chorzow*, the Court referred to "principle of international law" as well as to a "principle generally accepted in the jurisprudence of international arbitration, as well as by municipal courts", *Case Concerning the Factory at Chorzów (Germany v. Poland)* (1927), PCIJ (Ser. A) No. 9 at 21 and 31; see also *Gabčíkovo-Nagymaros Project (Hungary/Slovakia)*, [1997] ICJ Rep 7 at paras 75–76.

[128]See e.g. Karl Zemanek, "The legal foundations of the international system: general course on public international law" (1997) 266 Rec des Cours 9 at paras 242–243.

[129]See e.g. Humphrey Waldock, "General course on public international law" (1962) 106 Rec des Cours 1 at 69.

[130]Prosper Weil, "Le droit international en quête de son identité: cours général de droit international public" (1992) 237 Rec des Cours 11 at 150 ("Loin de relever d'une source autonome de droit international, tous ces principes ont en réalité le caractère de règles coutumières") [Weil, "Cours général"]; Waldock, ibid at 69 ("the formal source of the principle is customary or treaty law").

[131]Waldock, ibid at 69.

[132]Weil, "Cours général", *supra* note 130 at 150.

examining this action of the General Assembly it is appropriate to have regard to the general principles of international law regulating termination of a treaty relationship on account of breach".[133] Then, the Court explained that:

> [t]he rules laid down by the Vienna Convention on the Law of Treaties concerning termination of a treaty relationship on account of breach (adopted without a dissenting vote) may in many respects be considered as a codification of existing customary law on the subject.[134]

While it seems that the general principles of international law have a customary character both in nature and content, there have been arguments for the expansion of their content that are not inconsistent with the afore-cited jurisprudence. Bassiouni is of the view that general principles can be found in "expressions of other unperfected sources of international law enumerated in the statutes of the PCIJ and ICJ; namely, conventions, customs, writings of scholars, and decisions of the PCIJ and ICJ."[135] Considering that the VCLT was not in force yet at the time the Advisory Opinion on the *Presence of South Africa in Namibia* was delivered, it is perfectly valid to say that the general principle of international law enunciated by the Court sought to incorporate an unperfected multilateral treaty.

As the Court has not elaborated on its methods for identifying general principles, this is a matter open to speculation. At this point, it suffices to say that the indeterminacy as to their content and the fact that they have been used—alas sporadically—confirms the intended purpose of the drafter of the PCIJ Statute: minimize the possibility of *non-liquet*. Having said that, it has been noted that the PCIJ and the ICJ have not used general principles for the purpose Judge Lauterpacht conceived:[136] to fill *lacunae* in international law.[137] This, however, is a matter of appreciation, as the PCIJ relied on principles upon admitting to find a gap on its own Statute:

> Neither the Statute nor the Rules of Court contain any rule regarding the procedure to be followed in the event of an objection being taken *in limine litis* to the Court's jurisdiction. The Court therefore is at liberty to adopt the principle which it considers best calculated to

[133]*Legal Consequences for States of the Continued Presence of South Africa in Namibia (South West Africa) notwithstanding Security Council Resolution 276 (1970)*, Advisory Opinion, [1971] ICJ Rep 16. at para 94 (reprinted in 10 ILM 677).

[134]Ibid.

[135]M. Cherif Bassiouni, A Functional Approach to General Principles of International Law (1989–1990) 11 Mich J Int'l L 768 at 768; Reisman, while warning against the dangers in the use of unperfected legal acts by the judiciary, noted that "important information—possibly vital legal information—is often to be found in unperfected legal acts, much as vital information for medical research may be found in stem cells", W. Michael Reisman, "Unratified Treaties and Other Unperfected Acts in International Law: Constitutional Functions" (2002) 35 35 Vand J Transnat'l L 729 at 746 [Reisman, "Unratified Treaties"].

[136]Hersch Lauterpacht, "Some Observations on the Prohibition of 'Non Liquet' and the Completeness of the Law" in Frederick Mari van Asbek, ed, *Symbolae Verzijl, présentées au professeur J.H.W. Verzijl à l'occasion de son LXX-ième anniversaire* (The Hague: Martinus Nijhoff, 1958) 196 at 205.

[137]Raimondo, *supra* note 83 at 33.

> ensure the administration of justice, most suited to procedure before an international tribunal and most in conformity with the fundamental principles of international law.[138]

3.3.4 Subsidiary Means

When the issue of subsidiary means to discover law was initially discussed in the Advisory Committee of Jurists entrusted with drafting the Statute of the PCIJ, the formula on the table was the proposal of Baron Descamps on the inclusion of "international jurisprudence as a means for the application and development of law."[139] The initial reaction was not positive, as Root considered that such means, along with the general principles discussed above, enlarged the jurisdiction of the Permanent Court in such a manner that would ultimately destroy any possibility of States submitting to it. He added that "if the clauses were accepted, it would amount to saying to the States: 'You surrender your rights to say what justice should be.'"[140] It wasn't until two meetings after the initial introduction of the issue that a compromise formula was provisionally adopted, including both judicial decisions and the doctrine of the best-qualified writers,[141] on the understanding that these are not sources proper and merely auxiliary elements of interpretation.[142] The wording, as it was eventually adopted by the Advisory Committee, and amended by the Council of the League of Nations, was: "Subject to the provisions of Article 59, judicial decisions and the teachings of the most highly qualified publicists of the various nations, as subsidiary means for the determination of rules of law."[143] It has been pointed out that the reference made to Article 59 is of no relevance to the issue of judicial decisions as subsidiary sources, given that the said article deals strictly with the obligations generated by a decision and the limits of such obligations.[144] When the Inter-Allied Committee for the future of the PCIJ reviewed the subparagraph on subsidiary means contained in Article 38, it felt that the meaning of the provision had been misconstrued:

> What it means is not that the decisions of the Court have no effect as precedents for the Court or for international law in general, but that they do not possess the binding force of particular decisions in the relations between the countries who are parties to the Statute. The provision in question in no way prevents the Court from treating its own judgments as

---

[138] *Case of the Mavrommatis Palestine Concessions (Greece v. United Kingdom)* (1924), PCIJ (Ser. A) No. 2 at p. 16.

[139] *Procès-Verbaux*, *supra* note 25 at 294.

[140] Ibid.

[141] Ibid at 337.

[142] Ibid at 334.

[143] Protocol of Signature Relating to the Statute for the Permanent Court of International Justice Provided for by Article 14 of the Covenant of the League of Nations, 16 December 1920, [1921] 6 LNTS 379, (1923) 17 AJIL Supp 55 at art 38, online: United Nations Treaty Collection http://treaties.un.org/doc/Publication/UNTS/LON/Volume%206/v6.pdf.

[144] Jennings, "General course", *supra* note 19 at 341–342.

precedents, and indeed it follows from Article 38 […] that the Court's decisions are themselves "subsidiary means for the determination of rules of law."[145]

While it is widely accepted that the elements included as subsidiary means are not sources of law ("at least not in the strict sense of themselves creating new norms"[146]), any modern international lawyer would hesitate in denying the important role that they play in international law. This is especially true for judicial decisions of international courts and tribunals,[147] which can be said to "constitute the most important means for the determination of rules and principles of international law."[148] I will not discuss the writings of authors, as they do not carry the same weight[149] as judicial decisions and do not have the potential to crystallise nascent law in the same way that those decisions can.[150] However, I do recognise the important role that scientific organizations, such as the *Institut de Droit International* or the International Law Association, play in assisting in the codification of standards and the advancement of customary law.[151] However, in my view, this is less doctrinal writing and more private codification.[152]

---

[145]Inter-Allied Committee, *supra* note 21.

[146]Pauwelyn, *supra* note 115 at 90.

[147]See Rosenne, *The law and practice*, *supra* note 120 at 1551; see also *Military and Paramilitary Activities in and against Nicaragua (Nicaragua v. United States of America)*, Jurisdiction and Admissibility, [1984] ICJ Rep 392. at p 547 (In the Separate opinion of Judge Sir Robert Jennings: "Law develops by precedent, and it is that which gives it consistency and predictability") [*Nicaragua*, Jurisdiction and Admissibility].

[148]Cheng, *General principles*, *supra* note 129 at 1.

[149]Jennings has stated that although judicial decisions and writings are treated in the same way by the Statute, "in practice there need be no doubt that judicial decision is much the more important", Jennings, "General course", *supra* note 19 at 341.

[150]The age of Oppenheim is long gone: "there are no international courts in existence which can define these customary rules and apply them authoritatively to cases which themselves become precedents binding upon inferior courts. The writers on international law, and in especial the authors of treatises, have in a sense to take the place of the judges [… i]t is for this reason that text-books of international law have so much more importance for the application of the law than text-books of other branches of the law", Lassa Oppenheim, "The Science of International Law Its Tasks and Method" (1908) 2 AJIL 313 at 315.

[151]See e.g. Antonio Truyol Y Serra, "Théorie du droit international public: cours general" (1981) 173 Rec des Cours 9 at 255. Having said that, there are certain scientific institutions that enjoy more *prestige* than others, for instance, Mauritius unsuccessfully tried to use Guidelines of the International Bar Association in order to unseat ICJ Judge Christopher Greenwood as Arbitrator in the proceedings between that country and the United Kingdom, as: "In the Tribunal's view, Mauritius has not demonstrated that the rules adopted by non-governmental institutions such as the IBA have been expressly adopted by States, nor do they form part of a general practice accepted as law, nor fall within any other of the sources of international law enumerated in Article 38(1) of the Statute of the ICJ.", *The Republic of Mauritius v. The United Kingdom of Great Britain and Northern Ireland, Reasoned Decision on Challenge* (2011), [2012] 51 ILM 353 at para 167 (Permanent Court of Arbitration, operating under *UNCLOS*, Annex VII Arbitration) (Ivan Shearer, Judge Sir Christopher Greenwood, Judge Albert Hoffmann, Judge James Kateka, Judge Rüdiger Wolfrum) [*Mauritius v. United Kingdom*].

[152]See e.g. Gerald G. Fitzmaurice, "The contribution of the Institute of International Law to the development of international law" (1973) 138 Rec des Cours 203 at 220–221.

It is very common that international courts quote previous decisions as evidence of law already discovered or interpretation earlier constructed. This is an undeniable part of the international judiciary, as we know it today: "first, courts have the ability to create a dialogue which will result in an argued decision; and, secondly, this dialogue extends to several circles of interested actors."[153] Moreover, the privileged role that the ICJ plays in the international legal arena, as the only permanent universal[154] court of general jurisdiction currently in operation, has made it common that its decisions get used as precedent in specialised tribunals.[155] Cases when the ICJ has quoted arbitral tribunals have been scarce.[156] Aside from sporadic use of arbitral decisions, the Court has rarely quoted permanent specialised Courts,[157] and not until very recently when dealing with international criminal law[158] and international human rights law.[159]

With regard to method, the Court itself has explained in the case concerning the *Land and Maritime Boundary between Cameroon and Nigeria* (hereinafter, *Cameroon v. Nigeria*) that:

> It is true that, in accordance with Article 59, the Court's judgments bind only the parties to and in respect of a particular case. There can be no question of holding Nigeria to decisions reached by the Court in previous cases. The real question is whether, in this case, there is cause not to follow the reasoning and conclusions of earlier cases.[160]

---

[153] Hélène Ruiz Fabri, "Enhancing the Rhetoric of Jus Cogens" (2012) 23:4 EJIL 1049 at 1056; the point has been made that "judgments do not have an impact on the opinion of states about the law solely on the basis of the World Court's authority. Instead, the Court has to find acceptable solutions to problems of co-ordination or cooperation or propose acceptable ethical norms", Niels Petersen, "Lawmaking by the International Court of Justice—Factors of Success", in Armin von Bogdandy and Ingo Venzke, *International Judicial Lawmaking: On Public Authority and Democratic Legitimation in Global Governance* (Heidelberg: Springer, 2012) 411 at 436.

[154] This is, of course, universal as far as the United Nations is concerned.

[155] See Rosenne, *The law and practice*, *supra* note 120 at 1553 ("Reliance on previous decisions—particularly those of the International Court—is marked in ad hoc arbitration tribunals, but the organic permanence of the International Court and its status as the principal judicial organ of the United Nations have enabled this process to be followed with greater frequency"); although the case has been made that Court "is the foremost promoter of the authoritativeness of its own pronouncements", Villalpando, *supra* note 125 at 3.

[156] Rosenne enumerated the cases in which the PCIJ and the ICJ made use of arbitral awards in their decisions up until the last update of his book in 2005, Rosenne, ibid at 1556–1557.

[157] *Case concerning the Land, Island and Maritime Frontier Dispute (El Salvador v. Honduras: Nicaragua intervening)*, [1992] ICJ Rep 351 at paras 402–403.

[158] *Application of the Convention on the Prevention and Punishment of the Crime of Genocide* (Bosnia and Herzegovina v. Serbia and Montenegro), Merits, Judgment, [2007] ICJ Rep 43 (reprinted in 46 ILM 188). [*Application of the Genocide Convention*].

[159] *Ahmadou Sadio Diallo (Republic of Guinea v. Democratic Republic of the Congo)*, Merits, Judgment, [2010] ICJ Rep 639 (reprinted in 50 ILM 40) [*Ahmadou Sadio Diallo*, Merits]; *Jurisdictional Immunities*, *supra* note 103.

[160] The Court has clarified in a subsequent case that this is only by analogy, *Land and Maritime Boundary between Cameroon and Nigeria (Cameroon v. Nigeria)*, Preliminary Objections, [1998] ICJ Rep 275 at para 28 [*Cameroon v. Nigeria*, Preliminary Objections].

The Courts view seems to indicate that its past jurisprudence constitutes strong evidence of the law applicable to a particular situation.[161] That evidence is, of course, subject to an evaluation of the Court as to the similarities between the situation in past cases and the one sub judice.[162] Logically if the circumstances are so different that the reasoning of the Court in a previous case is not fully applicable to the situation, the use of the precedent is unnecessary:

> Perhaps the most obvious attempt to resist the argumentative burden is to claim it does not actually bear on the present situation. [...] Distinguishing is a dual process of reverse analogy whereby the precedent is not impugned as such but rather declared to be inapplicable. By pointing out relevant differences, the reach of the precedent is retrospectively shaped.[163]

From another point of view, tribunals "will not usually feel free to ignore a relevant decision, and will normally feel obliged to treat it as something that must be accepted, or else—for good reason—rejected".[164]

3.3.5 Normativity Beyond Article 38: Unilateral Declarations

There are a number of reasons for which scholars have criticised Article 38 of the ICJ Statute.[165] While it has been widely stated that there are many possible sources

---

[161]Or, as Thirlway put it, the role of the judicial decisions "is to provide examples of the application of international law", Hugh Thirlway, "Concepts, principles, rules and analogies: international and municipal legal reasoning" (2002) 294 Rec des Cours 265 at 345; see also, Gilbert Guillaume, "The Use of Precedent by International Judges and Arbitrators" (2011) 2:1 at J Int Disp Settlement 5 at 12 ("the International Court of Justice does not recognize any binding value to its own precedent. However, it takes it into great consideration"); Waldock, *supra* note 129 at 88 ("Unlike the latter, the "subsidiary means" are not themselves constitutional sources which can of their own force give to a principle the stamp of a legal rule. They are evidentiary sources which may assist in satisfying the Court as to the existence of a conventional or customary rule or of a general principle of law").

[162]As Shahabuddeen puts it, "the use of precedents involves a method of reasoning by analogy", Mohamed Shahabuddeen, *Precedent in the World Court* (New York: Cambridge University Press, 1996) at 102.

[163]Marc Jacob, "Precedents: Lawmaking Through International Adjudication", in Bogdandy and Venzke, *supra* note 153 at 64.

[164]Gerald G. Fitzmaurice, "Some Problems Regarding the Formal Sources of International Law" in Frederick Mari van Asbek, ed, *Symbolae Verzijl, présentées au professeur J.H.W. Verzijl à l'occasion de son LXX-ième anniversaire* (The Hague: Martinus Nijhoff, 1958) 124 at 172.

[165]Lady Fox provides us with a summarised critique of the sources of international law as reflected in the Statute: Hazel Fox, "Time, History and Sources of Law Peremptory Norms: Is There a Need for New Sources of International Law" in Matthew Craven, Malgosia Fitzmaurice and Maria Vogiatzi, eds., *Time, History and International Law* (Leiden: Martinus Nijhoff, 2007) 119 at 125-129.

of law not enumerated in Article 38,[166] one of the most inescapable criticisms is that it is not even exhaustive as to sources of strict law.[167] This recognition departs not only from aspirational views about the future of international law, but also from the realities that the PCIJ and the ICJ have had to deal with throughout the years:

> I would stress the related proliferation in the sources of international law, again in ways that would have been inconceivable to the generation that drafted what became Article 38 of the Court's statute. Read the recent decisions of the ICJ and recognise that it now routinely articulates international obligations on the basis of authorities that are not listed among the famous four of Article 38.[168]

One of the sources that has been used by both the PCIJ and ICJ, mostly uncontroversially, in order to recognise legal obligations are unilateral statements and declarations.[169] Indeed, since the times of the Permanent Court, the view was expressed that such statements could be binding.[170] However, it was the ICJ which elaborated a clear method of ascertaining legal obligations from a unilateral statement in the cases concerning *Nuclear Tests (Australia v. France and New Zealand v. France)* (hereinafter, *Nuclear Tests*):

> When it is the intention of the State making the declaration that it should become bound according to its terms, that intention confers on the declaration the character of a legal undertaking, the State being thenceforth legally required to follow a course of conduct consistent with the declaration. An undertaking of this kind, if given publicly, and with an intent to be bound, even though not made within the context of international negotiations, is binding.[171]

While it has been noted that it is up to the Court to "form its own view of the meaning and scope intended by the author of a unilateral declaration which may create a legal obligation",[172] it has also emphasised that it "all depends on the intention of the State in question."[173]

Between 1997 and 2006, the International Law Commission took up the topic of "Unilateral acts of States", under which it elaborated the 2006 Guiding Principles

---

[166]See e.g. Antonio Augusto Cançado Trindade, *International Law for Humankind: Towards a New Jus Gentium* (Leiden: Martinus Nijhoff, 2010) at 128.

[167]Jennings, "General course", *supra* note 19 at 344.

[168]Ralph G. Steinhardt, "The International Court of Justice at Several Crossroads" (2009) 103 Am Soc Int'l L Proc 397 at 398.

[169]Rubin, seeking to defend the integrity of the system of sources in Article 38 of the Statute, is of the view that unilateral statements do not fit within any of the sources enumerated in the aforementioned Article, Alfred P. Rubin, "The International Legal Effects of Unilateral Declarations" (1977) 71 AJIL 1 at 28–29.

[170]*Legal Status of Eastern Greenland (Denmark v. Norway)* (1933), PCIJ (Ser. A/B) No. 53 at p 71.

[171]*Nuclear Tests (Australia v. France)*, [1974] ICJ Rep 253 at para 43; *Nuclear Tests (New Zealand v. France)*, [1974] ICJ Rep 457 at para 46.

[172]*Military and Paramilitary Activities in and against Nicaragua (Nicaragua v. United States of America)*, Merits, [1986] ICJ Rep 14 at para 269 (reprinted in 25 ILM 1023) [*Nicaragua*, Merits].

[173]*Frontier Dispute (Burkina Faso v. Republic of Mali)*, [1986] ICJ Rep 554 at para 39.

applicable to unilateral declarations of States capable of creating legal obligations. The said Guidelines confirm that the two main elements of identification of a statement generating legal obligations are, as established by the *Nuclear Tests* cases, (1) the publicity of the statement and the (2) the manifestation of the will to the effect of creating legal obligations.[174]

Early views looked at statements as verbal treaties, which by implication, may have to be registered under Article 18 of the Covenant of the League of Nations[175]—predecessor of Article 102 of the Charter of the UN, providing for the registration of treaties and international agreements. However, unlike treaties, these statements need not be reciprocal or require any subsequent action in order to take effect,[176] and more importantly, that "a statement is made orally or in writing makes no essential difference, for such statements made in particular circumstances may create commitments in international law".[177] It has been noted that *Nuclear Tests* can be said to create new law in the sense that the cases "recognis[e] that a written or verbal undertaking may give rise to legal rights even when made without such reciprocal or mutual exchange of commitments…"[178] However, the recognition of unilateral declarations in *Nuclear Tests* was also the subject of criticism because such recognition deemed binding an 'unperfected legal act', the implication being that one:

> [M]ust question the constitutive effect of transforming unilateral statements by heads of state into potentially binding obligations and assigning the constitutional competence to make such determination, on a case-by-case basis, to the International Court of Justice.[179]

In his Declarations appended to the judgment of the ICJ on the merits of *Cameroon v. Nigeria*, Judge Francisco Rezek emphasised the difference between treaties and unilateral declarations:

> It is to be expected that the case concerning the Legal Status of Eastern Greenland […] would be referred to in a discussion of this sort. It is sometimes forgotten that the Court never said that one of the ways in which treaties could be concluded was by oral agreement. The Court did not state that the Ihlen Declaration was a treaty. It said that Norway was bound by the guarantees given by the Norwegian Minister to the Danish ambassador. Thus, there are other, less formal, ways by which a State can create international obligations for itself.[180]

---

[174] *Report of the ILC, 58th Session*, *supra* note 1 at para 176 (principle 1, p 368 of the Report).

[175] James W. Garner, "The International Binding Force of Unilateral Oral Declarations" (1933) 27:3 AJIL 493 at 494.

[176] *Nuclear Tests* (*Australia v. France*), *supra* note 171 at 43; *Nuclear Tests* (*New Zealand v. France*), *supra* note 171 at 46.

[177] *Nuclear Tests* (*Australia v. France*), ibid at para 45; *Nuclear Tests* (*New Zealand v. France*), ibid at para 48; see also, *Report of the ILC, 58th Session*, *supra* note 1 at p 374.

[178] Thomas M. Franck, "The Decision of the ICJ in the Nuclear Test Cases" (1975) 69 AJIL 612 at 615.

[179] Reisman, "Unratified Treaties", *supra* note 135 at 737.

[180] *Cameroon v. Nigeria*, Merits, *supra* note 86 at p 491.

The point has been raised that unilateral statements are not a source of international law per se, but a source of rights and obligations.[181] That is, they are usually seen as generators of discrete obligations rather than rules. However, on one side it is understood that a State can recognise the existence or applicability of a rule by a declaration to that effect,[182] and on the other "the usefulness of this dogmatic distinction is doubtful."[183]

3.3.6 Hierarchy, the Sources in Article 38 and Jus Cogens

An important feature of academic debate on the sources of international law since the mid-20th century has been the study of the relationships between sources or norms derived from those sources,[184] and specifically the study of hierarchical relationships between norms. While there has been ample and strong criticism of a view of international law that sees normativity as a sliding scale,[185] contemporary accounts recognise that "the growing complexity of the international legal system reflected in the increasing variety of forms of commitment adopted to regulate state behaviour in regard to an ever-growing number of transnational problems."[186] From the outset, there is more than one type of relationships between norms as well as legal techniques to deal with the conflicts between them.[187] This section is specifically concerned with the abstract relationship between sources in which one

---

[181]See e.g. Thirlway, *supra* note 161 at 337; see also Hugh Thirlway, *The Sources of International Law* (Oxford: Oxford University Press, 2014) at 44–52.

[182]*Nuclear Tests (Australia v. France)*, *supra* note 171 at 51 ("The Court finds that the unilateral undertaking resulting from these statements cannot be interpreted as having been made in implicit reliance on an arbitrary power of reconsideration. The Court finds further that the French Government has undertaken an obligation the precise nature and limits of which must be understood in accordance with the actual terms in which they have been publicly expressed."); *Nuclear Tests (New Zealand v. France)*, *supra* note 171 at 53 (with identical text).

[183]Zemanek, *supra* note 128 at 134 (he adds: "since the dogmatic characterization does not fit all [kinds of] unilateral acts, it does not warrant their total exclusion from the sources of international law").

[184]Especially under perspective of the fragmentation of international law, see e.g *Report of the ILC, 58th Session*, *supra* note 1.

[185]See e.g. Prosper Weil, "Towards relative normativity in international law?" (1983) 77 AJIL 413 at 421 ("There is now a trend towards the replacement of the monolithically conceived normativity of the past by graduated normativity. While is has always been difficult to locate the threshold beyond which a legal norm existed, at least there used to be no problem once the threshold could be pronounced crossed: the norm created legal rights and obligations; it was binding…") [Weil, "Relative normativity"].

[186]Dinah Shelton, "Normative Hierarchy in International Law" (2006) 100:2 AJIL 291 at 322.

[187]See Michael Akehurst, "The Hierarchy of the Sources of International Law" (1975) 47:1 BYIL 274 at 274; G.J.H. van Hoof, *Rethinking the Sources of International Law* (Deventer: Kluwer Law and Taxation Publishers, 1983) at 152.

has been designated as superior to the other. That is, the notion that "rules derived from one source prevail over rules derived from another source".[188]

While the ILC has recently recognised that "norms may thus exist at higher and lower hierarchical levels",[189] it has also pointed out that the "[t]he main sources of international law (treaties, custom, general principles of law as laid out in Article 38 of the Statute of the International Court of Justice) are not in a hierarchical relationship *inter se*."[190] However, peremptory norms of international law, or *jus cogens*, have been recognised to have an abstract hierarchical superiority over norms derived from the sources enumerated in the aforementioned Article 38.

During the work of the ILC on the topic of the law of treaties, peremptory norms were never treated as a source of law itself, but as a quality that certain norms or rules have. In fact the ILC noted that "the emergence of rules having the character of *jus cogens* is comparatively recent;"[191] and that while a new rule of *jus cogens* could be established "either by general multilateral treaty or by the development of a new customary rule",[192] their modification "would today most probably be effected through a general multilateral treaty."[193] Having said that, the nature, content and mechanisms by which a peremptory norm comes to life have been the subject of extensive debate. It has been argued that "peremptory norms, whether in becoming norms or in becoming peremptory or both, must be considered in terms of the sources of international law."[194] That is, irrespective of weather norms can be borne peremptory—which entails treating *jus cogens* as a source[195]—become peremptory—viewing *jus cogens* as a status that certain norms attain[196]—or a

---

[188]Akehurst, ibid at 374.

[189]*Report of the ILC, 58th Session, supra* note 1 at para 251 (conclusion 1).

[190]Ibid at para 251 (conclusion 31).

[191]*Commentaries, supra* note 88 at 248 (art 50, para 3).

[192]"*Report of the International Law Commission covering the work of its fifteenth session, 6 May–12 July 1963*" (UN Doc A/5509) in *Yearbook of the International Law Commission 1963*, vol 2 (New York: UN, 1964) at 211 [*Report of the ILC, 15th Session*].

[193]*Commentaries, supra* note 88 at 248 (art 50, para 4).

[194]Onuf and Birney add that "either new peremptory norms are generated or existing norms are made peremptory. In either case, that process is conveniently described as a "source" of international law. Note that the term "source" refers not simply to the named thing, like custom or customs, but to a dynamic, if structured, process of law coming into being through the agency of whatever that thing happens to be. In the instance at hand, the process is novel and not well-delineated", N.G. Onuf and Richard K. Birney, "Peremptory Norms of International Law: Their Source, Function and Future" (1974) 4 Denv J Int'l L & Pol'y 187 at 190 and 195; see also, Ulrich Scheuner, "Conflict of Treaty Provisions with a Peremptory Norm of General International Law" (1969) 29 ZaöRV 28 at 30 (recognising that the inclusion of the concept of *ius cogens* in the VCLT "involves considerable changes in the theory of the international order and of the sources of inter-national law").

[195]See e.g. Alexander Orakhelashvili, *Peremptory Norms in International Law* (Oxford: OUP, 2006) at 110–111.

[196]M. Cherif Bassiouni, "International Crimes: Jus Cogens and Obligation Erga Omnes" (1996) 59:4 L. & Cont. Probs 63 at 63. Akehurst, *supra* note 187 at 282–284.

combination of both,[197] there is a process that must be verified by the relevant legal actors in order to find that a particular norm is peremptory. In any event, *jus cogens* is treated as a category of norms which content is discoverable but infinite. Abstract hierarchical effects are attributed to the category because of the importance of the category itself, and not because in a particular clash of norms one norm is more important than the other. Moreover, peremptory norms are not hierarchical between them,[198] but in the unlikely scenario that there is a conflict between two peremptory norms in a specific case, they are subject to the same methods to solve such conflict than other norms. In short, it can be said that all *jus cogens* norms are superior to customary norms; whereas it cannot be said that all norms found in treaties are superior to customary norms. Therefore, as the hierarchy that all *jus cogens* norms enjoy is accorded a priori, independently of its content and opposable to any other non-peremptory norm, I will treat such hierarchy as abstract and at the source level. However, I want to leave clear that in my view *jus cogens* is not a source itself, and that the inclusion of a given norm in the peremptory category is, ultimately, a matter of content.

The argument I make in this sub section is that while international law has definitively moved away from formal hierarchy, it has acknowledged the existence of hierarchy in regards to a specific category or norms based on the importance of its content, although the actual content of the category is still open to progressive development. As evidenced in the procès-verbaux of the proceedings of the Advisory Committee, its members were indeed concerned about issues of hierarchy and possible conflicts between norms. With the consolidation of the concept of *jus cogens* in international law, the Court has been faced with arguments claiming the peremptoriness of the norm. However, the Court has fallen short of the expectations raised by the ILC in the draft articles on the law of treaties,[199] and has provided little clarification on the criteria to identify a peremptory norm.[200]

In this subsection, I will review the legislative history of the Statute of the Court, especially in regards to the attempts to establish hierarchy in the sources mentioned in the Statute. I will also review the jurisprudence of the Court concerning

---

[197]Orakhelashvili, *Peremptory Norms*, *supra* note 373 at 43 and 127 ("The nature of jus cogens can influence, adapt to itself or even predetermine, totally or partly, these law-making processes [referring to custom and general principles], such as the case of custom-generation, and even justify the autonomous mode of law-making. The relevant sources of jus cogens should be treated as mutually complementary and not as mutually exclusive.").

[198]*Fragmentation of International Law: Difficulties arising from the Diversification and Expansion of International Law: Report of the Study Group of the International Law Commission*, UNGAOR, 61st Sess, Supp. No. 10, UN Doc. A/CN.4/L.682 at para 367 [*Fragmentation Report*].

[199]As it will be shown below, the ILC "considered the right course to be [...] to leave the full content of this rule to be worked out in State practice and in the jurisprudence of international tribunals", *Commentaries*, *supra* note 88 at 248 (art 50, para 3).

[200]In making reference to three cases of the ICJ, Conklin points out that "the Court has failed to explain the point in time when a peremptory norm emerges, nor has the Court explained why", William E. Conklin, "The Peremptory Norms of the International Community" (2012) 23:3 EJIL 837 at 842–843.

jus cogens. Since this is the only abstract hierarchical relationship recognised by the Court and international law in general, I will analyse the methods by which the ICJ identified the existence of the *jus cogens* rule, and the effect that it had in the specific case.

By the 15th meeting of the Advisory Committee in charge of drafting the Statute of the PCIJ, its members had already agreed on most of the content of what would become Article 38 of the Statute. The only major issue aired by the participants was the fact that the draft being discussed at the time, which has based on the President's proposal, stated that the rules contained in the draft Article should be applied in successive order.[201] Such formulation put treaties at the forefront of the discussion as the first and therefore principal of the sources enumerated. Only in the absence of a conventional rule, either bilateral or multilateral, would the Court be able to pass to the next source. In defence of his draft, the President stated that the Committee "shall indicate in a order of natural précellence, without requiring in a given case the agreement of several sources".[202] This was, in the view of Baron Descamps, to absolve the Court from having to look at all enumerated rules if a clear solution is found in a treaty.[203] In defence of the opposite view, the delegate from Italy, Minister Arturo Ricci-Busatti, understood the words 'successive order' to "suggest the idea that the judge was not authorised to draw upon a certain source, for instance point 3 [general principles of law], before having applied conventions and customs mentioned respectively in points 1 and 2."[204] He also made the point that the chapeau of the Article seemed to ignore that rules derived from each source could be applied simultaneously.[205] However, it was Ricci-Busatti's alternate argument that caught the attention of the Committee members: the expression was superfluous as "it is a fundamental principle of law that a special rule goes before general law".[206] Professor de La Pradelle, along with Professor Francis Hagerup and Lord Phillimore joined Ricci-Busatti. While Professor Rafael Altamira y Crevea characterised the phrase as a pleonasm, he did not mind it.[207] Baron Descamps finally admitted that he did not attach much importance to the expression.[208]

At the end of the 15th session, and pending further modifications at the second reading, an amendment proposed by Elihu Root was provisionally adopted: "The following rules of law are to be applied by the Court within the limits of its competence, as described above, for the settlement of international disputes; they will be considered in the undermentioned [sic] order".[209]

---

[201]*Procès-Verbaux*, *supra* note 25 at 331.

[202]Ibid at 337.

[203]Ibid.

[204]Ibid at 337.

[205]Ibid.

[206]Ibid.

[207]Ibid at 338.

[208]Ibid.

[209]Ibid at 344.

Eventually draft Article 35, as finally adopted by the Advisory Committee, stated that the Permanent Court shall "apply in the order following", or in French "applique en ordre successif",[210] the sources as enumerated today in Article 38 of the ICJ Statute. The Report of the President of the Advisory Committee, which contained a commentary to each proposed article, stated that the then Article 35 "lays down an order in which the rules of law are to be applied"[211] and that: "the Court is to apply, firstly, the rules embodied in conventions; secondly, in the absence of general or special conventions, international custom in so far as its continuity proves a common usage…"[212]

However, the chapeau of the Article, stating that the rules enumerated should be applied in the order designated, was dropped by the Council of the League of Nations before adoption of the final text of the Statute at the Assembly of the League of Nations.[213] And while the chapeau of the Article was modified for the Statute of the ICJ, there was no mention of an order of application in the current version of Article 38.

It is undeniable that such a formula would have had the effect of establishing a hierarchy in the system of norms to be applied by the Permanent Court. However, the hierarchy was not one of value but of specificity. Under the international law that the members of the Advisory Committee knew and practiced, customary law was always general international law, and treaties—whether law-making or contract treaties—were always more specific than customary law. Above the generality of customary law were only the 'maxims du droit' that Professor de La Pradelle understood to be the content of the general principles of law enumerated in the draft Article.[214] The successive order of the sources, as understood by the drafters of the Statute of the PCIJ, was due to the principle lex specialis derogat lege generali. It was an absolute order because the knowledge of the time linked the specificity in the content of the norm to its form.[215] The hierarchy was abstract because, in their

---

[210]Ibid at 730.

[211]Ibid at. 729.

[212]Ibid.

[213]*Protocol of Signature Relating to the Statute for the Permanent Court of International Justice Provided for by Article 14 of the Covenant of the League of Nations*, 16 December 1920, *supra* note 143 at art 38.

[214]*Procès-Verbaux*, *supra* note 25 at 335; that view seems to still be accepted today, see e.g., Pauwelyn, *supra* note 115 at 129 ("Because of the vague nature of general principles of law, cases of genuine conflict between these principles and other norms of international law are rare. Where they arise, treaty and custom must prevail as lex specialis").

[215]Bishop made the point that "it is clear that treaties prevail over custom, as between the parties to the treaty; and in practice treaties and custom are the primary sources looked to. In general, one might say that general principles of law tend to come after decisions and publicist, and are counted upon as source of law only as something of a 'last resort'", WM.W. Bishop, General course of public international law, (1965) 115 Rec de Cours 147 at 241; contra Charles De Visscher, "Contribution a l'etude des sources du droit international" [1933] Rev de Dr int et de Leg Comparee 395 at 413.

view, there was no need to compare two norms from different sources in order to find out which was more specific; form controlled specificity.[216] This is further evidenced by the fact that most members of the Advisory Committee agreed that the meaning implied in the phrase "in successive order" was logical,[217] superfluous,[218] a pleonasm,[219] and self-evident as it "was already indicated in the enumeration."[220]

Initially, the ICJ appears to have rejected such a view in 1982, when it suggested in the *Continental Shelf* case between Tunisia and Libya that the sources listed in Article 38 are to be applied simultaneously: "the Court is, of course, bound to have regard to all the legal sources specified in Article 38, paragraph 1, of the Statute of the Court in determining the relevant principles and rules applicable".[221] However, just a couple of years later in the case concerning the *Delimitation of the Maritime Boundary in the Gulf of Maine Area* (hereinafter, *Gulf of Mai ne*), the Court stated that:

> A body of detailed rules is not to be looked for in customary international law which in fact comprises a limited set of norms for ensuring the co-existence and vital co-operation of the members of the international community, together with a set of customary rules whose presence in the *opinio juris* of States can be tested by induction based on the analysis of a sufficiently extensive and convincing practice, and not by deduction from preconceived ideas.
>
> […]
>
> As already noted, customary international law merely contains a general requirement of the application of equitable criteria and the utilization of practical methods capable of implementing them. It is therefore special international law that must be looked to, in order to ascertain whether that law, as at present in force between the Parties to this case, does or does not include some rule specifically requiring the Parties, and consequently the Chamber, to apply certain criteria or certain specific practical methods to the delimitation that is requested.[222]

---

[216]See H. Thirlway, 'The Sources of International Law', in M.D. Evans (ed.), *International Law*, 3nd ed (Oxford: Oxford University Press, 2010) 91 at 114 ("In the classical theory of international law, any priority of conflicting rules or norms was resolved simply according to the de facto hierarchy of the sources from which they derived, coupled with the principles of the overriding effect of lex posterior and lex specialis […]. For this purpose, the content of the rules in issue was irrelevant, except insofar as it was taken into account to judge […] whether one rule was specialis in relation to the other, and if so, which was which.").

[217]*Procès-Verbaux*, *supra* note 25 at 333 (Lord Phillimore).

[218]Ibid at 337 (Minister Ricci-Busatti).

[219]Ibid at 338 (Professor Altamira).

[220]Ibid at 338 (Professor de Lapradelle).

[221]*Continental Shelf* (*Tunisia v. Libyan Arab Jamahiriya*), [1982] ICJ Rep 18 at para 23.

[222]*Delimitation of the Maritime Boundary in the Gulf of Maine Area* (*Canada v. United States of America*), [1984] ICJ Rep 246 at para 111 and 114 (reprinted in 23 ILM 1197).

That, however, is not the current state of the discipline.[223] Today, regional custom can override general custom as a matter of *lex specialis*;[224] multilateral conventions may be considered the general framework within which all activities in a specific matter are carried out;[225] they can be the reflection of customary international law on a specific matter[226]; or can even establish the superiority of a principle of international law over subsequent treaties derogating it or modifying its scope.[227] Today, the source of the norm does not control the precedence of one norm over another,[228] nor does it dictate the level of specificity of one over the other.

While contemporary views challenge the idea that international law is absolutely horizontal,[229] treaties are not in the position that Baron Descamps proposed in a hierarchical system. The ILC has considered that "there are certain rules from which States are not competent to derogate at all by a treaty arrangement, and which may be changed only by another rule of the same character."[230] Such a view was eventually codified as law in the *VCLT*: "If a new peremptory norm of general international law emerges, any existing treaty which is in conflict with that norm becomes void and terminates."[231]

These developments, along with the discussions at the ILC on the topic of State Responsibility, caused Professor Prosper Weil to lament the path in which international law was heading. In this view, "whatever their formal origins, whatever their object of importance, all norms are placed on the same Plane, their relations ungoverned by any hierarchy."[232]

---

[223]There is an interesting comment in the dissenting opinion of Judge Moreno Quinta on Right of Passage: "In any case, although I agree that that Article establishes a legal order of precedence in the application of sources of international law, I consider that the validity of a general principle may take the place of international custom, and the existence of international custom the place of a treaty", *Case concerning Right of Passage over Indian Territory* (*Portugal v. India*), Merits, [1960] ICJ Rep 6 at p 90.

[224]*Fragmentation Report*, *supra* note 198 at para 85.

[225]Today, UNCLOS (*supra* note 43) is considered the framework upon which all compatible norms of international law concerning the oceans must be interpreted, *Oceans and the law of the Sea*, GA Res 69/245, UNGAOR, 69th Sess, UN Doc A/RES/69/245 (2014) at p 2; see also *Southern Bluefin Tuna* (*New Zealand-Japan, Australia-Japan*) (2000), XXIII RIAA 23 at para 52 (Arbitrators: Judge Stephen M. Schwebel, Judge Florentino Feliciano, The Rt. Hon. Justice Sir Kenneth Keith, Judge Per Tresselt, Chusei Yamada).

[226]*Nicaragua*, Merits, *supra* note 172 at para 56.

[227]*UNCLOS*, *supra* note 43 at art 311.6.

[228]See e.g., Pauwelyn, *supra* note 115 at 148 ("to build a theory of conflict of norms with reference solely to the source of these norms is unworkable. There would be too many exceptions and uncertainties, essentially because hierarchies in international law (unlike domestic law) are not based on form but on substance").

[229]Antônio Augusto Cançado Trindade, "International law for humankind: towards a new jus gentium (I). General course on public international law" (2005) 316 Rec des Cours 9 at 336.

[230]*Commentaries*, *supra* note 88 at 247 (art 50, para 1).

[231]*VCLT*, *supra* note 87 at art 53.

[232]Weil, "Relative normativity", *supra* note 185 at 432.

The movement of international law away from formal specificity based in hierarchy was confirmed by the ILC in its Fragmentation Report when it stated that "norms may thus exist at higher and lower hierarchical levels",[233] and that the "[t]he main sources of international law (treaties, custom, general principles of law as laid out in Article 38 of the Statute of the International Court of Justice) are not in a hierarchical relationship inter se."[234] In fact, the conventionally accepted knowledge in the field states that relationships between norms derived from the sources enumerated in Article 38 of the ICJ Statute are dependent on the specific content of such norms and that precedence or hierarchy cannot be determined abstractly.[235]

According to the *VCLT*, *jus cogens* is defined as "a norm accepted and recognised by the international community of states as a whole as a norm from which no derogation is permitted and which can be modified only by a subsequent norm of general international law having the same character."[236] Although this notion should apply exclusively for the purposes of the law of treaties, it remains the only definition adopted by States in a treaty, and "is generally regarded as having wider significance".[237]

Since the adoption of the draft articles on the law of treaties, the ILC has recognised that "there is no simple criterion by which to identify a general rule of international law as having the character of *jus cogens*."[238] This lead to the conclusion that including in the draft Articles a list of existing *jus cogens* norms would be counterproductive.[239] Already since its 15th session in 1963, the Commission agreed that the full content of rule providing for the absolute invalidity of treaties

[233] *Report of the ILC, 58th Session*, *supra* note 1 at para 251 (conclusion 1).

[234] Ibid at para 251 (conclusion 31).

[235] *Fragmentation Report*, *supra* note 198 at para 407. Mark Eugen Villiger, *Customary International Law and Treaties: A Study of their Interactions and Interrelations, with Special Consideration of the 1969 Vienna Convention on the Law of Treaties* (Dordrecht: Martinus Nijhoff Publishers, 1985) at 39 (Villiger explains the equality of all sources in Article 38 from the autonomy of each of them: "the autonomy of sources necessitates customary law and treaties being equivalents, and any relationship between the two depending on other criteria in casu"); see also Zdzislaw Galicki, "Hierarchy in International Law within the Context of its Fragmentation", in I. Buffard, et al. (eds.), *International Law between Universalism and Fragmentation Festschrift in Honour of Gerhard Hafner* (The Hague: Koninklijke Brill, 2008) 41 at 51 ("comprehensive hierarchy or hierarchical system within the realm of international law does in fact not exist").

[236] *VCLT*, *supra* note 87 at art 53.

[237] Hilary Charlesworth and Christine Chinkin, "The Gender of Jus Cogens" (1993) 15 Hum Rts Q 64 at fn. 4; see also Conklin, *supra* note 200 at 843 (noting that the VCLT is "invariably offered as the authority for the existence and the identity if peremptory norms").

[238] *Commentaries*, *supra* note 88 at 247–248 (art 50, para 2).

[239] "Fifth Report on the Law of Treaties, by Sir Humphrey Waldock, Special Rapporteur" (Un Doc A/CN.4/183 and Add. 1–4) in *Yearbook of the International Law Commission 1966*, *supra* note 88 at 25.

conflicting with a peremptory norm[240] would be better left for State practice and jurisprudence of international tribunals to develop.[241] The observations of the Special Rapporteur, then Sir Humphrey Waldock, included in his fifth report, clarifies that the ILC meant that to include "the identification of the norms which have become *jus cogens*"[242] In relation with the issue of the method of identification, the ILC only specified that the fact that a treaty provision is non-derogable does not entail that it is a jus cogens norms.[243] Such is the case, for instance, of the principle of common heritage of mankind as it appears in *UNCLOS*,[244] as States parties have committed themselves "not [to] be party to any agreement in derogation thereof."[245] That, however, does not make such principle peremptory.[246]

Having said that, the ILC has not resisted the temptation of providing some examples throughout the years. The commentary to the draft articles on the law of treaties only concluded definitively that the Charter prohibition of use of force is a peremptory norm of international law, while merely suggesting that the commission of acts considered criminal under international law, including trade in slaves piracy and genocide, could be peremptory. However, the 2001 commentaries to the draft articles on State responsibility went further stating that "peremptory norms that are *clearly accepted and recognised* include the prohibitions of aggression, genocide, slavery, racial discrimination, crimes against humanity and torture, and the right to self-determination."[247] The Commission, in the 2006 conclusions of the work of the Study Group on the Fragmentation of International Law, slightly modified the list and softened its views by stating that the examples of peremptory norms most frequently cited are the prohibitions of "aggression, slavery and the slave trade, genocide, racial discrimination apartheid and torture, as well as basic rules of international humanitarian law applicable in armed conflict, and the right to self-determination."[248]

---

[240]The rule would eventually be codified in Article 53 VCLT, and, as Suy points out, it states that a treaty conflicting with a existing peremptory norm at the time of its occlusion is void *ab intio* and *in toto*, Eric Suy, "Article 53 Convention of 1969", in Olivier Corten and Pierre Klein, eds., *The Vienna Conventions on the Law of Treaties: A Commentary* (Oxford: Oxford University Press, 2011) at 1231.

[241]*Report of the ILC, 15th Session*, *supra* note 192 at p 198–199; many scholars of the time agree, see e.g. Antonio Gómez Robledo, "Le ius cogens international: sa genèse, sa nature, ses fonctions" (1981) 172 Rec des Cours 9 at 167

[242]"Fifth Report on the Law of Treaties", *supra* note 239 at 25.

[243]*Commentaries*, *supra* note 88 at 248 (art 50, para 2).

[244]*UNCLOS*, *supra* note 43 at art 136.

[245]Ibid at art 311.6.

[246]Gennady M. Danilenko, "International Jus Cogens: Issues of Law-Making" (1991) 2 EJIL 42 at 59.

[247]"Report of the International Law Commission on the work of its fifty-third session (23 April–1 June and 2 July–10 August 2001)" (UN Doc A/56/10) in *Yearbook of the International Law Commission 2001*, vol 2, part 2 (New York and Geneva: UN, 2007) at 85 (UNDOC.A/CN.4/ SER. A/2001/Add. 1 (Part 2)) (emphasis is mine) [*Report of the ILC, 53th Session*].

[248]*Report of the ILC, 58th Session*, *supra* note 1 at para 251 (conclusion 33).

In elaborating those lists, the Commission did not provided any insight on the method of identification. In most cases, the ILC either referred itself in order to establish the peremptory character of the norms, or quoted judicial decisions of national or international Courts stating that a norm was part of *jus cogens*. It is noted though, that according to the aforementioned 2006 Conclusion, the ILC considers that expression designating norms as 'fundamental', expressive of 'elementary considerations of humanity' or 'intransgressible principles of international law', could mean that the norm is of peremptory character.[249] Such is the case of the principle of self-determination, which was qualified as peremptory in the ILC's 2001 Commentaries[250] on the basis of the ICJ's statement that it "is one of the essential principles of contemporary international law."[251]

Although it has been noted by scholars that the importance attached to peremptory norms requires an appropriate determination process,[252] the *VCLT* "is silent regarding the process through which [the international community] can accept and recognise that a norm of international law has fulfilled the criterion"[253] provided in its Article 53. This, coupled with the absence of guidance by the ILC itself on the method used to discover the peremptory character of the norms it has included in the category over the years, brings more questions than answers. "Paradoxically, one of the still unresolved questions concerns the definition of normative procedures by which rules of fundamental importance for the community of states may be created."[254] While the formation—or creation—of *jus cogens* is conceptually an issue separate from the method of identification of a peremptory norm; my view is that as the method should shed some light on the type of evidence needed to ascertain their existence. This in turn will clarify the relevant legal actors in the creation process and the means and ways in which these actors crystalise prospective *jus cogens* norms.

Some scholars have partially evaded the question of method by simply dissecting article 53 of the *VCLT* in order to spell out the requirements for the existence of a *jus cogens* norm.[255] It has been noted that such perspective looks for a

---

[249]Ibid at para 251 (conclusion 31).

[250]*Report of the ILC, 53th Session*, supra note 247 at 127.

[251]*East Timor (Portugal v. Australia)*, [1995] ICJ Rep 90 at para 29.

[252]Danilenko states that "As 'higher law' jus cogens clearly requires the application of higher standards for the ascertainment of the existence of community consensus as regards both the content and the peremptory character of the relevant rules", Danilenko, *supra* note 246 at 65; Engelen argues that "the establishment of a rule of general international law from which States are not competent to derogate at all by a treaty arrangement requires a stringent law-making process", Frank Engelen, *Interpretation of Tax Treaties under International Law* (Amsterdam: IBFD Publications, 2004) at 36.

[253]Anne Lagerwall, "Article 64 Convention of 1969", in Corten and Klein, eds., *supra* note 240 at 1480.

[254]Danilenko, *supra* note 246 at 43.

[255]Contra, Ulf Linderfalk, "The Creation of Jus Cogens—Making Sense of Article 53 of the Vienna Convention" (2011) 71 ZaöRV 359 at 374 (If international legal scholars regard as deficient the definition of *jus cogens* laid down in Art. 53 of the Vienna Convention, it is not because of what is actually stated in this provision. It is because of the wrongful assumption that Art. 53 can be used to explain something it does not pretend to explain: the creation of *jus cogens*) [Linderfalk, "Article 53"].

method to identify peremptory norms by reference of the legal consequences of the norm, by separating those norms that the community believes to have certain effects from those than do not.[256] Plain and simply, "a peremptory norm of general international law is [1.] a norm [2.] accepted and recognised by the international community of States as a whole [3.] as a norm from which no derogation is permitted and [4.] modifiable only by a new norm having the same status."[257] While most authors agree on the source of the criteria for identification and its content, some prefer to join the third and fourth requirements in a single requirement,[258] while others like them separated.[259] There is also the view that instead of being requirements, the third and fourth together are a pleonasm that expels out the legal consequences of a norm being peremptory.[260] Although it seems that the second requirement asks for *cuasi* universal acceptance, it is understood that wide majority would suffice to establish *jus cogens*,[261] regardless on whether its materialization comes from an existing rule of international law or as a new rule,[262] as it is evident that finding universal support for a norm in such a divided world would be extremely difficult in some cases.[263] This is still subject of extensive debate.[264]

---

[256]See Ulf Linderfalk, "What Is So Special About Jus Cogens?—On the Difference between the Ordinary and the Peremptory International Law" (2012) 14 Int'l Community L. Rev. 3 at 5–11.

[257]*VCLT*, *supra* note 87 at Art. 53.

[258]See Rafael Nieto-Navia, "International Peremptory Norms (Jus Cogens) And International Humanitarian Law", in Lal Chand Vohrah, et al. *Man's inhumanity to man: essays on international law in honour of Antonio Cassese* (The Hague: Kluwer Law International, 2003), 595 at 610–619.

[259]Carin Kahgan, "Jus Cogens and the Inherent Right to Self-Defense" (1997) 3 ILSA J Int'l & Comp L 767 at 775; Kamrul Hossain, "The Concept of Jus Cogens and the Obligation under the U. N. Charter" (2005) 3 Santa Clara J Int'l L 72 at 76.

[260]This is consistent with the view that Article 53 of the VCLT governs the formation of peremptory norms and their effects once they exist, See Jerzy Sztucki, *Jus Cogens and the Vienna Convention on the Laws of Treaties* (New York: Springer-Verlag, 1974) at 97.

[261]Kahgan, *supra* note 259 at 775–776; David S. Mitchell, "The Prohibition of Rape in International Humanitarian Law as a Norm of Jus Cogens: Clarifying the Doctrine" (2004) 15 Duke J Comp & Int'l L 219 at 231 (he speaks of a "general consensus of the international community").

[262]Hossain, *supra* note 259.

[263]Antonio Cassese, *International Law*, 2nd ed., (Oxford: OUP, 2004) at 202 [Cassese, *International Law*]; Karen Parker and Lyn Beth Neylon, "Jus Cogens: Compelling the Law of Human Rights" (1989) 12 Hastings Int'l & Comp L Rev 411 at 418.

[264]Linderfalk argues that Article 53 cannot be understood to mean "that the *opinio juris* establishing the existence a rule of law as *jus cogens* is either more express or more widespread than the *opinio juris* establishing customary international law in general", Linderfalk, "Article 53", *supra* note 255 at 375–376.

Under this logic, Article 53 of the *VCLT* requires the so-called 'double consent from States'.[265] That is, the existence of the norm is subject to the legal tests applicable to its respective source, and there has to be evidence of its peremptory character.[266]

Orakhelashvili rejects the exclusive reliance on the elements included in Article 53 of the *VCLT* for the identification of the norm. Instead, he proposes an identification criterion that rids itself from the need of affirmative evidence in international relations[267] and dismisses the arguments that identify *jus cogens* with the foundational elements of the system of international law.[268] His method focuses in the substance of norms, and investigates the—possible—collective reaction of actors in international relations to the breach of community interests protected by that norm. He states:

> In order to qualify as peremptory, a norm, while protecting a given actor, legal person or value, must safeguard interests transcending those of individual States, have a moral or humanitarian connotation, because its breach would involve a result so morally deplorable as to be considered absolutely unacceptable by the international community as a whole, and consequently not permitting division of these interests into bilateral legal relations.[269]

The stating point for Orakhelashvili, as well as for those authors suggesting a more formalistic view, is an existing norm. Moreover, a norm potentially subject to be breached. Therefore, as much as he means to advance the idea that *jus cogens* is the equivalent of international public policy,[270] the element of State consent—and consequently some form of source-like ascertainment method—is still present.

---

[265]See e.g. Orakhelashvili, *Peremptory Norms*, *supra* note 195 at 106; Linderfalk call is 'double *opinio juris*', Ulf Linderfalk, "The Effect of Jus Cogens Norms: Whoever Opened Pandora's Box, Did You Ever Think About the Consequences?" (2008) 18:5 EJIL 853 at 862 [Linderfalk, "The Effect"].

[266]"D'abord, le consentement toujours nécessaire pour approuver une norme de droit international général et, ensuite, l'autre consen- tement nécessaire pour voir en cette norme une norme impérative, à laquelle aucun accord contraire ne peut absolument pas déroger", Gómez Robledo, *supra* note 241 at 105.

[267]In his view, "If merely evidentiary criteria were adopted, then the reason for which a given norm is peremptory would be unclear (as practice often denotes as peremptory norms those which are not and vice versa)", moreover, the criteria he chooses "refer to an objective standard of identification of jus cogens based on the substance of a norm and hence independent of the will of States or judicial practice as an exclusive factor determining whether a norm is peremptory", Orakhelashvili, *Peremptory Norms*, *supra* note 195 at 43 and 47.

[268]He affirms that "[n]ot all rules which are important, or even indispensable, for the existence and working of international law are peremptory", ibid at 45; In D'Amato's autopioetic model, where "ultimate criterion of international legality is the self-perpetuation of the international legal system", he argues that "if *jus cogens* is on a *higher* plane than customary law and has any substantive content at all, then it would have to be taken as a superior imperative to the self-perpetuation of the system", Anthony D'Amato, "International Law as an Autopoietic System", in Wolfrum and Röben, *supra* note 1, 335 at fn 8. and p 394.

[269]Orakhelashvili, *Peremptory Norms*, *supra* note 195 at 50.

[270]Ibid at 30–31.

The mainstream knowledge in the field is that *jus cogens* can be identified in assertions of customary law, in provisions of multilateral treaties, or in resolutions of the UN General Assembly. It has been argued that the last two cannot in and of themselves generate a norm of *jus cogens*, but that "they serve as evidence of the community attitude to the relevant norms; content and status."[271] It seems that for modern international lawyers, the combination of as many manifestations of a norm as possible, especially if generated from different sources, makes a strong argument for the peremptory character of a norm.[272] An author has criticised the process of identification of *jus cogens* norms which simply relies in finding *locus* of legality in one or more recognised source of law:

> Once a peremptory norm is said to be identified as a right traceable to one of the sources accepted in Article 18 [I assume he meant 38] of the Statute of the International Court, our role, as lawyers, seems complete. [...] This very association of a peremptory norm with an institutional source as if the norm were discrete and self-standing constitutes a blind spot of contemporary legal analysis.[273]

The point can be made that such a critique is directed at establish *jus cogens* as an independent source. However, it is undeniable that what is most often described in legal scholarship as methods for the identification of *jus cogens*, is a tweaked version of the modern method to identify customary law.[274] From that perspective, it is more than justified to consider *jus cogens* nothing else than an enhanced customary norm.[275] That, of course, just changes the main question to how much *opinio juris* is necessary for a norm to cross from customary to peremptory. I agree with the proposition that:

> The binding character of a peremptory norm does not rest upon de number of time it is cited in legal rhetoric nor in a will of some make-believe international community 'out there' in some posited objectivity aggregated from the wills of the members.[276]

---

[271]Alexander Orakhelashvili, "Peremptory Norms of the International Community: A Reply to William E. Conklin" (2012) 23 EJIL 863 at 866 [Orakhelashvili, "A Reply"].

[272]Lagerwall, *supra* note 253 at 1469 ("Each of the sources of international law mentioned [treaties, custom and UN General Assembly resolutions] presents characteristics challenging the view that they alone could constitute a source of peremptory norms. Thus, it is preferable to combine different sources together in order to establish the peremptory character of those norms, as well as the time at which they emerged").

[273]Conklin, *supra* note 200 at 843.

[274]Linderfalk, "Article 53", *supra* note 255 at 372–373 ("The criteria governing the existence of *jus cogens* are very much the same as those governing the existence of customary international law"); Linderfalk, "The Effect", *supra* note 265 at 862 ("Stated somewhat differently, a norm of *jus cogens* may be said to presuppose the existence of two kinds of *opinio juris*").

[275]Orakhelashvili, "A Reply", *supra* note 271 at 866 ("If need be, international courts can, as they have repeatedly done, apply requirements of custom-generation—state practice and *opinio juris*—in the way that explains the emergence of *jus cogens* rules"); or putting it in reverse order, "second order rules of *jus cogens* are customary international law", Linderfalk, "Article 53", *supra* note 255 at 372.

[276]William E. Conklin, "The Peremptory Norms of the International Community: A Rejoinder to Alexander Orakhelashvili" (2012) 23:3 EJIL 869 at 870.

Professor Antonio Cassese suggested that the task of existence of a particular peremptory norm should be entrusted to the international judiciary.[277] In his view, such an authoritative determination cannot be left to the UN General Assembly (or other political international bodies) or to the individual statements of international actors.[278] In addressing the issue of method, Cassese favoured a two-stages method, similar to the double consent approach discussed above. In his words: "often the inquiry deals both with the question of whether a general rule or principle has evolved and, if so, of whether such rule or principle also has the status of *jus cogens*."[279]

Although he did not discuss at length the first stage of the process, he seems to favour customary law and general principles as sources of norms candidate to peremptory status. That being said, on the basis of Article 53 of the *VCLT*, he rejected the idea that the second-stage of the process was based on the method of identification of customary law.[280]

He instead proposes three parameters in order to verify the peremptory nature of a rule. By corollary of entrusting the international judiciary with the decision of the peremptory nature of a norm, he proposed that the first parameter should be whether international or national Courts have made a statement on the nature of a prospective norm. His second parameter is to determine whether the value protected by the prospective norm is 'fully congruous' with the goals or values of the international community. Finally, he proposes as the third parameter a comparative inquiry on whether the prospective norm is as crucial for the international community as an existing undisputed peremptory norm.[281]

As interesting as Cassese's views are, they are still confronted with the realities of international affairs: outside a very small number of norms, some of which are already found in the lists of the ILC, "very few states and other legal subjects take a stand on the peremptory nature of international rules, and authoritative pronouncements on the matter are few and far between."[282] The reliance on values behind norms and the critical importance for the community transfer the *locus* of legality outside the realm of State action.[283] By framing it in the function of international courts and tribunals, *jus cogens* norms have the possibility to transcend. This depends on the role that such courts and tribunals see themselves playing in international relations. While Cassese's perspective assumes an

[277]Antonio Cassese, *Realizing Utopia: The Future of International Law* (Oxford: OUP, 2012) at 164 [Cassese, *Realizing Utopia*].

[278]Ibid.

[279]Ibid (The task of the body charged with inquiring into jus cogens would only consist of establishing whether, in addition to being a customary rule or principle, the norm at issue has also been endowed with the higher rank of a peremptory norm).

[280]Ibid at 165.

[281]Ibid at 166.

[282]Ibid.

[283]Contra Bing Bing Jia, "The Immunity of State Officials for International Crimes Revisited" (2012) 10 J Int'l Criminal Just 1303 at 1320 ("there will be no jus cogens norms that can have a meaningful and effective existence, if they are wrought by others than states").

international judiciary deeply engaged in the role of identifying peremptory norms, he did warn about the need of persuasive argument: "Here, as in any other matter, the cogency of the court's reasoning has a decisive bearing on its likelihood to be taken up by other courts and tribunals."[284]

The ICJ has been seized in a number of occasions of cases in which the parties to the dispute argued that the norms applicable to the case were norms with peremptory status. That being said, in the history of the Court only three norms have conclusively been designated, in unequivocal terms, peremptory norms of international law. I will discuss them individually, and in reverse chronological order.

A note on method: I will exclude from this analysis *Nicaragua*, as my reading of the merits judgment is that that the Court took judicial note of the statements of the ILC, Nicaragua and the United States to the effect that the norm prohibiting the use of force was peremptory.[285] The Court's conclusion from those statements was that the norm was customary.[286] As there was no further discussion on the nature and effect of such norm *qua* peremptory, I do not assume the Court's position on the matter beyond the stated conclusion.[287]

Prohibition of Torture. In 2012, the Court delivered its judgment in the case concerning *Questions relating to the Obligation to Prosecute or Extradite (Belgium v. Senegal)* (hereinafter, *Prosecute or Extradite*),[288] which dealt with the alleged crimes committed by Mr. Hissène Habré, the former head of State of Chad, while he was in power. Mr. Habré, who was residing in Senegal under political asylum, was pursued in Belgium for having allegedly committed crimes against humanity, including torture. Belgian authorities issued an international arrest warrant in absentia, but the courts in Senegal ruled against it. Through diplomatic exchanges, Belgium requested Senegal to comply with the obligation to prosecute or extradite Mr. Habré under the United Nations Convention against Torture and Other Cruel, Inhuman or Degrading Treatment or Punishment (hereinafter, UNCAT). Since Belgium was of the view that no satisfactory action was taken by Senegal in this respect, it filed a case against the latter in the registry of the ICJ. Belgium relied on UNCAT for establishing the jurisdiction or the Court, but also made arguments on

---

[284]Ibid at 164.

[285]*Nicaragua*, Merits, *supra* note 172 at para 190.

[286]Ibid (the paragraph starts by saying that "[a] further confirmation of the validity as customary international law of the principle of the prohibition of the use of force expressed in Article 2, paragraph 4, of the Charter of the United Nations may be found in the fact that"); see also Dinah Shelton, "Righting Wrongs: Reparations in the Articles on State Responsibility" (2002) 96 AJIL 833 at fn. 57.

[287]*Contra*, Orakhelashvili, *Peremptory Norms*, *supra* note 195 at 42 ("It is furthermore inaccurate to read the *Nicaragua* judgment in such a way as to construe it as just referring to the ILC's emphasis on the peremptory character of the prohibition of the use of force and not itself expressing the similar attitude.").

[288]*Questions relating to the Obligation to Prosecute or Extradite (Belgium v. Senegal)*, Judgment, [2012] ICJ Rep 422 at para 39.

the basis of the customary and *jus cogens* norms prohibiting torture. That is because Belgium sought for the Court to establish the international responsibility of Senegal for not prosecuting or extraditing Mr. Habré on the basis of acts of torture allegedly committed before the entry into force of UNCAT for Senegal.

Although the Court dismissed the line of argument of Senegal on this point, it categorically stated that the prohibition of torture was not only part of customary international law, but that is had become a peremptory norm of international law.[289] The Court then stated:

> That prohibition is grounded in a widespread international practice and on the *opinio juris* of States. It appears in numerous international instruments of universal application ([…]), and it has been introduced into the domestic law of almost all States; finally, acts of torture are regularly denounced within national and international fora.[290]

The international instruments used by the Court include UN General Assembly resolutions and two human rights conventions adopted under the auspices of the UN: ICCPR and UNCAT. To those, the Court only added the Geneva Conventions of 1949. It is interesting that the Court does mention the regular condemnation of acts of torture, without referencing the case law of human rights bodies and tribunals, as well as the jurisprudence of the international and hybrid criminal law tribunals. It is not only that cases have been brought to those institutions against States and individuals because of their responsibility in acts of torture; these institutions have also themselves declared the peremptory character of the prohibition.[291] It is also interesting to contrast the mere mention—without any examples—of national legislation, with the work done by the International Committee of the Red Cross in surveying national legislation concerning torture.[292]

The final point that I wish to make in the case of the prohibition of torture is that the Court found in *Prosecute or Extradite* that such prohibition is customary and peremptory without much clarity in the method. The paragraph of the decision above quoted makes clear reference to the method used by the Court to find customary law (*opinio juris* and State practice) and then elaborated the elements of *opinio juris* and State practice already discussed.[293] It can be argued that the process followed by the Court is the same for both considerations, and it was the

---

[289] Ibid. at para 99.

[290] Ibid.

[291] See e.g. *Prosecutor v. Anto Furundžija ("Lašva Valley" Case), IT-95-17/1* Judgment (10 December 1998) at para 153–157 (International Criminal Tribunal for the former Yugoslavia, Trial Chamber) online: ICTR http://www.ictr.org; *Case of Maritza Urrutia (Guatemala)* (2003), Inter-Am Ct HR (Ser C) No 103, at para 92.

[292] Jean-Marie Henckaerts and Louise Doswald-Beck, eds., *Customary international humanitarian law* (Cambridge: Cambridge University Press, 2005) at vol. II, part 2, paras 1039–1247.

[293] As per *Nicaragua* (*supra* note 172), resolutions and multilateral conventions can be evidence of *opinio juris*; while, according to *Arrest Warrant* (*infra* note 295), national legislation is considered evidence of State practice. I do not know whether denunciations of acts of torture at the national and international level qualify as either *opinio juris* or practice.

overwhelmingly strong level of *opinio juris* what allowed such prohibition to cross the Rubicon of peremptoriness.[294] Alternatively, it can be argued that the method expressed by the Court in paragraph 99 of the judgment only proved the customary status of the prohibition of torture and that its peremptory status was axiomatic for the Court. I favour the latter of the two positions, since the Courts verification of 'widespread international practice' does not seem to match the requirement of acceptance and 'recognition by the international community of States as a whole' found in Article 53 of the *VCLT*.

Prohibition of committing war crimes and crimes against humanity. The express recognition of the peremptory status of the prohibition of committing war crimes and crimes against humanity is, without a doubt, the most bizarre of the three analysed in this section. As it was in the case of the prohibition of torture, it is impossible to indicate with precision what was the method used by the Court to establish that a norm has *jus cogens* character. And that is, because the Court recognised the status of such prohibitions by means of reference to a previous case.

In 2002, the Court delivered its judgment in the case concerning the *Arrest Warrant of 11 April 2000* (*Democratic Republic of Congo v. Belgium*) (hereinafter, *Arrest Warrant*).[295] The case filed by the Democratic Republic of Congo sought to cancel an international arrest warrant issued on 11 April 2000 by Belgian authorities against the then Minister for Foreign Affairs in office of the Democratic Republic of the Congo, Mr. Abdulaye Yerodia Ndombasi.[296]

Mr. Ndombasi was being prosecuted in Belgium for allegedly committing serious violations of international law. In many respects, the facts of *Arrest Warrant* are similar to those of *Prosecute or Extradite*; with the exception that in the latter case Chad had lifted the immunity of Mr. Habré, while in the latter the Democratic Republic of Congo was asserting the immunity enjoyed by Mr. Ndombasi as Minister of Foreign Affairs.

In *Arrest Warrant*, the Court did not investigate the nature of the norms allegedly transgressed by Mr. Ndombasi and for which he was been prosecuted in Belgium. Instead, the Court made a detailed analysis of the rules governing immunity from

---

[294]Alston and Simma are of the view that "we are safe in concluding that the threshold requirement for the emergence of *jus cogens*, namely the generality, or universality, of acceptance and recognition, is set at least as high as that necessary for the development of general (or universal) customary law", Bruno Simma and Phillip Alston, Sources of Human Rights Law. Custom, Jus Cogens, and General Principles, (1988–1989) 12 Aust. YBIL 82 at 103; D'Amato states that "it should be possible to argue that a rule of *jus cogens* simply means a *very strong* rule of customary international law", Anthony A. D'Amato, *The concept of custom in international law* (Ithaca, N. Y.: Cornell University Press, 1971) at 132; see also Jordan Paust, "The Reality of Jus Cogens", (1991–1992) 7 Conn J Int'l L 81 at 82–84 ("Yet *jus cogens* norms have an extra feature, unlike custom in general, it must be generally expected that such norms are peremptory").

[295]*Arrest Warrant of 11 April 2000* (*Democratic Republic of the Congo v. Belgium*), [2002] ICJ Rep 3 [*Arrest Warrant*].

[296]*Arrest Warrant of 11 April 2000* (*Democratic Republic of the Congo v. Belgium*), "Application Instituting Proceedings" at p 2 (17 October 2000), online: International Court of Justice http://www.icj-cij.org/docket/files/121/7081.pdf.

criminal jurisdiction. In the dispositive part of the judgment, the Court found that the issuance and circulation of the arrest warrant against Mr. Ndombasi failed to respect the jurisdictional immunities that he enjoyed.[297] Shortly after the judgment was delivered, Shelton noted that the Court avoided pronouncing itself on the peremptory nature of was crimes and crimes against humanities.[298]

Fast-forward ten years, when the Court delivered its judgment in the case concerning *Jurisdictional Immunities of the State* (*Germany v. Italy: Greece intervening*) (hereinafter, *Jurisdictional Immunities*). The case relates to the proceedings instituted against Germany in the Italian Courts relating illegal acts allegedly committed by the authorities of the Third Reich during World War II. In its application to the Court, Germany stated that "Italian judicial bodies have repeatedly disregarded the jurisdictional immunity of Germany as a sovereign State",[299] since the Italian courts found that Germany was not entitled to sovereign immunity and was liable to pay damages in a number of cases.[300] The line of reasoning of the Italian courts was that "jurisdictional immunity is not absolute and cannot be invoked by a State in the face of acts by that State which constitute crimes under international law."[301]

For the purposes of the case in the ICJ, Italy advanced the argument that since the acts committed by Nazi Germany constituted violations to *jus cogens* norms, the jurisdictional immunities claimed by Germany cannot prevail. In other words:

> Since *jus cogens* rules always prevail over any inconsistent rule of international law, whether contained in a treaty or in customary international law, so the argument runs, and since the rule which accords one State immunity before the courts of another does not have the status of *jus cogens*, the rule of immunity must give way.[302]

The Court was of the view that there was no conflict between the procedural rules according Germany jurisdictional immunity, and the substantive rules prohibiting the illegal acts committed by Nazi Germany, as the rules are meant to address different matters. In short, the rules of State immunity "do not bear upon the question whether or not the conduct in respect of which the proceedings are brought was lawful or unlawful."[303]

---

[297] *Arrest Warrant*, *supra* note 295 at paras 70–71.

[298] Shelton, *supra* note 286 at 843 (she further notes in footnote 58 that "[o]nly one of the ten opinions [...] mentions the concept of *jus cogens* norms despite its obvious relevance to the issues in the case").

[299] *Jurisdictional Immunities of the State* (*Germany v. Italy: Greece intervening*), "Application Instituting Proceedings" at p 4 (23 December 2008), online: International Court of Justice http://www.icj-cij.org/docket/files/143/14923.pdf.

[300] For a doctrinal view of the judgments of the Italian courts, see Pasquale De Sena and Francesca De Vittor, "State Immunity and Human Rights: The Italian Supreme Court Decision on the Ferrini Case" (2005) 16 EJIL 89; Annalisa Ciampi, "The Italian Court of Cassation Asserts Civil Jurisdiction over Germany in a Criminal Case Relating to the Second World War: The Civitella Case" (2009) 7:3 J. Int'l Criminal Just 597.

[301] *Jurisdictional Immunities*, *supra* note 103 at para 27.

[302] Ibid at para 92.

[303] Ibid at para 93.

To further sustain its point, the Court brought up the fact that in *Arrest Warrant* it had also decided to uphold the immunity of an individual, and stated that such reasoning was also applicable to State immunity. However, in explaining the similarities between *Arrest Warrant* and *Jurisdictional Immunities*, it stated that:

> In *Arrest Warrant*, the Court held, albeit without express reference to the concept of *jus cogens*, that the fact that a Minister for Foreign Affairs was accused of criminal violations of rules which undoubtedly possess the character of *jus cogens* did not deprive the Democratic Republic of the Congo of the entitlement which it possessed as a matter of customary international law to demand immunity on his behalf.[304]

At the end of the passage quoted above, reference is made to paragraph 58 of *Arrest Warrant*, were the Court stated that it was unable to find State practice supporting exceptions to the jurisdictional immunity enjoyed by "incumbent Ministers for Foreign Affairs, where they are suspected of having committed war crimes or crimes against humanity."[305] Under the circumstances, there is no other conclusion to draw that in *Jurisdictional Immunities* the Court recognised the peremptory character of the prohibition against war crimes or crimes against humanity. It is interesting that a commentator, in defending the argument that "judicial practice also actually deals with peremptory norms without mentioning the concept, but underlining the special character or effect of norms",[306] noted the reference made in the Join Separate Opinion of Judges Higgins, Kooijmans and Buergenthal in *Arrest Warrant* to the jurisdictional effects of war crimes and crimes against humanity,[307] but made no mention to the judgment of the Court itself.

However, the issue remains that in neither *Arrest Warrant* nor *Jurisdictional Immunities*, the Court explained the method by which concluded that the prohibition against such crimes are part of *jus cogens*. Once again, the Court seems to be of the view that the *jus cogens* character of a norm is self-evident.

The final point I wish to make concerning *Jurisdictional Immunities* is that, the Court did not investigate weather the acts committed by Nazi Germany were indeed violations of *jus cogens*. In deciding that there was no clash between norms, the Court only assumed for the purposes of analysing the argument that the prohibitions were of *jus cogens*, without definitively stating whether they were or not peremptory.[308] Although it could be argued that "the murder of civilians in occupied territory, the deportation of civilian inhabitants to slave labour and the

[304]Ibid at para 95.

[305]*Arrest Warrant*, *supra* note 295 at para 58.

[306]Orakhelashvili, *Peremptory Norms*, *supra* note 195 at 42.

[307]Ibid at 43.

[308]*Jurisdictional Immunities*, *supra* note 103 at paras 93 and 97; Boudreault also noted this fact, François Boudreault, "Identifying Conflicts of Norms: The ICJ Approach in the Case of the Jurisdictional Immunities of the State (Germany v. Italy: Greece Intervening)" (2012) 25 Leiden J Int'l L 1003 at 1005.

deportation of prisoners of war to slave labour"[309] are war crimes,[310] and therefore the prohibition to commit those crimes is part of *jus cogens* as per *Arrest Warrant*; the fact remains that the Court remained silent in this matter.

Prohibition of Genocide. The ICJ has specifically stated three times in the last decade the peremptory character of the prohibition of genocide. First in the case concerning *Armed Activities on the Territory of the Congo (New Application: 2002) (Democratic Republic of the Congo v. Rwanda)*, shortly after in the case concerning *Application of the Convention on the Prevention and Punishment of the Crime of Genocide (Bosnia and Herzegovina v. Serbia and Montenegro)* (hereinafter, *Application of the Genocide Convention*), and recently in *Application of the Convention on the Prevention and Punishment of the Crime of Genocide (Croatia v. Serbia)*. In all three judgements the Court un-controversially stated "the norm prohibiting genocide was assuredly a peremptory norm of international law (*jus cogens*)."[311]

To arrive to this conclusion, the Court relied in -all occasions- on its own *Advisory Opinion on the Reservations to the Convention on the Prevention and Punishment of the Crime of Genocide*, and the Preamble of the *United Nations Convention Against Genocide*. In the aforementioned Advisory Opinion, the Court was of the view "that the principles underlying the Convention are principles which are recognised by civilized nations as binding on States, even without any conventional obligation." That is, although the Court did not express in specify terms the peremptoriness of the norm, it already pointed out the heightened level that such prohibition universally enjoys.

It worth nothing that both in the aforementioned Advisory Opinion and in *Application of the Genocide Convention*, the Court also cited UN General Assembly resolution 96 (I) which declared that genocide is a crime under international law.

From the point of view of method, this is the least reproachable of the cases here discussed. In 1955, the Court made an articulate argument, making use of the legal tools available at the moment, in order to defend the idea that the prohibition of genocide needs not be in a treaty for it to be universally binding. Subsequent decisions have relied on this to defend the *jus cogens* character of the rule, with all that such label means in current international law.

The truth is that in order to perform its work, the Court does not need to call a norm *jus cogens*. The higher moral level is assigned to the norms preciously discussed is simply as a way to differentiate among international obligations and to

[309] *Jurisdictional Immunities*, *supra* note 103 at para 93.

[310] *Elements of Crimes*, Official Records of the Review Conference of the Rome Statute of the International Criminal Court, Kampala, 31 May–11 June 2010, ICC-ASP/1/3(part II-B), at articles 8(2)(a) (vii)-1 and 8(2)(b)(i) online: International Criminal Court http://www.icc-cpi.int/.

[311] *Application of the Genocide Convention*, *supra* note 158 at para 161; see also *Armed Activities on the Territory of the Congo (New Application: 2002) (Democratic Republic of the Congo v. Rwanda)*, [2006] ICJ Rep 6 at para 64 [*Armed Activities*]; *Application of the Convention on the Prevention and Punishment of the Crime of Genocide (Croatia v. Serbia)*, Merits, at para 87 online: International Court of Justice http://www.icj-cij.org/docket/files/118/18422.pdf.

assign an objective wrongness to certain violations. That being said, "peremptory norms identify the ethical underpinnings of the international system and legally obligate states to uphold them."[312] This means that in the view of the Court, there are particular violations that are objectively worse than others. "The emergence and assertion of *jus cogens* in contemporary international law fulfill the necessity of a minimum of verticalization in the international legal order, erected upon pillars in which the juridical and the ethical are merged."[313] This is not meant to diminish the effect of international law in general, as Weil feared,[314] but to recognise that human consciousness is nuanced and gives predominance to certain values above others.[315]

It must be noted that on 2015, the ILC decided to include the topic of '*Jus Cogens*' in its programme of work.[316] The syllabus prepared by the special rapporteur, Professor Dire D. Tladi, includes the nature, requirements for the identification, and the development of an illustrative list of norms which have achieved the status of *jus cogens*.[317] This development is promising as it would certainly bring some clarity as to the process to indentify a peremptory norm of international law.

3.4 The Jurisprudence of Incorporation

In the previous section, I briefly discussed the three first sources enumerated in Article 38 of the ICJ Statute, that is, the primary normative forms accepted as law by the contemporary doctrine of sources. I also briefly covered unilateral declarations, which are a source of law not mentioned in the Statute; jurisprudence, which is identified in the Statute as subsidiary means to identify norms; and *jus cogens*. The focus of the discussion was the nature and method of identification of each one of them, as seen by the drafters of Article 38 and by the Court itself, according to its jurisprudence. I explained as well that in the case of the general principles of law, such a discussion was more complicated to tackle due to the relative indeterminacy that they enjoy as a source of law in the context of the function of the Court. The purpose of that exercise was to introduce the rationale used by the Court in defining the scope and content of norms identified in Article 38—or at least, the ones susceptible to definition from the standpoint of tradition and current regulation—I also discussed how the subsidiary means were included in the Statute, particularly

[312]Mitchell, *supra* note 261 at 230.

[313]Cançado Trindade, "General course", *supra* note 229 at 336.

[314]Weil, "Relative normativity", *supra* note 185 at 413.

[315]See e.g. Weil, ibid at 424 (Although Weil is not totally comfortable with the hierarchization of international law he finds that "this normative differentiation is certainly inspired by unimpeachable moral concerns"); see also Theodor Meron, "On a Hierarchy of International Human Rights" (1986) 80 AJIL 1 at 21.

[316]*Report of the ILC, 67th session*, *supra* note 113 at para 286.

[317]*Report of the International Law Commission: Sixty-sixth session*, UNGAOR, 69th Sess, Supp. No. 10, UN Doc A/69/10 (2014) at annex, paras 13–16.

noting the positivistic voices that equated them with judge-made legislation. This was to show that the treatment given to other sources found in Article 38 is susceptible of replication in other contexts by operation of Article 38 itself.

This is, however, only one part of the complex reality in which the Court functions. It must be recognised that "the enumeration of 'sources' of International Law listed in Article 38 of the ICJ Statute was never meant to be, nor could it be, exhaustive."[318] Especially when the Court is, by its own admission, under the duty to take judicial notice of all the international law applicable to a case:

> It being the duty of the Court itself to ascertain and apply the relevant law in the given circumstances of the case, the burden of establishing or proving rules of international law cannot be imposed upon any of the parties, for the law lies within the judicial knowledge of the Court.[319]

From time to time the Court has encountered cases in which the determination as to the legal existence and binding nature of an instrument was subject to questioning under the framework presented in the previous section. Setting aside cases where the subject matter under litigation concerned violations of international human rights or humanitarian law, I argue that when dealing with normative forms not fulfilling the totality of the requirements for them to be considered a source under the elements enumerated in Article 38, the Court has treated them as one of these elements instead of as distinct normative forms.[320] The result has been the incorporation of diverse normative forms in the framework established by Article 38 of the ICJ Statute.[321] In defence of this argument, I will present in the following subsections three cases decided by the ICJ in which such operation took effect.

A note on method: in the following subsection I make extensive use of the pleadings of the parties as well as to their statements in the oral proceedings[322] in

---

[318]Cançado Trindade, "General course", *supra* note 229 at 150.

[319]*Fisheries Jurisdiction* (*United Kingdom v. Iceland*), Merits [1974] ICJ Rep 3 at para 17; *Fisheries Jurisdiction* (*Federal Republic of Germany v. Iceland*), Merits [1974] ICJ Rep 175 at para 18 (with identical text).

[320]Chodosh has already argued that when dealing with what he calls 'declarative international law', "these phenomena may be included in one of the two previously recognized categories", Hiram E. Chodosh, Neither Treaty nor Custom: The Emergence of Declarative International Law (1991) 26 Tex Int'l L J 90.

[321]See Klabbers, "Law-making", *supra* note 15 at 87–88 ("Yet with all these instruments, there is always some uncertainty as to whether they really constitute additional sources of international law, or whether they should not be somehow captured by the list of Article 38. […] In both cases, however, there is some element of stretching involved in categorizing unilateral declarations and decision-making practices within international organizations within the accepted sources catalogue of Article 38 ICJ").

[322]In discussing the function of the Court under Article 60 of its Statute, the ICJ was of the view that the pleadings and the record of the oral proceedings "are also relevant to the interpretation of the Judgment, as they show what evidence was, or was not, before the Court and how the issues before it were formulated by each Party", *Request for Interpretation of the Judgment of 15 June 1962 in the Case concerning the Temple of Preah Vihear* (*Cambodia v. Thailand*), [2013] ICJ Rep 281 at para 69.

order to show that, although the Court's action is governed by the principle *juria novit curiae*,[323] the majority decision often reflects the logic advanced in the arguments of the parties, each of which seeks to reduce the issue to the extreme that best serves their interest (for example, law vs. non-law). I also make use of dissenting opinions in order to demonstrate that a middle way was plausible in the view of the distinguished jurists that have, at different times, joined the bench.[324]

3.4.1 Military and Paramilitary Activities in and Against Nicaragua

The case on the *Military and Paramilitary Activities in and against Nicaragua* (hereinafter, *Nicaragua*) case has been characterised as the leading case in the jurisprudence of the ICJ.[325] The case was initiated by Nicaragua against the United States on 9 April 1984, relying on the declarations recognizing as compulsory the jurisdiction of the International Court of Justice under Article 36, paragraph 2, of the Statute of the Court.[326] Three days before Nicaragua filed its application in the Registry of the ICJ, the United States submitted a communication to the Secretary-General of the UN, with the purpose of modifying its declaration as to exclude "disputes with any Central American state or arising out of or related to events in Central America..."[327] Then, on 7 October 1985, the United States withdrew the said declaration.[328]

The sequence of events is explained by the text of the United States' declaration which provided that it "shall remain in force for a period of five years and thereafter until the expiration of six months after notice may be given to terminate this declaration."[329] In view of the fact that terminating the declaration would not have the effect of preventing a case by Nicaragua of being heard, the United States

[323] *Lotus*, *supra* note 101 at p 31.

[324] For a justification about this the method, see Villalpando, *supra* note 125 at 9 ("to fully assess the contribution of the Court to the development of our discipline, it is not sufficient to analyse in awe the repercussions of its explicit and categorical dicta as to the state of the law. These are only the tip of an iceberg made of implicit choices, silences, and innuendos, which may be understood only by a thorough reading not only of the judgment, but also of the opinions of judges and the pleadings of the parties, in light of the general debates in the legal scholarship of our times").

[325] The authors add "[E]ven outside the jurisprudence of the Court, Nicaragua ranks amongst the most important cases decided in the past century" Cristina Hoss, Santiago Villalpando and Sandesh Sivakumaran, *Nicaragua: 25 Years Late* (2012) 25 Leiden J Int'l L 131 at 133.

[326] *Declaration recognizing as compulsory the jurisdiction of the Court, in conformity with Article 36, paragraph 2, of the Statute of the International Court of Justice*, United States, 14 August 1946, 1 UNTS 9.

[327] *Declaration of the United States of America relating to the above-mentioned Declaration*, United States, 6 April 1984, 1354 UNTS 452.

[328] *Termination by the United States of America*, United States, 7 October 1985, 1408 UNTS 270.

[329] *Declaration*, *supra* note 326 at 12.

sought to first limit the possibility of such a case by means of a modification of the declaration. Admittedly an argument could be made about the applicability, or not, of the six-months notice to modifications as well as terminations.

During the jurisdiction and admissibility stage, several issues related to the validity of both Nicaragua's and the United States' declarations under Article 36, paragraph 2, were raised. I am particularly interested in the effect of the United States' modification and subsequent withdrawal, and the body of law governing such acts. In its memorial, Nicaragua argued that:

> In principle, questions of modification, invalidity termination, are to be determined on grounds substantially similar to those found in the law of treaties, that is to say, either as expressly provided for in the instrument or on legal grounds external to the terms of the declaration, such as fundamental change of circumstances.[330]

The United States, in its counter-memorial, stated categorically that Declarations under the Statute cannot be assimilated to treaties, and that the application of the law of treaties to such declarations is not warranted.[331]

During the oral arguments on jurisdiction and admissibility, Sir Ian Brownlie, on behalf of Nicaragua, defended the position that the modification and terminations of such declarations were governed by the principles of the law of treaties, relying mostly on the opinions of writers.[332] It is noted, though, that the argument Brownlie was trying to make was that there was no right to unilaterally modify the declarations made under Article 36, paragraph 2, of the Statute.[333]

Myres McDougal, on behalf of the United States, argued that it would be "incorrect and seriously misleading"[334] and a "grotesque miscalculation of common interest"[335] to assimilate to treaties the obligations established by unilateral declarations made under the ICJ Statute. McDougal went beyond that and suggested that the Court should advance the law in recognition of the *sui generis* nature of the declarations:

> I now propose to outline a developing international law, fashioned in specific relation to declarations by practice and Court decision, which honours modification and termination if exercised before the filing of an adversary claim and to establish that the international law

[330] *Military and Paramilitary Activities in and against Nicaragua* (*Nicaragua* v. *United States of America*), "Memorial of Nicaragua (Questions of Jurisdiction and Admissibility)" (30 June 1984), ICJ Pleadings (vol. 1) 361 at para 119.

[331] *Military and Paramilitary Activities in and against Nicaragua* (*Nicaragua* v. *United States of America*), "Counter-Memorial of the United States of America (Questions of Jurisdiction and Admissibility)" (17 August 1984), ICJ Pleadings (vol. 2) 3 at para 338 [*Nicaragua*, "Counter-Memorial"].

[332] *Military and Paramilitary Activities in and against Nicaragua* (*Nicaragua* v. *United States of America*), "Oral Arguments on Jurisdiction and Admissibility" (8 to 18 October and 26 November 1984), ICJ Pleadings (vol. 3) 5 at p 72.

[333] Ibid at p 70.

[334] Ibid at p 217.

[335] Ibid at p 219.

> of treaties, when properly understood, even if assumed to apply to declarations, does not preclude such modification and termination.[336]

In the judgment on jurisdiction and admissibility the Court, after evaluating the arguments of both parties and reviewing its judgments in the *Nuclear tests* cases,[337] decided that:

> It appears from the requirements of good faith that they [declarations under Article 36, paragraph 2] should be treated, by analogy, according to the law of treaties, which requires a reasonable time for withdrawal from or termination of treaties that contain no provision regarding the duration of their validity.[338]

The practical implication of the afore-cited statement was to effectively impose a six-months notice for the modification made by the United States on 6 April 1984 to take effect. Therefore, the United States was forced to submit to the contentious jurisdiction of the ICJ in the case.[339] Judges Oda, Jennings and Schwebel dissented from the Courts judgment on this point. Judge Oda was particularly critical of the application of treaty law to the declarations under Article 36, paragraph 2, as in his view a treaty granting a right to one of the parties to unilaterally terminate or modify its terms with immediate effect would not be a treaty, while this practice was at the time perfectly normal in the case of the said declarations.[340] Judge Schwebel relied on the fact that the Court had consistently referred to these declarations as unilateral acts[341] to state that in his own view the stronger argument was to treat them as *sui generis* legal acts rather than governed by the law of treaties.[342] In my view, the simplest yet most logical explanation of the issues at stake among the dissenting views came from Sir Robert Jennings, who stated:

> The declarations are statements of intention; and statements of intention made in a quite formal way. Obviously, however, they do not amount to treaties or contracts; or, at least, if one says they are treaties, or contracts, one immediately has to go on to say they are a special kind of treaty, or contract, partaking only of some of the rules normally applicable to such matters. Thus, however one starts, one ends by treating them as more or less *sui generis*. In short, it seems to me that, interesting as it might be to speculate about the

---

[336]Ibid at p 220.

[337]*Nuclear Tests* (*Australia v. France*), *supra* note 171 at 46; *Nuclear Tests* (*New Zealand v. France*), *supra* note 171 at 29 ("[j]ust as the very rule of *pacta sunt servanda* in the law of treaties is based on good faith, so also is the binding character of an international obligation assumed by unilateral declaration").

[338]*Nicaragua*, Jurisdiction and Admissibility, *supra* note 147 at para 63.

[339]Ibid at para 65.

[340]Ibid at p 510 (Separate opinion of Judge Sir Robert Jennings).

[341]*Anglo-Iranian Oil Co.* (*United Kingdom v. Iran*), Preliminary Objection, [1952] ICJ Rep 93 at 105; *Case concerning Certain Norwegian Loans* (*France v. Norway*), [1957] ICJ Rep 9 at p 23; *Barcelona Traction, Light and Power Company, Limited* (*Belgium v. Spain*), Preliminary Objections, [1964] ICJ Rep 6 at p 29.

[342]*Nicaragua*, Jurisdiction and Admissibility, *supra* note 147 at p 620 (Dissenting opinion of Judge Schwebel).

juridical taxonomy of Optional-Clause declarations, it is better to begin the inquiry not from a label but from the actual practice and expectation of States today.[343]

Sir Jennings' point was that framing the argument on the law of treaties was a disservice to the practice of States and especially to the jurisprudence of the Court, which had sustained in previous occasions the "well-established principle of international law embodied in the Court's Statute, namely, that the Court can only exercise jurisdiction over a State with its consent."[344]

Another important feature of the United States' declaration under Article 36 was that, when originally made, it specified it shall not apply to "Disputes arising under a multilateral treaty, unless (i) all parties to the treaty affected by the decision are also parties to the case before the Court, or (2) the United States of America specially agrees to jurisdiction".[345] This reservation was of pivotal importance for the United States, as Nicaragua had argued in its application that the actions of the former constituted a flagrant violation of the Charter of the UN and the Charter of the Organization of American States[346] (hereinafter, OAS). After the United States objected to the jurisdiction of the Court on the basis of the said reservation, the Court decided at the preliminary stage that the objection was not of an exclusive preliminary character.[347] In lay terms, the Court left the determination of the validity of the said objection to the merits stage, as, in the view of the Court, it involved matters of substance.

Nothing of the above boded well for the United States. Something quite radical—yet not unique[348]—then occurred. As is widely known, the government of the United States was of the view that "the judgment of the Court [on jurisdiction and

---

[343]Ibid at p 547 (Separate opinion of Judge Sir Robert Jennings).

[344]See also, *Monetary Gold Removed from Rome in 1943* (*Italy v. France, United Kingdom of Great Britain and Northern Ireland and United States of America*), [1954] ICJ Rep 19 at p 32; see also *Aerial Incident of 27 July 1955* (*Israel v. Bulgaria*), [1959] ICJ Rep 127 at p 142.

[345]*Declaration*, *supra* note 326 at 10 and 12.

[346]*Military and Paramilitary Activities in and against Nicaragua* (*Nicaragua v. United States of America*), "Application instituting proceedings" (9 April 1984), ICJ Pleadings (vol. 3) online: International Court of Justice http://www.icj-cij.org/docket/files/70/9615.pdf at para 9.

[347]*Nicaragua*, Merits, *supra* note 172 at para 76.

[348]For instance Iceland failed to make any written submissions and to appear in both the jurisdiction and merits hearing for the *Fisheries Jurisdiction* cases, the Court took note of that: *Fisheries Jurisdiction* (*United Kingdom v. Iceland*), Jurisdiction of the Court, [1973] ICJ Rep 3 at para 12; *Fisheries Jurisdiction* (*Federal Republic of Germany v. Iceland*), Jurisdiction of the Court, [1973] ICJ Rep 49 at para 13; *Fisheries Jurisdiction* (*United Kingdom v. Iceland*), *supra* note 319 at para 17; *Fisheries Jurisdiction* (*Federal Republic of Germany v. Iceland*), *supra* note 319 at para 18; France also failed to submit pleadings and participate in the hearings of the *Nuclear Tests* cases, the Court took note: *Nuclear Tests (Australia v. France)*, *supra* note 386 at 15; *Nuclear Tests (New Zealand v. France)*, *supra* note 386 at 15; the Court noted in *Aegean Sea Continental Shelf* that "[n] o pleadings were filed by the Government of Turkey, and it was not represented at the oral proceedings; no formal submissions were therefore made by that Government", *Aegean Sea Continental Shelf*, *supra* note 82 at paras 14–15; in the *Hostages case*, Iran also refused to participate in the written and oral proceedings, *United States Diplomatic and Consular Staff in Tehran* (*United States of America v. Iran*), [1980] ICJ Rep 18 at para 33.

admissibility] was clearly and manifestly erroneous as to both fact and law,"[349] and therefore refused to participate in the merits stage. In view of the rights conferred to the appearing party in the Statute of the ICJ, Nicaragua asked the Court to decide in favour of its claim. However, as the Court is bound to satisfy itself that the claim of the non-rebellious party is well founded in both fact and law,[350] and considering that the objection of the United States was properly made while still being party to the proceedings,[351] the Court considered the validity of the objection.[352]

On 27 June 1986, the Court delivered its judgment on the merits of the case, and upheld the objection of the United States based on the reservation made in its Declaration to disputes arising from multilateral treaties. However, the Court made the point that:

> [T]he effect of the reservation in question is confined to barring the applicability of the United Nations Charter and Organization of American States Charter as multilateral treaty law, and has no further impact on the sources of international law which Article 38 of the Statute requires the Court to apply.[353]

By that, the Court not only meant that it was still free to apply customary international law and general principles of international law, but that the content of both Charters could be informative about the content of customary international law.[354]

When analysing the content of customary international law in a diversity of topics, which included the prohibition of the use of force, the principle of non-intervention, and the right to self-defence, the Court made use of the text of certain UN General Assembly[355] and OAS[356] General Assembly resolutions and the attitude of the parties to the dispute towards them in order to ascertain the opinio juris of both States. For instance, the Court was of the view that the "description, contained in Article 3, paragraph (g), of the Definition of Aggression annexed to

---

[349] *Nicaragua*, Merits, *supra* note 172 at para 10.

[350] *Statute of the ICJ*, *supra* note 3 at art 53.2.

[351] *Nicaragua*, "Counter-Memorial", *supra* note 331 at paras 20–23 and 252–278.

[352] See e.g. *Aegean Sea Continental Shelf*, *supra* note 82 at para 47 ("It would not discharge its duty under Article 53 of the Statute if it were to leave out of its consideration a reservation, the invocation of which by the Respondent was properly brought to its notice earlier in the proceedings").

[353] *Nicaragua*, Merits, *supra* note 172 at para 56.

[354] Ibid at para 183 and 196; the opinion has been expressed, in fact, that for the purposes of the threat of use of force, the UN Charter expresses the modern customary law, *Report of the ILC, 18th Session*, *supra* note 88 at 247.

[355] *Nicaragua*, ibid at para 188 ("This *opinio juris* may, though with all due caution, be deduced from, inter alia, the attitude of the Parties and the attitude of States towards certain General Assembly resolutions").

[356] Ibid at para 189, 192 and 204 ("As regards the United States in particular, the weight of an expression of *opinio juris* can similarly be attached to its support of the resolution of the Sixth International Conference of American States condemning aggression (18 February 1928)", also, the principle of non-intervention "was confirmed by resolution 78 adopted by the General Assembly of the Organization of American States on 21 April 1972.").

General Assembly resolution 3314 (XXIX), may be taken to reflect customary international law."[357] It is also noteworthy that in order to ascertain the scope of forms of use of force less grave than aggression, the Court drew inspiration from the formulations contained in the General Assembly resolution 2625 (XXV)—entitled Declaration on Principles of International Law concerning Friendly Relations and Co-operation among States in accordance with the Charter of the United Nations[358]

Finally, the Court also made use of the text of the declaration on principles governing the mutual relations of States participating in the Conference on Security and Co-operation in Europe, and the United States' acceptance of the principle of the prohibition of the use of force, contained therein.[359]

*

The judgment on the merits in *Nicaragua* has been widely discussed from the point of view of sources throughout the years. Human rights scholars have praised the manner in which customary international law was developed from UN General Assembly resolutions.[360] Also, international humanitarian law scholars have widely acknowledged that the merits judgment in Nicaragua upheld the customary nature and wide content[361] of Common Article 3 to the Geneva Conventions of 1949. Notwithstanding these and other important issues raised by the Court in the *Nicaragua* case, my view is that both the jurisdiction and admissibility and the merits judgments show interesting examples of the incorporation and treatment of distinctive normative forms as if they were one of the elements enumerated in Article 38.

It has been shown above that in the jurisdiction and admissibility judgment it was decided that, as a matter of good faith, the declaration made under Article 36, paragraph 2, of the Statute was to be governed by the law of treaties,[362] at least in the aspects related to termination and modification. This determination holds a special weight. This sort of declaration is not to be treated only as a source of legal obligations for the State, but also as the source of the Court's jurisdiction. Given the

---

[357]Ibid at para 195 (For the completeness of the statement, what the Court considered customary was: "it may be considered to be agreed that an armed attack must be understood as including not merely action by regular armed forces across an international border, but also 'the sending by or on behalf of a State of armed bands, groups, irregulars or mercenaries, which carry out acts of armed force against another State of such gravity as to amount to' (inter alia) an actual armed attack conducted by regular forces, 'or its substantial involvement therein'.").

[358]Ibid at para 191 and 193.

[359]Ibid at para 189 and 204.

[360]See e.g. Lori Bruun, "Beyond the 1948 Convention Emerging Principles of Genocide in Customary International Law" (1993) 17 Md J Int'l L & Trade 193 at 216–217; Richard B. Lillich, "The Growing Importance of Customary International Human Rights Law" (1995/96) 25 Ga J Int'l & Comp L 1 at 8.

[361]Theodor Meron, "Editorial Comment: Revival of Customary Humanitarian Law" (2005) 99 AJIL 817 at 819 [Meron, "Revival"].

[362]Klabbers, "Law-making", *supra* note 15 at 88 ("the binding force of unilateral declarations may be constructed as a form of treaty. The ICJ has done so explicitly when it comes to declarations accepting its compulsory jurisdiction"); see also *Cameroon v. Nigeria*, Preliminary Objections, *supra* note 160 at para 30.

seriousness of the matter, and the jurisprudence of the Court concerning the nature and significance of this declaration, an argument could be made for the Court to specifically address the special character of the Declaration. This is further evidenced by the fact that subsequent jurisprudence of the Court, specifically in the *Fisheries Jurisdiction* case, upheld "the *sui generis* character of the unilateral acceptance of the Court's jurisdiction."[363]

To me, the issue of whether the case was admissible has very little to do with the assertion by Nicaragua concerning the applicability of treaty law to the declarations. The Court could have decided either way without having to make recourse to the law of treaties. Sir Robert Jennings was particularly eloquent on the point that, even by analogy, it makes little sense to start the analysis of the validity of the declaration by a body of law specifically designed to deal with legal acts involving at the very least one more party. In my view, the decision that the Court made was defensible on the basis of good faith alone.[364] The reference to the law of treaties, and subsequently the VCLT,[365] as applicable by analogy, has only complicated the body of law applicable to unilateral declarations in general and the declarations under Article 36, paragraph 2, of the ICJ Statute in particular. An example of this is the fact that in the *Fisheries Jurisdiction* case, Spain argued for the application of the interpretative rule found in the VCLT, based on the jurisprudence of the ICJ.[366] The Court had to explain that the special character of the declarations made the analogy to treaties, and the law applicable to both, dependent on compatibility.[367] As axiomatic as this statement may sound, it is necessary, as the partial analogy made by the Court in *Nicaragua* now requires an explanation, on a case-by-case basis, of the extent to which treaty law applies to unilateral declarations.

The judgment of the Court in *Nicaragua* and subsequent cases has found its way to general international law. When reviewing the Commentary by the ILC to its Guiding Principles applicable to unilateral declarations of States capable of creating legal obligations,[368] it is evident that treaty law has greatly influenced this

---

[363] *Fisheries Jurisdiction (Spain v. Canada)*, [1998] ICJ Rep 432 at para 46; see also *Cameroon v. Nigeria*, ibid at para 30.

[364] This, while keeping in mind that the Court itself has stated that good faith is "one of the basic principles governing the creation and performance of legal obligations [...] it is not in itself a source of obligation where none would otherwise exist", *Border and Transborder Armed Actions (Nicaragua v. Honduras)*, Jurisdiction and Admissibility, Judgment, [1988] ICJ Rep 105 at para 94.

[365] *Cameroon v. Nigeria*, Preliminary Objections, *supra* note 160 at para 30.

[366] *Fisheries Jurisdiction (Spain v. Canada)*, "Memorial of the Kingdom of Spain (Competence)" (28 September 1995) at para 32, online: International Court of Justice http://www.icj-cij.org/docket/files/96/8591.pdf ("*Or, cela ne signifie pas que les règles juridiques et de l'art de l'interprétation des déclarations (et des réserves) ne coïncident pas avec celles qui régissent l'interprétation des traités ou qu'on ne puisse appliquer, le cas échéant, une extension analogique desdites règles. La jurisprudence de la Cour n'offre aucun doute à ce propos*").

[367] *Fisheries Jurisdiction (Spain v. Canada)*, *supra* note 363 at para 46.

[368] *Report of the ILC, 58th Session*, *supra* note 1 at p 369.

codification project.[369] I find particularly puzzling that Guiding Principle eight, concerning the invalidity of a unilateral act that is contrary to a peremptory norm of international law, was derived from "the analogous rule contained in article 53 of the [VCLT]".[370] Although Article 53 of the VCLT was drafted exclusively for the purposes of the law of treaties, it remains the only norm describing *jus cogens* adopted by States in a treaty, and "is generally regarded as having wider significance".[371] This, however, does not justify saying that since the VCLT does not allow States to contract out of a *jus cogens* norm, individual acts of a State cannot have that effect either. It is an essential feature of *jus cogens* that it invalidates normative forms with content contrary to a norm having a peremptory status.[372] In other words, "the concept of invalidity for conflict with jus cogens is not an invention of the Vienna Convention; it is an aspect of general international law."[373] Orakhelashvili is of the view that:

> The correct approach is not to enquire whether *jus cogens* applicable to treaties also applies to unilateral actions of States, but to acknowledge that *jus cogens* applies to treaties precisely because the fundamental illegality attached to certain acts is so grave that it is not capable of being legitimized even if supported by a legal rule embodied in a derogatory agreement.[374]

The ILC's commentaries to the Guiding Principles applicable to unilateral declarations contain other conclusions under a similar logic. That is, deducing the

---

[369]It must be noted that the ILC did not intend for the Guidelines to cover declarations accepting the compulsory jurisdiction of the ICJ made under Article 36 of the Statute of the Court. However, the ILC was of the view that the Court's reasoning in its interpretation of such declarations is fully applicable to unilateral acts and declarations *stricto* sensu.

[370]*Report of the ILC, 58th Session*, *supra* note 1 at p 378.

[371]Charlesworth and Chinkin, *supra* note 237 at fn. 4; see also Giorgo Gaja, "Jus Cogens Beyond de Vienna Convention" (1981) 172 Rec des Cours 279 at 290–291 (noting that the ILC, in its work on State Responsibility, has expressly referred to the definition contained in Article 53 of the *VCLT*); see also Conklin, *supra* note 200 at 843 (noting that the VCLT is "invariably offered as the authority for the existence and the identity of peremptory norms"); Jochen A. Frowein, "Reactions by not directly affected states to breaches of public international law" (1994) 348 Rec des Cours 345 at 365.

[372]See, Mark W. Janis, *An Introduction to International Law* (New York: Aspen Publishers, 2003) 62–63; for those authors that believe that *jus cogens* is just an enhanced form of customary law, it is self-evident that it can derogate regular customary law, see Jordan Paust, "The Reality of Jus Cogens" (1991–1992) 7 Conn J Int'l L 81 at 84; In *Jurisdictional Immunities* (*supra* note 103) the Court did not rejected Italy's argument on the basis that *jus cogens* could not derogate customary law, but on the basis that there was no conflict between norms.

[373]Orakhelashvili, *Peremptory Norms*, *supra* note 195 at 205; see also S.E. Nahlik, "The Grounds of Invalidity and Termination of Treaties" (1971) 65 AJIL 736 at 745 ("Even though it may appear new to supporter of traditional doctrines, the provision of the Vienna Convention declaring void treaties which are contrary to a norm of international *jus cogens* is not an invention of either the International Law Commission or the Vienna Conference. It reflects a state of affairs which was slowly coming into being at a much earlier date and which, with the entry into force of the United Nations Charter, is no longer subject to any doubt.").

[374]Ibid at 205–206.

law applicable to unilateral declarations by analogy to treaty law in diverse issues, such as the capacity to undertake obligations, competent authorities, and rescission on the basis of *rebuc sic stantibus*, among others.

Interestingly enough, the issue of unilateral declarations was also raised in the early stages of the discussion on the law of treaties at the ILC. When Sir Gerald Fitzmaurice took over the rapporteurship on the law of treaties, he found that the reports delivered so far by Professors Brierly and Sir Hersch Lauterpacht were not intended to cover the topic in detail. In his first report to the Commission, he proposed a detailed draft code, which defined the concept of treaties at length, and stated that:

> A unilateral instrument, declaration, or affirmation may be binding internationally, but it is not a treaty, though it may in some cases amount to, or constitute, an adherence to a treaty, or acceptance of a treaty or other international obligation.[375]

In sum, the alerts raised by the dissenting opinions in *Nicaragua* have actually been confirmed. The *sui generis* character of the unilateral declaration has eventually been recognised by the Court itself and the codification, or progressive development, of a law governing their application by the ILC has been effected in reference to treaty law, but with a considerable number of caveats.

Turning now to the merits judgment in *Nicaragua*, I am interested in discussing the multiple means used by the Court to find evidence of customary international law. Leaving aside the opinions both inside[376] and outside[377] the bench, stating that in some aspects, the Court simply applied the UN Charter in *Nicaragua*, I am interested specifically in the Court's use of resolutions of organs of international organizations. It must be recalled that the Court specifically stated that the attitude of the litigants and other States to resolutions of the UN and OAS General Assemblies could be used so as to ascertain the opinio juris of states in a particular matter. Since before the judgment in *Nicaragua*, there has been a widespread view among international scholars that "such resolutions play an important role in the formation of customary law, a role which is comparable with the role of multilateral treaties."[378] International organizations being creatures of relatively recent creation,

[375]"*Law of Treaties: Report by G.G. Fitzmaurice, Special Rapporteur*" (UN Doc A/CN.4.101) in *Yearbook of the International Law Commission 1956*, vol 2 (New York: UN, 1957) at 117 (A/CN.4/SER.A/1956/Add.1) (he added: "[b]ut a purely unilateral instrument, neither referring to or connected with any other, can never amount to an international agreement, still less a treaty. It may be the source of an international obligation but the obligation cannot be a treaty obligation").

[376]*Nicaragua*, Merits, *supra* note 172 at p 304 (Dissenting opinion of Judge Schwebel).

[377]Wladyslaw Czapliński, "Sources of International Law in the Nicaragua Case" (1989) 38 ICLQ 151 at 166.

[378]Czapliński, ibid at 160; at the beginnings of the 20th century, speaking about proceedings of international congresses, Fiore stated that "even when certain rules have not the character of law and of positive law by virtue of the consent of the government represented, one must, nevertheless, consider as very important the authority arising from the accord existing in the wording of a draft agreement…", Pasquale Fiore, *International law codified and its legal sanction, or, The legal organization of the society of states*, 5th ed., trans by Edwin M, Borchard (New York: Baker, Voorhis, 1918) at 81–82.

especially when compared with the long history of custom in international law,[379] the approach taken by the Court was not without criticism.[380]

Nicaragua has been identified by many as the transitional point between traditional and modern approaches of ascertainment of customary international law[381]—the former an inductive process deriving law from the specific practice of States, the latter a deductive process deriving law from statements of rules.[382] From the point of view of institutional international law, resolutions emanating from political organs of an international organization are valid sources of law for the purposes of the organization.[383] However, when it comes to the enactment of general rules applicable to the relations among States, the ILC was of the view that the "[r]ecords of the cumulating practice of international organizations may be regarded as evidence of customary international law with reference to States' relations to the organizations."[384] Less restrictive opinions see in these resolutions

[379]Judge Kotaro Tanaka's dissenting opinion in *South West Africa* is often cited for his statement that the United Nations was "replacing an important part of the traditional individualistic method of international negotiation by the method of 'parliamentary diplomacy' [... which] is bound to influence the mode of generation of customary international law", *South West Africa*, *supra* note 122 at p 291.

[380]See e.g. Anthony D'Amato, "Trashing Customary International Law" (1987) 81 AJIL 101 ("The Court thus completely misunderstands customary law. First, a customary rule arises out of state practice; it is not necessarily to be found in UN resolutions and other majoritarian political documents."); see also Anthony D'Amato, "Nicaragua and International Law: The "Academic" and the 'Real'" (1985) 79 AJIL 657 [D'Amato, "Nicaragua"].

[381]See, e.g. J. Patrick Kelly, "The Twilight of Customary International Law" (1999–2000) 40 Va J Int'l L 449 at 484–485; See also Meron, "Revival", *supra* note 361 at 820; Niels Petersen, "Customary Law Without Custom? Rules, Principles, and the Role of State Practice in International Norm Creation" (2008) 23 Am U Int'l L Rev 275 at 280; John A. Perkins, "The Changing Foundations of International Law: From State Consent to State Responsibility" (1997) 15 BU Int'l LJ 433 at 467; Sohn noted the change in the methods of ascertainment of customary international law, and suggested that UN General Assembly resolutions of a declaratory nature supplement the treaty-making process by international conferences, Sohn, *supra* note 110 at 1078–1079.

[382]Anthea Elizabeth Roberts, "Traditional and Modern Approaches to Customary International Law: A Reconciliation" (2001) 95:4 AJIL 757 at 758.

[383]*Effect of Awards of Compensation Made by the United Nations Administrative Tribunal*, Advisory Opinion, [1954] ICJ Rep 47 at paras 56–62; *Certain Expenses of the United Nations (Article 17, paragraph 2, of the Charter)*, Advisory Opinion, [1962] ICJ Rep 151 at paras 175–177.

[384]*Report of the International Law Commission covering its second session, 5 June–19 July 1950* (UN Doc A/1316) in *Yearbook of the International Law Commission 1950*, vol 2 at 372 (A/CN.4/SER.A/1950/Add.1) (reference is made to the Report of the ILC to the General Assembly on ways and means for making the evidence of customary international law more readily available).

"recommendations contributing to the progressive development of international law."[385] It is in the context of the so-called modern approaches to international customary law that resolutions of international organizations, especially those of a general character at both the universal and regional levels, gain importance. As it is their regular order of business to make general statements about issues within the scope of their mandate (a mandate often given by the organs of the organization itself[386]), the accumulation of opinions in a given topic can be of relevance.

In *Nicaragua*, the Court indeed looked at the statement made by the United States at the time of adoption at the first committee of the draft that would become UN General Assembly resolution 2131 (XX), specifically challenging the legal value of its content.[387] However, the Court did not draw any conclusions from this statement because the United States did not react in a similar way to the adoption of UN General Assembly resolution 2625 (XXV), declaring similar language as that of the former resolution as basic principles of international law.[388] Leaving aside the question as to whether the attitude towards the latter resolution was clear enough to invalidate the expressed opinion in the former, I find that the method used in that specific instance was in accordance with the expressed goals of the Court. It is often the case that during the debates at the General Assembly of the UN, States make general statements or explanations of vote with the purpose of reinforcing their views on the legal nature of the content of the resolutions being discussed. In other cases, and when the circumstances warrant it, the resolution itself will be clear on the

[385] See e.g., Institut de Droit International, "The Elaboration of General Multilateral Conventions and of Non-contractual Instruments Having a Normative Function or Objective", Session of Cairo —1987, online: Institut de Droit international http://www.idi-iil.org/idiE/resolutionsE/1987_caire_02_en.PDF.

[386] For example, in 2010, the UN General Assembly established the 'Regular Process for Global Reporting and Assessment of the State of the Marine Environment, including Socio-economic Aspects' under the United Nations, and decided that it would be "accountable to the General Assembly and shall be an intergovernmental process guided by international law, including [*UNCLOS*] and other applicable international instruments, and take into account relevant Assembly resolutions", *Oceans and the law of the Sea*, GA Res 65/37A, UNGAOR, 65th Sess, UN Doc A/RES/65/37A (2010) at para 202.

[387] During the debates at the First Committee, the United States made a declaration to the effect that the said resolution was "only a statement of political intention and not a formulation of law", UNC1OR, 20th Sess, 1423 Mtg, UN Doc A/C. 1/SR. 1423 (1965); for a discussion on the effect of the statement, see Marko Divac Öberg, "The Legal Effects of Resolutions of the UN Security Council and General Assembly in the Jurisprudence of the ICJ" (2006) 16:5 EJIL 879 at 901–902.

[388] *Nicaragua*, Merits, *supra* note 172 at para 203.

exceptionality of a measure as to exclude it from becoming evidence of customary law,[389] or on the special nature of a principle being put forward.[390]

The Court, however, did more than look at the attitude of the parties to the dispute during the adoption of UN General Assembly resolution 2625. The Court was also of the view that "[t]he effect of consent to the text of such resolution […] may be understood as an acceptance of the validity of the rule or set of rules declared by the resolution by themselves."[391] Shortly after that, the Court reproduced a number of paragraphs of the aforementioned resolution, as well as OAS General Assembly resolution 78,[392] while reminding the reader that the "adoption by States of this text affords an indication of their *opinio juris* as to customary international law on the question."[393]

In a more recent Advisory Opinion, the Court would go on to expand the doctrine set in *Nicaragua*, by explaining the conditions in which a resolution could be considered part of customary international law:

> They can, in certain circumstances, provide evidence important for establishing the existence of a rule or the emergence of an *opinio juris*. To establish whether this is true of a given General Assembly resolution, it is necessary to look at its content and the conditions of its adoption; it is also necessary to see whether an *opinio juris* exists as to its normative

[389]When the Security Council authorised Member States of the United Nations to adopt a series of measures regarding piracy off the coast of Somalia, it underscored that the granting of such authorisation "shall not be considered as establishing customary international law", *Somalia*, SC Res 1816 (2008), UNSCOR, 2008, UN Doc S/RES/1816 (2008) at para 9; the General Assembly repeated the wording when it noted that the Securitty Council had adopted such authorization, *Oceans and the law of the Sea*, GA Res 63/111, UNGAOR, 63th Sess, UN Doc A/RES/63/111 (2008) at para 66; similarly, when the Security Council authorized measures to confront migrant smugglersand human traffickers on the high seas off the coast of Libya, it affirmed that such adoption "shall not affect the rights or obligations orresponsibilities of Member States under international law", *Maintenance of international peace and security*, SC Res 2240 (2015), UNSCOR, 2015, UN Doc S/RES/2240 (2015) at para 11.

[390]For instance, in 1970, the General Assembly solemnly declared that the sea-bed, ocean floor and subsoil beyond areas of national jurisdiction are common heritage of mankind [the area] and that "[n]o State or person, natural or juridical, shall claim, exercise or adquire rights with respect to the area or its resources incompatible with the international regime to be established and the principles of this Declaration", *Declaration of Priciples Governing the Sea-Bed and the ocean Floor, and the Subsoil Thereof, beyond the Limits of National Jurisdictions*, GA Res 2749 (XXV), UNGAOR, 25th Sess, UN Doc A/RES/2749 (XXV) (1970) at para 1–3; also in 1961, the General Assembly declared that that if a State uses nuclear or thermo-nuclear weapons "is to be considered as violating the Charter of the United Nations, as acting contrary to the laws of humanity and as committing a crime against mankind and civilization", *Declaration on the prohibition of the use of nuclear and thermo-nuclear weapons*, GA Res 1653 (XVI), UNGAOR, 16th Sess, UN Doc A/RES/1653 (XVI) (1961) at para 1.d; but see Richard A. Falk, "On the Quasi-Legislative Competence of the General Assembly" (1966) 60:4 AJIL 782 at 787 (discussing the limited claim of such statement as there were "negative votes of several powerfull states").

[391]*Nicaragua*, Merits, *supra* note 172 at para 188.

[392]Ibid at para 191–192.

[393]Ibid at para 191.

character. Or a series of resolutions may show the gradual evolution of the opinio juris required for the establishment of a new rule.[394]

While I do not wish to deny the customary value of some of the principles contained in UN General Assembly resolution 2625, I find it problematic to justify the direct quote of the text of the resolution as the embodiment of such principles.[395] Having already determined that the Charter could be informative of the content of customary international law, and keeping in mind that the attitude of the parties during the adoption of resolution 2625 was informative of the *opinio juris* of States, there was absolutely no need to derive it from its content.[396] Interestingly, a subsequent opinion of the Court dealing with the UN Charter's prohibition of use of force, has also seen the elevation of passages of resolution 2625 as the 'reaffirmation' of a customary rule.[397]

While the Court's stated position in *Nicaragua* was in accordance with what has been identified as the traditional approach,[398] the overwhelming opinion of scholars was that such a position was nothing more than lip service. It is clear that the ICJ's decision had the effect of diminishing the value of conflicting *opinio juris*,[399] conflicting practice, or strict adherence to the rule[400] in disproving the existence of the rule. The consequence is that the element of State consent in the elaboration of the rule seems to dilute as the Court has paid more attention to what States say in international fora[401] and "the 'attitude' of states to a rule of law, it seems, may be determined by their voting behaviour in the General Assembly."[402] As Charlesworth puts it: "The *Nicaragua* analysis suggests that voting for a resolution in an international forum without more provides both adequate state practice and *opinio juris*

---

[394] *Legality of the Threat or Use of Nuclear Weapons Case*, Advisory Opinion, [1996] ICJ Rep 226 at para 70 (reprinted in 35 ILM 809) [*Nuclear Weapons*].

[395] See Fred L. Morrison, "Legal Issues in the *Nicaragua* Opinion" (1987) 81 AJIL 160 at 161 ("The source of the new obligation is not that usually argued in the literature, uniform state practice as evidenced by declaration and subsequent conduct [… n]or is it to be found in the crystallization or interpretation of Charter obligations.").

[396] See e.g. Thomas M. Franck, "Some Observations on the ICJ's Procedural and Substantive Innovations" (1987) 81 AJIL 116 at 118; before *Nicaragua* was decided, Judge Schwebel noted that in the context of non-self governing territories, the Court had not articulated the reasons for its use of UN General Assembly resolution 2625, Stephen M. Schwebel, The Effect of Resolutions of the U.N. General Assembly on Customary International Law, (1979) 73 Am Soc Int'l L Proc 301 at 303–304.

[397] *Legal Consequences of the Construction of a Wall in the Occupied Palestinian Territory*, Advisory Opinion, [2004] ICJ Rep 136 at paras 86–88 [*A Wall in the OPT*].

[398] *Nicaragua*, Merits, *supra* note 172 at para 207.

[399] Ibid at para 203.

[400] Ibid at para 186.

[401] D'Amato, "Nicaragua", *supra* note 380.

[402] Franck, *supra* note 396 at 118; see also Jonathan I. Charney, "Universal International Law" (1993) 87 AJIL 529 at 537 [Charney, "Universal"].

for the formation of customary rules."[403] For this reason, it has been argued that the modern approach lacks legitimacy.[404]

Above and beyond all that, the issue I wish to raise is the fact that *Nicaragua*, along with other decisions of the Court, has successfully mainstreamed the legal understanding that under certain conditions the text of General Assembly resolutions is legally binding as customary international law.[405] It has been extensively argued that such an approach could eventually downplay the role of custom in international law. It has not been discussed, though, that while *Nicaragua* has given increasing importance to resolutions such as UN General Assembly resolution 2625, it diminishes the normative possibilities of other resolutions. Especially those falling short of the tall requirements set up by the Court in *Nuclear Weapons*. It is not my point that all UN General Assembly resolutions—or those of the assembly of any international body, for that matter—are legally binding engagements under international law. They are not. My point is that resolutions need not be binding—as customary law or anything else—for them to play a role in international law and governance.[406] Whether international judicial institutions should recognise that role in their respective adjudicative processes is still a contested issue.[407]

That being said, a number of scholars have expressed support for the authority of certain UN General Assembly resolutions. Opinions range between considering them merely as crystallizers of prospective rules[408] and naming them the content of a declaratory international law.[409]

---

[403]H.C.M. Charlesworth, "Customary International Law and the Nicaragua Case" (1984–1987) 11 Austl YB Int'l L 1 at 24.

[404]Arthur A. Weisburd, "Customary International Law: The Problem of Treaties" (1988) 21 Vand J Transnat'l L 1.

[405]Joyner, writing before *Nicaragua*, noted that "several authors have attempted to link the legal essence of General Assembly resolutions with variant expressions of treaty law, customary law, or 'general principles of law'", Christopher C. Joyner, "U.N. General Assembly Resolutions and International Law: Rethinking the Contemporary Dynamics of Norm-Creation" (1981) 11 Cal W Int'l LJ 445 at 456.

[406]Anne-Marie Slaughter, "International Law and International Relations" (2000) 285 Rec des Cours 9 at 217 ("Soft law is neither the mark of a failed "hard law" negotiation; nor it is automatically the baby version of what will ultimately be a full-fledged legal régime. It serves its own distinct purposes in addition to its potential for evolution into hard law. Both as an instrument of desired international outcomes and as the expression of global values, 'international law' should encompass both hard and soft rules and associated practices."); see also Alan Boyle, "Some Reflections on the Relationship of Treaties and Soft Law" in Vera Gowlland-Debbas, *Multilateral Treaty-making* (The Hague: Martinus Nijhoff Publishers, 2000) at 38.

[407]W. Michael Reisman, "Soft Law and Law Jobs" (2011) 2:1 J Int'l Disp Settlement 25 at 30 ("So my plea to international jurists is as follows: take account of the law job you are performing. When your law job is to sit as judges and arbitrators, eschew the adjectives; apply law, not soft law.").

[408]See Joyner, *supra* note 405 at 477–478; see also, Alan Boyle and Christine Chinkin, *The Making of International Law* (Oxford: Oxford University Press, 2007) at 210.

[409]See Chodosh, *supra* note 320; see also Charney, "Universal", *supra* note 402 at 551 ([G]eneral international law may be established on the basis of less formal indications of consent or acquiescence. This makes worldwide law possible; it cannot be done through treaties alone).

However, it is still argued that "there are several ways in which a resolution, by being linked to one or more of the traditional sources of international law, can serve as a law-creating mechanism."[410] The most widely discussed of these is the suggestion made by Professor Bin Cheng of the concept of 'instant custom'; that is, UN General Assembly resolutions are to be considered immediately customary law if there is a strong indication of *opinio juris*, especially in the event that meaningful expressions of State practice are not possible[411]—that is, a concept that sustains the incorporation of resolutions into a recognised source of international law, without the need to go beyond its topic and voting record.

To finalise this section, it must be said that *Nicaragua* can alternatively be understood as the initial step in a trend adopted by the Court that has progressively increased the value afforded to resolutions in its adjudicatory process. That is, the stated approach of the Court, even when the Court itself did not necessarily follow it, has been to expand the realm of action of resolutions—mostly from the UN—in international law. In *Nuclear Weapons*, the Court noted "that General Assembly resolutions, even if they are not binding, may sometimes have normative value."[412] Some time later, in the Advisory Opinion on the *Legal Consequences of the Construction of a Wall in the Occupied Palestinian Territory* (hereinafter, *A Wall in the OPT*), the Court was asked to detail the legal consequences of the construction of the wall around East Jerusalem "considering the rules and principles of international law, including the Fourth Geneva Convention of 1949, and relevant Security Council and General Assembly resolutions."[413] That is, in the view of the General Assembly, its own resolutions, as well as those of the Security Council, are not necessarily part of the rules and principles of international law, or at least not at the same level as Geneva Conventions.[414] The Court, however, was of the view that for the purposes of the requested assessment, the relevant rules and principles of

---

[410] Samuel A. Bleicher, The Legal Significance of Re-Citation of General Assembly Resolutions, (1969) 63:3 AJIL 444 at 452; Arangio-Ruiz, considers it natural that "the text of a non-binding Assembly resolution as well as the attitudes manifested by States in the vote or in the debate concerning such a resolution merge—at some stage—into one or the other of the processes universally accepted as the law-making processes of international law", Gaetano Arangio-Ruiz, "The normative role of the General Assembly of the United Nations and the Declaration of Principles of Friendly Relations" (1972) Rec des Cours 419 at 470.

[411] Bin Cheng, "United Nations Resolutions on Outer Space: 'Instant' International Customary law?" (1965) 5 Indian J Int'l L 23; contra Pellet, "Article 38", *supra* note 10 at 752; see also Robert Y. Jennings, "What is International Law and How Do We Tell It When We See It?" (1981) 37 Ann suisse dr int 59 at 71 ("When Professor Cheng felt impelled to invent the paradox, 'instant custom', for the laws governing space, we should have taken the hint that perhaps it was instant because it was not custom").

[412] *Nuclear Weapons*, *supra* note 394 at para 70.

[413] *Illegal Israeli actions in Occupied East Jerusalem and the rest of the Occupied Palestinian Territory*, GA Res ES-10/14, UN GAOR, 10th Sp. Sess., UN Doc. A/RES/ ES-10/14 (2003) at p 3.

[414] It could be said that I am interpreting too much from the position of a couple of comas in a UN General Assembly resolution, but my experience is that every single character of these resolutions matter.

international law: "can be found in the United Nations Charter and certain other treaties, in customary international law and in the relevant resolutions adopted pursuant to the Charter by the General Assembly and the Security Council."[415]

More recently, when the Court was asked in the *Kosovo* Advisory Opinion whether the unilateral declaration of independence made by the Provisional Institutions of Self-Government of Kosovo was in accordance with international law,[416] it stated that "Security Council resolution 1244 (1999) and the Constitutional Framework[417] form part of the international law which is to be considered in replying to the question".[418] This, of course, with due regard to the fact that the Security Council invoked its powers under Chapter VII of the Charter in resolution 1244 (1999).

3.4.2 Maritime Delimitation and Territorial Questions Between Qatar and Bahrain

On 8 July 1991 Qatar filed a case against Bahrain in the Registry of the ICJ. The case dealt with an existing territorial dispute between the two States, specifically over a group of islands and sandbanks, and the delimitation of their respective maritime areas.

As neither of the States in the dispute have made, still to this date, a declaration recognizing as compulsory the jurisdiction of the ICJ under Article 36, paragraph 2, of the Statute of the Court,[419] the jurisdiction of the Court needed to be triggered by means of a referral or of a provision to that effect in a treaty or convention in force.[420] At the moment of the filing, Qatar relied on two alleged Agreements concluded on 19 December 1987 and 25 December 1990 in order to establish the jurisdiction of the Court in the case.

The jurisdiction of the Court was immediately challenged by Bahrain on the basis that the document characterised by Qatar as "The Agreement in the form of Minutes (…) [or] 'Doha Agreement'" (hereinafter, the Minutes of 25 December

---

[415] *Legality of the Wall*, *supra* note 397 at para 86.

[416] Request for an advisory opinion of the International Court of Justice on whether the unilateral declaration of independence of Kosovo is in accordance with international law, GA Res 63/3, UN GAOR, 63th Sess., UN Doc. A/RES/63/3.

[417] United Nations Interim Administration Mission in Kosovo, *Regulation 2001/9 on Constitutional Framework on Interim Self-Government in Kosovo*, online: Assembly of Kosovo http://www.assembly-kosova.org/common/docs/FrameworkPocket_ENG_Dec2002.pdf.

[418] *Accordance with International Law of the Unilateral Declaration of Independence in Respect of Kosovo*, Advisory Opinion, [2010] ICJ Rep 403 at para 93.

[419] *Multilateral Treaties Deposited with the Secretary-General*, at chapter I, 4, online: United Nations Treaty Collection: http://treaties.un.org/pages/ParticipationStatus.aspx [*MTDSG* online].

[420] *Statute of the ICJ*, *supra* note 3 at Art. 36.1.

1990)[421] was the signed record of a meeting held among the Foreign Ministers of Bahrain, Qatar and Saudi Arabia.[422] From Bahrain's point of view "the Minutes do not have the status of a binding agreement and cannot, therefore, serve as a basis for the Court's jurisdiction",[423] and "even if they possess such a status, their content does not support the Qatari submission that the text accords each Party the right unilaterally to commence proceedings".[424] The legal nature of the Agreement by exchange of letters of 19 December 1987 was not challenged by Bahrain; however, it must be noted that it was never registered with the Secretariat of the UN in accordance with Article 102 of the Charter of the UN[425]

The said Minutes provided that in the consultations held between 23 and 25 December 1990:

> The following was agreed:
>
> [...]
>
> (2) [...] After the end of this period [that is, until the end of 1991], the parties may submit the matter to the International Court of Justice in accordance with the Bahraini formula, which has been accepted by Qatar, and the proceedings arising therefrom.[426]

In the course of the oral proceedings concerning the Court's jurisdiction and admissibility of the case, Sir Ian Sinclair, for the Qatari side, and Sir Elihu Lauterpacht, for the Bahraini side, provided the views of the contending States concerning the legal nature of the Minutes of 25 December 1990. During the re-joinder, Lauterpacht, in a passionate defence of the view that the Agreement was not of a legal nature, stated:

> (...) I respectfully adhere to the submission that there is a clear distinction between content and intent. The mere fact that the "content" of an instrument is of a kind that could be legally binding if deliberately made so does not mean that it is legally binding. The result depends upon context, form and expression. Sir Ian was good enough to bring to the attention of the Court an article that I had quite forgotten that I had written some eighteen

---

[421] *Maritime Delimitation and Territorial Questions between Qatar and Bahrain (Qatar v. Bahrain)*, "Memorial of the Government of the State of Qatar", (10 February 1992) at p 57 online: International Court of Justice http://www.icj-cij.org/docket/files/87/7023.pdf.

[422] "Every treaty and every international agreement entered into by any Member of the United Nations after the present Charter comes into force shall as soon as possible be registered with the Secretariat and published by it", *Charter*, *supra* note 3 at Art. 102.1.

[423] *Maritime Delimitation and Territorial Questions between Qatar and Bahrain (Qatar v. Bahrain)*, "Counter-Memorial of the Government of the State of Bahrain", (11 June 1992) at p 52 online: International Court of Justice http://www.icj-cij.org/docket/files/87/7025.pdf.

[424] Ibid.

[425] *United Nations Treaty Series Database*, online: United Nations Treaty Collection: http://treaties.un.org/ [UNTS online].

[426] *Minutes on settlement of disputes regarding joint boundaries*, Bahrain, Qatar and Saudi Arabia, 25 December 1990, 1641 UNTS 239 (English translation at p 251); also available in *Maritime Delimitation and Territorial Questions between Qatar and Bahrain (Qatar v. Bahrain)*, "Application Instituting Proceedings", (8 July 1991) at p 56, online: International Court of Justice http://www.icj-cij.org/docket/files/87/7021.pdf [*Qatar v. Bahrain*, Application].

> years ago entitled "Gentlemen's Agreements". How the follies of one's youth return to haunt one. Unfortunately, apart from reminding me of its existence, Sir Ian did not provide me with a text and time has not permitted me to look it up again. But now that he has put the idea in my mind, I can of course recall that there are many international texts of what may be called 'sub-binding' quality. Often they are called 'soft law'—prescriptions which are clearly intended to be a guide to conduct, often very specific in content, but not intended to have legal force. The Stockholm Declaration on the Environment would be one example. The so-called 'Compromis de Luxembourg' on voting within the Council of the European Community would be another. Other examples will, I am sure, readily occur to the Members of the Court.[427]

The Court rendered a judgment on jurisdiction and admissibility on 1 July 1994, finding by fifteen votes to one that it had jurisdiction to entertain the case, with Judge Oda dissenting on that point. As for the legal nature of the Minutes of 25 December 1990, the Court was of the view that it constituted an "international agreement creating rights and obligations for the Parties."[428] This was after specifically quoting its own statement in the *Aegean Sea Continental Shelf* (*Greece v. Turkey*) (hereinafter, *Aegean Sea Continental Shelf*) case on the freedom of form in international agreements[429] and the definition of a treaty found in the VCLT, even though the parties to the dispute are not—still to this date[430]—signatories or parties to that convention.[431]

The approach of the Court was simple and in accordance with its own jurisprudence: its task is to look at the terms of the contested document and the circumstances in which it was drawn up in order to discern its legal nature.[432] The Court was of the view that the Minutes of 25 December 1990 enumerated legal commitments to which Qatar and Bahrain had consented, thus creating rights and obligations in the international arena and governed by international law for both States. Therefore, the said Minutes had to be considered an international agreement.[433]

Judge Oda's dissenting opinion explained in a rather entertaining manner his particular views concerning the Minutes of 25 December 1990: "Quite simply, the

---

[427] *Maritime Delimitation and Territorial Questions between Qatar and Bahrain* (*Qatar v. Bahrain*), "Oral argument of Professor Elihu Lauterpacht" (11 March 1994) at p 29, online: International Court of Justice http://www.icj-cij.org/docket/files/87/5447.pdf.

[428] *Qatar v. Bahrain*, Jurisdiction and Admissibility (1 July 1994), *supra* note 82 at para 25.

[429] *Aegean Sea Continental Shelf*, *supra* note 82 at para 96 (The Court "knows of no rule of international law which might preclude a joint communiqué from constituting an international agreement to submit a dispute to arbitration or judicial settlement"); see also, *Customs Regime between Germany and Austria*, Advisory Opinion, (1931), PCIJ (Ser. A/B) No. 41 at p 47.

[430] *MTDSG* online, *supra* note 419 at chapter XXIII, 1.

[431] Compare *Sovereignty over Pulau Ligitan and Pulau Sipadan* (*Indonesia v. Malaysia*), Merits, [2002] ICJ Rep 625 at para 37 (The Court acknowledged the situation of one of the parties when states that it "notes that Indonesia is not a party to the Vienna Convention of 23 May 1969 on the Law of Treaties; the Court would nevertheless recall that, in accordance with customary international law, reflected in Articles 31 and 32 of that Convention…").

[432] *Aegean Sea Continental Shelf*, *supra* note 82 at para 96.

[433] *Qatar v. Bahrain*, Jurisdiction and Admissibility (1 July 1994), *supra* note 82 at para 25.

Foreign Minister of Bahrain signed the Minutes without so much as thinking that they were a legally binding international agreement",[434] and he adds that "the 1990 Agreement [did not constitute] a treaty or convention within the meaning of Article 36(1) of the Statute".[435]

Oda did recognise that in the meetings, the three Ministers agreed upon certain issues. However, he questions whether such agreement is of significance for the purposes of international law:

> In fact, the three Foreign Ministers, in attestation of that agreement, did sign the Minutes of the meeting (i.e., the agreed record of the discussion that had taken place during that tripartite meeting) and, in my view, they certainly did so without the slightest idea that they were signing a tripartite treaty or convention.[436]

Although the ICJ was of the view that the Parties had undertaken to submit the whole territorial dispute between them by virtue of the Minutes of 25 December 1990, it also considered that the Qatari submission was not reflective of the whole of the dispute.[437] To guarantee that the Court was seized of the case in the manner envisaged by the Minutes of 25 December 1990,[438] the Parties were authorised to further submit, either individually or jointly, all the matters to be decided.[439]

Even though several meetings were held in order to draft a special agreement or a joint act defining the scope of the dispute to be decided, the parties were ultimately unable to agree and Qatar made an individual submission before the deadline set by the Court. Also before the deadline, Bahrain submitted to the Court a report on the failed negotiations, as it was its view that the judgment of 1 July 1994 required the parties to agree on terms of reference for the Court to adjudicate the dispute.

On 15 February 1995, the Court delivered a second judgment on jurisdiction and admissibility, in which the content of the Minutes of 25 December 1990 was further examined. Having left aside the issue of the legal nature of the Minutes in the previous judgment, the Court noted that the parties held different views on the method of seisin that was provided for in the said Minutes.[440] In order to decide on this point, the Court quoted its judgment in the *Territorial Dispute* case between the Libyan Arab Jamahiriya and Chad identifying the customary methods of

[434] Ibid at p 139 (Dissenting opinion of Judge Oda).

[435] Ibid.

[436] Ibid at 138. (Dissenting opinion of Judge Oda).

[437] Ibid at para 33–34.

[438] That is, in accordance with the so-called Bahraini formula: "The Parties request the Court to decide any matter of territorial right or other title or interest which may be a matter of difference between them; and to draw a single maritime boundary between their respective maritime areas of seabed, subsoil and superjacent waters", *Qatar v. Bahrain*, Application, *supra* note 426 at 50.

[439] *Qatar v. Bahrain*, Jurisdiction and Admissibility (1 July 1994), *supra* note 82 at para 38.

[440] *Maritime Delimitation and Territorial Questions between Qatar and Bahrain* (*Qatar v. Bahrain*), Jurisdiction and Admissibility, [1995] ICJ Rep 6 at para 23 [*Qatar v. Bahrain*, Jurisdiction and Admissibility (15 February 1995)].

interpretation of treaties, as reflected in the VCLT.[441] The Court reaffirmed its previous findings that the Minutes of 25 December 1990 were an international agreement containing the undertaking of the parties to submit the territorial dispute to the Court.[442] It further found that the aforementioned Minutes allowed for unilateral seisin and therefore decided,[443] by ten votes to five, that the Court was now seized of the whole of the dispute and that it had jurisdiction to adjudicate the dispute as defined by Qatar in its latest submission.[444]

*

Scholars have extensively questioned the judgments of the Court on jurisdiction and admissibility in *Qatar v. Bahrain*, specifically on whether the Minutes of 25 December 1990 authorised the parties to the dispute to unilaterally seise the jurisdiction of the Court, or if they constituted an outline for an eventual joint submission to the ICJ. Such line of criticism is reinforced by the fact that the Court, in view of the content of the Minutes of 25 December 1990, afforded the Parties the opportunity to ensure that the entire dispute was submitted to the Court in the judgment of 1 July 1994.[445] Moreover, the Court ultimately relied on an individual submission for the seisin of the Court in its judgment of 15 February 1995. However, few scholars have focused on the aspect of the judgments that I find more troubling, that is, the manner in which the Court decided that the Minutes of 25 December 1990 comprised an international agreement governed by the customary law of treaties,[446] and the consequences that it has for the identification and categorization of international agreements.

Although, as Judge Oda has pointed out, there may have been issues of form with the Agreement by exchange of letters of 19 December 1987,[447] I have excluded it from the analysis because none of the parties registered the Agreement with the Secretariat of the UN Since both Parties to the Agreement of 19 December 1987 are member States of the UN and both recognised its binding legal nature,[448]

---

[441] *Territorial Dispute (Libyan Arab Jamahiriya v. Chad)*, [1994] ICJ Rep 6 at para 41 ("in accordance with customary international law, reflected in Article 31 of the 1969 Vienna Convention on the Law of Treaties, a treaty must be interpreted in good faith in accordance with the ordinary meaning to be given to its terms in their context and in the light of its object and purpose. Interpretation must be based above all upon the text of the treaty. As a supplementary measure recourse may be had to means of interpretation such as the preparatory work of the treaty and the circumstances of its conclusion.").

[442] *Qatar v. Bahrain*, Jurisdiction and Admissibility (15 February 1995), *supra* note 440 at para 24.

[443] Ibid at para 43.

[444] Ibid at para 50.

[445] *Qatar v. Bahrain*, Jurisdiction and Admissibility (1 July 1994), *supra* note 82 at para 38.

[446] See, e.g. Jan Klabbers, "Qatar v. Bahrain: the concept of 'treaty' in international law" (1995) 33 Archiv des Völkerrechts 361 [Klabbers, "Qatar v. Bahrain"].

[447] *Qatar v. Bahrain*, Jurisdiction and Admissibility (15 February 1995), *supra* note 440 at p 44 (Dissenting opinion of Judge Oda).

[448] *Qatar v. Bahrain*, Jurisdiction and Admissibility (1 July 1994), *supra* note 82 at para 21 ("The Parties agree that the exchanges of letters of December 1987 constitute an international agreement with binding force in their mutual relations").

it is a registrable agreement in the sense of Article 102 of the Charter of the UN[449] As the Charter clearly states that unregistered treaties and international agreements cannot be invoked before any of the organs of the Organization,[450] I maintain that the ICJ should not have accepted any arguments based on it and therefore the mere reference by the Court to the said Agreement is contrary to the Charter.[451]

Returning to the issue of the Minutes of 25 December 1990, it must be recalled that Bahrain challenged the characterization of the Minutes of 25 December 1990 as a treaty, both at the Court[452] and at the UN Secretariat, when Qatar registered them as a treaty in accordance with Article 102 of the Charter of the UN[453] It has been noted that the Court started its analysis of the said Minutes by quoting the definition of treaties found in the VCLT. Since neither of the parties to the dispute has become a party to the VCLT,

> one can hardly escape the conclusion that for purposes of international law, the definition of the Vienna Convention was treated as coming close to a definition with the force of customary law, which is somewhat surprising given the fact that it is, after all, but a definition, and moreover, a definition for the purposes of the Vienna Convention only.[454]

On this particular point, Gautier has recently stated that "this position reflects the state of general international law",[455] as the ICJ has confirmed in a subsequent case that Article 2.1.a reflects customary international law.[456]

---

[449]"Every treaty and every international agreement entered into by any Member of the United Nations after the present Charter comes into force shall as soon as possible be registered with the Secretariat and published by it", *Charter*, *supra* note 3 at 102.1; see also Michael Brandon, "Analysis of the Terms 'Treaty' and 'International Agreement' for Purposes of Registration Under Article 102 of the United Nations Charter" (1953) 47 AJIL 49; David Hutchinson, "The Significance of the Registration or Non-registration of an International Agreement in determining whether or not is a Treaty" (1993) 46 Curr Legal Probs 257.

[450]"No party to any such treaty or international agreement which has not been registered in accordance with the provisions of paragraph 1 of this Article may invoke that treaty or agreement before any organ of the United Nations", *Charter*, *supra* note 3 at 102.2.

[451]But see, Anthony Aust, *Handbook of International Law* (Cambridge: Cambridge University Press, 2005) at 112–113.

[452]"It is not correct to say that 'the two States (Qatar and Bahrain) were engaged in the drafting of the Doha Agreement'. What happened at Doha cannot be likened to a treaty-drafting exercise", *Maritime Delimitation and Territorial Questions between Qatar and Bahrain* (*Qatar v. Bahrain*), "Oral argument of H.E. Dr. Husain Mohammed Al-Baharna" (4 March 1994) at p 27, online: International Court of Justice http://www.icj-cij.org/docket/files/87/5431.pdf.

[453]*Minutes on settlement of disputes regarding joint boundaries between Qatar, Bahrain and Saudi Arabia, Objection by Bahrain*, 9 August 1991,1647 UNTS 422.

[454]Klabbers, "Qatar v. Bahrain", *supra* note 446 at 365.

[455]Philippe Gautier, "Article 1 Convention of 1969" in Corten and Klein, eds., *supra* note 240 at 37 [Gautier, "Article 1"].

[456]*Cameroon v. Nigeria*, Merits, *supra* note 86 at para 263.

Irrespective of its customary status, it must be kept in mind that the definition in the ILC Draft Articles on the Law of Treaties, which served as the basis for the VCLT, is a maximalist one. That is, it envisaged covering "all forms of international agreement in writing concluded between States."[457]

Throughout the seventeen years that the topic of the Law of Treaties was on the agenda of the ILC, several formulations appeared in the draft article dedicated to the definition of the terms to be used in the Convention. For instance, already in Sir Humphrey Waldock's first report to the Commission in 1962, the draft contained a broader definition for 'international agreement' and a more restrictive one for 'treaties', while the comments recognised that "there also exist international agreements, such as exchanges of notes, which are not a single formal instrument nor usually subject to ratification, and yet are certainly agreements to which the law of treaties applies."[458] Sir Waldock used the term 'agreements in simplified form' to describe instruments which "could not appropriately be called formal instruments, and yet they are undoubtedly international agreements subject to the law of treaties."[459] At that session, the Commission would adopt a draft article containing definitions for 'treaty' and for 'treaty in simplified form', simply stating that the latter "means a treaty concluded by exchange of notes, exchange of letters, agreed minutes, memorandum of agreement, joint declaration or other instrument concluded by any similar procedure."[460] The commentary to the article specifies that "the law of treaties for the most part applies in the same manner to formal treaties and to treaties in simplified form, but in the sphere of conclusion and entry into force some differences may be found to exist."[461] Indeed, draft article 4 (authority to negotiate, draw up, authenticate, sign, ratify, accede to, approve or accept a treaty) and 12 (ratification) contained specific provisions applicable to treaties in simplified form. The draft articles established that "in the case of treaties in simplified form, it shall not be necessary for a representative to produce an instrument of full powers",[462] and that such treaties shall be presumed not to require ratification.[463] A few years later, and in view of the comments received from member States of the UN to the draft articles, Sir Waldock proposed deleting the

---

[457]*Commentaries*, *supra* note 88 at 188 (art 2, para 2).

[458]"First Report on the Law of Treaties by Sir Humphrey Waldock, Special Rapporteur" (UN Doc A/CN.4/144) in *Yearbook of the International Law Commission 1962*, vol 2 (New York: UN, 1964) at 33 (UN Doc A/CN.4/SER.A/1962/Add.1).

[459]Ibid.

[460]"Report of the International Law Commission covering the work of its Fourteenth Session, 24 April–29 June 1962" (UN Doc A/5209) in *Yearbook of the International Law Commission 1962*, *supra* note 458 at 161.

[461]Ibid at 163.

[462]Ibid at 165.

[463]Ibid at 171.

definition of treaties in simplified form.[464] The Commission adopted the proposal,[465] and the definition never made it to the Draft Articles adopted in 1968 or to the VCLT.

The position of the Commission, up until 1965, seemed to recognise that international agreements come in many different forms, and as such, special rules apply to particular forms. But the end result of the codification endeavour was the recognition of one set of rules that would apply to all binding international agreements in written form. Alternatives and variations of specific rules are included in the VCLT, but contrary to early ILC drafts, their applicability is dictated by the expressed will of the parties and not by the form of the agreement. The ICJ, in the *Cameroon v. Nigeria* case, eventually confirmed this notion:

> Thus while in international practice a two-step procedure consisting of signature and ratification is frequently provided for in provisions regarding entry into force of a treaty, there are also cases where a treaty enters into force immediately upon signature. Both customary international law and the Vienna Convention on the Law of Treaties leave it completely up to States which procedure they want to follow.[466]

Whether the legal recognition of agreements in simplified form was desirable or not is beyond the scope of this study; but I wish to highlight that in the current state of international law, and especially after *Qatar v. Bahrain*, there is only one type of binding international agreement not covered by the customary law of treaties, as reflected in the Vienna Conventions: oral agreements.[467]

With the adoption by the Court of Article 2.1.a of the VCLT as its working definition of a treaty, and eventually as the reflection of customary law, the elements of form were confirmed to be irrelevant for the task of differentiating between political agreements and binding international agreements. As the ICJ had previously stated in *Aegean Sea Continental Shelf*, to determine the nature of the act or transaction embodied in a document submitted to it, "the Court must have regard above all to its actual terms and to the particular circumstances in which it was drawn up".[468]

This, however, did not prevent the Court from reviewing the formal aspects of an instrument in the *Cameroon v. Nigeria* case. As it was argued by Nigeria that the so-called Maroua Declaration[469] had not been perfected because the appropriate

---

[464]"Fourth Report on the Law of Treaties, by Sir Humphrey Waldock, Special Rapporteur" (UN Doc A/CN.4/177) in *Yearbook of the International Law Commission 1965*, vol 2 (New York: UN, 1967) at 13 (UN Doc A/CN.4/SER.A/1965/Add.1) ("The five Governments which have commented upon the present paragraph are at one in thinking that the definition of an informal treaty which it contains is inadequate, either in general or as a basis for the rules formulated in articles 4 and 12").

[465]Ibid at 159–160 (showing that Article 1.1.(b) was deleted).

[466]*Cameroon v. Nigeria*, Merits, *supra* note 86 at para 264.

[467]See Anthony Aust, *Modern Treaty Law and Practice, 2nd ed*, (Cambridge: Cambridge University Press, 2007) at 9 [Aust, *Treaty Law*].

[468]*Aegean Sea Continental Shelf*, *supra* note 82 at para 96.

[469]*Maroua Declaration (with chart)*, Nigeria and United Republic of Cameroon, 1 June 1975, 1236 UNTS 319.

authorities never ratified it, the Court noted that the VCLT leaves the matter of form to the will of the contracting States. The Court then concluded from the text of the Declaration that it is an international agreement in the sense of the VCLT, and that it had entered into force immediately upon its signature,[470] even though there was no indication of a method or date of entry into force.[471] On this specific point it must be recalled that according to the VCLT, entry into force by definitive signature is not to be presumed,[472] and it is ultimately subject to proof of the collective will of the participants or the individual will of a signing State.[473] The Court also relied on the fact that the then Presidents of Nigeria and Cameroon effected a correction to the Maroua Declaration by an exchange of letters, in order to sustain its conclusion that the said Declaration was a treaty.[474]

When the Court indeed looked at the content of the Minutes of 25 December 1990 in *Qatar v. Bahrain*, it was of the view that they constituted an international agreement because they "enumerate the commitments to which the Parties have consented."[475] Kabblers is of the opinion that the quoted passage means that "[a]s soon as there are commitments, the Court argued, those commitments amount to legal rights and obligations. There are no two ways about it: commitments, once consented to, are by definition legal commitments."[476] The point to be made here is that the fact that the jurisdiction of the Court needs to be established by means of a treaty or a special agreement referring the case to the ICJ, does not mean that an instrument referencing to such a possibility is a treaty or special agreement. If content is to rule over form, there must be a certainty that the content was meant to

---

[470] *Cameroon v. Nigeria,* Merits, *supra* note 86 at para 264.

[471] On this point, it has been noted that "[t]he intention of the parties as to the status of an instrument is often most easily ascertained by examining the form and wording. In British practice use of terms such as 'shall', 'agree' and 'enter into force' denote an intention to conclude a treaty", Anthony Aust, "The Theory and Practice of Informal International Instruments", (1986) 35 ICLQ 787 at 800.

[472] "The consent of a State to be bound by a treaty is expressed by the signature of its representative when: (a) the treaty provides that signature shall have that effect; (b) it is otherwise established that the negotiating States were agreed that signature should have that effect; or (c) the intention of the State to give that effect to the signature appears from the full powers of its representative or was expressed during the negotiation", *VCLT, supra* note 87 at Art. 12.1.

[473] See Cedric Van Assche, "Article 12 Convention of 1969", in Corten and Klein, eds., *supra* note 240 at 218; See also, Gerald G. Fitzmaurice, "Do Treaties Need Ratification?" (1934) 15 Brit YB Int'l L 113; Hans Blix, "The Requirement of Ratification" (1953) 30 Brit YB Int'l L 352.

[474] *Cameroon v. Nigeria,* Merits, *supra* note 86 at para 267.

[475] *Qatar v. Bahrain,* Jurisdiction and Admissibility (1 July 1994), *supra* note 82 at para 25.

[476] Klabbers, "Qatar v. Bahrain", *supra* note 446 at 368 and 376-376 (he adds: "As soon as there is a text indicating some sort of obligations, the Court infers from that circumstance an intention to become bound, and, what is more, and intention to become legally bound, Or rather, to put the matter in more accurate words, it would seem that as soon as some commitment can be discerned, the Court operates from the presumption that the agreement in question must be legally binding.").

be of a legally binding nature. In other words, content shall be looked at together with the circumstances of its adoption. That is the true meaning of the Court's dictum in *Aegean Sea Continental Shelf*.[477]

Before the VCLT, it was possible to differentiate between formal agreements—treaties strictu senso—and informal agreements—treaties in simplified form.[478] The provisions of the UN Charter on the registration obligations reflect this division as it is meant to apply to "every treaty and every international agreement".[479] While the ILC had considered specific rules on modalities of conclusion and entry into force applicable to treaties in simplified form, by the time the discussions on the topic of the law of treaties had concluded, most of these rules had been eliminated from the draft articles by integrating them with the rules applicable to formal instruments.[480]

Personally, I am not convinced that the Minutes of 25 December 1990 were a treaty in force in the sense of the VCLT. Especially considering that in the absence of an entry into force formula, the VCLT does not allow for the presumption that the parties intended the signature to legally bind them in the international arena.[481] In my view, if all 'international agreements concluded between States in written form and governed by international law' are subject to the customary law of treaties, as reflected in the VCLT, then all international agreements must meet the conditions of validity found in the customary law of treaties, as reflected in the VCLT. Under that logic, the Court should have considered whether the parties had agreed that the Minutes were to enter into force by signature.[482] The Court expressly rejected this line of argument.[483] However, if the ILC or the Vienna Conference had retained the rules applicable to treaties in simplified form, there would be no doubt that the Minutes of 25 December 1990 constituted an international agreement of this kind, and that entry into force by signature was presumed.

For both parties to the dispute, the definition in Article 2.1.a of the VCLT had no authority until the Court itself applied it as customary international law. It is my view that had the Court not adopted the VCLT's definition of a treaty as its working definition—and the binary logic that comes with it—a broader concept of

[477]*Aegean Sea Continental Shelf*, *supra* note 82 at para 96.

[478]See Aust, *Treaty Law*, *supra* note 467 at 17.

[479]*Charter*, *supra* note 3 at 102.1.

[480]Gautier, "Article 1", *supra* note 455 at 35–36; without expressly stating it so, Article 7.1.b of the *VCLT* provides for an exception to the customary rules on full powers, which is not considered applicable to formal multilateral agreements, See Aust, *Treaty Law*, *supra* note 467 at 77–78.

[481]*VCLT*, *supra* note 87 at art. 24.2; Mark Eugen Villiger, *Commentary on the 1969 Vienna Convention on the Law of Treaties* (Leiden: Martinus Nijhoff Publishers, 2009) at 345.

[482]Ibid at art 12.1.b.

[483]See *Qatar v. Bahrain*, Jurisdiction and Admissibility (1 July 1994), *supra* note 82 at para 27 ("The Court does not find it necessary to consider what might have been the intentions of the Foreign Minister of Bahrain or, for that matter, those of the Foreign Minister of Qatar. The two Ministers signed a text recording commitments accepted by their Governments, some of which were to be given immediate application").

international agreements could have been advanced in international law.[484] However, the Court went that way, and by adopting the logic of the VCLT as applicable to all binding agreements under international law, blurred the line between formal and informal agreements. The diversity in form, language and nature of commitments has been reduced to a single relevant normative form: the treaty. That is, the treaty as defined by the VCLT. The result is that in the universe of written international agreements, the only important line is that dividing binding from non-binding agreements.

Finally, none of the above necessarily means that the Court did not have jurisdiction to entertain the case. It could be argued that paragraph two of the Minutes of 25 December 1990, providing for the jurisdiction of the Court, was in and of itself a reference satisfying the requirements of Article 36, paragraph 1, of the Statute of the Court. Both the PCIJ and the ICJ had in the past rejected the argument that specific formalities are required for a case to be refered.[485] Moreover, legally binding commitments could be found to coexist with non-binding or general provisions in a given instrument.[486] And for this to happen, such instrument would not need to be a treaty in the sense of the VCLT.

3.4.3 *Judgment No. 2867 of the Administrative Tribunal of the International Labour Organization upon a Complaint Filed Against the International Fund for Agricultural Development*

On 23 April 2010, the Chairman of the Executive Board of the International Fund for Agricultural Development (hereinafter, IFAD), informed the Registry of the ICJ about a resolution adopted by that body[487] challenging the decision of the International

[484]See Oscar Schachter, "The Twilight Existence of Nonbinding International Agreements" (1977) 71 AJIL 296.

[485]*Rights of Minorities in Upper Silesia* (*Minority Schools*) (*Germany v. Poland*) (1928), PCIJ (Ser. A) No. 12 at 23 ("The acceptance by a State of the Court's jurisdiction in a particular case is not, under the Statute, subordinated to the observance of certain forms, such as, for instance, the previous conclusion of a special agreement"); *Corfu Channel case* (*United Kingdom v. Albania*), Preliminary Objection [1948] ICJ Rep 15 at 27 ("While the consent of the parties confers jurisdiction on the Court, neither the Statute nor the Rules require that this consent should be expressed in any particular form").

[486]See e.g. R.R. Baxter, International Law in Her Infinite Variety, (1980) 29 ICLQ 549 at 550 ("It seems well to refer to the norms contained in international agreements, because one instrument may contain both provisions creating precise legal obligations and norms of such a vague and general character that it is clear that they were not intended to be enforced").

[487]*Appeal of Judgment No.2867 of the International Labour Organization Administrative Tribunal to the International Court of Justice*, IFAD Doc EB 2010/99/R.43/Rev.1, online: International Fund for Agricultural Development http://www.ifad.org/gbdocs/eb/99/e/EB-2010-99-R-43-REV-1.pdf.

Labour Organization Administrative Tribunal (hereinafter, ILOAT) in *Judgment No. 2867 on the case of Mrs A.T.S.G. v. President of IFAD* (hereinafter, *No. 2867*).[488]

By virtue of Article XII of the Statute of ILOAT,[489] the governing bodies of the international organizations under the jurisdiction of this Tribunal[490] have the possibility of challenging the validity of its decisions before the ICJ. The Statute of ILOAT specifies that the ICJ should decide by means of an Advisory Opinion, which shall be binding.

ILOAT's Judgment *No. 2867* specifically dealt with the complaint made by Ana Teresa Saez García, an international civil servant working at the Global Mechanism (hereinafter, GM), which is a specialised body established by the United Nations Convention to Combat Desertification[491] (hereinafter, UNCCD). At this point, it must be noted that the aforementioned Convention did not provide for the establishment of a Secretariat for the GM, and instead instructed the Conference of its parties to identify an organization to house and perform the administrative operations of the GM.[492] At the first session of the conference of the Parties to the UNCCD, it was decided to select IFAD to house the GM.[493]

Saez García had been pursuing an administrative process to the effect of rescinding the decision of the managing director of the GM not to extend her contract. As she was not successful, she appealed the decision at the ILOAT, identifying IFAD as its counterparty. This was due to the fact that all her letters of appointment were clear that such an appointment was with IFAD. At the Administrative Tribunal, IFAD argued that the decision-making process of the GM was outside the jurisdiction of ILOAT and that, as per the UNCCD, the authorities of the GM are not accountable to IFAD. The Administrative Tribunal found in *No. 2867* that the personnel of GM are staff members of IFAD and that the decisions of the authorities of the GM relating to staffing matters were, in law, decisions of IFAD. This specific issue was the decision that IFAD challenged before the ICJ.

---

[488] *Mrs A.T.S.G. v. President of the International Fund for Agricultural Development*, Judgment of 3 February 2010, ILOAT Judgment No. 2867.

[489] "Statute of the Administrative Tribunal of the International Labour Organization", online: International Labour Organization http://www.ilo.org/public/english/tribunal/about/statute.htm.

[490] "Membership", online: International Labour Organization http://www.ilo.org/public/english/tribunal/membership/index.htm.

[491] *United Nations Convention to Combat Desertification in those Countries Experiencing Serious Drought and/or Desertification*, Particularly in Africa, 14 October 1994, 1954 UNTS 3 at art 21.4, 33 ILM 1328.

[492] Ibid at art 21.6.

[493] *Report of the Conference of the Parties on its First Session, Held in Rome from 29 September to 10 October 1997*, ICCD Doc ICCD/COP(1)/11/Add.1, at 67–69, online: United Nations Convention to Combat Desertification http://archive.unccd.int/cop/officialdocs/cop1/pdf/11add1eng.pdf; Organization to house the Global Mechanism and agreement on its modalities, ICCD Doc Dec 24/COP.1, para 1. online: United Nations Convention to Combat Desertification http://www.unccd.int/cop/officialdocs/cop1/pdf/11add1eng.pdf#page=67.

The Court had already dealt with revisions of four judgments of the ILOAT[494] as well as with three judgments of the defunct UN Administrative Tribunal.[495] The Court had noted before that there are conceptual challenges between the judicial role of the ICJ, as established in the Charter of the UN, and the request to review a case between an individual and an international organization. Namely, two issues related to procedural equality are prominent: (1) in accordance with the Statute of ILOAT, only the employer can make use of the revision process, and (2) in accordance with the Statute of the Court, only States or international organizations are entitled to appear before the Court in advisory proceedings.[496]

In order to remedy the judicial inequalities, the Court decided in the Advisory Opinion in *Judgment No. 2867 of the Administrative Tribunal of the International Labour Organization upon a Complaint Filed against the International Fund for Agricultural Development* (hereinafter, *Judgment No. 2867 of ILOAT*) that no oral proceedings were to be held, and that IFAD "was to transmit to the Court any statement setting forth the views of Ms. Saez García which she might wish to bring to the attention of the Court".[497] That has been the practice of the Court since its 1956 Advisory Opinion on the Judgments of the Administrative Tribunal of the ILO upon Complaints Made against UNESCO (hereinafter, UNESCO), its first case

---

[494]All of them cumulated in a single case at the ICJ: *Judgments of the Administrative Tribunal of the I.L.O. upon complaints made against the U.N.E.S.C.O.*, Advisory Opinion, [1956] ICJ Rep 77 [*Judgments of the Administrative Tribunal of the I.L.O.*]; the cases subject of review were: *Duberg v. Director-General of the United Nations Educational, Scientific and Cultural Organisation*, Judgment of 26 April 1955, ILOAT Judgment No. 17; *Leff v. Director-General of the United Nations Educational, Scientific and Cultural Organisation*, Judgment of 26 April 1955, ILOAT Judgment No. 18; *Wilcox v. Director-General of the United Nations Educational, Scientific and Cultural Organisation*, Judgment of 26 April 1955, ILOAT Judgment No. 19; *Bernstein v. Director-General of the United Nations Educational, Scientific and Cultural Organisation*, Judgment of 29 October 1955, ILOAT Judgment No. 21.

[495]The first being, *Application for Review of Judgment No. 158 of the United Nations Administrative Tribunal*, Advisory Opinion, [1973] ICJ Rep 166 [*Application for Review of Judgment No 158*]; relating to: *Fasla v. Secretary-General of the United Nations*, Judgment of 28 April 1972, UNAT Judgment No. 158, [1972] U.N. Jur. Yb. 127, UN Doc. AT/DEC/158; the second being, *Application for Review of Judgment No. 273 of the United Nations Administrative Tribunal*, Advisory Opinion, [1982] ICJ Rep 325; relating to: *Mortished v. Secretary-General of the United Nations*, Judgment of 15 May 1981, UNAT Judgment No. 273, [1981] UN Jur Yb 115, UN Doc. AT/DEC/273; and the third being, *Application for Review of Judgment No. 333 of the United Nations Administrative Tribunal*, Advisory Opinion, [1987] ICJ Rep 18 [*Application for Review of Judgment No. 333*]; relating to: *Yakimetz v. Secretary-General of the United Nations*, Judgment of 8 June 1984, UNAT Judgment No. 333, [1984] UN Jur Yb 146, UN Doc. AT/DEC/273.

[496]*Statute of the ICJ*, *supra* note 3 at Art. 66; See also Yaël Ronen, "Participation of Non-State Actors in ICJ Proceedings" (2012) 11 L and Practice of Int'l Courts and Tribunals 77; Hugh Thirlway, "The International Court of Justice 1989–2009: at The Heart Of The Dispute Settlement System?" (2010) 57 NILR 347 at 387–390.

[497]*Judgment No. 2867 of the Administrative Tribunal of the International Labour Organization upon a Complaint Filed against the International Fund for Agricultural Development*, Order of 29 April 2010, [2010] ICJ Rep 298 at Operative Paragraph 4.

of revision of the judgment of an administrative tribunal. This is regardless of the fact that on that first judgment, the Court made clear that it was "not bound for the future by any consent which it gave or decisions which it made with regard to the procedure thus adopted."[498]

In previous cases of revision, the Court was of the view that: "General principles of law and the judicial character of the Court do require that, even in advisory proceedings, the interested parties should each have an opportunity, and on a basis of equality, to submit all the elements relevant to the questions which have been referred to the review tribunal."[499] What makes the Advisory Opinion on the *Judgment No. 2867 of ILOAT* remarkable is that in order to discover the content of the general principle of law relating to the equality of access to justice, the ICJ made use of two general comments of the HRC. The Court looked at the evolution in the content of General Comments No. 13[500] and No. 32,[501] and noted that the latter gives detailed attention to the concept of equality before courts and tribunals.[502] This, in the view of the Court, is due to 30 years of experience of the Committee in the application of Article 14 of the ICCPR. Such analysis led the Court to conclude that the principle of equality of the parties "must now be understood as including access on an equal basis to available appellate or similar remedies unless an exception can be justified on objective and reasonable grounds."[503]

*

Substantively, the Advisory Opinion on the *Judgment No. 2867 of ILOAT* dealt with more than the possible violation of the terms of contract of a staff member. An important point of international law was at the core of the request for the Advisory Opinion: the responsibility of international organizations for the actions of hosted institutions.[504] This is particularly important due to the increased use of similar institutional arrangements in multilateral treaties concluded under the auspices of

---

[498] *Judgments of the Administrative Tribunal of the I.L.O., supra* note 494 at p 86.

[499] *Application for Review of Judgment No. 158, supra* note 495 at para 36.

[500] CCPR, *General Comment No. 13: Equality before the courts and the right to a fair and public hearing by an independent court established by law (Art. 14)*, (13 April 1984) in *Compilation Of General Comments and General Recommendations adopted by Human Rights Treaty Bodies*, UN Doc HRI/GEN/1/Rev.9 (Vol. I) (2008) at 63.

[501] CCPR, *General Comment No. 32: Right to equality before courts and tribunals and to a fair trial (Art. 14)*, (23 August 2007) in *Compilation, vol I*, ibid at 248.

[502] *Judgment No. 2867 of the Administrative Tribunal of the International Labour Organization upon a Complaint Filed against the International Fund for Agricultural Development*, Advisory Opinion, [2012] ICJ Rep 10 at para 39 [*Judgment No. 2867 of ILOAT*].

[503] Ibid at para 44.

[504] The Legal Counsel of the United Nations has already clarified the relationship between IFAD and GM as far as treaty-making capacity and applicability of administrative and financial rules and regulations: "Interoffice memorandum to the Executive Secretary of the United Nations Convention to Combat Desertification Secretariat regarding questions posed by the Joint Inspection Unit" [2009] UN Jur Yb 450.

the UN,[505] and especially taking into account the recent codification project concluded by the ILC on the responsibility of international organizations.[506] However, my interest in the Advisory Opinion comes from the Court's use of the General Comments of the HRC.

Judge Cançado Trindade, in his separate opinion to the Advisory Opinion, summarised the evolution of the principle of equality between the parties in the jurisprudence of the ICJ related to the revision of judgments of administrative tribunals.[507] It is interesting how, in the previous cases, the actual content of such a principle was never investigated, or rather was presented as self-evident. The transparency of the Court in *Judgment No. 2867 of ILOAT*, specifically in demonstrating the means by which the general principle of laws can be identified, is of great use to litigants. It has been noted that the few specific norms that have general principles as their source "seem generally to be procedural guidelines for international tribunals."[508] There is, however, another evolution to consider. In *A Wall in the OPT*, the first advisory opinion in which a general comment of the HRC was quoted, the Court did so in order to supplement its own interpretation of the ICCPR.[509] More recently, in *Diallo*, the Court saw fit to extensively justify its use of the HRC interpretation of the ICCPR to inform its own, the only difference being that the views of the HRC were found in recommendations addressing individual complaints.[510] However, in *Judgment No. 2867 of ILOAT*, the ICCPR did not constitute a binding legal instrument between the parties to the dispute at the ILOAT, nor did the Court attempt to justify its use. Although admittedly there are points of coincidence between the concept of free access to justice in general international law[511] and the human rights jurisprudence concerning judicial remedies and the existence of reasonable alternative means for staff members of

---

[505]See, for example, the modalities adopted in the Convention on Biological Diversity, which resulted in the provision of administrative secretariat services by the United Nations Environment Programme to the Secretariat of the aforementioned Convention, initially in an interim basis and then permanently, *Convention on Biological Diversity*, 5 June 1992, 1760 UNTS 79 at art 24 and 41, 31 ILM 818; *Selection of a competent international organization to carry out the functions of the Secretariat of the Convention*, CBD Doc COP1 Dec I/4, online: Convention on Biological Diversity http://www.cbd.int/decision/cop/default.shtml?id=7064.

[506]*International Law Commission: Sixty-third session*, UNGAOR, 66st Sess., Supp. No. 10, UN Doc. A/66/10 (2011) at para 87.

[507]*Judgment No. 2867 of the Administrative Tribunal of the International Labour Organization upon a Complaint Filed against the International Fund for Agricultural Development*, Dissenting Opinion of Judge Cançado Trindade, [2012] ICJ Rep 10 at paras 32–46.

[508]Onuf and Birney, *supra* note 194 at 191.

[509]*A Wall in the OPT*, *supra* note 397 at para 136.

[510]*Ahmadou Sadio Diallo*, Merits, *supra* note 159 at para 66.

[511]See, e.g. *Ambatielos Case* (*Greece v. United Kingdom*) (1956), XII RIAA 83 at 110, (Arbiters: Ricardo J. Alfaro, Algot J. F. Bagge, Maurice Bourquin, John Spiropoulos, Gerald Thesiger).

international organizations,[512] the hermeneutical route followed by the Court in *Judgment No. 2867 of ILOAT* is still far from its traditional approach.

As to the actual effect of the Court's analysis of the general comments, the judgment in UNESCO had stated that "it is not necessary for the Court to express an opinion upon the legal merits of Article XII of the Statute of the Administrative Tribunal."[513] However, in *Judgment No. 2867 of ILOAT*, after reviewing the content of General Comment 32, the Court was "unable to see any such justification for the provision for review of the Tribunal's decisions which favours the employer to the disadvantage of the staff member."[514] The result, however, was not as satisfactory to Judge Cançado Trindade as it was to the Court as a whole. In his view, "[t]he result is the prehistoric and fossilized procedure that defies logic, common sense and the basic principle of the good administration of justice."[515] This is hardly surprising as during his period as judge at the IACHR, he defended on multiple occasions the idea that access to justice is part of jus cogens,[516] until the dicta was finally adopted by that human rights Court.[517]

But the point I wish to make is that the Court did not need to make reference to the general comments in order to corroborate its views on the principle of equality. Unlike the case of UN General Assembly resolutions, the Court did not state as an abstract rule that general comments could inform the content of general principles.[518] But the fact remains that in this particular case it did inform the content of a principle. On one hand, such operation disconnected the general comment from its intended purpose within the legal regime in which the HRC operates: that is, interpreting the obligations contained in the ICCPR. On the other, the analysis of the Court further shows that normative forms are recognised legal norms as long as

[512]See, e.g. *Waite and Kennedy v. Germany* (1999), (2000) 30 EHRR 26 at para 50; *Golder v. United Kingdom* (1975), (1979–1980) 1 EHRR 524 at paras 35–36; *Osman v. United Kingdom* (1998), (2000) 29 EHRR 245 at para 136; see also August Reinisch, The Immunity of International Organizations and the Jurisdiction of their Administrative Tribunals, (2008) 7:2 Ch J Int'l L 285.

[513]*Judgments of the Administrative Tribunal of the I.L.O.*, *supra* note 494 at p 85.

[514]*Judgment No. 867 of ILOAT*, *supra* note 502 at para 39.

[515]*Judgment No. 2867 of ILOAT*, Dissenting Opinion of Judge Cançado Trindade, *supra* note 507 at para 48.

[516]See e.g. *Case of the Pueblo Bello Massacre* (*Colombia*) (2006), Inter-Am Ct HR (Ser C) No 159, Opinion of Judge Cançado Trindade at para 64, *Case of López-Álvarez* (*Honduras*) (2006), Inter-Am Ct HR (Ser C) No 141, Opinion of Judge Cançado Trindade at paras 53–55; *Case of the Sawhoyamaxa Indigenous Community* (*Paraguay*) (2006), Inter-Am Ct HR (Ser C) No 146, Opinion of Judge Cançado Trindade at paras 35–36; *Case of Ximenes-Lopes* (*Brazil*) (2006), Inter-Am Ct HR (Ser C) No 149, Opinion of Judge Cançado Trindade at paras 44–47; *Case of Servellón-García* et al. (*Honduras*) (2006), Inter-Am Ct HR (Ser C) No 152, Opinion of Judge Cançado Trindade at para 13.

[517]*Case of Goiburú* et al. (*Paraguay*) (2006), Inter-Am Ct HR (Ser C) No 153, at para 131 [*Goiburú*]; *Case of La Cantuta* (*Peru*) (2006), Inter-Am Ct HR (Ser C) No 162, at para 160 [*La Cantuta*].

[518]Although the argument has been made that UN General Assembly resolutions could have the effect of informing the content of general principles, Bleicher, *supra* note 410 at 451–452.

they can be incorporated into one of the sources enumerated in Article 38 of the Statute of the Court.

The general interpretative view of a universal human rights treaty body was taken out of its regular context—interpreting the conventional norm it attempts to develop—and used to justify the evolution of the content of a general principle of law already recognised by the Court. In practical terms, the process followed by the Court was exactly the same as the one used half a century ago. To paraphrase the Court itself, as the legal and factual situation was—to the extent of the applicability of the Court's regular procedure—identical to UNESCO, there was no reason to disregard the reasoning and conclusions adopted in the earlier case.[519] Therefore, the weight of the precedent would have been enough to sustain the use of such a procedure. As for its newly asserted views on Article XII of the Statute of ILOAT, the Court as a whole had previously disapproved such a provision in softer terms[520] and judges independently have called for a proper two-stage system,[521] such as the one eventually adopted by the UN General Assembly in 2009.[522] The fact that the review process for the defunct UN Administrative Tribunal was abolished in 1995,[523] coupled with the creation of the new system of Administration of Justice at the UN applicable to staff members of the Secretariat, of the civilian component of Peacekeeping Operations and Special Political Missions, and of the Funds and Programmes, would have been enough to justify such views.

It could be argued, as Christenson has, that

> some principles of general international law are or ought to be so compelling that they might be recognised by the international community for the purpose of invalidating or forcing revision in ordinary norms of treaty or custom in conflict with them.[524]

Even though the Court made a rather strong statement of disapproval of the revision process provided in the Statute of ILOAT,[525] it still relied on the tools already provided in its Statute to diminish the inequality of the parties at the procedural level. It seems from the tenor of paragraph 44 of the judgment that the

---

[519] *Cameroon v. Nigeria*, Preliminary Objections, *supra* note 160 at para 28.

[520] See e.g. *Judgments of the Administrative Tribunal of the I.L.O.*, *supra* note 494 at p 85.

[521] See e.g. *Application for Review of Judgment No. 333*, *supra* note 495 at p 109 (Separate Opinion of Judge Ago).

[522] *Administration of justice at the United Nations*, GA Res 63/233, UNGAOR, 64th Sess, UN Doc A/RES/63/233 (2009).

[523] *Review of the procedure provided for under article 11 of the statute of the Administrative Tribunal of the United Nations*, GA Res 50/54, UNGAOR, 50th Sess, UN Doc A/RES/50/54 (1995).

[524] Gordon A. Christenson, "Jus Cogens. Guarding Interests Fundamental to International Society" (1988) 28 Va J Int'l L 585 at 586.

[525] De Branadere notes that the Court was "very critical of the review mechanism" and that it is "without doubt a legitimate reproach to the ILOAT review system", Eric De Brabandere, Individuals in Advisory Proceedings Before the International Court of Justice: Equality of the Parties and the Court's Discretionary Authority, (2012) 11:2 Law & Prac Int'l Courts & Trib 253 at 279.

only role the Court see itself playing in the face of such systemic inequality in the revision process is "to attempt to ensure, so far as possible, that there is equality in the proceedings before it."[526] That is because the Court found itself in no position to reform the system established by the ILOAT Statute, or to abstain from deciding on the matter. In other words, the measures of the Court were meant to address "the only inequality which the Court can guarantee since it cannot alter the relevant provisions of the ILOAT Statute to that effect."[527]

If the afore-cited statement by Christenson is to be taken seriously, a general principle of international law should be more than able to trump a resolution adopted by the International Labour Conference. Even more so if it is taken into account that the Inter-American Court has ruled that equal access to justice is a peremptory rule of international law.[528]

However, Bordin asks not to underestimate the criticism made by the Court of the review procedure, as:

> It suggests that the Court's perception of its judicial role in proceedings that directly concern the rights of individuals is keeping up with the evolving human rights standards to which it so vehemently referred in its Opinion of 1 February.[529]

That is to say, the Court's opinion in *Judgment No. 2867 of ILOAT* can be considered a fair warning to prospective litigants under Article XII of the ILOAT Statute: "[i]t is thus likely that, if the ILOAT Statute is not amended, the Court may consider to refuse to reply to the request in future cases"[530]

3.5 Conclusion

As has been explained above, a widely accepted statement of the sources of international law is found in Article 38 of the ICJ Statute.[531] Being simply a copy of the same article of the Statute of the PCIJ, this list was never intended to become

---

[526] *Judgment No. 2867 of ILOAT*, *supra* note 502 at para 44.

[527] De Brabandere, *supra* note 525 at 279.

[528] *Goiburú*, *supra* note 517, at para 131 ("Access to justice is a peremptory norm of international law and, as such, gives rise to obligations *erga omnes* for the States to adopt all necessary measures to ensure that such violations do not remain unpunished, either by exercising their jurisdiction to apply their domestic law and international law to prosecute and, when applicable, punish those responsible, or by collaborating with other States that do so or attempt to do so."); *La Cantuta*, *supra* note 7, 160 (with similar text).

[529] Fernando Lusa Bordin, "Procedural Developments at the International Court of Justice" (2012) 11:2 Law & Prac Int'l Courts & Trib 325 at 363.

[530] De Brabandere, *supra* note 525 at 279.

[531] Shaw, *supra* note 114 at 66; *contra* Ross, *supra* note 113 at 83 (Ross categorically rejects the idea that art 38 of the PCIJ and ICJ statutes can ever constitute the foundations of the doctrine of sources).

the monolithic statement of what the law is.[532] In the face of what could be constructive uncertainty, the legal actors in the international arena have found refuge in Article 38 as if it were "a quasi-constitutional provision on law-making in the global community."[533] This is something it was never meant to be:

> Where in that list shall we shoehorn the resolutions and declarations of intergovernmental organizations and their subsidiary agencies? Where in that Article 38 list are the decisions of other international courts and arbitral tribunals on issues of general or specialized international law? Where in that list are the expert submissions of non-governmental organizations on legal issues? The point is not that the work product from these contemporary actors is binding. They obviously aren't that, but the recent decisions of the ICJ couldn't be clearer that international lawyers of every stripe ignore at their peril this evidence of what the law in its contemporary forms requires.[534]

Saying that the ICJ will use these sources is not the same as granting States—or anyone, for that matter—the authority to create law through those means. There is no other way to explain epistemologically why treaties and custom are the basic sources of international law[535] than just referring to the practice of States. With regard to this paradox, Professor Fitzmaurice concluded that the sources of international law cannot be exhaustively stated "for any rule purporting to limit them will, ex hypothesi, have itself to derive from one of the very sources it purports to validate, and will therefore require for its own validity an antecedent rule, independently derived, or having a separate and further source."[536]

I reject the way in which the ICJ has incorporated normative forms in the elements contained in Article 38 because I am of the view that all international instruments have a legal effect. Now, legal effect should not to be mistaken for legal obligation.[537] In any case, when a legal obligation exists, the content of the obligation is not restricted to the instrument that formally brought it to life. As Abi-Saab has put it: "le caractère obligatoire ou non obligatoire d'un acte ou d'un instrument n'épuise pas tous ses effets juridiques, et que ceux-ci à leur tour ne recouvrent pas toute la signification juridique de l'instrument."[538]

For the purposes of this chapter, my concern is the wide use of ICJ dicta by other jurisdictional entities in the determination of what sources are. As has been mentioned above, it is normal for the Court to quote *Nuclear Tests* in order to explain the method it uses to identify unilateral declarations that create binding legal

---

[532]Frede Castberg, "La méthodologie du droit international public" (1933) 43 Rec des Cours 309.

[533]Klabbers, "Law-making", *supra* note 15 at 89.

[534]Steinhardt, *supra* note 168 at 398 (emphasis is from the original).

[535]Heilborn, *supra* note 77 at 20.

[536]Fitzmaurice, "Some Problems", *supra* note 164 at 161.

[537]See also, Mohammed M. Gomaa, "Non-Binding Agreements in International Law" in Laurence Boisson de Chazonrnes and Vera Gowlland-Debbas, eds., *The International Legal System in Quest of Equity and Universality: Liber Amicorum Georges Abi-Saab* (The Hague: Martinus Nijhoff, 2001) 229 at 243.

[538]George Abi-Saab, "Cours général de droit international public" (1987) 207 Rec des Cours 9 at 155.

obligations, and assess their validity. By virtue of its own repetition,[539] the repetition by other judicial actors in international law[540] and, to a certain extent, the assistance of extensive academic commentary—whether positive or negative—subsidiary means have contributed to the consolidation of dicta such as the one in *Nuclear Tests* as definitive law on the matter. For instance, the dictum in *North Sea Continental Shelf* concerning the elements of customary law has also been quoted in subsequent ICJ judgments and other international judgments and awards as evidence of the state of the law on the matter.[541] The said dictum was also quoted as the method of ascertainment used by the authors of the International Committee of the Red Cross study on Customary International Humanitarian Law.[542] Charney has raised the point that:

> [N]on-ICJ international dispute settlement tribunals invariably rely heavily on international treaty law because their role is to apply treaty-based legal régimes. Nevertheless, at times these forums are required to rely on other sources of law, either because their constitutive treaties mandate it or the applicable treaty does not provide all of the law needed to resolve the dispute. Under these circumstances, they turn to other sources of law. If the sources used are not the generally accepted primary sources of international law, they are close analogues to them. When these forums rely on those sources, they explicitly or implicitly rely on norms developed by the ICJ.[543]

There is, in principle, nothing wrong with such a consolidation of opinions, as legal certainty is not only expected but also demanded by the rule of law. However, in the topic of sources specifically, Sir Robert Jennings has stated that Article 38 "may also be referred to by other tribunals and generally, because it can now be

---

[539] *Armed Activities*, *supra* note 311 at para 46.

[540] See e.g. *United States—Sects. 301–310 of the Trade Act of 1974* (*Complaint by the European Communities*) (1999), WTO Doc. WT/DS152/R at para 7.118 (Panel Report), [2000] 39 ILM 452; *Arbitration between Barbados and the Republic of Trinidad and Tobago, Award of the Tribunal* (2006), 45 ILM 800 at para 291 (Permanent Court of Arbitration, operating under *UNCLOS*, Annex VII Arbitration) (Arbitrators Judge Stephen Schwebel, Sir Ian Brownlie, Vaughan Lowe, Francisco Orrego Vicuña, Sir Arthur Watts); *Dispute Concerning Access to Information Under Article 9 of the OSPAR Convention between Ireland and the United Kingdom of Great Britain and Northern Ireland, Final Award* (2003), XXIII RIAA 59 at para 89, (Permanent Court of Arbitration) (Arbitrators: W. Michael Reisman, Gavan Griffith, Rt Hon. Lord Mustill).

[541] In footnote 102 I mentioned already an ad hoc arbitral award and a decision of the European Court of Human Rights and the Extraordinary Chambers in the Court of Cambodia making use of the *North Sea Continental Shelf* dictum; *Nicaragua*, Merits, *supra* note 172 at paras 177, 185 and 207; interestingly, after the identification criterion elaborated in *North Sea Continental Shelf* was found to be 'axiomatic' in *Libya v. Malta* (*supra* note 105 at para 29), the Court has quoted the latter for explaining the elements of the criterion in *Nuclear Weapons* (*supra* note 394 at para 64); but has recently returned to quote the former in *Jurisdictional Immunities* (*supra* note 103 at para 55).

[542] Henckaerts and Doswald-Beck, *supra* note 292 at vol. I p xxxviii ("The approach taken in this study to determine whether a rule of general customary international law exists is a classic one, set out by the International Court of Justice in a number of cases, in particular in the *North Sea Continental Shelf* cases").

[543] Charney, "Multiple tribunals", *supra* note 116 at 190–191.

regarded as an authoritative statement of sources of international law as a consequence of the backing of general practice accepting it as such".[544] This is especially worrying when it is taken into account that the Court is rarely transparent with regard to the methods of ascertaining a customary norm. It has been noted that the ICJ often relies on its own authority to sustain pronouncements about the content of the law, and that such pronouncements "generally become instant classics in our discipline and trustworthy references as to the state of the law."[545]

The arbitral tribunal constituted under Annex VII of UNCLOS to deal with the case between Mauritius and the United Kingdom seems to have taken the suggestion wholeheartedly. While such a tribunal is mandated to apply UNCLOS "and other rules of international law not incompatible with this Convention",[546] upon a challenge to the appointment of one of the arbiters, the tribunal was of the view that "the system of inter-State dispute settlement is based upon the consent of the Parties, and more specifically upon the rules of public international law, the sources of which are set out in Article 38(1) of the Statute of the ICJ."[547] It is doubtful that the phrase 'other rules of international law' in UNCLOS meant Article 38 of the Statute of the ICJ, especially when taking into account that other parts of the convention do refer specifically to that article of the ICJ Statute.[548]

My argument is that the exaggerated value that has been placed in Article 38 of the Statute of the ICJ has contributed to the belief that it can plausibly provide a constitutional framework for general international law. As many pages have been written stating its paramount importance as those claiming its incompleteness. Yet Article 38 "has been taken as a convenient catalogue of international legal sources generally, and as such, has been the starting point for most discussion in this area",[549] if not the final one.

[544]Jennings, "General course", *supra* note 19 at 330.

[545]Villalpando, *supra* note 125 at 3.

[546]*UNCLOS*, *supra* note 43 at art 293.

[547]*Mauritius v. United Kingdom*, *supra* note 151 at 167.

[548]*UNCLOS*, *supra* note 43 at art 74 and 83.

[549]David Kennedy, "The Sources of International Law" (1987) 2 Am U J Int'l L & Pol'y 2.

Chapter 4
Human Rights as a New Paradigm

Abstract In this chapter, I discuss certain relevant cases of international human rights courts that challenge the way in which the doctrine of sources is understood. The common element in the cases to be discussed is the use of both binding and non-binding instruments which are external to the jurisdiction of the respective court in order to re-frame the obligations of States. International human rights courts have justified such use by invoking the customary rules of treaty interpretation, as reflected in the Vienna Convention on the Law of Treaties, and specifically the principle of systemic integration. In this chapter I engage in a substantive analysis of how actions taken by human rights bodies in the creation of standards through resolutions, general comments, recommendations, and guidelines have been used by human rights courts to complement the meaning of international human rights conventions. I argue that the advances brought by international human rights courts and bodies portrays a broader understanding of normativity which has been present in other self-contained regimes and might eventually be present in general international law.

4.1 Introduction

In the last six decades, International Law has gone through a process of expansion that has seen not only a growth in the number of topics which are today subject to some degree of international regulation,[1] but also a increasing number of instruments and institutions designed to regulate the international life of States.[2]

---

[1]Already in 1923, Kelsen noted that "on ne peut pas parler d'objets ou d'affaires *qui ne peuvent* être règlementés par le droit international, mas seulement par le droit interne…", Hans Kelsen, "Théorie générale du droit international public. Problèmes choisis" (1932) 42 Rec des Cours 117 at 303 [Kelsen, "Problèmes choisis"].

[2]One of the premises of the study of the ILC on fragmentation of international law, as initially conceived, was that "[a] major factor generating this fragmentation is the increase of international regulations", "Report of the International Law Commission on the work of its fifty-second session (1 May–9 June and 10 July–18 August 2000)" (UN Doc A/55/10) in *Yearbook of the International Law Commission 2000*, vol 2, part 2 (New York and Geneva: UN, 2006) at 143 (UN Doc A/CN.4/SER.A/2000/Add. 1 (Part 2)/Rev.1).

C.I. Fuentes, *Normative Plurality in International Law*,
Ius Gentium: Comparative Perspectives on Law and Justice 57,
DOI 10.1007/978-3-319-43929-7_4

International Human Rights Law itself is a result of such expansion. Before the creation of the UN, the conduct of States with regard to its own citizens was largely outside the realm of international action.[3] The adoption of the Universal Declaration on Human Rights has marked a turning point for the protection of human rights worldwide. Today, there is a universal system for the protection and promotion of human rights which operates through ten core treaties, each of them creating monitoring bodies to ensure the compliance of States,[4] as well as several other conventions and protocols providing for specialised rules for issues as diverse as apartheid in sports or the involvement of children in armed conflict.[5]

All of this without forgetting that there are three fully operational regional systems for the protection of human rights, with judicial entities operating at the top of each system, as well as political processes constantly discussing human rights-related issues in international fora both at the universal and regional levels.

In the previous chapters I described a general trend in the evolution of international law from its origins up until 1945, and another since then until today. The first trend found normative value in an expanding catalogue of sources. The second trend restricted the catalogue of authorised sources to a small list, and struggled to fit diverse normative forms within the list. In this chapter, I will discuss a number of international human rights court cases that challenge the way in which the doctrine of sources is understood. The main argument of this chapter is that the jurisprudence of international human rights courts in recent years portrays a broader understanding of normativity that could be used as a conceptual model to elaborate a better theoretical description of the realities of general international law.

That is, parallel to the trend described in the previous chapter, the theory and practice of international human rights law has developed in a manner that allows for a plurality of norms to shape the content of the legal obligations of States. It has been noted that international human rights law has had an impact on general international law.[6] I argue that this understanding of normativity can be considered a complement to the doctrine of sources in international law, by assisting in

[3]A.W. Brian Simpson, *Human Rights and the End of Empire: Britain and the Genesis of the European Convention* (Oxford: Oxford University Press, 2004) at 91 ("In 1939 there were, at the international level, no universal or even regional arrangements for the general protection of individuals against ill treatment by their own governments. There was no general international law of human rights"); See also Ed Bates, *The Evolution of the European Convention on Human Rights: From Its Inception to the Creation of a Permanent Court of Human Rights* (Oxford: Oxford University Press, 2010) at 33–34.

[4]See "The Core International Human Rights Instruments and their monitoring bodies", online: Office of the High Commissioner on Human Rights <http://www.ohchr.org/EN/ProfessionalInterest/Pages/CoreInstruments.aspx>.

[5]*Multilateral Treaties Deposited with the Secretary-General*, at chapter IV, online: United Nations Treaty Collection: <http://treaties.un.org/pages/ParticipationStatus.aspx> [*MTDSG* online].

[6]Menno T. Kamminga, "Final Report on the Impact of International Human Rights Law on General International Law" in Menno T. Kamminga and Martin Scheinin, eds, *The Impact of Human Rights Law on General International Law* (Oxford: Oxford University Press, 2009)1 at 21–22.

explaining the treatment that certain sources receive in international courts and arbitral tribunals of general jurisdiction as well as in other decision-making bodies at the international level, such as the UN Security Council.

In order to make this argument, I will show that international human rights courts are doing something conceptually different from, yet factually similar to, what has been done by the ICJ. That is, I will try to show that international human rights courts, unlike the ICJ, have made use of a diversity of instruments that are external to their respective regimes in order to construct the content of legal obligations applicable to States. At the same time, I will try to show that such construction, although conceptualised as interpretation by the international human rights courts, has provided legal effect to otherwise non-applicable (or even non-binding) norms by virtue of their specificity in relation to an applicable norm. However, as the ICJ itself has been an actor in international human rights law, and since it has dealt recently with a case in which it had to decide on the protection of the rights of an individual, I will also show that what the ICJ has done specifically in human rights law cases differs from its general practice in cases related to other areas of international law.

International human rights law is, in the words of the ILC, a self contained regime within the international legal system.[7] As such, human rights rest on the same general rules of the system, to the extent that the regime has not created a special rule for itself.[8] However, little has been said about the theoretical assumptions that underlie the general system and the self-contained regime,[9] and to what extent there may be a theoretical incompatibility between them.[10] While the goals of the chapter are those stated above, the argument rests on the assumption that the current understanding of the rule of interpretation found in article 31(3)(c) of the VCLT[11] (often called the principle of systemic integration of international

[7] *Report of the International Law Commission: Fifty-eight session*, UNGAOR, 61st Sess, Supp. No. 10, UN Doc A/61/10 (2006) at para 251 (conclusion 11 and 12) [*Report of the ILC, 58th session*].

[8] Ibid at para 251 (conclusions 14, and 8–10).

[9] Speaking against the special character of human rights treaties: Michael K. Addo, *The Legal Nature of International Human Rights* (Leiden: Martinus Nijhoff Publishers, 2010) at 472.

[10] Speaking against the proposition that human rights treaties are to be treated "as a 'special branch' of international law, widely immune to the principles of general international law", Daniel Rietiker, "The Principle of 'Effectiveness' in the Recent Jurisprudence of the European Court of Human Rights: Its Different Dimensions and Its Consistency with Public International Law—No Need for the Concept of Treaty *Sui Generis*" (2010) 79 Nordic J Int'l L 245.

[11] According to which, "[t]here shall be taken into account, together with the context: (…) any relevant rules of international law applicable in the relations between the parties", *Vienna Convention on the Law of Treaties*, 23 May 1969, 1155 UNTS 331 at art 31.3(c), (1969) 8 ILM 679 [*VCLT*].

law[12]) and other related interpretation techniques,[13] as applied by international human rights courts, go beyond the simple interpretation of relevant norms.

In the first section, I will discuss the international courts' practice of using diverse instruments that are not within their jurisdiction in order to interpret the content of human rights obligations. I will pay attention to the concept of interpretation in modern international law and to how the practice of human rights tribunals relates to the general understanding of the principle of systemic integration in general international law.

The second section discusses the jurisprudence of regional courts on five specific topics in order to show the manner in which treaty obligations are expanded by virtue of the content of instruments otherwise inapplicable to the specific case. It is argued here that international human rights law is understood as a network of obligations that extend from the general rights enshrined in their conventions, to the specific aspect of the obligation in diverse instruments of different normative value.

The analysis in this chapter largely excludes the African Court because it has not had yet the opportunity to decide on issues related to the substantive topics discussed herein. The African Court has used judgments of the ECHR[14] and the IACHR,[15] as well as General Comments[16] and Recommendations[17] of the HRC in order to contrast and compare the interpretation of similar provisions. However, when allegations of violations of "other relevant Human Rights instrument ratified by the States concerned"[18] have been brought, the Court has not deemed necessary to consider the application of these treaties if it has already found a violation of a comparable provision in the African Charter.[19] That being said, in *Femi Falana v.*

---

[12]*Fragmentation of International Law: Difficulties arising from the Diversification and Expansion of International Law: Report of the Study Group of the International Law Commission*, UNGAOR, 61st Sess, Supp. No. 10, UN Doc. A/CN.4/L.682 at para 413 [*Fragmentation Report*]; aee also Campbell McLachlan, "The Principle of Systemic Integration and Article 31(3)(c) of the Vienna Convention" (2005) 54:2 ICLQ 279 at 280.

[13]*American Convention on Human Rights*, 22 November 1969, 36 OASTS 1 at art 29, 1144 UNTS 123 [*American Convention*].

[14]*Tanganyika Law Society and The Legal and Human Rights Centre v. the United Republic of Tanzania; and Reverend Christopher R. Mtikila v. the United Republic of Tanzania*, Nos 009/2011 and 011/2011, Judgment, at paras 82.1 and 106.2–106.4, online: African Court on Human and People's Rights <http://www.african-court.org/> [*Tanganyika Law Society*]; *Lohé Issa Konate v. Burkina Faso*, No 004/2013, Judgment, at paras 147, 154, 158, online: African Court on Human and People's Rights <http://www.african-court.org/> [*Lohé Issa Konate*].

[15]*Tanganyika Law Society*, ibid at paras 82.1, 106.5, and 107.3; *Lohé Issa Konate*, ibid at paras 147 and 159.

[16]*Tanganyika Law Society*, ibid at para 105.4; *Lohé Issa Konate*, ibid at paras 152 and 164.

[17]*Lohé Issa Konate v. Burkina Faso*, ibid at paras 128 and 147.

[18]*Protocol on the Establishment of an African Court*, *supra* note 43 at art 3.

[19]*Benefiniciaries of late Norbert Zongo, Abdoulaye Nikiema alias Ablassé, Ernest Zongo and Blaise Ilboudo and the Bukinabè Human and Peoples' Rights Movement v. Burkina Faso*, No. 013/2011, Judgment, at para 188, online: African Court on Human and People's Rights <http://www.african-court.org/>; *Tanganyika Law Society*, *supra* note 14 at paras 122–123; except

African Union[20] the African Court made use of an Advisory Opinion of the ICJ[21] as well as a UN codification convention[22]; while in *Lohé Issa Konate Burkina Faso*[23] the African Court found direct violations to the Revised ECOWAS Treaty.[24] This already shows the African Court's willingness to take into account a diversity of sources of international law beyond those within the system in which it operates.

4.2 Interpretation as Normative Expansion

In 2010, the ICJ delivered its decision on the *Diallo* case, which, by most accounts, constitutes the first decision of the Court in a contentious case concerning the violation of human rights of an individual.[25] While other human rights cases have followed,[26] *Diallo* stands alone in the aspects related to the nature of the adjudication itself: that is, the Court had to decide if State actions were against the rights of an individual under both a regional and an universal human rights treaty. This, however, is the normal order of business in the European, Inter-American, and African courts of human rights, which were established with the mandate of deciding whether there has been a violation of the protected rights of an individual.[27]

(Footnote 19 continued)

in *Lohé Issa Konate* (*supra* note 14), where the Court found violations to both the African Charter and the ICCPR for exactly the same rights.

[20]*Femi Falana v. the African Union*, No 001/2011, Judgment, online: African Court on Human and People's Rights <http://www.african-court.org/> [*Femi Falana*].

[21]Ibid at para 68; See also *Reparations for Injuries Suffered in the Service of the United Nations*, Advisory Opinion, [1949] ICJ Rep 174 at 182.

[22]*Femi Falana*, *supra* note 22 at para 70 TA; see also *Vienna Convention on the Law of Treaties between States and International Organizations or between International Organizations*, 21 March 1986, in *MTDSG Online*, supra note 5 at chapter XXIII.3 (not in force).

[23]*Lohé Issa Konate*, *supra* note 14 at para 176.

[24]*Revised Treaty of the Economic Community of West African States (ECOWAS)*, 24 July 1993, 2373 UNTS 233.

[25]*Ahmadou Sadio Diallo (Republic of Guinea v. Democratic Republic of the Congo)*, Merits, Judgment, [2010] ICJ Rep 639 at p 730–732 (Separate Opinion of Judge Cançado Trindade) (reprinted in 50 ILM 40) [*Ahmadou Sadio Diallo*, Merits].

[26]Specifically, *Questions relating to the Obligation to Prosecute or Extradite (Belgium v. Senegal)*, Judgment, [2012] ICJ Rep 422 [*Prosecute or Extradite*]; and *Case concerning the application of the International Convention on the Elimination of all Forms of Racial Discrimination (Georgia v. Russian Federation)*, [2011] ICJ Rep 70.

[27]Bruno Simma "Human Rights before the International Court of Justice: Community Interest Coming to Life?" in Holger Hestermeyer, et al, *Coexistence, cooperation and solidarity: Liber Amicorum Rüdiger Wolfrum* (Leiden: Martinus Nijhoff Publishers, 2012) 577 at 588–589.

While other international courts seem to believe that they themselves constitute self-contained regimes,[28] *Diallo* shows that the methods followed by international human rights courts are not necessarily linked to the institutions themselves but to the body of law in which they operate.[29] As discussed above,[30] in *Diallo* the ICJ took into account the opinion of the HRC in interpreting the ICCPR and corroborated that its own reading of the obligation in that treaty and the African Convention were consistent with the interpretation given by the ECHR and the Inter-American Court of the rights as expressed in their respective systems.[31] Recently, in other human rights-related cases—*Prosecute or Extradite* and *Jurisdictional Immunities*—and cases containing aspects which could be analysed using human rights law—*Judgment No. 2867 of ILOAT*—, the ICJ also took into account the interpretation given by the HRC,[32] the UN Committee against Torture,[33] and the ECHR[34] and decided in the same manner as those bodies. Although the judgment of the Court in *Diallo* has been praised for expressly referring to and following the interpretation of international human rights institutions,[35] this process by which "judges from very different regimes entered into mutual observation of other regimes"[36] is nothing new in international human rights

---

[28]*The Prosecutor v. Duško Tadić (Prijedor Case)*, IT-94-1, Decision on the Defense Motion for Interlocutory Appeal on Jurisdiction (2 October 1995) at para 11 (International Tribunal for the of Former Yugoslavia, Appeals Chamber).

[29]For example, an Arbitral Tribuna established under Annex VII to UNCLOS, found that there is a right to protest at sea on the basis of Articles 19 and 21 of the ICCPR and resolutions of the International Maritime Organization and the International Whaling Commission, *The Arctic Sunrise Arbitration*, Award on the Merits at para 227 (Permanent Court of Arbitration, operating under UNCLOS, Annex VII Arbitration) (arbitrators: Thomas A. Mensah, Henry Burmester, Alfred H.A. Soons, Janusz Symonides and Dr. Alberto Székely) online: Permanent Court of Arbitration <http://www.pcacases.com>; *contra* Jonas Christoffersen, "The Impact of Human Rights Law on General International Law", in Kamminga and Scheinin, *supra* note 6 at 42 (arguing that the methods of treaty interpretation applicable to the European Convention, because of its special character as a human rights treaty, are in fact not particular to human rights treaties).

[30]*Supra* p 6.

[31]*Ahmadou Sadio Diallo*, Merits, *supra* note 25 at para 66–68.

[32]*Judgment No. 2867 of the Administrative Tribunal of the International Labour Organization upon a Complaint Filed against the International Fund for Agricultural Development*, Advisory Opinion, [2012] ICJ Rep 10 at para 39.

[33]*Prosecute or Extradite*, *supra* note 26 at para 101.

[34]*Jurisdictional Immunities of the State (Germany v. Italy: Greece intervening)*, Judgment, [2012] ICJ Rep 99 at para 78.

[35]Bruno Simma, "Mainstreaming Human Rights: The Contribution of the International Court of Justice" (2012) 3:1 J Int Disp Settlement 7 at 20–21; Eirik Bjorge, *Ahmadou Sadio Diallo (Republic of Guinea v. Democratic Republic of the Congo)*, 105 AJIL 534 at 539.

[36]Andreas Fischer-Lescano and Gunther Teubner, "Regime-Collisions: The Vain Search for Legal Unity in the Fragmentation of Global Law" (2004) 25:4 Mich J Int'l L999 at 1041–1042.

law. In fact, with due regard to the regional differences of each regime, international human rights institutions constantly refer to or cite one another in their decisions.[37]

There is, however, an important difference between the ICJ and the regional courts in the context of this discussion. While the ICJ can possibly decide on any issue or instrument of international law, depending on the will of the parties, the competence *ratione materiae* of international human rights courts is limited by the content of the regional human rights treaties that have authorised their respective jurisdictions.[38] In the case of the European Court, it is authorised "to ensure the observance of the engagements undertaken [...] in the [European] Convention and the Protocols thereto",[39] as the latters' content is considered additional Articles to the Convention.[40] In the case of the Inter-American Court, the issue of jurisdiction is slightly more complicated, as its jurisdiction comprises the interpretation and application of the provisions of the American Convention,[41] as well as certain rights contained in other Inter-American instruments.[42] The African Court's jurisdiction is much more ample, as in accordance with the 1998 Protocol to the Banjul Charter on the Establishment of an African Court on Human and Peoples' Rights, its jurisdiction "shall extend to all cases and disputes submitted to it concerning the

---

[37]Carlos Iván Fuentes, René Provost and Samuel G. Walker, "E Pluribus Unum – Bhinneka Tunggal Ika? Universal Human Rights and the Fragmentation of International Law" in René Provost and Colleen Sheppard, eds., *Dialogues on Human Rights and Legal Pluralism* (Dordrecht: Springer, 2012) 37 at 55; see also Lucius Caflisch and Antônio Augusto Cançado Trindade, "Les conventions américaine et européenne des droits de l'homme et le droit international general" (2004) 108 RGDP 5.

[38]Bruno Simma and Theodore Kill, "Harmonizing Investment Protection And International Human Rights: First Steps Towards a Methodology" in Christina Binder, Ursula Kriebaum, August Reinisch, and Stephan Wittich, eds, *International Investment Law for the 21st Century: Essays in Honour of Christoph Schreuer* (Oxford: Oxford University Press, 2009) 678 at 682.

[39]*European Convention for the Protection of Human Rights and Fundamental Freedoms*, Europ TS No 5 at art 19, 213 UNTS 211 [*European Convention*].

[40]*Protocol to the Convention for the Protection of Human Rights and Fundamental Freedoms*, 20 March 1952, 213 UNTS 221 at art 5; *Protocol No. 4 to the Convention for the Protection of Human Rights and Fundamental Freedoms securing certain rights and freedoms other than those already included in the Convention and in the First Protocol thereto*, 16 September 1963, 1496 UNTS 263 at art 6; *Protocol No. 6 to the Convention for the Protection of Human Rights and Fundamental Freedoms concerning the Abolition of the Death Penalty*, 28 April 1983, 1496 UNTS 281 at art 6; *Protocol No. 7 to the Convention for the Protection of Human Rights and Fundamental Freedoms*, 22 November 1984, 1525 UNTS 195 at art 7; *Protocol No. 12 to the Convention for the Protection of Human Rights and Fundamental Freedoms*, 4 November 2000, 2465 UNTS 207 at art 3; *Protocol No. 13 to the Convention for the Protection of Human Rights and Fundamental Freedoms concerning the abolition of the death penalty in all circumstances*, 3 May 2002, 2246 UNTS 112 at art 5.

[41]*American Convention*, *supra* note 13 at art 62.3.

[42]*Additional Protocol to the American Convention on Human Rights in the Area of Economic, Social, and Cultural Rights "Protocol of San Salvador"*, 17 November 1988, OASTS 69 at art 19.6, (1989) 28 ILM 156; *Inter-American Convention on the Prevention, Punishment and Eradication of Violence Against Women "Convention of Belém do Pará"*, 9 June 1994, (1994) 33 ILM 1534 at art 19 [*CBP*].

interpretation and application of the Charter, this Protocol and any other relevant Human Rights instrument ratified by the States concerned."[43] Once the African Court on Human Rights and the African Court of Justice merge by virtue of the entry into force of the 2008 Protocol on the Statute of the African Court of Justice and Human Rights, its human rights jurisdiction will be just as ample as it concerns: "the provision or provisions of the African Charter on Human and Peoples' Rights, the Charter on the Rights and Welfare of the Child, Protocol to the African Charter on Human and Peoples' Rights on the Rights of Women in Africa or any other relevant human rights instrument, ratified by the State concerned."[44]

It is beyond the scope of this chapter to enumerate all the rights protected in each system. It suffices to say that the action of international human rights courts would theoretically be delimited by the specific content of a given obligation in accordance with the human rights treaty that provides for their respective jurisdiction, and the choices that the respective court makes as to the interpretation of the obligations contained in those treaties. This section deals with a subset of these choices, specifically those that involve the use of a source of law external to the competence ratione materiae of the courts.

For example, the Inter-American Court recently decided in the Case of *Atala Riffo and daughters v. Chile* [hereinafter, *Atala Riffo*], that Article 1.1 of the American Convention also prohibits discrimination on basis of sexual orientation.[45] The IACHR arrived at that conclusion after quoting the interpretation that the European Court gave to Article 14 of the European Convention in two cases.[46] The Inter-American Court also reviewed recommendations and general comments of UN treaty-based bodies for the protection of human rights such as the HRC, the Committee on Economic, Social, and Cultural Rights, the Committee on the Rights of the Child, the Committee against Torture, and the Committee on the Elimination of Discrimination against Women,[47] as well as other documents from the UN Charter-based bodies for the protection of human rights.[48] Finally the Court also quoted a statement read at a Plenary Meeting of the UN General Assembly by the

---

[43] *Protocol to the African Charter on Human and Peoples' Rights on the Establishment of an African Court on Human and Peoples' Rights*, 10 June 1998, (1997) 9 Afr J Int'l & Comp L 953 at art 3.

[44] *Protocol on the Statute of the African Court of Justice and Human Rights*, 1 July 2008, 48 ILM 317 at annex, art 34 (not in force); it must be noted that the article will remain unchanged upon the entry into force of the *Protocol on Amendments to the Protocol on the Statute of the African Court of Justice and Human Rights*, 27 June 2014 (not in force) online: African Union <http://www.au.int/en/treaties>.

[45] *Case of Atala Riffo and daughters (Chile)* (2012), Inter-Am Ct HR (Ser C) No 239 [*Atala Riffo*].

[46] Ibid at 87; the cases specifically quoted are: *Salgueiro Da Silva Mouta v. Portugal*, No 33290/96, (2001) 31 EHRR 47 at para 28; *Clift v. United Kingdom*, No 7205/07, 13 July 2003 at para 57.

[47] *Atala Riffo*, ibid at para 88–89.

[48] Ibid at para 90.

Permanent Representative of Argentina, on behalf of sixty-six Member States,[49] as an explanation of a vote under the rules of procedure of the Assembly,[50] but incorrectly identified in the judgment as a "Declaration on Human Rights, Sexual Orientation, and Gender Identity adopted by the Assembly."[51] To sum it up, the IACHR stated:

> Bearing in mind the general obligations to respect and guarantee the rights established in Article 1.1 of the American Convention, the interpretation criteria set forth in Article 29 of that Convention, the provisions of the Vienna Convention on the Law of Treaties, and the standards established by the European Court and the mechanisms of the United Nations, the Inter-American Court establishes that the sexual orientation of persons is a category protected by the Convention.[52]

While Article 1.1 of the Convention does not mention sexual orientation as a category specifically protected against discrimination, it does prohibit discrimination on the basis of "any other social condition." With due regard to the obligation of the Inter-American Court to give reasons for its judgments,[53] I find it curious that IACHR made use of so many instruments and cases external to the Inter-American System for the protection of human rights in order to support their conclusion. Considering that the list provided in Article 1.1 of the American Convention is open to categories not already mentioned, it would not have been problematic to justify the findings of the IACHR on the basis of an interpretation emphasizing teleological elements.[54] For instance, the Court could have made use of its own jurisprudence establishing that "when interpreting the Convention it is always necessary to choose the alternative that is most favourable to protection of the rights enshrined in said treaty."[55]

---

[49]UNGAOR, 63th Sess, 70 Mtg, UN Doc A/63/PV.70 (2008) at p 30; see also *Letter dated 18 December 2008 from the Permanent Representatives of Argentina, Brazil, Croatia, France, Gabon, Japan, the Netherlands and Norway to the United Nations addressed to the President of the General Assembly*, UNGAOR, 63th Sess, UN Doc A/63/635 (2008).

[50]*Rules of Procedure of the General Assembly, embodying amendments and additions adopted by the General Assembly up to September 2007*, UNGAOR, UN doc A/520/Rev.17 at rule 88.

[51]*Atala Riffo*, supra note 52 at para 90.

[52]Ibid at 91.

[53]*American Convention*, *supra* note 13 at art 66.1.

[54]"According to the teleological principle, a treaty must be interpreted-and not only interpreted, but as it were assisted or supplemented-by reference to its objects, principles, and purposes, as declared, known, or to be presumed. In this way, gaps can be filled, corrections made, texts expanded or supplemented, always so long as this is consistent with, or in furtherance of, the objects, principles, and purposes in question", Gerald G. Fitzmaurice, "Law and Procedure of the International Court of Justice: Treaty Interpretation and Certain Other Treaty Points" (1951) 28 Brit YB Int'l L 1 at 8; see also Francis G. Jacobs, "Varieties of Approach to Treaty Interpretation: With Special Reference to the Draft Convention on the Law of Treaties before the Vienna Diplomatic Conference" (1969) 18 ICLQ 318 at 319.

[55]*Case of the Mapiripán Massacre (Colombia)* (2005), Inter-Am Cr HR (Ser C) No. 134, at para 106 [*Mapiripán Massacre*].

In order to advance a particular interpretation of the American Convention, the Inter-American Court made use, in *Atala Riffo*, of non-binding instruments and the case law and documents of institutions which were developing standards in treaties not belonging to the Inter-American System. All of these instruments, which are outside the material competence of the Inter-American Court, expand on general obligations similar to those found in the American Convention and develop in detail the issue under discussion by the IACHR. However, these instruments remain external to the legal framework on which the Inter-American Court is mandated to operate. As Samson has put it:

> the law objectively applicable between the parties in dispute is not judicially cognizable in its totality when the jurisdiction to consider the applicable law is limited. This is the case because the authority attached to the judicial determination of the meaning of law is a function of the jurisdiction of the tribunal.[56]

As noted above, the Inter-American Court has made use of external sources in its judgments on the basis of interpretative rules applicable to the American Convention.[57] Specifically in *Atala Riffo*, the IACHR referred to the interpretative rules found in the VCLT and Article 29 of the American Convention. Before analysing further the nature of the interpretative process followed by the international human rights courts, it is necessary to discuss the content of the rules of interpretation and their reception in the case law of the Courts.

Initially, I must point out that the VCLT, as conventional law, does not apply to the American Convention. Since the American Convention was concluded over a decade before the VCLT entered into force, it does not fulfil the rule of non-retroactivity of the VCLT.[58] However, it is considered that certain provisions of the VCLT reflect customary treaty law, among them those applicable to the interpretation of treaties.[59] Therefore, the customary rule on the interpretation of treaties, as codified in the VCLT provides:

---

[56]Mélanie Samson, "High Hopes, Scant Resources: A Word of Scepticism about the Anti-Fragmentation Function of Article 31(3)(c) of the Vienna Convention on the Law of Treaties" (2011) 24 Leiden J Int'l L 701 at 709–710.

[57]Similarly, "[t]he [European] Court's consideration of external sources is dependent to a large extent on the ECHR interpretation process developed by the Court over the years", Magdalena Forowicz, *The Reception of International Law in the European Court of Human Rights* (Oxford: Oxford University Press, 2010) at 4.

[58]*VCLT, supra* note 11 at art 4.

[59]*Case concerning the question whether the re-evaluation of the German Mark in 1961 and 1969 constitutes a case for application of the clause in article 2 (e) of Annex I A of the 1953 Agreement on German External Debts between Belgium, France, Switzerland, the United Kingdom of Great Britain and Northern Ireland and the United States of America on the one hand and the Federal Republic of Germany on the other* (1980), XIX RIAA 67 at para 16 (arbitrators: Erik Castrén, Karl Arndt, Marc J. Robinson, Hedwig Maier, Maurice E. Bathurst, Albert D. Monguilan, Wilhelm A. Kewenig); *Arbitral Award of 31 July 1989 (Guinea-Bissau v. Senegal)*, [1991] ICJ Rep 53 at para 48; *Territorial Dispute (Libyan Arab Jamahiriya v. Chad)*, [1994] ICJ Rep 6 at para 41; *Maritime Delimitation and Territorial Questions between Qatar and Bahrain (Qatar v. Bahrain)*, Jurisdiction and Admissibility, [1995] ICJ Rep 6 at para 33; *Oil Platforms (Islamic Republic of Iran v. United States of America)*,

General rule of interpretation

1. A treaty shall be interpreted in good faith in accordance with the ordinary meaning to be given to the terms of the treaty in their context and in the light of its object and purpose.
2. The context for the purpose of the interpretation of a treaty shall comprise, in addition to the text, including its preamble and annexes:

   (a) any agreement relating to the treaty which was made between all the parties in connection with the conclusion of the treaty;
   (b) any instrument which was made by one or more parties in connection with the conclusion of the treaty and accepted by the other parties as an instrument related to the treaty.

3. There shall be taken into account, together with the context:

   (a) any subsequent agreement between the parties regarding the interpretation of the treaty or the application of its provisions;
   (b) any subsequent practice in the application of the treaty which establishes the agreement of the parties regarding its interpretation;
   (c) any relevant rules of international law applicable in the relations between the parties.

4. A special meaning shall be given to a term if it is established that the parties so intended.[60]

However, the totality of the interpretation rule is not relevant for the purposes of this chapter. The focus of this section is the afore-cited paragraph (3)(c), which provides that other relevant rules of international law applicable between the parties shall be taken into account together with the context at the moment of interpretation.

(Footnote 59 continued)

Preliminary Objection, Preliminary Objection, [1996] ICJ Rep 803 at para 23; *Kasikilil-Sedudu Island (Botswana v. Namibia)*, Judgment, [1999] ICJ Rep 1045 at para 18; *LaGrand (Germany v. United States of America)*, Judgment, [2001] ICJ Rep 466 at para 99; *Sovereignty over Pulau Ligitan and Pulau Sipadan (Indonesia v. Malaysia)*, Judgment, [2002] ICJ Rep 625 at para 37; *Avena and other Mexican Nationals (Mexico v. United States of America)*, Judgment, [2004] ICJ Rep 48 at para 83; *Award in the Arbitration regarding the Iron Rhine ("Ijzeren Rijn") Railway between the Kingdom of Belgium and the Kingdom of the Netherlands* (2005), XXVII RIAA 35 at para 45 (arbitrators: Judge Rosalyn Higgins, Guy Schrans, Judge Bruno Simma, Alfred H.A. Soons, Judge Peter Tomka) [*Iron Rhine*]; *Certain Questions of Mutual Assistance in Criminal Matters (Djibouti v France*, [2008] ICJ Rep 177 at para 112 [*Mutual Assistance in Criminal Matters*]; *Question of the Delimitation of the Continental Shelf between Nicaragua and Colombia beyond 200 nautical miles from the Nicaraguan Coast (Nicaragua v. Colombia)*, Preliminary Objections, Judgment of 17 March 2016 at para 33, online: ICJ <http://www.icj-cij.org/docket/files/154/18956.pdf>; *Alleged Violations of Sovereign Rights and Maritime Spaces in the Caribbean Sea (Nicaragua v. Colombia)*, Preliminary Objections, Judgment of 17 March 2016 at para 35, online: ICJ <http://www.icj-cij.org/docket/files/155/18948.pdf>.

[60] *VCLT*, *supra* note 11 at art 31.3.

The ILC has stated that "article 31(3)(c) may be taken to express what may be called the principle of 'systemic Integration'",[61] which "points to a need to take into account the normative environment more widely."[62] According to McLachlan:

> The foundation of this principle is that treaties are themselves creatures of international law. However wide their subject matter, they are all nevertheless limited in scope and are predicated for their existence and operation on being part of the international law system.[63]

The first express use of the principle by the ICJ is found in the 2003 *Oil Platforms Case*.[64] After considering the aforementioned Article, the ICJ was of the view that "application of the relevant rules of international law relating to this question thus forms an integral part of the task of interpretation entrusted to the Court."[65] In the specific case, it meant having regard to the customary and conventional law on the use of force, when interpreting the clauses of the Treaty of Amity, Economic Relations and Consular Rights between the United States and Iran.[66] Moreover, Article 31(3)(c) has recently been used by the ICJ to interpret the content of a treaty in light of another treaty.[67]

Scholars have argued that Article 31(3)(c) of the VCLT was a forgotten clause up until the ICJ made use of it in 2003.[68] However, this may be true only as far as general international courts and arbitral tribunals are concerned. Both the Inter-American and the European Court of Human Rights have recognised in unequivocal terms the applicability of the general rule of interpretation codified in

---

[61] *Fragmentation Report*, *supra* note 12 at para 413.

[62] Ibid at para 415.

[63] McLachlan, *supra* note 12 at 280.

[64] Orakhelashvili has argued that "it was applied by the International Court of Justice in the Namibia case", Alexander Orakhelashvili, "Restrictive Interpretation of Human Rights Treaties in the Recent Jurisprudence of the European Court of Human Rights" (2003) 14:3 EJIL 529 at 536; indeed, when discussing the *Mandate for South West Africa*, the Court was of the view that "its interpretation cannot remain unaffected by the subsequent development of law, through the Charter of the United Nations and by way of customary law" *Legal Consequences for States of the Continued Presence of South Africa in Namibia (South West Africa) notwithstanding Security Council Resolution 276 (1970)*, Advisory Opinion, [1971] ICJ Rep 16. at para 53 (reprinted in 10 ILM 677).

[65] *Oil Platforms (Islamic Republic of Iran v. United States of America)*, Merits, [2003] ICJ Rep 161 at para 41.

[66] *Treaty of Amity, Economic Relations and Consular Rights between the United States and Iran*, 15 August 1955, 284 UNTS 93.

[67] *Mutual Assistance in Criminal Matters*, *supra* note 59 at para 112.

[68] See e.g. McLachlan, *supra* note 12 at 279–280; see also Philippe Sands; "Treaty, Custom and the Cross-fertilization of International Law" (1998) 1 Yale Human Rts & Dev LJ 85 at 87; Orakhelashvili, *supra* note 64 at 536.

the VCLT to their respective regional treaties.[69] In fact, both Courts have specifically recognised the value of paragraph 3(c) before *Oil Platforms*.[70]

In the context of the European Court, it has been noted that "[t]he most influential principle in terms of reception of international law has been the rule contained in Article 31(3)(c) of the VCLT".[71] On this point, the European Court has stated that:

> [T]he [European] Convention has to be interpreted in the light of the rules set out in the Vienna Convention of 23 May 1969 on the Law of Treaties and that Article 31(3)(c) of that treaty indicates that account is to be taken of "any relevant rules of international law applicable in the relations between the parties". The Convention, in including Article 6, cannot be interpreted in a vacuum. The Court must be mindful of the Convention's special character as a human rights treaty, and it must also take the relevant rules of international law into account. The Convention should so far as possible be interpreted in harmony with other rules of international law of which it forms part...[72]

It has been noted that explicit references to Article 31(3)(c) in the case law of the ECHR are scarce.[73] However, it has been argued that "once the Court incorporated this provision into its case law, it no longer felt the need to refer to it explicitly in subsequent decisions."[74]

On the other side of the Atlantic, the Inter-American Court, since its first judgment, has used Article 31 of the VCLT to sustain that the American Convention "must, therefore, be interpreted so as to give it its full meaning and to enable the system for the protection of human rights entrusted to the Commission

---

[69]See e.g. *Golder v. United Kingdom* (1975), 18 Eur Ct HR (Ser A) at para 29; *Johnston and Others v. Ireland*, 112 Eur Ct HR (Ser A) at para 51; *Lithgow and Others v. United Kingdom*, 102 Eur Ct HR (Ser A) at paras 114 and 117; *Witold Litwa v. Poland*, No 26629/95, ECHR 2000–III at para §§ 57–59; *"Other treaties" subject to the advisory jurisdiction of the Court (Art. 64 American Convention on Human Rights)* (1982), Advisory Opinion OC-01/82, Inter-Am Ct HR (Ser A) No 1, at para 33.

[70]For example, *Al-Adsani v. United Kingdom* [GC], No 35763/97, [2001] 34 EHRR 11 at para 55 [*Al-Adsani*]; *Case of the "Street Children" (Villagrán-Morales et al.) (Guatemala)* (1999) Inter-Am Ct HR (Ser C) No 63, at para 192 [*Street Children*].

[71]Forowicz, *supra* note 57 at 13.

[72]*Al-Adsani*, *supra* note 70 at para 55; see also *Loizidou v. Turkey*, No 15318/89, (1997) 23 EHRR 513 at para 43 [*Loizidou*]; *Georgia v. Russia* (dec), No 38263/08, (2012) 54 E.H.R.R. SE10 at para 72 (the European Convention shall "be interpreted insofar as possible in the light of the general principles of international law") [Georgia v Russia]; *Banković and others v. Belgium and 16 Other Contracting States*, No 52207/99, (2001) XII Reports 333 at para 43; *Saadi v. United Kingdom* [GC], No. 13229/03, at para 62; *Bosphorus Hava Yolları Turizm ve Ticaret Anonim Şirketi (Bosphorus Airways) v. Ireland* [GC], 45036/98, ECHR 2005-VI at para 150; *Case of Hirsi Jamaa and others v. Italy*, No 27765/09, (2012) 55 EHRR 21 at paras 170–171.

[73]Forowicz, *supra* note 57 at 13.

[74]Ibid; The ILC has suggested that in certain circumstances reference to Article 31(3)(c) is not need: "customary law, general principles of law and general treaty provisions form the interpretative background for specific treaty provisions and it often suffices to refer to them to attain systemic integration", *Fragmentation Report*, *supra* note 12 at para 421.

and the Court to attain its 'appropriate effects'."[75] That is, the Inter-American Court has been of the view that although it

> lacks competence to declare that a State is internationally responsible for the violation of international treaties that do not grant it such competence, it can observe that certain acts or omissions that violate human rights, pursuant to the treaties that they do have competence to apply, also violate other international instruments for the protection of the individual.[76]

Furthermore, Inter-American Court has expanded the scope of the principle of systemic integration,[77] and applied the customary interpretation rule together with Article 29 of the American Convention,[78] which states that:

> No provision of this Convention shall be interpreted as:
>
> a. permitting any State Party, group, or person to suppress the enjoyment or exercise of the rights and freedoms recognised in this Convention or to restrict them to a greater extent than is provided for herein;
> b. restricting the enjoyment or exercise of any right or freedom recognised by virtue of the laws of any State Party or by virtue of another convention to which one of the said states is a party;
> c. precluding other rights or guarantees that are inherent in the human personality or derived from representative democracy as a form of government; or
> d. excluding or limiting the effect that the American Declaration of the Rights and Duties of Man and other international acts of the same nature may have.[79]

---

[75] *Case of Velásquez-Rodríguez, (Honduras)*, (1987), Inter-Am Ct HR (Ser C) No 1, at para 30 (Preliminary Objections); see also *Case of the Ituango Massacres (Colombia)* (2006) Inter-Am Ct HR (Ser C) No 148, at para 156 ("the interpretation of a treaty must take into account not only the agreements and instruments related to the treaty (paragraph 2 of Article 31 of the Vienna Convention), but also the system of which it is part (paragraph 3 of Article 31 of said Convention)") [*Ituango Massacres*]; *Case of the Indigenous Community Yakye Axa (Paraguay)* (2005) Inter-Am Ct HR (Ser C) No 125, at para 126 [*Yakye Axa*]; *Case of Tibi (Ecuador)* (2004) Inter-Am Ct HR (Ser C) No 114, at para 144; *Street Children, supra* note 70 at para 192.

[76] *Case of Bámaca-Velásquez (Guatemala)* (2000), Inter-Am Ct HR (Ser C) No 70, at para 115 [*Bámaca-Velásquez*].

[77] *Case of Apitz Barbera et al. ("First Court of Administrative Disputes") (Venezuela)* (2008), Inter-Am Ct HR (Ser C) No 182, at para 217 ("pursuant to subparagraph (b) of the Article, the Court has construed the guarantees contained in the Convention in accordance with the standards established in other international instruments") [*Apitz Barbera*].

[78] See, e.g. *Yakye Axa, supra* note 75 at para 125 ("Previously this Court as well as the European Court of Human Rights have asserted that human rights are live instruments, whose interpretation must go hand in hand with evolution of the times and of current living conditions. Said evolutionary interpretation is consistent with the general rules of interpretation embodied in Article 29 of the American Convention, as well as those set forth in the Vienna Convention on Treaty Law.")

[79] *American Convention, supra* note 13 at art 29; the Commission has occasionally called Article 29 the "most-favorable-to-the-individual-clause", as it "provides that no provision of the American Convention shall be interpreted as 'restricting the enforcement or exercise of any right or freedom recognized by virtue of the laws of any State Party of another convention which one of the said states is a party'", *Juan Carlos Abella v. Argentina (La Tablada)* (1997), Inter-Am Comm HR No 24/98, at para 164.

On the basis of paragraph (d) of the aforecited Article 29 of the American Convention, the IACHR has invoked specifically the content of the American Declaration of the Rights and Duties of Man in order "to construe ['interpret' in the Spanish version] the Articles of the American Convention."[80] However, the Court has rejected the argument that Article 29(d), read in conjunction with the Inter-American Democratic Charter, another non-binding instrument adopted by the OAS General Assembly, allows the Court to infer a right to democracy in the Inter-American System.[81]

The reception of the systemic integration principle by the international human rights courts must be analysed in the context of the concept of evolutive interpretation of treaties. Since 1978, the European Court has been of the view that the European Convention is a "living instrument which (…) must be interpreted in the light of present-day conditions."[82] That is, when interpreting a right in the European Convention, the ECHR takes into account the emergence of consensus among States parties on a particular topic.[83] The Inter-American Court has adopted the same views with regard to the American Convention.[84] The concept of evolutive

---

[80] *Case of Bueno-Alves (Argentina)* (2007), Inter-Am Ct HR (Ser C) No 164, at para 60 (Based on the foregoing, the Court considers that the American Declaration may be applied in the instant contentious case, if deemed appropriate, to construe the Articles of the American Convention which the Commission and the representative consider that have been violated) [*Bueno-Alves*]; see also *Interpretation of the American Declaration of the Rights and Duties of Man within the Framework of Article 64 of the American Convention on Human Rights* (1989), Advisory Opinion OC-10/89, Inter-Am Ct HR (Ser A) No 10, at paras, 46–47 ("[G]iven the provisions of Article 29 (d), these States cannot escape the obligations they have as members of the OAS under the Declaration […]. That the Declaration is not a treaty does not, then, lead to the conclusion that it does not have legal effect, nor that the Court lacks the power to interpret it within the framework of the principles set out above"); see also Lucas Lixinski, "Treaty Interpretation by the Inter-American Court of Human Rights: Expansionism at the Service of the Unity of International Law" (2010) 21:3 EJIL 585 at 603 (In his view, "The Court has systematically invoked treaties outside the Inter-American system as a means to expand its jurisdiction, using Article 29 of the American Convention as a catapult for expanding its mandate", I however only partially agree as he seems to disregard the role that Article 31(3)(c) of the *VCLT* has played in the jurisprudence of the Court).

[81] *Apitz Barbera*, *supra* note 77 at paras 216–223.

[82] *Tyrer v. United Kingdom*, Ser A No 26, (1979–1980) 2 EHRR 1 at para 31.

[83] "The concept of European consensus in the case law of the ECtHR may be defined as a general agreement among the majority of Member States of the Council of Europe about certain rules and principles identified through comparative research of national and international law and practice", Kanstantsin Dzehtsiarou, "European Consensus and the Evolutive Interpretation of the European Convention on Human Rights" (2011) 12 German LJ 1730 at 1733.

[84] *The Right to Information on Consular Assistance in the framework of the guarantees of the Due Process of Law* (1999), Advisory Opinion OC-16/99, Inter-Am Ct HR (Ser A) No 16, at para 114.

interpretation (also called a principle,[85] method[86] or tool[87]) is often considered a deviation from the general rules of interpretation due to the special character of human rights treaties.[88] However, the argument has been made that the interpretation of human rights treaties do not "require different rules, but simply a reasonable understanding of the 'object and purpose' of the respective treaty when applying the general rule".[89] Moreover, in the context of studying the impact of human rights in general international law, a commentator has expressed the view that the evolutionary interpretation is not unique to human rights treaties, as its use is consistent with the general rule of interpretation.[90] Indeed it has been noted that although the act creative of a right is subject to the law in force at the time of its creation, "its continued manifestation, shall follow the conditions required by the

[85]Yutaka Arai, "The Margin of Appreciation Doctrine in the Jurisprudence of Article 8 of the European Convention on Human Rights" (1998) 16 Neth Q Hum Rts 41 at 51; Ernst-Ulrich Petersmann, "Human Rights, International Economic Law and 'Constitutional Justice'" (2008) 19:4 EJIL 769 at 779; Luzius Wildhaber, "European Court of Human Rights" (2002) 40 Can YB Int'l L 309 at 311.

[86]George Letsas, *A Theory of Interpretation of the European Convention on Human Rights* (Oxford: Oxford University Press, 2007) at 75; Malgosia Fitzmaurice, "The Tale of Two Judges: Sir Hersch Lauterpacht and Sir Gerald Fitzmaurice Human Rights and the Interpretation of Treaties" (2008) 61 Rev Hell D I 125 at 126; Vassilis P. Tzevelekos, "The Use of Article 31(3)(c) of the VCLT in the Case Law of the ECtHR: An Effective Anti-Fragmentation Tool or a Selective Loophole for the Reinforcement of Human Rights Teleology? Between Evolution and Systemic Integration" (2010) 31 Mich J Int'l L 621 at 634–635; Paolo Palchetti, "Interpreting 'Generic Terms': Between Respect for the Parties' Original Intention and the Identification of the Ordinary Meaning", in "Jurisdictional Immunities of the State and Exequatur of Foreign Judgments: a private International Law Evaluation of the Recent ICJ Judgment in Germany v. Italy" Nerina Boschiero, et al. (eds), *International Courts and the Development of International Law, Essays in Honour of Tullio Treves* (T.M.C. Asser Press, The Hague, The Netherlands, 2013) 91 at 91.

[87]Dzehtsiarou, *supra* note 83 at 1731.

[88]*Soering v. United Kingdom*, No. 14038/88, (1989) 161 Eur Ct HR (Ser A) at para. 87; in aspects of treaty law other than interpretation, the Court has held similar views, see *Belilos v. Switzerland*, No 10328/83, (1988) 132 Eur Ct HR at para 60; *Loizidou, supra* note 82 at para 67; see also *RosInvest Company UK Limited v. Russian Federation*, [2007] IIC 315 at para 40 (Arbitration Institute of the Stockholm Chamber of Commerce) (arbitrators: Prof. Dr. Böckstiegel, The Rt. Hon. Lord Steyn, Sir Franklin Berman KCMG, QC).

[89]Oliver Dörr, "Article 31. General rule of interpretation", in Oliver Dörr and Kirsten Schmalenbach, eds, *Vienna Convention on the Law of Treaties* (Berlin: Springer-Verlag, 2012) 521 at 536; in the context of the ECHR, see also Rietiker, *supra* note 10 at 276 ("the [European] Court's approach can be regarded as a proper application of the VCLT, and for this reason there is absolutely no need to have recourse to the doctrine of a treaty *sui generis* as far as the ECHR is concerned").

[90]Christoffersen, *supra* note 29 at 37.

evolution of law."[91] Both the ICJ[92] and arbitral tribunals[93] have applied evolutionary interpretation to treaties in subjects other than human rights law.

It has been noted that:

> Based on the practice of international courts in applying Article 31(3)(c) VLCT, two different relationships between "external" law and the treaties being interpreted can be distinguished: first, courts determine the meaning of a discrete or individual term appearing in a treaty by recourse to external law, referring to the normative content of the external rule to clarify the meaning of a specific term as used in the treaty. Second, external law may exert a sort of "gravitational pull" on a treaty rule, resulting in a treaty interpretation that coheres more closely with the external rule.[94]

The use of article 31(3)(c) by the international human rights courts has been in line with the second relationship above described. Specifically, in *Atala Rifo*, the result of the interpretative operation was to construct the meaning of Article 1.1 of the American Convention in the same sense as the standards established by universal and European bodies in the interpretation of their respective treaties.[95]

However, scholars have been cautions in when discussing the notion that norms external to the jurisdiction of a tribunal can have such effect in the interpretation of a treaty. Some have warned that the use of such interpretative methods could overreach the jurisdiction of a particular court,[96] and may constitute direct

---

[91] *Island of Palmas case (Netherlands, USA)* (1928), II RIAA 829 at 845 (arbitrator: Max Huber); see also Institut de Droit International, "The Intertemporal Problem in Public International Law", Session of Wiesbaden—1975, at Art. 1 online: Institut de Droit International <http://www.idi-iil.org/idiE/resolutionsE/1975_wies_01_en.pdf> ("Any interpretation of a treaty must take into account all relevant rules of international law which apply between the parties at the time of application").

[92] *Dispute regarding Navigational and Related Rights (Costa Rica v. Nicaragua)*, [2009] ICJ Rep 213 at paras 66 and 71; see also *Aegean Sea Continental Shelf (Greece v. Turkey)*, [1978] ICJ Rep 3 at para 77; see also Bruno Simma "Human Rights before the International Court of Justice: Community Interest Coming to Life?" in Holger Hestermeyer, et al, Coexistence, cooperation and solidarity: Liber Amicorum Rüdiger Wolfrum (Leiden: Martinus Nijhoff Publishers, 2012) 577 at 600 ("I would submit that the way in which the ICJ engaged in an exercise of dynamic, or evolutionary, treaty interpretation in its recent *Judgment on Navigational and Related Rights* on the San Juan River between Costa Rica and Nicaragua bodes well in this regard and may indicate the willingness of the Court to test the application of progressive traits originally developed in specialized human rights jurisprudence to other branches of international law").

[93] *Iron Rhine, supra* note 59 at para 84; *Merrill & Ring Forestry LP v. Canada*, [2010] IIC 427 at para 190 (ICSID) (arbitrators: Francisco Orrego Vicuña, Kenneth W. Dam, J. William Rowley QC).

[94] Thomas Kleinlein, "Judicial Lawmaking by Judicial Restraint? The Potential of Balancing in International Economic Law", 12:5 Ger LJ 1141 at 1158.

[95] *Atala Riffo*, supra note 52 at para 91.

[96] McLachlan, *supra* note 12 at 288; see also Duncan French, "Treaty Interpretation and the Incorporation of Extranous Legal Rules" (2006) 55 ICLQ 281 at 287.

application of external norms[97] or modification of the interpreted treaty.[98] In this regard, the view has been expressed that:

> the purpose of interpreting by reference to 'relevant rules' is, normally, not to defer the provisions being interpreted to the scope and effect of those 'relevant rules,' but to clarify the content of the former by referring to the latter. 'Relevant rules' may not, generally speaking, override or limit the scope or effect of a provision for whose clarification they are referred.[99]

The ILC does not share such a view, as it has categorically stated that "although a tribunal may only have jurisdiction in regard to a particular instrument, it must always interpret and apply that instrument in its relationship to its normative environment—that is to say "other" international law."[100] On the issue of actual meaning of interpretation in treaty law, Lord McNair has noted that:

> Strictly speaking, when the meaning of the treaty is clear, it is 'applied', not 'interpreted'. Interpretation is a secondary process which only comes into play when it is impossible to make sense of the plain terms of the treaty or when they are susceptible of different meanings.[101]

In that sense, "[i]nterpretation is a legal operation designed to determine the precise meaning of a rule, but it cannot change its meaning."[102] Although Article 31 (3)(c) of the VCLT provides for recourse to other rules of international law as a means of interpreting the text of a treaty, we should not lose sight of the fact that "the mere presence of the 'relevant rules' of international law does not mean that

---

[97]Philippe Sands and Jeffery Commission, "Treaty, Custom and Time: Interpretation/Application?" in Malgosia Fitzmaurice, Olufemi Elias and Panos Merkouris, eds, *Treaty Interpretation and the Vienna Convention on the Law of Treaties: 30 Years on* (Leiden: Koninklijke Brill, 2010) 39 at 41.

[98]Simma and Kill, *supra* note 38 at 692–694.

[99]Orakhelashvili, *supra* note 64 at 537.

[100]*Fragmentation Report, supra* note 12 at para 423.

[101]Arnold McNair, *The Law of Treaties* (Oxford: Claredon Press, 1961) at 365.

[102]*Case concerning a boundary dispute between Argentina and Chile concerning the delimitation of the frontier line between boundary post 62 and Mount Fitzroy* (1994), XXII RIAA 3 at para 75 (Arbitrators: Mr. Rafael Nieto Navia, Mr. Reynaldo Galindo Pohl, Mr. Santiago Benadava, Mr. Julio A. Barberis and Mr. Pedro Nikken); It is noted that the ICJ has also recognised the difference by stating in the *Kasiliki-Sedudu Islands* that the Special Agreement providing for its seisin "in referring to the 'rules and principles of international law', not only authorises the Court to interpret the 1890 Treaty in the light of those rues and principles but also to apply those rules and principles independently", *Kasikilil-Sedudu Island, supra* note 59 at para 91; specifically in the relationship between customary and treaty law, an Arbitral Tribunal stated that "[i]f customary international law were applied not to circumscribe, but to negate rights expressly granted in the Treaty, this would no longer be 'interpretation or application' of the Treaty but the substitution of customary law in place of the Treaty", *Indus Waters Kishenganga Arbitration (Pakistan v. India)*, Final Award, 20 December 2013 (Arbitrators: Judge Stephen M. Schwebel, Sir Franklin Berman Howard S. Wheater, Lucius Caflisch, Jan Paulsson, Judge Bruno Simma, Judge Peter Tomka) online: Permanent Court of Arbitration <http://www.pcacases.com>.

they have to be applied as if they formed part of treaty relations."[103] While the distinction between application and interpretation is crucial,[104] it has been argued—in the context of Article 31(3)(c)—that there is no easy way to determine when the interpretation by reference to other rules becomes application.[105] Kammerhofer has a rather extreme view on the matter: he is of the opinion that "systemic integration is not about interpretation properly speaking", as it constitutes "a technique for incorporating external norms into the norms of a treaty."[106]

The Inter-American Court has respected the distinction between application and interpretation. In its 30-plus years of existence, none of its over 250 judgments in contentious cases has mentioned in the *operative part* any legal instrument that the IACHR is not authorised to apply. However, *Atala Riffo* is a clear example in which several international instruments outside the jurisdiction of the Inter-American Court—even non-binding ones—assisted in delimiting the scope of the obligations in the American Convention and other Inter-American instruments providing for its jurisdiction. Neuman has specifically discussed the interpretative methods of the Inter-American Court and noted that the "notion of an ever-expanding 'corpus juris' of binding and non-binding norms available for consideration in the regulation of states underlies much of the Court's practice in interpreting the [American Convention]".[107] He has questioned whether Article 31 of the VCLT sustains the extensive use of the Convention of the Rights of the Child[108] (hereinafter, CRC),[109] or if Article 29 of the American Convention does authorise the use of global non-binding norms.[110] As for Article 29, he is of the view that "any consent expressed in this provision would appear to be limited to actual treaty obligations of OAS member states, and would not extend to the importation of European regional norms or global soft law."[111]

It is worth noting that the ILC Conclusions on the topic of Fragmentation of International Law [hereinafter, the Conclusions] have been criticised precisely for

---

[103]Alexander Orakhelashvili, *The Interpretation of Acts and Rules in Public International Law* (Oxford: Oxford University Press, 2009) at 366.

[104]In *Pulp Mills*, the ICJ stated: "In the interpretation of the 1975 Statute, taking account of relevant rules of international law applicable in the relations between the Parties, whether these are rules of general international law or contained in multilateral conventions to which the two States are parties, nevertheless has no bearing on the scope of the jurisdiction conferred on the Court under Article 60 of the 1975 Statute, which remains confined to disputes concerning the interpretation or application of the Statute.", *Pulp Mills on the River Uruguay (Argentina v. Uruguay)*, [2010] ICJ Rep 14 at para 66; see also French, *supra* note 96 at 290.

[105]Sands and Commission, *supra* note 97 at 41 and 58.

[106]Jörg Kammerhofer, "Systemic Integration, Legal Theory and the International Law Commission", 19 Finnish YB Int'l L 157 at p 13.

[107]Gerald L. Neuman, "Import, Export, and Regional Consent in the Inter-American Court of Human Rights" (2008) 19:1 EJIL 101 at 114.

[108]*Convention on the Rights of the Child*, 20 November 1989, 1577 UNTS 3 [CRC].

[109]Ibid at 112.

[110]Ibid at fn. 68.

[111]Ibid at 105.

advancing the principle of systemic integration in a manner that blurs the distinction between application and interpretation, and encouraging the use of external sources.[112] The critique is not totally undeserved, as the Report of the Study Group accompanying the Conclusions suggests that it may be impossible to distinguish between application and interpretation in the context of Article 31(3)(c).[113] However, the ILC discussed Article 31(3)(c) as a technique for the harmonization of international law.[114] That is, the Conclusions are premised on the existence of two or more norms that are valid and applicable with respect to a given situation.[115] Systemic integration, from the point of view of the ILC, is an objective to be accomplished when interpreting a group of norms[116] that both factually cover the situation and "have a binding force in respect of the legal subjects finding themselves in the relevant situation."[117] In more abstract terms, it is a requirement to integrate "a sense of coherence and meaningfulness" in the process of legal reasoning. There is, however, a tension between the nature of Article 31(3)(c) as an interpretative rule and the purpose which the ILC proposes in the Fragmentation study.[118] It has been noted that:

> Deploying external rules to guide legal reasoning in other adjudicative functions may be desirable to promote coherence within international law, but such an activity must rely on a source other than Article 31(3)(c) for its normative foundation. The Vienna Convention rules of interpretation have been accepted as customary international law, but only *qua* rules of interpretation.[119]

The reality is that today, sources external to the Inter-American system and the European system play an important role in the judgments of each court. Recently, the Inter-American Court noted that:

---

[112]Jan Klabbers, "Reluctant Groundnormen: Articles 31(3)(c) and 42 of the Vienna Convention on the Law of Treaties and the Fragmentation of International Law" in Matthew Craven, Malgosia Fitzmaurice and Maria Vogiatzi, eds., *Time, History and International Law* (Leiden: Mastinus Nijhoff, 2007) 141 at 159–160 ("Treaty interpretation would cease to be a search for the intentions of the parties; it would, instead, become a quasi-legislative exercise, a search for the best way to keep the system intact, and would thus be vulnerable to the criticism that it does away with what the parties may have had in mind"); see also, Anastasios Gourgourinis, "The Distinction between Interpretation and Application of Norms in International Adjudication" [2011] 2:1 J Int'l Dispute Settlement 31 at 37–43.

[113]*Fragmentation Report*, *supra* note 12 at fn 580.

[114]According to the Conclusions, the principle of harmonization is "a generally accepted principle that when several norms bear on a single issue they should, to the extent possible, be interpreted so as to give rise to a single set of compatible obligations", *Report of the ILC, 58th Session*, *supra* note 7 at para 251 (conclusion 4).

[115]Ibid at para 251 (conclusion 2).

[116]Ibid at para 251 (conclusion 12).

[117]Ibid at fn. 1.

[118]Tzevelekos, *supra* note 86 at 631–632.

[119]Simma and Kill, *supra* note 38 at 694.

> [T]he need for comprehensive protection of the individual under the Convention has led the Court to interpret its provisions through their convergence with other norms of international law, particularly with regard to the prohibition of crimes against humanity, which is *ius cogens*, without this implying that it has exceeded its powers, [...]. What the Court does, in accordance with treaty-based law and customary law, is to employ the terminology used by other branches of international law in order to assess the legal consequences of the alleged violations vis-à-vis the State's obligations.[120]

I do not believe that this is merely an issue of terminology. As the passage reproduced above and other judgments reveal,[121] it is in fact an operation beyond mere interpretation which gives legal effect to both binding and non-binding instruments that are outside the scope of the jurisdiction of the Inter-American and European Courts. The reliance on the principle of systemic integration is interesting, as it has been noted in the scholarship that it simply is "a tool of interpretation not explicitly vested with the power to modify."[122]

4.3 Five Examples

In the next subsections, I will give five examples in which international human rights courts have made use of the interpretative methods discussed above in order to expand the content of instruments that grant them jurisdiction, on the basis of instruments that do not. The examples are presented as broad areas of human rights law that have been expanded by making direct reference to the content of binding instruments, non-binding instruments or a combination of both.

For the purposes of the next subsections it would not be enough that a human rights court cites or even quotes a given instrument. I am interested in those occasions in which the courts actually understood that the content of a given human right in one of the regional conventions incorporates an obligation expressed in an instrument external to the operation of its jurisdiction.

4.3.1 The Protection of Human Rights in Times of War

The relationship between international human rights law and international humanitarian law has been the subject of extensive debate in the jurisprudence of

[120] *Case of Manuel Cepeda-Vargas (Colombia)* (2010), Inter-Am Ct HR (Ser C) No 213, at para. 42.

[121] *Case of Perozo et al. (Venezuela)* (2009), Inter-Am Ct HR (Ser C) No 195, at para 288.

[122] Simma and Kill, *supra* note 38 at 694.

international institutions[123] and in scholarship.[124] Today, it is accepted that in times of war, both normative bodies apply concurrently for the protection of the individual.[125] This is especially the case for the protection of civilians.

However, the practice of human rights institutions in incorporating the use of international humanitarian law to supplement the content of human rights instruments has been inconsistent. Such is the example of the Inter-American System. In its landmark 1997 decision in *La Tablada*, the Inter-American Commission made an extensive analysis of the relationship between international human rights law and international humanitarian law in order to conclude that "the American Convention necessarily require [sic] the Commission to take due notice of and, where appropriate, give legal effect to applicable humanitarian law rules."[126] While it is noted that the Inter-American Commission did not find a violation of the American Convention or applicable international humanitarian law in *La Tablada*, the lengthy analysis on the Commission's competence to apply international humanitarian law constituted a decisive step forward in the application of such rules.

The Inter-American Court, however, was not of the same view in the first case that the Commission brought to it alleging a violation of the Geneva Conventions. In *Las Palmeras (Colombia)*, the Inter-American Commission sought a declaration that Colombia had violated the right to life as established in the American Convention and of common article 3 of the Geneva Conventions,[127] due to the execution of six persons by members of the Colombian Armed Forces.[128] In the preliminary exceptions judgment of 2000, the Inter-American Court was of the view that the American Convention "has only given the Court competence to determine whether the acts or the norms of the States are compatible with the Convention itself, and not with the 1949 Geneva Conventions."[129] The

[123]See e.g. *Legality of the Threat or Use of Nuclear Weapons Case*, [1996] ICJ Rep 226 (reprinted in 35 ILM 809); *Legal Consequences of the Construction of a Wall in the Occupied Palestinian Territory*, Advisory Opinion, [2004] ICJ Rep 136 at paras 86–88.

[124]See especially, René Provost, *International Human Rights and Humanitarian Law* (Cambridge: Cambridge University Press, 2002).

[125]*Basic Principles for the protection of civilian populations in armed conflicts*, GA Res 2675 (XXV), UNGAOR, 25th Sess, UN Doc A/RES/2675 (XXV) (1970).

[126]*Juan Carlos Abella v. Argentina*, *supra* note 79 at para 164.

[127]*Geneva Convention for the Amelioration of the Condition of the Wounded and Sick in Armed Forces in the Field (Geneva Convention I)*, 12 August 1949, 75 UNTS 31; *Geneva Convention for the Amelioration of the Condition of Wounded, Sick and Shipwrecked Members of Armed Forces at Sea (Geneva Convention II)*, 12 August 1949, 75 UNTS 85; *Geneva Convention relative to the Treatment of Prisoners of War (Geneva Convention III)*, 12 August 1949, 75 UNTS 135; *Geneva Convention relative to the Protection of Civilian Persons in Time of War (Geneva Convention IV)*, 12 August 1949, 75 UNTS 287.

[128]Dinah Shelton, "Humanitarian Law in the Jurisprudence of the Inter-American Human Rights System" at 3 online: University of Pretoria <http://web.up.ac.za/sitefiles/file/47/15338/Humanitarian_Law_in_the_Jurisprudence.pdf>.

[129]*Case of Las Palmeras (Colombia)* (2000), Inter-Am Ct HR (Ser C) No 67, at para 33.

Inter-American Court reminded the Commission in strong terms that when triggering the contentious jurisdiction of the IACHR, it "should refer specifically to rights protected by [the American] Convention" or other treaties providing for its jurisdiction.[130] However, later that year, the IACHR clarified that *Las Palmeras* is to be read as stating "that the relevant provisions of the Geneva Conventions may be taken into consideration as elements for the interpretation of the American Convention."[131]

The stance of the Inter-American Court with regard to international humanitarian law seemed to soften again in 2004. In the Merits judgment of the *Case of De La Cruz-Flores (Peru)*, the IACHR noted "for information only" that the First Geneva Convention[132] as well as Additional Protocol I[133] and II[134] protect medical activities in times of war, regardless of the beneficiary.[135] Shortly after, in the *Case of the Mapiripán Massacre (Colombia)*, the IACHR made clear that Common Article 3 is "useful to interpret the Convention, in the process of establishing the responsibility of the State and other aspects of the violations alleged."

In one of its latest decisions, the IACHR strengthened the position of international humanitarian law in the process of defining the obligations of the State by stating in the *Case of Massacre of Santo Domingo (Colombia)* that, although it could not decide that the State had violated the Geneva Convention, "the Court can observe the regulations in International Humanitarian Law, as the specific norms in the subject, in order to give specific application to the conventional rules [that is, the American Convention] that define the scope of the obligations of the State."[136]

As for the substantive content of their respective human rights conventions in conditions of armed conflict, both the Inter-American and European Court have expanded the content of the right to life by using the provisions of the Geneva Conventions and Additional Protocols on the protection of civilians and those hors

---

[130] Ibid at para 34.

[131] *Bámaca-Velásquez*, *supra* note 76 at para 209 (in *Bamaca Velazques* and subsequent cases, the Inter-American Court stated that this was its view in *Las Palmeras*, however, a close look at the paragraphs of the judgment referred by the Court show no statement to that effect).

[132] *Geneva Convention for the Amelioration of the Condition of the Wounded and Sick in Armed Forces in the Field*, *supra* note 127 at art 18.

[133] *Protocol Additional to the Geneva Conventions of 12 August 1949, and Relating to the Protection of Victims of International Armed Conflicts*, 8 June 1977, 1125 UNTS 3 at art 16, (1977) 16 ILM 1391.

[134] *Protocol Additional to the Geneva Conventions of 12 August 1949, and Relating to the Protection of Victims of Non-International Armed Conflicts*, 8 June 1977, 1125 UNTS 609, (1977) 16 ILM 1442.

[135] Case of *De La Cruz-Flores (Peru)* (2004), Inter-Am Ct HR (Ser C) No 115, at para 95.

[136] *Case of Massacre of Santo Domingo (Colombia)* (2012), Inter-Am Ct HR (Ser C) No 259, at para 24 [*Santo Domingo*].

de combat.[137] In general, it has been stated that the right to life "must be interpreted insofar as possible in the light of the general principles of international law, including the rules of international humanitarian law which play an indispensable and universally accepted role in mitigating the savagery and inhumanity of armed conflict."[138] In that sense, it has also been established by both Courts that obligations of States emanating from the right to life continued to apply even where the security conditions are difficult, including in the context of armed conflict.[139]

Specifically, in the case of *Varnava and others v. Turkey*, the European Court linked the right to life in the European Convention to the provision of medical assistance to the wounded.[140] The Inter-American Court has also built a connection between the right to life and the conventional and customary provisions of international humanitarian law providing for the application of the principles of distinction between civilians and combatants, proportionality and precautions in attack.[141] That is, an attack planned or executed in disregard of these principles could constitute a violation to the right to life of civilians, if they are affected.

The Inter-American Court has also specifically linked other rights to the content of the Geneva Conventions. It has stated that the principle of distinction between civilian and military objects as well as the prohibition of pillage, found in both customary and conventional humanitarian law, could inform the content of the right to private property.[142] Other expansions include the right to circulation and residence and the rights of the child, but those will be dealt with in subsequent sections.

The Inter-American Court has also noted that the prohibition of torture is found not only in international human rights instruments, but also in the Geneva Conventions and its Additional Protocols I and II.[143] And while the IACHR has

---

[137] *Varnava v. Turkey*, Nos 16064/90, 16065/90, 16066/90, 16068/90, 16069/90, 16070/90, 16071/90, 16072/90 and 16073/90, (2010) 50 E.H.R.R. 21 at para 185 ("in a zone of international conflict Contracting States are under obligation to protect the lives of those not, or no longer, engaged in hostilities") [*Varnava*]; *Bámaca-Velásquez, supra* note 76 at para 207 ("confronted with an internal armed conflict, the State should grant those persons who are not participating directly in the hostilities or who have been placed hors de combat for whatever reason, humane treatment, without any unfavorable [sic.] distinctions"); see also Andrea Gioia, "The Role of the European Court of Human Rights in Monitoring Compliance with Humanitarian Law in Armed Conflict" in Orna Ben-Naftali, *International Humanitarian Law and International Human Rights Law* (Oxford: Oxford University press, 2011) 201 at 236–238.

[138] *Georgia v. Russia, supra* note 72 at 72.

[139] Ibid at para 72; *Bámaca-Velásquez, supra* note 76 at para 207 ("The Court considers that it has been proved that, at the time of the facts of this case, an internal conflict was taking place in Guatemala. As has previously been stated, instead of exonerating the State from its obligations to respect and guarantee human rights, this fact obliged it to act in accordance with such obligations" [references removed]); see also *Ergi v. Turkey*, No 23818/94, (2001) 32 EHRR 18 at para 79 and 82; *Isayeva v. Russia*, No 57950/00, (2005) 41 EHRR 38 at para 180 and 210; *Al-Skeini v. United Kingdom*, No.55721/07, (2011) 53 EHRR 18 at para 164.

[140] *Varnava, supra* note 137 at para 185; Goia, *supra* note 137 at 237.

[141] *Santo Domingo, supra* note 136 at para 211.

[142] Ibid at paras 270–272.

[143] *Bueno-Alves, supra* note 80 at para 77.

been of the view that in order to define the concept of torture as enshrined in the American Convention it should consider the content of all other international instruments on the topic,[144] it has never derived direct meaning from the Geneva Conventions in this regard.

As a final point in this subsection, it must be noted that when making reference to customary international humanitarian law, the Inter-American Court often quotes directly from the ICRC study on the subject,[145] without verifying the existence of opinio juris and practice.[146] The Court also found evidence of authoritative interpretation of the Additional Protocols to the Geneva Conventions in the commentaries prepared by the ICRC.[147]

4.3.2 The Protection of Children

It has been noted in the scholarship that the Inter-American System has been particularly expansive in its interpretation of the rights of children. In the view of the IACHR, "their condition demands special protection by the [State], which must be understood as an additional right and complementary to the other rights recognised to all persons under the Convention."[148] This is a particularly interesting issue considering that in the Inter-American System there is no specific treaty dealing with the rights of children, and that the American Convention contains a very general provision on the rights of the child: "Every minor child has the right to the measures of protection required by his condition as a minor on the part of his family, society, and the state."[149]

By basing itself on the principle of systemic integration, as codified in the VCLT, the Inter-American Court made use of the CRC to give content to the rights of the child in the merits decision of the case of Street Children:

> Both the American Convention and the Convention on the Rights of the Child form part of a very comprehensive international corpus juris for the protection of the child that should help this Court establish the content and scope of the general provision established in Article 19 of the American Convention.[150]

---

[144]Ibid at para 78.

[145]*Case of the "Las Dos Erres" Massacre (Guatemala)* (2009), Inter-Am Ct HR (Ser C) No 211, at para 184 [*Las Dos Erres*]; see also, *Case of the Girls Yean and Bosico (Dominican Republic)* (2005) Inter-Am Ct HR (Ser C) No 130 at 133.

[146]*Case of Gelman (Uruguay)* (2011), Inter-Am Ct HR (Ser C) No 221, at para 210 [*Gelman*].

[147]*Case of Contreras et al. (El Salvador)* (2011), Inter-Am Ct HR (Ser C) No 232 at fn. 158 [*Contreras*].

[148]*Las Dos Erres*, *supra* note 145 at para 184.

[149]*American Convention*, *supra* note 13 at art 19.

[150]*Street Children*, *supra* note 70 at para 194.

I have discussed Street Children elsewhere[151] from the point of view of the State's obligation to ensure the right to life of children in the wider sense—that is, including the minimum conditions for a dignified life.[152] Although the IACHR based its obligation in the American Convention, the specific content of those minimum conditions for a dignified life was constructed by making direct reference to Articles 2, 3, 6, 20, 27 and 37 of the CRC.[153]

The CRC is not a static instrument. As with other UN human rights conventions, a Committee has been established for the purpose of examining the progress made by State Parties. Pursuant to its mandate, the Committee on the Rights of the Child has issued a number of general observations interpreting the scope of the obligation in that Convention. In a number of cases, the Inter-American Court has adopted the interpretation of the Committee so as to broaden the scope of rights pertaining to children in the Inter-American System.[154] In cases related to indigenous peoples, the Inter-American Court has taken note of the interpretation of the Committee on the Rights of the Child of the obligations found in the CRC and has expanded the content of Article 19 of the American Convention on the basis of its General Comment 11.[155] In the *Case of Chitay Nech et al. (Guatemala)* the IACHR found, based on the aforementioned General Comment, that "within the general obligation of States to promote and protect the cultural diversity of indigenous persons, there is also a special obligation to guarantee the right to cultural life of indigenous children."[156] Therefore a deprivation of the enjoyment of that cultural life constitutes a violation of Article 19 of the American Convention. In this connection, the IACHR has also found that such deprivation of cultural life can also be the result of lack of territory.[157] As I have discussed elsewhere,[158] the IACHR is specifically concerned

[151]Carlos Iván Fuentes, "Silent Wars in Our Cities: Alternatives to the Inadequacy of International Humanitarian Law to Protect Civilians during Endemic Urban Violence", in Benjamin Perin, ed., *Modern Warfare: Armed Groups, Private Militaries, Humanitarian Organizations and the Law* (Vancouver: UBC Press, 2012) 287 at 303–304.

[152]*Street Children, supra* note 70 at para 191.

[153]Ibid at para 195 and 198.

[154]Besides the specific general comments specifically mentioned in this section, in developing the obligations of States concerning children, the Court has referenced the Committee on the Rights of the Child's General Comment No. 3, 5, 4, 7 and 12.

[155]CRC, *General Comment No. 11: Indigenous children and their rights under the Convention*, (12 February 2009) UN Doc CRC/C/GC/11 (The Court specifically quoted para 82: "[t]he effective exercise of the rights of indigenous children to culture, religion, and language constitute essential foundations of a culturally-diverse State").

[156]*Case of Chitay Nech et al. (Guatemala)* (2012), Inter-Am Ct HR (Ser C) No 212, at para 168 [*Chitay Nech*].

[157]*Case of the Xákmok Kásek Indigenous Community (Paraguay)* (2010), Inter-Am Ct HR (Ser C) No 214, at para 263.

[158]Carlos Iván Fuentes, *Redefining Canadian Aboriginal title: a critique towards an Inter-American doctrine of indigenous right to land* (LL.M. Thesis, McGill University, Faculty of Law, 2006) online: eScholarship@McGill <http://digitool.library.mcgill.ca/R/>.

with the special relationship between indigenous peoples and their traditional territories.

There are also cases in which the Inter-American Court has encountered a situation in which the rights of a child were particularly affected because of internal armed conflict. In this context, the IACHR has understood that the provisions of international human rights must be complemented by those of international humanitarian law:

> The content and scope of Article 19 of the American Convention must be specified, in cases such as the instant one, taking into account the pertinent provisions of the Convention on the Rights of the Child, especially its Articles 6, 37, 38 and 39, and of Protocol II to the Geneva Conventions.[159]

In the *Case of Contreras et al. (El Salvador)*, the IACHR specified that "in the context of internal armed conflicts, the State's obligations to children are defined in Article 4(3) of Protocol II additional to the Geneva Convention."[160]

It is particularly important that the IACHR has identified, in the *Case of Gelman (Peru)*, that the right to identity expressed in the CRC does not find similar express provisions in the conventions of the Inter-American System. This however, has not been seen as a bar to its recognition. By making direct reference to resolutions of the OAS General Assembly[161] and an Opinion of the Inter-American Juridical Committee[162] as well as the provisions of the CRC,[163] the IACHR reached the conclusion that the right to identity is "an enforceable basic human right *erga omnes* as an expression of a collective interest of the overall international community that does not admit derogation or suspension in cases provided in the American Convention on Human Rights."[164]

The Inter-American Court took a similar route when it encountered alleged violations of civil and political rights found in the Convention, which required a special duty of care in the case of children. The case of the *Juvenile Reeducation Institute (Paraguay)* dealt with death and injuries suffered, as well as the general situation, of children in the Panchito López juvenile detention centre. The Inter-American Commission was of the opinion that this centre "embodied a system that was the antithesis of every international standard pertaining to the incarceration

---

[159]*Mapiripán Massacre*, *supra* note 55 at para 153.

[160]*Contreras*, *supra* note 147 at para 107.

[161]OASGA, "Inter-American Program for Universal Civil Registry and 'Right to Identity,'" GA Res AG/RES. 2286 (XXXVII O/07) of June 5, 2007; OASGA, "Inter-American Program for Universal Civil Registry and 'Right to Identity,'" GA Res AG/RES. 2362 (XXXVIII-O/08) of 3 June 2008; OASGA, "Follow-up Program for Universal Civil Registry and 'Right to Identity,'" GA Res AG/RES. 2602 (XL-O/10) of 8 June 2010.

[162]OASIAJC, "On the scope of the right to identity", CJI/Res. 137 (LXXI-O/07) of 10 August 2007, in *Annual Report of the Inter-American Juridical Committee to the General Assembly 2007*, OAS Doc OEA/Ser.Q/VII.38 at 28.

[163]*CRC*, *supra* note 108 at art 8.

[164]*Gelman*, *supra* note 146 at para 123; see also OASIAJC, "On the scope of the right to identity", supra note 162 at para 12.

of juveniles."[165] When deciding the case, instead of looking at the individual violation of the right of the child, the IACHR analysed the violation of other rights through the enhanced standard that international human rights law contemplates in the case of children.[166]

The Inter-American Court had already stated that, regarding the detention of children, several specific considerations have to be taken into account by the State,[167] and that the American Convention "requires applying the highest standard in determining the seriousness of actions that violate their right to humane treatment."[168] However, in *Juvenile Reeducation Institute*, when reviewing the violation to the right to humane treatment contained in Article 5 of the American Convention as "compounded by the added obligation established in Article 19 [rights of the child] of the American Convention",[169] the IACHR expanded the content of those rights to include the standards found in Articles 6 and 27 of the CRC and the interpretation given by the Committee of the Rights of the Child, namely, the "State's obligation to ensure to the maximum extent possible the survival and development of the child",[170] as understood in accordance with the Committee's definition of development as per its General Comment No. 5.[171]

In light of this broad definition of development adopted by the Committee, the IACHR made use of two UN General Assembly resolutions in order to pinpoint the specific measures expected to be adopted by States in the case of children under detention: Resolution 45/113 on the UN Rules for the Protection of Juveniles Deprived of Their Liberty[172] and Resolution 40/33 on the UN Standard Minimum Rules for the Administration of Juvenile Justice,[173] also known as the Beijing Rules—all of this to arrive to the conclusion that "[i]n the case of the right to humane treatment of a child deprived of his or her liberty, the State's obligations are intimately related to

---

165 *Case of the "Juvenile Reeducation Institute" (Paraguay)* (2004), Inter-Am Ct HR (Ser C) No 112 at para 4 [*Juvenile Reeducation Institute*].

166 Ibid at 148–150.

167 *Case of Bulacio (Argentina)* (2003), Inter-Am Ct HR (Ser C) No 100, at para 135.

168 *Case of the Gómez-Paquiyauri Brothers (Peru)* (2004), Inter-Am Ct HR (Ser C) No 110, at para 170.

169 Ibid at 160.

170 Ibid at 161.

171 CRC, *General Comment No. 5: General measures of implementation of the Convention on the Rights of the Child (arts. 4, 42 and 44, para. 6)*, (27 November 2003) in *Compilation Of General Comments and General Recommendations adopted by Human Rights Treaty Bodies*, UN Doc HRI/GEN/1/Rev.9 (Vol. I) (2008) at 424 ("The Committee expects States to interpret 'development' in its broadest sense as a holistic concept, embracing the child's physical, mental, spiritual, moral, psychological and social development. Implementation measures should be aimed at achieving the optimal development for all children.)

172 *United Nations Rules for the Protection of Juveniles Deprived of their Libert*, GA Res 45/113, UNGAOR, 45th Sess, UN Doc A/RES/45/113 (1990).

173 *United Nations Standard Minimum Rules for the Administration of Juvenile Justice ("The Beijing Rules")*, GA Res 40/33, UNGAOR, 40th Sess, UN Doc A/RES/40/33 (1985).

quality of life."[174] The European Court, while noting that the Beijing Rules are not binding, was of the view that they, along with the CRC, reflect an "international tendency in favour of the protection of the privacy of juvenile defendants."[175]

The European Court has also taken note of the provisions of the CRC in a number of cases. Specifically, in *KT v. Norway* the ECHR noted that Article 19 of the CRC, dealing with the State measures to avoid all forms of violence against children, places an emphasis on the effectiveness of the measures.[176] The case dealt with two successive investigations of a family pursued by the Norwegian child welfare services. The investigations reviewed the possible deficiencies in the care of two children. The parent subject to the investigations claimed that there was a violation of his right to respect for private and family life under Article 8 of the ECHR, especially considering that the first of such investigations found that the minors under his care had not been put in a situation of danger. The European Court was of the view that the investigations "fell within the range of measures envisaged in Article 19 of the UN Convention on the Rights of the Child for States to take in order to prevent abuse and neglect of children",[177] and therefore found no violation of Article 8 of the ECHR.[178] In *Maslov v. Austria*, the ECHR noted that the CRC provides for the obligation to have regard for the best interest of the child, and then considered that "where expulsion measures against a juvenile offender [who is a settled migrant] are concerned, the obligation to take the best interests of the child into account includes an obligation to facilitate his or her reintegration."[179]

In sum, although the European Convention contains no specific mention of the rights of children, and the American Convention contains a general right to the measures of protection required by his condition as a minor[180]; both Courts have made use of binding and non-binding instruments in order to shape the content of the obligations of States with regard to children.

4.3.3 Violence Against Women, Including Domestic Violence

The protection of women in international human rights law, especially in cases of domestic violence, has often been described as inadequate. In addressing this critique, international human rights tribunals have responded by building normative linkages between the rights provided in general conventions and the specific

[174] *Juvenile Reeducation Institute, supra* note 165 at 162.
[175] *T. v. United Kingdom*, No 24724/94, 16 December 1999 at para 75.
[176] *KT v. Norway*, No 26664/03, (2009) 49 EHRR 4 at paras 63 and 67.
[177] Ibid at para 63.
[178] Ibid at para 70.
[179] *Maslov v. Austria* [GC], No 1638/03, (2008) 47 EHR.R 20 at 82–83.
[180] *American Convention, supra* note 13 at art 19.

measures demanded from States in specific instruments. Besides the prohibition against discrimination in general instruments, two specific instruments have been concluded that address rights specific to women: the Convention on the Elimination of All Forms of Discrimination against Women (hereinafter, CEDAW), in the framework of the UN, and the Inter-American Convention on the Prevention, Punishment, and Eradication of Violence against Women, also known as the Convention of Belém do Pará (hereinafter, CBP). CBP is so far the only regional multilateral human rights treaty to deal solely with violence against women.

The first important decision in this field came from the Inter-American Court in the *Case of the Miguel Castro-Castro Prison (Peru)*, which dealt with the planned transfer of a number of female inmates from a maximum security prison for persons accused or convicted of terrorism and treason, to a maximum security prison for women. It was later proven that the transfer was a cover-up for an operation planned by the government with the objective of executing part of the prison population. From the outset, the IACHR stated that with regard to the alleged violence against women, it would apply:

> Article 5 of the American Convention and will set its scope, taking into consideration as a reference of interpretation the relevant stipulations of the Inter-American Convention to Prevent, Punish, and Eradicate Violence Against Women, ratified by Peru on June 4, 1996, and the Convention on the Elimination of all Forms of Discrimination against Women, ratified by Peru on September 13, 1982, in force at the time of the facts, since these instruments complement the international corpus juris in matters of protection of women's right to humane treatment, of which the American Convention forms part.[181]

When dealing with the specific allegations in the case, the Inter-American Court started by making use of General Recommendation 12[182] of the Committee on the Elimination of Discrimination against Women in order to establish that gender-based violence is a form of discrimination,[183] from which women should be protected in any situation.

In continuing its analysis, the IACHR, "following the line of international jurisprudence and taking into account that stated in [CEDAW]",[184] adopted the ICTR's definition of sexual violence as contained in the judgment of the case *The Prosecutor v. Jean-Paul Akayesu.*[185] Then, by making direct reference to the European Court's judgment in *Aydin v. Turkey*[186] and the 1998 report of the UN

[181] *Case of the Miguel Castro-Castro Prison (Peru)* (2006), Inter-Am Ct HR (Ser C) No 160, at para 276 [*Miguel Castro-Castro Prison*].

[182] CEDAW, *General Recommendation No. 19: Violence against women*, (1992) in *Compilation, vol II, supra* note 171 at 331–336.

[183] *Miguel Castro-Castro Prison, supra* note 181 at para 303.

[184] Ibid.

[185] *Prosecutor v. Jean-Paul Akayesu*, ICTR-96-4-T, Judgment (2 September 1998) at para 688 (International Criminal Tribunal for Rwanda, Trial Chamber), online: ICTR <http://www.ictr.org>.

[186] *Aydin v. Turkey*, No.25660/94, (2006) 42 EHRR 44 at para 83 [*Aydin*].

Special Rapporteur on violence against women,[187] the IACHR concluded that the sexual violence to which the inmates were subjected constituted torture, and therefore was a violation of the right to humane treatment in the American Convention and the provisions of the Inter-American Convention to Prevent and Punish Torture.[188]

Another interesting aspect was added to the jurisprudence on the protection of women when the Inter-American Court was seized of a case dealing with multiple killings of women in Ciudad Juarez, Mexico. In the *Cotton Field (Mexico)* case, the IACHR dealt with the violations of the right to life, liberty and personal integrity as enshrined in the American Convention, from the perspective of the obligation of the State to prevent such violations from occurring. The IACHR had already established that obligations to prevent relate to the means used by the State to address the possible violation and not to the outcome.[189] That is, the fact that a right has been violated does not necessarily mean that the State has not adopted reasonable measures to ensure the protection of those rights.

In order to define the scope of prevention of violence against women as established in CBP, the IACHR first used General Recommendation 19[190] of the Committee on the Elimination of Discrimination against Women to establish that the State can be responsible for acts of private persons if there is no due diligence in the investigation of such acts.[191] After reviewing a number of instruments adopted in the framework of the UN General Assembly, as well as reports of the Secretary-General and a Special Rapporteur, the IACHR concluded that:

> States should adopt comprehensive measures to comply with due diligence in cases of violence against women. In particular, they should have an appropriate legal framework for protection that is enforced effectively, and prevention policies and practices that allow effective measures to be taken in response to the respective complaints.[192]

As the IACHR found that Mexico did not adopt reasonable measures[193] (including the adoption of appropriate legislation[194]) in order to address the situation of systematic violence against women in Ciudad Juarez, it ruled that the State had

[187]UNHRC, "Report presented by Mrs. Radhika Coomaraswamy, Special Rapporteur on violence against women, with the inclusion of its causes and consequences, pursuant to resolution 1997/44 of the Commission" UN Doc E/CN.4/1998/54, 54th Sess, 26 January 1998 at para. 14.

[188]*Miguel Castro-Castro Prison*, *supra* note 181 at para 312.

[189]*Case of Velásquez-Rodríguez (Honduras)* (1988), Inter-Am Ct HR (Ser C) No 4, at para 166 (Merits) [Velásquez-Rodríguez, Merits].

[190]CEDAW, *General Recommendation No. 19*, *supra* note 182.

[191]*Case of González et al. ("Cotton Field") (Mexico)* (2009), Inter-Am Ct HR (Ser C) No 205, at para 258.

[192]Ibid.

[193]Ibid at para 284.

[194]Ibid at para 285.

violated the rights to life, personal integrity and personal liberty recognised in the American Convention.[195]

The European Court has also dealt with cases of violence against women, adopting a broad line of interpretation. In *Opuz v. Turkey*, the ECHR stated that:

> [i]n interpreting the provisions of the Convention and the scope of the state's obligations in specific cases the Court will also look for any consensus and common values emerging from the practices of European states and specialised international instruments, such as the CEDAW, as well as giving heed to the evolution of norms and principles in international law through other developments such as the Belém do Pará Convention, which specifically sets out states' duties relating to the eradication of gender-based violence.[196]

That is, as the European Convention does not specifically define discrimination against women, the ECHR made use of Article 1 of CEDAW[197] along with the aforementioned General Recommendation No. 19 as well as a resolution of the UN Commission on Human Rights[198] to establish that violence against women, including domestic violence, is a form of discrimination against women.[199] The ECHR also noted that CBP "describes the right of every woman to be free from violence as encompassing, among others, the right to be free from all forms of discrimination."[200] This led the ECHR to conclude "from the abovementioned rules and decisions that the state's failure to protect women against domestic violence breaches their right to equal protection of the law and that this failure does not need to be intentional."[201]

4.3.4 Forced Disappearances

One of the most important contributions of the Inter-American System to international human right law has been the case law dealing with forced disappearances. The cases of *Velásquez-Rodríguez* and *Godínez-Cruz*, both against Honduras, preceded all international law in the matter and established the basis upon which the regional conventional law was drafted. Since then, the IACHR considers that the forced disappearance of a person "is a multiple and continuous violation of many

[195] Ibid at para 286.

[196] *Opuz v. Turkey*, No 33401/02, (2010) 50 EHRR 28 at para 164 [*Opuz*].

[197] Ibid at para 186.

[198] UNHRC, "Elimination of violence against women", Res 2003/45, 59th Mtg, 23 April 2004, UN Doc E/CN.4/2003/L.11/Add.4 at para. 8 ("all forms of violence against women occur within the context of de jure and de facto discrimination against women and the lower status accorded to women in society and are exacerbated by the obstacles women often face in seeking remedies from the State").

[199] *Opuz, supra* note 196 at para 187–188.

[200] Ibid at para 189.

[201] Ibid at para 191.

rights under the Convention that the States Parties are obligated to respect and guarantee".[202]

However, the most interesting case in this regard has been *Blake v. Guatemala*, in which the IACHR noted that no treaty in force at the moment contained a precise legal definition of forced disappearance.[203] The IACHR then took note of the definitions contained in the UN Declaration on the Protection of All Persons from Enforced Disappearance, and the then recently adopted Inter-American Convention on Forced Disappearance of Persons[204] (hereinafter, CFD).

Guatemala raised a preliminary objection in the case since the victim, Nicholas Blake, had disappeared some time before the State had recognised the competence of the Inter-American Court. The victim was found dead after Guatemala had accepted the Court's jurisdiction. The IACHR, nevertheless, was of the view that it could not limit the temporal effects of the Declaration on the Protection of All Persons from Enforced Disappearance, particularly in considering such acts as continuing offences.[205]

The foregoing means that, in accordance with the principles of international law which are also embodied in Guatemalan legislation, forced disappearance implies the violation of various human rights recognised in international human rights treaties, including the American Convention, and that the effects of such infringements—even though some may have been completed, as in the instant case—may be prolonged continuously or permanently until such time as the victim's fate or whereabouts are established.[206]

In consequence, the IACHR found that it had competence to decide the responsibility of Guatemala for the disappearance of Nicholas Blake, even though it occurred almost two years before the State accepted the jurisdiction of the IACHR.[207] Eventually, in the judgment on the merits, the Inter-American Court also used the Declaration to interpret Article 8 of the American Convention as granting the relatives of Mr. Blake a right to have his disappearance and death

[202] *Velásquez-Rodríguez*, Merits, *supra* note 189 at para 155; *Case of Godínez-Cruz (Honduras)* (1988), Inter-Am Ct HR (Ser C) No 5, at para 163.

[203] *Case of Blake (Guatemala)* (1996), Inter-Am Ct HR (Ser C) No 27, at paras 36 (Peeliminary Objections) [*Blake*, Preliminary Objections].

[204] *Inter-American Convention on Forced Disappearance of Persons*, 9 June 1994, 22 ILM 1429 [CFD].

[205] *Blake*, Preliminary Objections, *supra* note 203 at para 36–37; *Case of Blake* (Guatemala) (1998), Inter-Am Ct HR (Ser C) No 36, at para 64 [*Blake*, Merits].

[206] *Blake*, Preliminary Objections, ibid at para 38.

[207] Similar conclusions were reached in the case of *Heliodoro Portugal*, and even though the Inter-American Convention on the Forced Disappearance of Persons was in force for Panama and would sustain the decision, the Court also quoted the Declaration on the Protection of All Persons from Enforced Disappearance, *Case of Heliodoro Portugal (Panama)* (2008), Inter-Am Ct HR (Ser C) No 186, at paras 108–109 [*Heliodoro Portugal*].

effectively investigated and to prosecute those responsible.[208] The obligation cannot be found in the text of Article 8, as it deals exclusively with judicial guarantees.

Over a decade after Blake, the IACHR noted that, besides the aforementioned instruments, the Rome Statute and International Convention for the Protection of all Persons from Enforced Disappearance contain the same constitutive elements for this violation.[209]

In *Silih v. Slovenia*, the European Court took note of the case law developed by the Inter-American Court and the recommendations of the HRC in the sense that they "accepted jurisdiction *ratione temporis* over the procedural complaints relating to deaths which had taken place outside their temporal jurisdiction"[210]—this to the effect that the procedural obligation to carry out an effective investigation is detachable from the substantive violation and therefore "capable of binding the state even when the death took place before the critical date."[211]

The European Court has also taken note of provisions of the Declaration on the Protection of All Persons from Enforced Disappearance, specifically its Article 11, to further elaborate the obligation of the authorities to release individuals from custody in a manner permitting verification.[212]

4.3.5 Forced Displacement

As a final example, I will discuss the interpretation that the Inter-American Court has given to the liberty of movement, enshrined in Article 22 of the American Convention, to encompass specific protection against forced displacement.

In this regard, the IACHR has stated that it shares the views of the HRC concerning the content of the right to freedom of movement as set out in General Comment No. 27,[213] therefore finding that such right encompasses, among other things: "a) the right of all those lawfully within a State to move freely in that State, and to choose his or her place of residence; and b) the right of a person to enter his or her country and the right to remain in one's country."[214]

Moreover, in a number of cases the Inter-American Court has been confronted with situations of internally displaced persons, which are: "persons or groups of persons who have been forced or obliged to flee or to leave their homes or places of

---

[208] *Blake*, Merits, *supra* note 205 at para 97.

[209] *Heliodoro Portugal*, *supra* note 207 at paras 106–110.

[210] *Silih v. Slovenia*, No 71463/01, (2009) 49 EHRR 37 at para 160.

[211] Ibid at para 159.

[212] *Aydin*, *supra* note 186 at para 153; *ER v. Turkey*, No 23016/04, (2013) 56 EHRR 13 at para 72.

[213] CCPR, *General comment No. 27: Article 12 (Freedom of movement)*, (1999) in *Compilation, vol I, supra* note 171 at 223.

[214] *Case of the Moiwana Community (Suriname)* (2005), Inter-Am Ct HR (Ser C) No 124, at para 111 [*Moiwana Community*].

habitual residence, in particular as a result of or in order to avoid the effects of armed conflict, situations of generalized violence, violations of human rights or natural or human-made disasters, and who have not crossed an internationally recognized State border".[215]

The IACHR has found that for the purposes of defining the obligations of States under the American Convention, the content of the Guiding Principles on Internal Displacement is important.[216] The IACHR has further considered that some of the Guiding Principles allow it to interpret the content and scope of Article 22 in the context of forced internal displacements.[217]

While the IACHR has noted that the Guiding Principles are based on existing international human rights law and international humanitarian law standards,[218] it has continued to make reference to the Guiding Principles rather than to the normative standards that sustain them.[219]

When the internal displacement has occurred in the framework of an armed conflict, the IACHR has also found that the regulations contained in Additional Protocol II to the Geneva Conventions are useful in the definition of the content of Article 22 of the American Convention.[220]

The European Court, by making direct reference to Principles 18 and 28, has found that "the authorities have the primary duty and responsibility to establish conditions, as well as provide the means, which allow the applicants to return voluntarily, in safety and with dignity, to their homes or places of habitual residence, or to resettle voluntarily in another part of the country."[221]

4.4 Conclusion

In this chapter I noted that international human rights courts have developed a set of interpretative tools in order to advance the protection of human rights in the face of changing circumstances and regardless of the inherent temporal limitations of legal solutions. While there are other important interpretation methods and criteria, I am interested only in those methods that could plausibly be conceptualized in terms of sources.

---

[215] UNHRC, "Report of the Representative of the Secretary-General, Mr. Francis M. Deng, submitted pursuant to Commission resolution 1997/39" UN Doc E/CN.4/1998/53/Add.2, 54th Sess, 11 February 1998, reprinted in (1999) 33:2 Int'l Migration Rev 484, 37 ILM 1482.

[216] *Mapiripán Massacre*, *supra* note 55 at para 171; *Chitay Nech*, *supra* note 156 at para 140.

[217] *Santo Domingo*, *supra* note 136 at para 256.

[218] *Moiwana Community*, *supra* note 214 at para 111.

[219] See e.g. *Case of Serrano-Cruz Sisters (El Salvador)* (2005), Inter-Am Ct HR (Ser C) No 120, at para 146.

[220] *Mapiripán Massacre*, *supra* note 55 at para 172; *Ituango Massacres*, *supra* note 55 at para 209.

[221] *Dogan and others v. Turkey*, Nos 8803/02 etc., 29 June 2004 at para 154.

The method of systemic integration, whether a principle, rule or objective, is indeed the prime candidate because it asks the interpreter to construe the meaning of a treaty provision by reference to other binding and situationally relevant norms of international law. Even in its most conservative application, systemic integration requires a verification of the nature and content of the rule which will be used to interpret a treaty norm. Attention must be paid to the fact that whenever the courts have made use of a legally binding instrument outside their respective jurisdiction, they verified that the State was a party to the instrument.

Arguably, the normative expansions described in previous sections constitute clear examples in which the content of treaties external to their respective regional systems—and, strictly speaking, not applicable to the judicial operation in question—assisted in defining the scope of the legal obligations contracted by the State in a multilateral convention. To which extent the Guiding Principles on Internal Displacement or the CRC constitute valid and applicable law for the European or Inter-American Courts in the sense of the ILC Conclusions is a matter of debate.

The relevance of the issues discussed in this chapter to the international legal system has usually being neglected in studies concerning the impact of human rights in international law. Speaking on the *sui generis* standing of the obligations contained in the ECHR, and the possibility of a 'spill-over' effect on the international legal system, De Wet stated:

> The true test for this development would lie in the extent to which courts and tribunals outside the system of human rights (ranging from national courts to international tribunals with a different or broader functional mandate) acknowledge the normatively superior standing of human rights obligations.[222]

[222]Erika de Wet, "The Emergence of International and Regional Value Systems as a Manifestation of the Emerging International Constitutional Order" (2006) Leiden J Int'l L 611 at 632.

Chapter 5
Normative Plurality in International Law

Abstract While the practice of human rights courts promotes coherence among the regional and the universal human rights regimes, the principle of systemic integration is not meant to expand the normative content of the interpreted treaty on the basis of external instruments, especially non-binding instruments. Therefore, such practice cannot be conceptualised as interpretation, but as the application of external instruments. To defend this argument, I rely in the theory of Alf Ross concerning the sources of international law. Then, after adjusting Ross's theory to the specific problems of the 21st century, and proposing three mutually reinforcing notions (specificity, completeness and purpose) that assist the judge in determining the applicable law to a case, I develop the content of the normative plurality hypothesis.

5.1 Introduction

It is widely accepted that the doctrine of sources of international law has failed to provide a plausible explanation that sustains the validity of traditional sources while taking into account recent phenomena.[1] And while many theories have been developed to explain the ultimate foundation of the doctrine "[n]o single theory has received general agreement and sometimes seems as though there are as many theories or at least formulations as there are scholars."[2]

[1]Martti Koskenniemi, "Introduction" in Martti Koskenniemi, ed., *Sources of International Law* (Aldershot. Ashgate, 2000) xi at xi; Robert Y. Jennings, "What is International Law and How Do We Tell It When We See It?" (1981) 37 Ann suisse dr int 59 at 60 [Jennings, "What is International Law"]; Duncan B. Hollis, "Why State Consent Still Matters—Non-State Actors, Treaties, and the Changing Sources of International Law" (2005) 23:1 Berkeley J Int'l L 137 at 142–144; Harlan Grant Cohen, "Finding International Law: Rethinking the Doctrine of Sources" (2007) 93 Iowa L Rev 65 at 70 ("Largely unchanged, the doctrine has struggled to identify and categorize modern international phenomena. The result, this Article argues, is a disconnect between the rules identified as law by the doctrine of sources and the rules actually treated as law by the actors in the international system").

[2]Oscar Schachter, "Towards a Theory of International Obligation" in Stephen M. Schwebel, ed., The Effectiveness of international decisions; papers of a conference of the American Society of International Law and the proceedings of the conference (Leiden: Sijthoff, 1971) 9 at 9.

C.I. Fuentes, *Normative Plurality in International Law*,
Ius Gentium: Comparative Perspectives on Law and Justice 57,
DOI 10.1007/978-3-319-43929-7_5

Many scholars agree that international law is in a process of evolution due to the impact of human rights.[3] A recent study by the International Law Association concluded that "[t]he permeation of international human rights law through general international law constitutes a quiet revolution which invariably targets international law's most 'statist' features."[4] The changing nature of general international law makes it possible, now more than ever before, to successfully theorise about the sources of international law beyond sovereignty and consent.[5] I argue that the recent phenomena provide a starting point upon which it should be possible to build a hypothesis about how norms are applied in international law. Moreover, since the ICJ itself—which, along with the ILC, "may be regarded as the guardians of general international law"[6]—has progressively adopted the methods of international human rights courts in cases concerning human rights issues, it is possible to argue that the conditions are ripe for the advance of such a theory.

In Chap. 3, I described the methods followed by the ICJ to identify rules of law in the exercise of its functions. I noted that when the Court found itself with normative forms that arguably do not conform to the standards of its own jurisprudence, it assimilated them to one of the sources enumerated in Article 38 of its Statute, instead of excluding them from its analysis or treating them as a *sui generis* normative form. In my view, this reveals the doctrine's failure to perform its function: "providing objective standards of legal validation."[7]

In Chap. 4, I described the recent phenomena I am most concerned with: namely, the extensive use by international human rights courts of binding and non-binding instruments outside their material jurisdiction in order to construct the meaning of instruments under their jurisdiction. I noted that the Courts rarely discussed the validity or applicability of the instruments external to their system, and that admittedly the use of external instruments can be conceptualised from different

---

[3]See generally Theodor Meron, "General Course on Public International Law: International Law in the Age of Human Rights" (2003) 301 Rec de Cours 1 at 21 [Meron, "General Course"]; Theodor Meron, *The Humanization of International Law* (Leiden: Martinus Nijhoff, 2006) at XV [Meron, *Humanization*]; René-Jean Dupuy, "Conclusions of the Workshop" in René-Jean Dupuy, ed., L'Avenir du Droit International Dans un Monde Multiculturel: Colloque de la Académie de Droit International de la Haye, 17–19 Novembre 1983 (The Hague : Martinus Nijhoff, 1983) at 478–487; René-Jean Dupuy, La Communauté internationale entre le mythe et l'histoire (Paris: UNESCO, 1986) at 171–173; Antônio Augusto Cançado Trindade, "Hacia el nuevo Jus Gentium del siglo XXI: El derecho universal de la humanidad" in Secretaria General de la OEA, Jornadas de Derecho Internacional 2003 (Washington: OEA, 2005) at 235–242; Antônio Augusto Cançado Trindade, A Humanização do Dereito Internacional (Belo Horizonte: Del Rey, 2006) at 135.

[4]Menno T. Kamminga, "Final Report on the Impact of International Human Rights Law on General International Law", in Menno T. Kamminga and Martin Scheinin, eds, The Impact of Human Rights Law on General International Law (Oxford: Oxford University Press, 2009) at 22;

[5]Although not specifically addressing the issue of sources, Peters has argued that humanity has displaced sovereignty as the new normative foundation of international law, Anne Peters, "Humanity as the A and Ω of Sovereignty" (2009) 20:3 EJIL 513 at 514.

[6]Kamminga, *supra* note 4 at 3.

[7]Oscar Schachter, "International law in theory and practice: general course in public international law" (1982) 178 Rec des Cours 9 at 60.

perspectives.[8] The international human rights courts have conceptualized this use from the point of view of interpretation, making use particularly of an expansive understanding of the principle of systemic integration. There are two possible ways to see this. The first is to accept the narrative presented by international human rights courts and classify the use of any external instrument—regardless of its nature—as a valid interpretation exercise in accordance with the customary law of treaties, as codified in the VCLT.[9] The second is to acknowledge that international human rights courts are giving effect to instruments that, according to the doctrine of sources and jurisdictional constraints emanating from their respective constitutive treaties, should not have any effect on a particular case.

In this chapter I will make use of the theory of international law advanced by Alf Ross in the 1940s in order to argue in favour of the second alternative. That is, I contend that the practice of international courts requires acknowledging the role played in international decision-making by factors other than those recognised in the doctrine of sources. The theory developed by Ross is critical in this respect because he argued that the content of a given judicial decision is determined by a number of factors which the judge leans on in the process of materializing legal meaning. A central aspect of his source theory is that rules properly formulated and enacted as valid law are one of these factors, along with other non-formulated rules which can be either partially objectified or non-objectified. In his view, non-objectified factors such as natural law "will after all become more or less masked as an 'interpretation' of the objectivated sources"[10] such as treaty law.

I argue that the framework provided by Ross explains the choices that the international human rights judge makes in a given case regarding the norms that influence its outcome. Yet it also explains the manner in which the judge—as an agent of the system in which he/she operates—justifies and defends his or her choices as to what constitutes a relevant norm in a particular case. In my view, this does not necessarily mean that international courts and tribunals are modifying the obligations contained in treaties under their jurisdiction. I argued in the previous chapter that international human rights courts, in order to advance the purposes of the international legal system, have understood international obligations as networks that extend from formal acceptance to broad agreement, and from general obligations to specific aspects thereof. That is, the response of international courts and tribunals to the ever-increasing activity of international actors is to use normative forms deriving from such activity in order to give specificity to formally accepted obligations accepted by States in the treaties under their jurisdiction. In this sense, sources external to the system of State responsibility established by the

---

[8]See especialy, Ingo Venzke, *How Interpretation Makes International Law. On Semantic Change and Normative Twists* (Oxford: Oxford University Press, 2012).

[9]See e.g. Oliver Dörr, "Article 31. General rule of interpretation", in Oliver Dörr and Kirsten Schmalenbach, eds, *Vienna Convention on the Law of Treaties* (Berlin: Springer-Verlag, 2012) 521.

[10]Alf Ross, *A textbook of international law: general part* (London: Longmans and Green, 1947) at 94.

American and European Convention are determining the scope of the obligations of States. Those interpretative methods are, in fact, used to justify a phenomenon of normative expansion by which judges are allowed to attach the content of external sources to general obligations found in the system. It has been indicated that the African Court was largely ignored in the analysis of the previous chapter because, to date, it has not had yet dealt with the issues related to the substantive topics discussed there. But it must be noted that such analysis would be different in the case of the African Court because it is allowed to interpret and apply "any other relevant Human Rights instrument ratified by the States concerned."[11] In other words, the 1998 Protocol to the Banjul Charter on the Establishment of an African Court on Human and Peoples' Rights contains a rule of systemic application of relevant and binding treaties.[12]

In the first section of this chapter, I will situate my argument in reference to the dominant theories of international law and the model on which they rely in order to explain normativity. I start by describing some recent contributions to the theoretical studies about the sources of international law, noting that they coincide with each other in their criticism of the doctrine of sources. Then, I turn to the theory developed by Alf Ross as a means of explaining the phenomena described in Chap. 4.

However, in order to supplement Ross's theory and allow it to respond to the modern challenges faced by international law, three mutually complementary notions need to be discussed in the second section: specificity, completeness and purpose. From there, I describe the normative plurality hypothesis, which is based on the idea that law-appliers must understand international law as a complete system with a purpose. That is, the normative plurality hypothesis does not seek to define the processes or instruments that are able to produce legal norms. Instead, norms are considered capable of having a legal effect with respect to a particular case or dispute to the extent that they address the specific factual situation of that case or dispute. At the end of this section, I will briefly discuss the differences between the normative plurality hypothesis and the principle of systemic integration.

5.2 Situating the Argument

The general design of this book is to present an alternative framework for the operation of norms in international law by contrasting it with the doctrine of sources of international law. However, before presenting the constitutive elements of the normative plurality hypothesis, I will briefly situate the arguments raised so far in

---

[11] *Protocol on the Establishment of an African Court*, *supra* note 43 at art 3.

[12] See *Lohé Issa Konate v. Burkina Faso*, No 004/2013, Judgment, online: African Court on Human and People's Rights <http://www.african-court.org/> (In this case, the African Court found violations African Charter, the ICCPR and the Revised ECOWAS Treaty).

the context of recent theoretical contributions to the study of sources of international law. At the risk of over-simplifying the framework in which the debate has operated, I will broadly classify these contributions as rule-based and process-based approaches.[13]

Rule-based approaches have in common that the identification of relevant normative forms is largely based on the intent of relevant actors. International legal theories based on such an approach endeavour to prove the existence and validity of legal norms by reference to constitutional norms providing for their creation[14] or the social practice of the law-applying authorities in creating norms.[15] The doctrine of sources is largely accommodated by rule-based approaches to international law,[16] as the function of the doctrine is to differentiate legal norms from non-legal norms.

In contrast, process-based approaches, such as the policy-oriented jurisprudence developed by the New Haven School, reject the idea that "international law is properly conceived as a body of inherited rules"[17] and instead regard the discipline as "a comprehensive process of authoritative decision in which rules are continuously made and remade".[18] In the view of the New Haven School, "the analytical jurist is not concerned with the process of decision-making but rather with the exposition, in a syntactic pattern, of the products of a limited number of decision

[13] I borrow the classification from: Benedict Kingsbury, "Concept of Compliance as a Function of Competing Conceptions of International Law" (1997–1998) 19 Mich J Int'l L 345 at 348.

[14] Kelsen identified the presumed basic norm as providing that "the states ought to behave as they have customarily behaved", Hans Kelsen, *Principles of international law* (New York: Rinehart, 1952) at 418; in this regard, neo-Kelsenism assumes that *there is* a basic norm, it may just be that it is epistemologically difficult to perceive, and therefore impossible—at this point in time—to accurately represent it as a rule in the descriptive sense: Jörg Kammerhofer, "The Benefits of the Pure Theory of Law for International Lawyers, Or: What Use Is Kelsenian Theory" (2006) 12 Int'l L Theory 5 at 52; at a more abstract level, Kammerhofer states that the fundamental problem of the system is that "there is no objective criterion to cognize the coherence of a normative order", Jörg Kammerhofer, "Kelsen—Which Kelsen? A Reapplication of the Pure Theory to International Law" (2009) 22:2 Leiden J Int'l L 225 at at 243.

[15] d'Aspremont argues that "grounding the ultimate law-ascertaining rule in a social practice constitutes [H.L.A.] Hart's most important contribution to the theory of law as well as the theory of the sources of international law", Jean d'Aspremont, *Formalism and the Sources of International Law: A theory of the Ascertainment of Legal Rules* (Oxford: Oxford University Press, 2011) at 51 [Aspremont, *Formalism*].

[16] Kelsen, however, dismissed the doctrine as it "n'est qu'une paraphrase de la théorie bien connue de l'auto-limitation de l'État, suivant laquelle l'État ne pourrait être obligé que par sa propre volonté", Hans Kelsen, "Les rapports de système entre le droit interne et le droit international public" (1926) 14 Rec des Cours 227; also, my reading of neo-Kelsenism is that it would be uncomfortable with the formulation of Article 38 of the ICJ Statute stating that international custom is evidence of a general practice accepted as law, as "norms are not corporeal objects whose existence we can verify simply by way of an act of observation", Jörg Kammerhofer, "Uncertainty in the Formal Sources of International Law: Customary International Law and Some of Its Problems" (2004) 15:3 EJIL 523 at 524.

[17] Myres S. McDougal, "A Footnote" (1963) 57 AJIL 383 at 383.

[18] Ibid.

sources."[19] The critique is relevant to this book in that I agree with their position that "a useful theory about law must avoid the temptation, so common in conventional legal method, to drastically reduce the universe of variables to a text or a few purportedly key social factors."[20]

A recent process-based contribution worth discussing is Jutta Brunnée and Stephen Toope's interactional theory of international law. Their theory, although heavily process-based, does try to bridge the gap between the two approaches, as it attempts to "make sense of the contemporary practice of international law, and distinguishes between legal and other social norms."[21] At the heart of the interactional theory of international law is the idea that law "can exist only when actors collaborate to build shared understandings and uphold a practice of legality."[22] A norm emerges under the interactional theory when shared understandings meet the criteria of legality and the practice of legality.[23] Their theory tries to describe the dynamic aspect of a source discourse, which they propose to be the operation of the different actors who are part of the modern international community in constructing the legal norm.[24] What is interesting about interactional theory for the

---

[19]Myres S. McDougal, Harold D. Lasswell and W. Michael Reisman, "Theories about International Law: Prologue to a Configurative Jurisprudence" (1967–1968) 8 Va J Int'l L 188 at 254; further to that, it has been noted that "In contrast with traditional schools of jurisprudence, the New Haven school takes into account, in its comprehensive analysis, many variables which affect the process of decision-making, other than 'legal norms'", Eisuke Suzuki, "The New Haven School of International Law: An Invitation to a Policy-Oriented Jurisprudence" (1974) 1 Yale Stud World Pub Ord 6.

[20]Michael Reisman, "The View from the New Haven School of International Law" (1992) 86 Am Soc Int'l L Proc 118 at 121.

[21]Jutta Brunnée and Stephen J. Toope, *Legitimacy and Legality in International Law: An Interactional Account* (Cambridge: Cambridge University Press, 2010) at 350 [Brunnée and Toope, *Legitimacy and Legality*].

[22]Ibid at 7.

[23]Jutta Brunnée and Stephen J. Toope "Interactional international law: An introduction" (2011) 3:2 Int'l Theory 307 at 308 [Brunnée and Toope, "An Introduction"]; the criteria of legality they adopt are those proposed by Lon Fuller in: *The Morality of Law*, rev ed (New Haven: Yale University Press, 1969); the criteria, as described by H.L.A. Hart are: "Rules should be (i) general; (2) made known or available to the affected party (promulgation); (3) prospective, not retroactive; (4) clear and understandable; (5) free from contradictions; and they should not (6) require what is impossible; (7) be too frequently changed; finally (8) there should be congruence between the law and official action", H.L.A. Hart, "Book Reviews" (1964–1965) 78 Harv L Rev 1281 at 1284.

[24]Jutta Brunnée and Stephen J. Toope, "International Law and Constructivism: Elements of an Interactional Theory of International Law" (2000–2001) 39 Colum J Transnat'l L 19 at 47; their view is similar to McDougal, who once dismissed certain schools of jurisprudence that "continue to present 'law' as a 'autonomous science or art, cleanly severable from the community processes which condition it and it in turn affects", Myres S. McDougal, "The Ethics of Applying System of Authority: The Balanced Opposites of a Legal System" in Harold D. Lasswell and Harland Cleveland, eds, *The Ethics of Power: The Interplay of Religion, Philosophy, and Politics* (New York: Harper 1962) 221 at 228.

purposes of the argument in this book is that it provides a convincing explanation of legal obligations regardless of the normative form in which it is expressed; it "instructs that it is crucial not to mistake the formal representation of law for successful law-making".[25]

Since the later part of the 20th century, a number of scholars collectively identified as NAIL[26] (New Approaches to International Law) have constructed a critique to both approaches that focuses on the structure of the legal argument. Epistemologically speaking, the critique situates itself above sources discourse, and addresses the possibility of mutually contradictory positions based on the same materials.[27] For NAIL, "[n]orms are legally binding which fit within one of a series of doctrinally elaborated categories, not when a persuasive argument about political interest or theoretical coherence can be made about their observance."[28] That is, it accepts the substantive indeterminacy of the law, while proposing a theory of legal argument based on language in order to account for the coherence of the system.[29] In that sense, the New Approaches are less interested with the identification of law as a task of the legal operator, but in how such a task reveals the deep structure of the legal argument. Both source theory and the practice of international tribunals in identifying the law are used by NAIL to show how the contradiction between consent and sovereignity as the ultimate foundation of legal authority.[30]

An interesting common thread among the theories described above is the general dissatisfaction with the doctrine of sources,[31] and particularly the challenges this doctrine faces in accommodating "the growing normative activity outside the classical law-making framework."[32]

[25]Brunnée and Toope, *Legitimacy and Legality*, *supra* note 7 at 47.

[26]See José María Beneyto, et al (eds), *New Approaches to International Law: The European and the American Experiences* (The Hague: TMC Asser Press, 2012).

[27]Martti Koskenniemi, "Letter to the Editors of the Symposium" (2004) 36 Stud Transnat'l Legal Pol'y 109 at 114.

[28]David Kennedy, "A new stream of international law scholarship" (1988–1989) 7 Wis Int'l LJ 1 at 31.

[29]Kennedy uses unilateral declarations to illustrate this point in David Kennedy, "The Sources of International Law" (1987) 2:1 Am U Int'l L Rev 1 at 50–51.

[30]Ibid at 88; see also David Kennedy, "Theses about International Law discourse" (1980) 23 Ger Yb Int'l L 353 at 378–382; Martti Koskenniemi, *From apology to Utopia: the structure of international legal argument* (Cambridge: Cambridge University Press, 2005) at 303–387.

[31]From the process-based camp, see e.g. Myres S. McDougal, "International law, power, and policy: a contemporary conception" (1953) 82 Rec des Cours 133 at 143 ("The most fundamental obscurity in contemporary theory about international law secretes itself in over-emphasis, by most writers and many decision-makers, upon the potentialities of technical "legal" rules, unrelated to policies, as factors and instruments in the guiding and shaping of decisions."); Rosalyn Higgins, *Problems and Process: International Law and How We Use It* (Oxford: Oxford University Press, 1994) at 18; for similar views from the rule-based approaches, see the text in: *supra* note 16.

[32]Aspremont, *Formalism*, *supra* note 15 at 221–222.

5.3 The Theory of Alf Ross

Although I have pointed out that there are interesting aspects in the above-described theories, which have influenced my reasoning to some extent, the work of Alf Ross has provided the most important insights upon which my hypothesis is based.

Ross, who has been described as having a "'realist' view based on 'socio-psychological experiences'",[33] was of the opinion that a source of law "means the general factors (motive components) which guide the judge when fixing and making concrete the legal content in judicial decisions."[34] This conclusion was based on his belief that judicial decisions play a decisive role in the international legal system in making concrete legal ideas out of the different factors, which include but are not limited to existing rules.[35] Interestingly, such a belief was partially shared by Kelsen.[36] Admittedly, Ross' rejection of the taxonomy embraced by rule-based approaches make his views akin to the those of the New Haven school,[37] with the exception that he was not concerned with all international decision-making but exclusively with the judicial decision. In his view, "the concrete decisions arise largely out of impulses not previously established by rules."[38] Instead of restricting the elements that play a role in the judicial decision to certain normative forms, Ross stated that three types of factors determine the judicial decision:

1. "The legal maxims authoritatively formulated in accordance with certain rules."[39] Treaties would fall under this category.

---

[33]Ole Spiermann, "A National Lawyer Takes Stock: Professor Ross' Textbook and Other Forays into International Law" (2003) 14:4 EJIL 675 at 677.

[34]Ross, *supra* note 10 at 80 (emphasis from the original).

[35]Ibid at 80–81.

[36]Hans Kelsen, *Law and Peace in International Relations: The Oliver Wendell Holmes Lectures, 1940–41* (Cambridge: Harvard University Press, 1942) at 162 ("One should not overlook the important fact that in the last analysis the law is not only and exclusively what the legislator more or less clearly sets forth or what the general rule of customary law more or less comprehensibly implies. Law is also what the courts finally decide in a concrete case.") [Kelsen, *Law and Peace*]; see also Lars Vinx, *Hans Kelsen's Pure Theory of Law: Legality and Legitimacy* (Oxford: Oxford University Press, 2007) at 197 (Kelsen "explicitly rejects the claim that a system of general positive legal norms could fully and precisely determine the legal meaning of all particular acts in advance of judicial proceedings.")

[37]Rosalyn Higgins, "Policy Considerations and the International Judicial Process" (1968) 17:1 ICLQ 58 at 59 (For Higgins, "[w]hen, however, decisions are made by authorized persons or organs, in appropriate forums, within the framework of certain established practice and norms, then what occurs is *legal* decision-making"); see also Harold D. Lasswell and Myres S. McDougal, "Legal Education and Public Policy: Professional Training in the Public Interest" (1943) 52 Yale LJ 203 at 266.

[38]Ross, *supra* note 10 at 80.

[39]Ibid at 81.

2. "The not formulated, yet partially objectified, rules of conduct emerging from the precedents of courts themselves, and from legal customs of those subject to them."[40] Under this category, he included all those rules that would have to be deduced from previous judicial decisions or from the social practice of subjects of international law.
3. "The free, not formulated, not objectified factors spontaneously arising in the judge as the mouthpiece of the community to which he belongs and to which he serves."[41] He included legal principles in this category.

The most interesting aspect of the group of three factors presented by Ross is that, although defined by their level of 'formulation' and 'objectification', their hierarchical application does not seem to flow from their nature but from the manner in which free factors are rationalized in mainstream legal discourse. That is:

> The effects of the free factors especially manifest themselves in the "interpretation" of the objective sources. That is to say, the result actually emerging from a co-operation between the objectivated sources and the free factors is — in order to conceal the creative activity — fictitiously ascribed to the objectivated sources alone and is said to be "deduced" from these by "interpretation".[42]

It flows from Ross' theory on sources that the expectations of the international community as to the role of the judge in the decision-making process heavily influence how he/she understands his/her own function. Otherwise, there will be no need to 'conceal the creative activity' of the judge, or much less, justify it on the basis of interpretation. That is, the judge is conscious of the need to base his/her decisions on the formulated law applicable to a dispute, but he/she is also aware that other factors may influence his/her decision. Such factors will ultimately be incorporated by means of interpretation without much regard to their actual normative value. Ross is silent on the motives of the judge for maintaining this fiction: perhaps the judge attempts to remain faithful to the tradition in which he/she operates or to ensure that his/her activity not become self-defeating by avoiding methodological critiques. In any case, Ross' theory does not reject the doctrine of sources, but merely displaces it from its canonical position to a psychosocial fact that shapes the judge's activity. Holterman, in discussing Ross's general legal theory, has stated that his is "a doctrine of how judges believe that they ought to behave in their capacity as judges; of which rights and duties they believe that they have (and hence, but only indirectly, which rights and duties they believe that the citizens have)."[43] In this sense, NAIL coincides with Ross in that "*[f]inalement, ce*

---

[40]Ibid at 81.

[41]Ibid at 81–82.

[42]Ibid at 92.

[43]Holtermann, Jakob v. H. "Getting Real Or Staying Positive Legal Realism(s), Legal Positivism And The Prospects Of Naturalism In Jurisprudence" online: University of Copenhagen <http://curis.ku.dk/ws/files/40358538/HOLTERMANN_Getting_real_or_staying_positive_DRAFT_2012_05_27.pdf>.

seront les preferences politiques du tribunal qui constitueront les facteurs les plus importants de la constitution de la decision".[44]

Having said that, the use of external sources by international human rights courts discussed in Chap. 3 provide the context upon which Ross's ideas can be tested. That is, it is plausible to conceptualise the phenomena described in the previous chapter as the masked interaction of objectivated and non-objectivated factors, instead of accepting them as interpretation.

The postulate is not without problems as external sources are often treaties, which would fall in the category of objectivated factors. Such is the example of the use of CRC by the Inter-American Court to interpret the content of Article 19 of the American Convention. Ross' factors make no difference with regard to applicability, but as his approach was by definition casuistic, it would not be illogical to assume that his factors are delimited by the boundaries of formal applicability to the specific case. In other words, as the CRC is neither valid nor applicable law in the context of the judicial function of the Inter-American Court, its content cannot be said to reflect formulated and objectivated law, but a factor equal to general legal principles in Ross's theory. This is so because the development of what follows from the rules of the CRC, as far as they are reflected in Article 19 of the American Convention, "would only be possible in relation to a concrete situation or at any rate in relation to particular legal questions and would in any case have an extremely vague, very subjective character."[45]

The same logic can be applied when discussing norms external to the jurisdiction of the human rights courts by virtue of their capacity to bind the State —that is, when the courts have based their interpretation of the norms contained in an instrument covered by their jurisdiction by reference to non-binding instruments collectively called 'soft law', or by reference to the precedent of other regional courts in the application of their respective regional instruments. In these cases it is even clearer that the level of objectivation is trumped by the fact that rules derived from these factors highly depend on the particular legal question and cannot be abstractly defined. In the case of an external precedent, the use of a particular dicta will depend on whether the right of the treaty being interpreted is substantively similar to the right interpreted by the external decision and whether the motives presented in the external decision are applicable to the regional particularities and normative environment in which the treaty being interpreted operates.

In sum, the framework provided by Ross allows for an analysis of the use of external sources by the international human rights courts beyond the traditional doctrine of sources and the customary rules of interpretation of treaties. In this framework, interpretation would be considered the rhetorical strategy by which the creative activity of the judge is justified and subsumed under the traditional doctrine of sources.

---

[44]Rémi Bachand, "La Critique en Droit International: Réflexions autour des Livres de Koskenniemi, Anghie et Miéville", (2006) 19 RQDI 1 at 12.

[45]Ross, *supra* note 10 at 91.

5.4 Adjusting the Theory

Although Ross's ideas on international law received mixed reviews during his lifetime[46] they provide an interesting insight to the way in which international law is conceived as a discipline and how it operates. They are, however, still a product of a time when international organizations and bodies did not play such an important role as they do today in international governance. In order to do justice to his theory in the light of new phenomena in international law, I will adjust the specifics of his source theory in international law to the realities faced today by international jurists.

5.4.1 From Judicial Decisions to International Decision-Making

More than half a century after the publication of Ross's international law manual, the iconic place that judicial decisions play in his theory is reminiscent of the treatment that those decisions received in the ILC Report on Fragmentation. In his view, "[t]he judicial decision is the pulse of legal life",[47] as "it is never merely 'application of the law', but always to a certain extent 'creation of law' also."[48] The ILC report discussed relationships between norms "especially by reference to the practice of international courts and tribunals".[49] Moreover, in order to illustrate the issue of fragmentation, the report cited the three cases initiated in three different fora concerning the MOX Plant nuclear facility at Sellafield, UK.[50]

In this regard, it has been argued that Ross's reliance on the jurisprudence of international courts produces results that are similar to the traditional doctrine of sources, as Ross's theory concentrates the inquiry on a limited number of judicial decisions.[51] Leaving aside the fact that the number of international courts and tribunals has grown exponentially since the publication of Ross's textbook, in modern international law the judicial decision is one of many instances where legal

---

[46]Kunz said of the book that it is "a work which no serious student of international law can afford to ignore", Josef L. Kunz, "Book Reviews and Notes: A Text Book of International Law. By Alf Ross" (1949) 43 AJIL 197 at 199; however, Green described the book as "ordinary nonsense", L.C. Green, "Book Reviews: A Text-Book of International Law. By Professor Alf Ross" (1948) 2:2 Int'l L Q 275 at 277.

[47]Ross, *supra* note 10 at 80.

[48]Ibid at 82.

[49]*Fragmentation of International Law: Difficulties arising from the Diversification and Expansion of International Law: Report of the Study Group of the International Law Commission*, UNGAOR, 61st Sess, Supp. No. 10, UN Doc. A/CN.4/L.682 at para 20 [*Fragmentation Report*].

[50]Ibid at paras 10–12.

[51]Clive Parry, *The Sources and Evidences of International Law* (Manchester: Manchester University Press, 1965) at 7.

norms are discussed, applied and developed. International institutions nowadays include bodies such as binational river commissions, regional fisheries management organizations or arrangements, multilateral peace and security fora and treaty review bodies. Their functions range from advisory to quasi-judicial, but they remain *loci* in which the content and extent of the law is debated and clarified.

To exclude such fora from this analysis would go against the logic that Ross himself advances through his factors. Therefore, I propose that insights about the structure of international legal obligations are not exclusively found in judicial decisions. That is, every situation in which a body created by international law is called to evaluate facts in the light of international law is a relevant place to inquire about the identification of the scope of a legal obligation and about law-creation itself. Admittedly, this adjustment brings Ross closer to process-based approaches such as International Legal Process, as one of its representatives is of the view that: "[i]nternational law is the whole process of competent persons making authoritative decisions in response to claims which various parties are pressing upon them".[52] However, critical differences exist between the process-based approaches and the re-statement of Ross that I propose. In regards to the New Have School, McDougal defended his policy-oriented framework as a theory *about* international law (as opposed to a theory *of* international law) in which "the scholarly inquirer assumes an observational stand-point relatively apart from the process of authoritative decision being observed, attempting to free himself in the highest degree possible from the limiting perspectives of internal participants".[53]

5.4.2 From Free Factors to External Instruments

Up to now, this book has adopted the language used by Ross in the description of the factors. In Chap. 2, divine law, natural law and general principles of law—up until 1945—were described as non-objectified sources that provided flexibility to the international jurist. In Chap. 3, I argued that the development of general principles of law from 1945 to the present has made them partially objectified. In the same chapter, I discussed the objectification that the constant citing of judicial decisions has lent to certain customary rules. These, however, were instances in which the sources were classified by their level of 'formulation' and 'objectification', but not on the basis of their applicability to a particular case.

---

[52]Higgins, *supra* note 27 at 59; as for the New Haven school, see also W. Michael Reisman, "The View from the New Haven School of International Law, The Jurisprudence of International Law: Classic and Modern Views" (1992) 86 ASIL Proc. 118 at 119 ("The New Haven School of jurisprudence is an entirely secular theory of law but it takes the perspective long associated with natural law, that of the decision maker.")

[53]Myres S. McDougal, "Some Basic Theoretical Concepts About International Law: A Policy-Oriented Framework of Inquiry" 4:3 J Conflict Resolution 337 at 337.

I have already argued in the current chapter that sources external to the jurisdiction of an international court can be conceptualized as free or non-objectivated factors in the language of Ross, as their normative value can be described only in relation to a particular situation. Having said that, I want to frame this argument with the socio-psychological aspects of Ross' theory, and specifically in the behaviour of the judge both as a jurist and as an institution of international law.

It is evident that Ross does not completely do away with all aspects related to the doctrine of sources. Although the level of objectivation is the defining character of his factors, it does not mean that the judge ignores the rules that govern his own function and the tradition in which he operates. That is to say, if the judge is bound to make a decision on the basis of a treaty, his decision—independent of the factors that motivated such a decision—will be framed on the basis of that treaty. However, in defining the scope of the legal obligation contained in the treaty, factors beyond the treaty itself will come into play. In Ross' theory, the judge is so cautious that any operation that includes non-objectivated norms will be labelled as interpretation. Ross' judge is by no means an automaton, but a rational being who follows his particular understanding of what the law is. He does not blindly follow the doctrine of sources, nor does he rebel against it: his is a gentle evolution in which the law is constantly reshaped by the influx of ideas that may or may not come in the form of legal rules.

Reading Ross' first factor as encompassing all treaties, regardless of their general validity and applicability to a given case, would mean that the judge is only partially aware of the tradition in which he operates. That is, the same judge who would advance the idea that an international obligation found in a treaty must be applied to a case as 'interpreted' in accordance with a general principle of law, cannot rationally decide to directly apply a non-ratified treaty to a case.

5.5 The Normative Plurality Hypothesis

As discussed above, the theory of sources developed by Ross provided a framework in which norms that otherwise would not have effect in a given dispute are used by the judge in crafting his/her decision. However, Ross' theory does not develop the guiding notions that assist the judge in determining the norms that are relevant for a given case.

Departing from the framework provided by Ross's theory, with the adjustments already discussed, I will develop in this section the normative plurality hypothesis which is based in the mutually reinforcing notions that guide the judge in determining the scope and extent of the law applicable to a particular case.

5.5.1 Three Guiding Notions

Since the introductory chapter, I have argued that the ICJ's understanding of what constitutes international law is preconditioned by three interdependent aspects: the legal tradition in which the Court operates, the rules that define the scope of its functions, and the Court's understanding of its role in the international legal system. I have also argued that these aspects precondition the definition of international law that persists in all international decision-making. I acknowledge that each of these aspects is very broad and encompasses many notions. My argument in this section is that the changes in the international legal system brought about by the influence of human rights on public international law have also changed the understanding of the aspects that precondition the definition of what constitutes international law. That is to say: in theorizing the means by which modern international-decision making understands and reflects normativity, what has changed is not the general aspects that determine the outcome, but the importance given to certain notions within such aspects. In the next subsections, I will discuss three interdependent notions that guide the decision-maker in defining what constitutes the norms applicable to a particular situation: specificity, completeness and purpose.

5.5.1.1 Reframing the Tradition Towards Specificity

In this subsection I will develop specificity as one of the guiding notions that assist the decision-maker in defining the relevant norms. The notion of specificity corresponds to the traditional aspect of international law. H.P. Glenn has defended a concept of legal tradition as "normative information that may be gathered or capture over a long period of time".[54] In Glenn's concept, a particular tradition already provides knowledge as to what constitutes normative information, but takes into account the effect that time has had on the information.

Admittedly, more often than not a decision-maker will not think of the international legal system as a tradition, or even consider the implications of information gathered before the 20th century. However, this does not mean that the decision-maker does not rely on an understanding of what constitutes relevant information, which can only be acquired by that information being transmitted to him/her.[55] In turn, his/her decision becomes part of the information that feeds the tradition.

Initially, I discussed the aspect of the tradition in reference to the *Nuclear Weapons* advisory opinion, arguing that the opinion of the Court identified international law as a law of coordination on the point concerning "an extreme circumstance of self-defence, in which the very survival of the State would be at

[54] H. Patrick Glenn, "A Concept of Legal Tradition" (2008–2009) 34 Queen's LJ 427 at 438.
[55] Ibid.

stake."[56] That is, while not specifically quoting the *Lotus* dictum, the decision suggested[57] that "[t]he rules of law binding upon States therefore emanate from their own free will".[58] This is true, of course, if international law is understood as "the aggregate of legal norms governing international relations"[59] and not as a full-fledged system.[60] What this means in terms of the tradition is that the normative information was only that emanating from States, and in certain defined forms.[61] In the absence of such normative information prohibiting certain conduct, States are at liberty to act. However, I have shown in the previous chapter that the decisions of international human rights courts—and the ICJ itself in human rights cases—have expanded the normative information of the tradition so as to encompass forms other than those mentioned in the *Lotus* dictum.

The expansion is not tremendously adventurous. Most of the normative information that has been included emanates from international bodies, which have been established by States or in which States participate as members. It is granted here that the intention of the States is not for these bodies to create international legal obligations, but it can be reasonably expected from the mandate given by the States to these bodies that specific aspects of obligations already contracted be discussed and clarified. It is my view that the normative information of the tradition is not formed exclusively by the obligations contracted by States, but also by the specific aspects of such obligations as developed by bodies created by States with the purpose, express or implied, of discussing and clarifying the specific content of an obligation.

I must note that the notion of specificity is not alien to the source doctrine. There has been much discussion about the specificity of international norms as a consequence of the hierarchy of its sources.

The notion of specificity advanced here is eminently substantive—that is, on whether substantively speaking, a normative instrument provides for a specific understanding of an existing obligation in international law. In the *Diallo* judgement, the ICJ provided an interesting example of the type of specificity here

---

[56] *Legality of the Threat or Use of Nuclear Weapons Case*, Advisory Opinion, [1996] ICJ Rep 226 (reprinted in 35 ILM 809) at 105.2.E.

[57] Contra, Ige F. Dekker and Wouter G. Werner, "The Completeness of International Law and Hamlet's Dilemma—Non Liquet, The Nuclear Weapons Case and Legal Theory" (1999) 68 Nordic J Int'l L 225 at 234.

[58] *The Case of the S.S. "Lotus"* (France v. Turkey) (1927), PCIJ (Ser. A) No. 10 at 18 [*Lotus*].

[59] Ibid at 413; quoting Paul Guggenheim, Traité de droit international public (Geneve: Librarie Georg, 1967) at 1.

[60] See *Report of the International Law Commission: Fifty-eight session*, UNGAOR, 61st Sess, Supp. No. 10, UN Doc A/61/10 (2006) at para 251 (conclusion 1) [*Report of the ILC, 58th Session*].

[61] *Lotus*, *supra* note 58 at 18 ("…as expressed in conventions or by usages generally accepted as expressing principles of law…").

discussed. When dealing with the possible violation of Article 9 of the ICCPR[62] and Article 6 of the African Charter,[63] the Court stated:

> First of all, it is necessary to make a general remark. The provisions of Article 9, paragraphs 1 and 2, of the Covenant, and those of Article 6 of the African Charter, apply in principle to any form of arrest or detention decided upon and carried out by a public authority, whatever its legal basis and the objective being pursued (see in this respect, with regard to the Covenant, the Human Rights Committee's General Comment No. 8 of 30 June 1982 concerning the right to liberty and security of person (Human Rights Committee, CCPR General Comment No. 8: Article 9 (Right to Liberty and Security of Person))). The scope of these provisions is not, therefore, confined to criminal proceedings; they also apply, in principle, to measures which deprive individuals of their liberty that are taken in the context of an administrative procedure, such as those which may be necessary in order to effect the forcible removal of an alien from the national territory.[64]

The statement of the ICJ echoes what international human rights institutions have understood for decades: that judicial guarantees such as the ones found in Article 9 of the ICCPR are to be understood as applying to any legal proceedings, unless, because of their nature, they are specifically tailored for criminal proceedings.[65] While the extension of general procedural guarantees to all types of judicial proceedings constitutes settled law in the Universal and Inter-American systems for the protection of human rights, the idea is not without controversy. Many of the guarantees that are considered general in both systems are included in an article or paragraph that unequivocally refers to criminal proceedings.[66] In the case of

---

[62] *International Covenant on Civil and Political Rights*, 16 December 1966, 999 UNTS 171 at art 9, (1967) 6 ILM 368 ("1. Everyone has the right to liberty and security of person. No one shall be subjected to arbitrary arrest or detention. No one shall be deprived of his liberty except on such grounds and in accordance with such procedure as are established by law. 2. Anyone who is arrested shall be informed, at the time of arrest, of the reasons for his arrest and shall be promptly informed of any charges against him.")

[63] African Charter on Human and Peoples' Rights, 27 June 1981, 1520 UNTS 271 at art 6, (1982) 21 ILM 58 ("Every individual shall have the right to liberty and to the security of his person. No one may be deprived of his freedom except for reasons and conditions previously laid down by law. In particular, no one may be arbitrarily arrested or detained.")

[64] *Ahmadou Sadio Diallo (Republic of Guinea v. Democratic Republic of the Congo)*, Merits, Judgment, [2010] ICJ Rep 639 at para 77 (reprinted in 50 ILM 40) [*Ahmadou Sadio Diallo*, Merits].

[65] *Exceptions to the Exhaustion of Domestic Remedies (Arts. 46(1), 46(2)(a) and 46 (2)(b) of the American Convention on Human Rights)* (1990), Advisory Opinion OC-11/90, Inter-Am Ct HR (Ser A) No 11, at para 28; see also *Case of Ivcher-Bronstein (Peru)* (2001), Inter-Am Cr HR (Ser C) No. 74, at paras 103–105.

[66] *Case of Ivcher-Bronstein*, ibid at para 104 ("The Court has established that, although this article does not stipulate minimum guarantees in matters which concern the determination of the rights and obligations of a civil, labor, fiscal or any other nature, the minimum guarantees established in paragraph 2 of the article should also apply to those categories and, therefore, in that respect, a person has the right to due process in the terms recognized for criminal matters, to the extent that it is applicable to the respective procedure."); see also Human Rights Committee, General Comment No. 32, Article 14: Right to equality before courts and tribunals and to a fair trial, U.N. Doc. CCPR/C/GC/32 (2007).

guarantees specifically linked to the right of liberty and security of persons, both the ICCPR and American Convention contain language vague enough to raise the question as to whether the arrest or detention has to be linked to a criminal proceeding. In contrast, the European Convention provides for protection against unlawful arrest or detention, except in six specific situations.[67]

In other words, Article 5 of the European Convention provides the judges of the European Court with enough specific normative information on the types of detention or arrest that are considered unlawful as to render the question of the nature of the proceedings superfluous. Inversely, the ICCPR and the American Convention lack such specificity and are, at best, constructively ambiguous.

In *Diallo*, the ICJ addressed the ambiguity in the ICCPR by making direct reference to the 1982 General Comment No. 8 of the HRC, which states that the guarantees found in paragraph 1 and 4 of Article 9 of the Covenant are "applicable to all deprivations of liberty, whether in criminal cases or in other cases such as, for example, mental illness, vagrancy, drug addiction, educational purposes, immigration control, etc".[68] While the Court had already stated that it "is in no way obliged [...] to model its own interpretation of the Covenant on that of the Committee",[69] the fact remains that it chose to refer specifically to the General Comment when arriving at the same conclusion. I argue that such a gesture by the Court is evidence of a broadening of the tradition to include the normative information generated by bodies whose existence and operation have been accepted by States.

Admittedly, the expansion of the normative information in the tradition here proposed is similar to the outcomes proposed by the New Haven School. Richard Falk, in critiquing Myres McDougal as a theorist, stated that "because of his insistence upon contextual analysis, McDougal makes the environment of world affairs relevant to any particular decision about the meaning of a legal rule".[70] The

---

[67]*European Convention for the Protection of Human Rights and Fundamental Freedoms*, Europ TS No 5, 213 UNTS 211 at art 5 ("(a) the lawful detention of a person after conviction by a competent court; (b) the lawful arrest or detention of a person for non-compliance with the lawful order of a court or in order to secure the fulfilment of any obligation prescribed by law; (c) the lawful arrest or detention of a person effected for the purpose of bringing him before the competent legal authority on reasonable suspicion of having committed an offence or when it is reasonably considered necessary to prevent his committing an offence or fleeing after having done so; (d) the detention of a minor by lawful order for the purpose of educational supervision or his lawful detention for the purpose of bringing him before the competent legal authority; (e) the lawful detention of persons for the prevention of the spreading of infectious diseases, of persons of unsound mind, alcoholics or drug addicts or vagrants; (f) the lawful arrest or detention of a person to prevent his effecting an unauthorised entry into the country or of a person against whom action is being taken with a view to deportation or extradition.") [ECHR].

[68]Human Rights Committee, General Comment No. 8: Right to liberty and security of persons (Art. 9), U.N. Doc. U.N. Doc. HRI/GEN/1/Rev.1 at 8 (1994).

[69]*Ahmadou Sadio Diallo*, Merits, *supra* note 64 at para 66.

[70]Richard A. Falk, "The Adequacy of Contemporary Theories of International Law—Gaps in Legal Thinking" (1964) 50 Va L Rev 231 at 234.

difference lies in the weight given to the notion of specificity. The notion is crucial to understanding the extent to which the normative information in the tradition, as a socio-psychological fact available to the decision-maker, assists in the determination of the law in a specific case, instead of becoming a blanket statement about the relevance of multilateral diplomacy in international law. In other words, there is no need for the decision-maker to consider redundant or irrelevant normative information. Only information that clearly serves the purpose of giving specific content to an obligation for a particular case should be considered part of the tradition by the decision-maker. While the repetition of identical normative information produced by different international institutions may calm the anxieties of fragmentation theorists, it accomplishes very little in terms of clarifying the scope of a legal obligation.

There are also clear problems when mistaking the substantive specificity here proposed with the formal specificity advanced in the *Gulf of Maine* case.[71] Firstly, it reinforces structural arguments suggesting that "rules derived from one source prevail over rules derived from another source".[72] Secondly, and if taken to extremes, it could suggest that non-binding instruments constitute lower-level normativity irrespective of their author and content.[73]

In sum, the decision-maker cannot understand the tradition of international law as a static element. Instead, it must search for the specific content that gives sense to the obligations contracted by States, especially in situations where constructive ambiguity has been used as a means of arriving at consensus and of engendering wide participation among members of the international community in a given binding instrument.[74]

---

[71]"As already noted, customary international law merely contains a general requirement of the application of equitable criteria and the utilization of practical methods capable of implementing them. It is therefore special international law that must be looked to, in order to ascertain whether that law, as at present in force between the Parties to this case, does or does not include some rule specifically requiring the Parties, and consequently the Chamber, to apply certain criteria or certain specific practical methods to the delimitation that is requested.", *Delimitation of the Maritime Boundary in the Gulf of Maine Area (Canada v. United States of America)*, [1984] ICJ Rep 246 at para 111 and 114 (reprinted in 23 ILM 1197).

[72]Michael Akehurst and Peter Malanczuk, *Modern Introduction to International Law*, 7th ed (New York: Rutledge, 2007) at 374.

[73]Especially because if we accept that soft law is lower-level normativity, in practical term law cannot be more or less binding and more or less complied with, see Jan Klabbers, 'The Redundancy of Soft Law' (1996) 65 Nordic J Int'l L 167; Jan Klabbers, 'The Undesirability of Soft Law' (1998) 67 Nordic J Int'l L 381; interestingly, Dupuy has argued that the criteria to identify soft law should be "*substantial, i.e., dependent on the nature and specificity of the behavior requested of the State*", Pierre Marie Dupuy, "Soft Law and the International Law of the Environment" (1990–1991) 12 Mich J Int'l L 420 at 430.

[74]In the context of the Rome Statute, it has been argued that "by resorting to the use of 'constructive ambiguity,' the drafters did leave open opportunities for a positive and precedent-setting approach", Valerie Oosterveld, "The Definition of Gender in the Rome Statute of the International Criminal Court: A Step Forward or Back for International Criminal Justice" (2005) 18 Harv Hum Rts J 1 at 58.

5.5.1.2 The First Rule Is Completeness

In this subsection, I will develop completeness as the second guiding notion to assist the decision-maker in defining the relevant norms in a particular case. The notion of completeness corresponds to the aspect of regulation of the decision-maker's activity in international law. In the introductory chapter, I discussed regulation by introducing Article 38 of the Statute of the ICJ and by discussing prohibitions of *non-liquet* and of judicial legislation. Evidently, these are not the only rules governing the judicial functions of the ICJ, but my analysis demonstrated the inherent tension that arises when an international court must find legal answers to all legal questions put to their consideration, while the sources in which these answers can be sought are limited.

At this stage, it is impractical, if not impossible, to state all the rules that govern decision-making activities of international bodies. It suffices to state that international bodies are generally bound to perform their functions in accordance with rules created by them or imposed on them by a governing entity. Such rules remain an important socio-psychological factor for decision-makers, especially when choosing how to better reflect their decision in written form. However, the idea that I wish to advance in this section is that among the rules applicable to decision-makers in the exercise of their functions, there is a principle of completeness of international law.[75] This principle, which constitutes the paramount notion for the decision-maker when weighing the restrictions to his activity, provides that "every international situation is capable of being determined as a matter of law".[76]

The concept of completeness has been extensively discussed in international law, principally from two opposing approaches: the formal completeness developed by Kelsen and the theory of material completeness[77] elaborated by Judge Lauterpacht.

The issue of gaps in international law specifically preoccupied Kelsen. He considered the existence of a case in which neither conventional nor general law was applicable to be logically impossible. From that point of view, it was always possible to know whether a State was obliged to act in a particular way or not.[78] Kelsen's claim of the completeness of international law depends on the existence of a compulsory judiciary,[79] as he relies on judicial actors for its effective

[75]Contra Julius Stone, "Non Liquet and the Function of Law in the International Community" (1959) 35 Brit YB Int'l L 124.

[76]Lassa Oppenheim, Robert Y. Jennings and C.A.H. Watts, *Oppenheim's international law*, 9th ed (London: Longmans, 1993) at 13.

[77]Martti Koskenniemi, "'The Lady Doth Protest Too Much' Kosovo, and the Turn to Ethics in International Law" (2002) 65:2 Modern L Rev 159 at fn 10.

[78]See Hans Kelsen, "Théorie du droit international public" (1953) 84 Rec des Cours 1 at 120 [Kelsen, "Théorie"].

[79]Kelsen, *Law and Peace*, *supra* note 36 at 117–119; see also Vinx, *supra* note 36 at 198; Jochen von Bernstorff, *The Public International Law Theory of Hans Kelsen: Believing in Universal Law*, trans by Thomas Dunlap (Cambridge: Cambridge University Press, 2010) at 212–213.

application.[80] However he noted that in the hypothetical case that an organ was authorized to fill *lacunae* by reference to norms other than treaties and custom, the implication was that the organ could create new norms if it did not find that the existing norms were satisfactory.[81] Kelsen found this to be in accordance with his own positivistic theories, as there was a norm authorizing the creation of a new norm, which would logically be a lower level norm than those providing for the jurisdiction of the organ.

Judge Lauterpacht advanced the idea of a principle of completeness of international law with regard to disputes submitted to a judicial entity—the positive formulation of the prohibition of *non-liquet*. In his view "once the parties have submitted a dispute for judicial determination, the principle of the completeness of the legal order fully applies, with the result that all disputes thus submitted are capable of a legal solution."[82] In Judge Lauterpacht's view, this was a consequence of the inherent powers of the international judicial entities to fill imperfections in lawmaking—or what he called 'real gaps'—by means of genuine interpretation "even if, as the result, the function of interpretation seems to assume the character of judicial legislation proper."[83]

In my view, there is a risk in adopting the Kelsenian approach, as it suggests that the *Lotus* dictum, stating that "[r]estrictions upon the independence of States cannot [...] be presumed"[84] operates as a residual rule in the system, providing for a fail-safe solution to all disputes.[85] Judge Lauterpacht denounced such reasoning as "intellectual inertia or short-sightedness",[86] and warned that if such a view is adopted "we come dangerously near to lending ourselves to the use of a narrow and unscientific method which will defeat the very end of law".[87] Instead, the notion of completeness advanced here corresponds to Judge Lauterpacht's recognition that

---

[80]Vinx, *supra* note 36 at 198 ("It is true that the claim to completeness can be sustained only through partly discretionary exercises of authority on the part of courts. But this is not a special defect of international law; rather, it is a general truth about any kind of legal order."); Bernstorff, ibid at 212–213 ("As Kelsen saw it, the decision by the court created an individual legal norm by concretizing a norm of customary law or an international legal treaty").

[81]Kelsen, "Théorie", *supra* note 78 at 120.

[82]Hersch Lauterpacht, *The Development of International Law by the International Court* (New York: Cambridge University Press, 1982) at 4–5.

[83]Hersch Lauterpacht, *The Function of Law in the International Community* (Oxford: Clarendon Press, 1933) at 84 [Lauterpacht, *The Function*].

[84]*Lotus*, *supra* note 58 at 18; Hernandez has recently noted that in a recent advisory opinion, "the Court took a strong step in resuscitating *Lotus*" and the binary conception of legality; Gleider I. Hernandez, *The International Court of Justice and the Judicial Function* (Oxford: Oxford University Press, 2014) at 265.

[85]See Dekker and Werner, *supra* note 57.

[86]Lauterpacht, *The Function*, *supra* note 83 at 94.

[87]Ibid at 95.

the law is never formally complete and falls to the judge to come up with just, scientific and creative solutions within the limits provided by existing legal materials.

In order to illustrate the notion of completeness proposed in this section, I will discuss the judgment of the ICJ in the case concerning the *Pulp Mills on the River Uruguay*. It is a particularly interesting case because of the competing views between the parties as to how to supplement the provisions of a bilateral treaty, as well as the ultimate reliance by the Court on general international law.

In the early 2000s, the government of Uruguay authorized two international firms, ENCE and Oy Metsä-Botnia AB, to construct and operate pulp mills on its side of the Uruguay River.[88] The dispute became international because the Uruguay River marks the border between Uruguay and Argentina. Although all border issues between the two countries were settled in 1961,[89] a treaty was signed on 26 February 1975 to establish a joint administration of the river and clarify the rights of both States. Indeed, the Statute of the Uruguay River[90] establishes a joint administration of the river through an international commission called the *Comisión Administrativa del Río Uruguay*. The treaty accords many substantive rights to the parties and procedural mechanisms are set in place to comply with the purposes of the Statute.

The dispute became the center of attention among scholars on the fields of environmental law and sustainable development law, as it focuses on the tension between the three elements of sustainable development: ecological, economic and social concerns. As Allan Boyle put it to the Court, one of the issues was whether Uruguay has a right to "pursue sustainable economic development while doing everything possible to protect the environment of the river for the benefit of present and future generations of Uruguayans and Argentines alike."[91]

On its application to the ICJ, Argentina argued that Uruguay had failed to comply with the Statute of the Uruguay River, as well as with "other obligations deriving from the procedural and substantive provisions of general, conventional and customary international law which are necessary for the application of the Statute."[92]

[88]Maria A. del-Cerro, "Paper Battle on The River Uruguay: The International Dispute Surrounding the Construction of Pulp Mills" (2007) 20 Geo Int'l Envtl L Rev 161 at 172–173.

[89]*Treaty between the Argentine Republic and the Eastern Republic of Uruguay concerning the boundary constituted by the River Uruguay*, Argentina and Uruguay, 7 April 1961, 1970 UNTS 332.

[90]*Statute of the River Uruguay*, Argentina and Uruguay, 26 February 1975, 1295 UNTS 339.

[91]*Pulp Mills on the River Uruguay, Verbatim Record of the Public sitting*, at 30–31 (Jun. 8, 2006), online: International Court of Justice <http://www.icj-cij.org/docket/files/135/13128.pdf>; see also *Pulp Mills on the River Uruguay*, Order of 13 July 2006, 45 ILM 1025, at para 80, online: International Court of Justice <http://www.icj-cij.org/docket/files/135/11235.pdf>.

[92]Application Instituting Proceedings, Pulp Mills on the River Uruguay, (May 4, 2006) online: International Court of Justice <http://www.icj-cij.org/docket/files/135/10779.pdf>.

As a general point, Argentina relied on Articles 1[93] and 41 (a)[94] of the Statute of the Uruguay River, which it considered "referral clauses"[95] incorporating four multilateral agreements binding on the parties.[96] The Court was of the view that the language of the Statute did not suggest that the parties intended to incorporate obligations contracted in other treaties under the Statute of the Uruguay River.[97]

However, the most interesting part of the decision was the treatment of sources on the issue of environmental impact assessments. In this regard, both parties accepted that there is an obligation under the Statute of the Uruguay River to conduct environmental impact assessments, but they disagreed on the scope and content of such obligation.[98] Argentina argued that the Espoo Convention on Environmental Impact Assessment in a Transboundary Context and UNEP Governing Council decision 14/25 (Goals and Principles of Environmental Impact Assessment) provided guidance as to the requirements for environmental impact assessments in international law. It must be noted that neither of the parties to the dispute are—or can be—parties to the Espoo Convention. Uruguay's position was that the only requirements in international law are found in the International Law Commission 2001 draft Articles on Prevention of Transboundary Harm from Hazardous Activities.

On the issue of the existence of an obligation to conduct environmental impact assessments, the Court did not expressly confirm the belief of the parties that the Statute of the Uruguay River contains such an obligation.[99] Instead the Court was of the view that "in order for the Parties properly to comply with their obligations under Article 41 (a) and (b) of the 1975 Statute, they must [...] carry out an environmental impact assessment". This was so because:

---

[93]*Statute of the River Uruguay*, supra note 90 at art 1 ("The Parties agree on this Statute, in implementation of the provisions of article 7 of the Treaty concerning the Boundary Constituted by the River Uruguay, of 7 April 1961, 3 in order to establish the joint machinery necessary for the optimum and rational utilization of the River Uruguay, in strict observance of the rights and obligations arising from treaties and other international agreements in force for each of the Parties").

[94]Ibid at art 41 ("Without prejudice to the functions assigned to the Commission in this respect, the Parties undertake: (a) To protect and preserve the aquatic environment and, in particular, to prevent its pollution, by prescribing appropriate rules and measures in accordance with applicable international agreements and in keeping, where relevant, with the guidelines and recommendations of international technical bodies; ...").

[95]*Pulp Mills on the River Uruguay (Argentina v. Uruguay)*, [2010] ICJ Rep 14 at para 56 [*Pulp Mills*].

[96]*Convention on International Trade in Endangered Species of Wild Fauna and Flora*, 3 March 1973, 993 UNTS 243; *Convention on Wetlands of International Importance especially as Waterfowl Habitat*, 2 February 1971, 996 UNTS 245, (1972) 11 ILM 963; *Convention on Biological Diversity*, 5 June 1992, 1760 UNTS 79, 31 ILM 818; *Stockholm Convention on Persistent Organic Pollutants*, 22 May 2001, 2256 UNTS 119, (2001) 40 ILM 532.

[97]*Pulp Mills*, *supra* note 95 paras 59 and 62.

[98]Ibid at para 203.

[99]Cymie R. Payne, "Pulp Mills on the River Uruguay (Argentina v. Uruguay)" (2011) 105:1 AJIL 94 at 98.

> [T]he obligation to protect and preserve, under Article 41 (a) of the Statute, has to be interpreted in accordance with a practice, which in recent years has gained so much acceptance among States that it may now be considered a requirement under general international law to undertake an environmental impact assessment where there is a risk that the proposed industrial activity may have a significant adverse impact in a transboundary context, in particular, on a shared resource.[100]

The statement could not have been cause of surprise for the litigants, as both parties understood that an obligation existed in the Statute of the Uruguay River. Moreover, from the point of view of the source of the norm, it seems uncontroversial to say that "[g]eneral international law fills the gaps left by treaties."[101] However, it has been noted that "[o]ne of the most significant outcomes of the case is the Court's recognition that [environmental impact assessment] is a practice that has become an obligation of general international law"[102] in certain situations.[103]

It is clear that, in order to advance the objectives set forth in the Statute of the Uruguay River, the conclusion of environmental impact assessments is desirable for certain projects. But it seems that the Court was reluctant to find, even by interpretation, that the Statute contained an actual legal obligation to conduct such assessments. As the parties to the dispute proposed to draw the content of the obligation by reference to diverse instruments, the Court saw fit to first justify the existence of the obligation in general international law. The key aspect of the judgement is that it constitutes the first authoritative recognition of the existence of an obligation in international law to conduct environmental impact assessments under certain circumstances. As it is within the freedom of the Court to arrive at such a conclusion, it is debatable whether the ICJ ever recognised the existence of a gap in the Statute of the Uruguay River and whether the gap triggered the crystallization of the norm. No tribunal would happily announce the existence of a gap or suggest that it resorted to judicial creativity in order to fill it. However, I argue that the judgement in *Pulp Mills* constitutes a perfect example of the principle of completeness in operation. In the end, by virtue of the weight of the opinion of the

---

[100]*Pulp Mills*, *supra* note 95 para 205; see also.

[101]Joost Pauwelyn, "The Role of Public International Law in the WTO: How far can we go?" (2001) 95:3 AJIL 535 at 536.

[102]Payne, *supra* note 99 at 99; see also Laura Pineschi, "The Duty of Environmental Impact Assessment in the First ITLOS Chamber's Advisory Opinion: Towards the Supremacy of the General Rule to Protect and Preserve the Marine Environment as a Common Value?" in "Jurisdictional Immunities of the State and Exequatur of Foreign Judgments: a private International Law Evaluation of the Recent ICJ Judgment in Germany v. Italy" Nerina Boschiero, et al. (eds), *International Courts and the Development of International Law, Essays in Honour of Tullio Treves* (T.M.C. Asser Press, The Hague, The Netherlands, 2013) 425 at 427.

[103]Which was later expanded by the ICJ to any activityhaving the potential adversely to affect the environment of another State; *Certain Activities Carried Out by Nicaragua in the Border Area (Costa Rica v. Nicaragua)* and *Construction of a Road in Costa Rica along The San Juan River (Nicaragua v. Costa Rica)*, Judgment of 16 December 2015, online: ICJ <http://www.icj-cij.org/docket/files/150/18848.pdf> ("Although the Court's statement in the Pulp Mills case refers to industrial activities, the underlying principle applies generally to proposed activities which may have a significant adverse impact in a transboundary context.")

Court and the repetition of the Court findings by ITLOS, the obligation to conduct environmental impact assessments in certain circumstances is now considered customary law, including for industrial activities in areas beyond national jurisdiction.[104]

5.5.1.3 The Regime's Sense of Purpose

In this subsection, I will develop purpose as the last of the guiding notions that assist the decision-maker in defining the relevant norms in a particular case. The notion of purpose corresponds to the aspect of the decision-maker's understanding of his/her role in the international community.

Although the notion of purpose seems to be the most abstract of the ones discussed in this section, it is in fact the only one that has been codified in a multilateral convention. The VCLT contains several provisions in which the object and purpose of a treaty limit the freedom of States to perform acts such as reservations[105] and agreements modifying[106] or suspending[107] a multilateral treaty between certain of the parties only. Moreover, the customary rule of interpretation of treaties, as reflected in the VCLT, provides that treaties must be interpreted, *inter alia*, in light of their object and purpose.[108]

The notion of purpose here advanced is better explained by reference to two judicial decisions in which the purpose of the regime in which the tribunal operates or the purpose of the tribunal itself had an impact on the manner in which the judges understood the obligations of the parties to the dispute. In the following paragraphs, I will briefly discuss the judgment of the defunct UNAT in *Andronov*, and the decision of the ICTY on the defence motion for interlocutory appeal on jurisdiction in *Tadić*.

On 20 November 2003, the now defunct UNAT rendered its judgment on the *Andronov* case, which dealt with a series of administrative decisions affecting the rights of a former staff member of the UN Office in Geneva. In that case, the Administration initially argued that since there was no specific administrative decision to challenge, UNAT had no jurisdiction to decide. Although the Tribunal would adopt the view that there was indeed a series of implied administrative decisions that could be challenged, it made a point on the position adopted by the Administration:

---

[104]The customary nature of the obligation of conducting environmental impact assessments was confirmed by ITLOS in: *Responsibility and Obligations of States Sponsoring Persons and Entities with Respect to Activities in the Area, Seabed Dispute Chamber*, Advisory Opinion, [2011] ITLOS Rep 10 at paras 145 and 148.

[105]*Vienna Convention on the Law of Treaties*, 23 May 1969, 1155 UNTS 331 at art19 (c), (1969) 8 ILM 679.

[106]Ibid at art 41 (b) ii.

[107]Ibid at art 58.

[108]Ibid at art 31.

> The Respondent seems to indicate that there is a *lacuna* in the legal system of the United Nations, but fails to suggest how this *lacuna* would be filled.
>
> The Tribunal believes that the legal and judicial system of the United Nations must be interpreted as a comprehensive system, without *lacunae* and failures, so that the final objective, which is the protection of staff members against alleged non-observance of their contracts of employment, is guaranteed.[109]

As I previously stated, the message of UNAT is that there are indeed gaps in the law governing the relations between the United Nations and its staff members. However, the Tribunal suggests that it is impossible to say that no legal obligation exists in a given case, even if it needs to be constructed so as to give effect to the underlying purpose of the system in which the Tribunal operates.

The ICTY's decision on the defence motion for interlocutory appeal on jurisdiction in the *Tadić* case dealt with several challenges against the very existence of the Tribunal as well as its competence. One of the grounds of the appeal was that the Security Council gave jurisdiction to the Tribunal only over crimes committed in the context of an international armed conflict. The accused argued that, if proven, his alleged crimes were committed in the context of a non-international armed conflict. The issue actually deserved some clarification, as the Appeals Chamber recognised that "some provisions of the Statute are unclear as to whether they apply to offences occurring in international armed conflicts only, or to those perpetrated in internal armed conflicts as well."[110]

Although the Trial Chamber had decided that the Tribunal had jurisdiction regardless of the nature of the conflict,[111] the Appeals Chamber conducted an extensive teleological analysis of the Statute of the ICTY adopted by the Security Council,[112] especially in light of previous resolutions concerning the situation in the former Yugoslavia. The Appeals Chamber concluded:

> that the conflicts in the former Yugoslavia have both internal and international aspects, that the members of the Security Council clearly had both aspects of the conflicts in mind when they adopted the Statute of the International Tribunal, and that they intended to empower the International Tribunal to adjudicate violations of humanitarian law that occurred in either context. To the extent possible under existing international law, the Statute should therefore be construed to give effect to that purpose.[113]

---

[109] *Andronov v. Secretary-General of the United Nations*, Judgment of 20 November 2003, UNAT Judgment No. 1157, [2003] U.N. Jur. Yb. 497, UN Doc. AT/DEC/1157 at p 9 (emphasis is from the original).

[110] *The Prosecutor v. Duško Tadić (Prijedor Case)*, IT-94-1, Decision on the Defense Motion for Interlocutory Appeal on Jurisdiction (2 October 1995) at para 71 (International Tribunal for the of Former Yugoslavia, Appeals Chamber) [*Tadić*].

[111] *The Prosecutor v. Duško Tadić (Prijedor Case)*, IT-94-1, Decision on the Defense Motion on Jurisdiction (10 August 1995) at para 74 (International Tribunal for the Former Yugoslavia, Trial Chamber).

[112] *International Criminal Tribunal for the former Yugoslavia (ICTY)*, SC Res 827 (1993), UNSCOR, 1992Un Doc S/RES/827/ (1993), reprinted in (1993) 32 ILM 1159.

[113] *Tadić*, *supra* note 110 at para 77.

Admittedly, in both of the cases discussed above, the operation of the Tribunal was a clear-cut teleological interpretation of an instrument within its jurisdiction. However, the cases are important in that they demonstrate two distinct approaches for understanding the notion of purpose. While *Andronov* emphasizes the purpose of the substantive legal regime applicable to the dispute, *Tadić* highlights the purpose of the institution itself within the legal regime. I argue that the notion of purpose guiding the decision-maker can be based on either of these approaches.

In recent years, international law scholarship has focused its attention on the perception of fragmentation in international law. In speaking about the relationship between apparently competing standards, both the ICJ[114] and the ILC[115] have stated that there is a need to achieve coherence or essential consistency in international law. In the language of the ILC, the need is to achieve "consistency of the conclusion with the perceived purposes or functions of the legal system as a whole."[116] The reality of the international legal order is that there are fundamental differences in the purpose of different regimes and institutions.[117] In this regard, I see a danger in overemphasising the role of coherence in legal reasoning. By no means should coherence be understood as a purpose of the system. That is, even when dealing with competing norms, the decision-maker must coherently determine their normative value, but by reference to the notion of purpose based in either the *Andronov* or the *Tadić* approach.[118]

5.5.2 *The Hypothesis*

In discussing the treatment of sources by the ICJ, the former President of the Court, Judge Rosalyn Higgins, expressed the view that:

> Where the status of a treaty or a resolution at the heart of the very issue under consideration by the Court is invoked, a rather rigorous analysis of its status will ensue. But where resolutions or treaties are invoked somewhat incidentally as evidence of law, a much looser approach will suffice.

Modern international theory has not been able to elaborate a framework that explains the different measures of legality used by the ICJ and other international courts and tribunals. The statement above by Dame Higgins demonstrates a practice

---

[114] *Ahmadou Sadio Diallo*, Merits, *supra* note 64 at para 66.

[115] *Fragmentation Report*, *supra* note 49 at para 35.

[116] Ibid.

[117] See, *Loizidou v. Turkey*, No 15318/89, (1997) 23 EHRR 513 at para 67; *The MOX Plant Case (Ireland v. United Kingdom)*, Provisional Measures, [2001] ITLOS Rep 95 at para 50.

[118] See *Al-Jedda v. United Kingdom*, No. 27021/08, (2011) 53 EHRR 23 at para 102 ("In the event of any ambiguity in the terms of a Security Council Resolution, the Court must therefore choose the interpretation which is most in harmony with the requirements of the Convention and which avoids any conflict of obligations.")

that is either considered an unsustainable double standard or broadly classified as within the interpretative powers of the judge. Such practice reveals one of the most positive characteristics of international law: flexibility. I argue that it is possible to elaborate a theory that reflects the flexibility of international tribunals in deciding what constitutes applicable law on the basis of the growing practice of international institutions, especially those operating at the centre of systems for the promotion and protection of human rights.

So far in this chapter I have relied on the socio-psychological realism of Alf Ross to explain that the decisions about what constitutes applicable law in a given case are ultimately made by human beings, based on factors that include—but are not exhausted by—positive law. I have adjusted Ross's theory to the challenges of the 21st century by expanding his views to all international decision-making, and by broadening its 'free factors' to include any normative instrument not formally binding to a case. I then proposed that the choice as to what constitutes relevant international law for a decision-maker rests on three mutually reinforcing notions: specificity, completeness and purpose. That is how I arrive at the central statement of the normative plurality hypothesis:

> Decision-makers must survey the *acquis* of international law in order to identify all the instruments containing relevant normative information for a particular situation. The set of rules of law applicable to the situation must then be complemented with other instruments containing specific normative information relevant to the situation, resulting in a complete system of norms advancing a common purpose.

The application of the hypothesis leads us to the recognition than in modern international law, norms from different sources coexist in a unordered space, and that legal meaning is produced by the free interaction of those norms around a given problem.[119]

[119]Boaventura de Sousa Santos proposes "a constellation of local and mutually intelligible local meanings, and networks of empowering normative references", Boaventura de Souza Santos, "Toward a Multicultural Conception of human rights" in Berta Esperanza Hernández-Truyol, ed., *Moral imperialism: a critical anthology* (New York City: New York University Press, 2002) at 47; which is clearly based on Theodor Adorno's concept of the constellation: "The unifying moment survives without a negation of negation, but also without delivering itself to abstraction as a supreme principle. It survives because there is no step-by-step progression from the concepts to a more general cover concept. Instead, the concepts enter into a constellation. The constellation illuminates the specific side of the object, the side which to a classifying procedure is either a matter of indifference or a burden. The model for this is the conduct of language. Language offers no mere system of signs for cognitive functions. Where it appears essentially as a language, where it becomes a form of representation, it will not define its concepts. It lends objectivity to them by the relation into which it puts the concepts, centered about a thing. Language thus serves the intention of the concept to express completely what it means", Theodor W. Adorno, *Negative dialectics* (London: Taylor & Francis, 2004).

As the hypothesis I advance is not a normative theory,[120] it does not contain a definitive description of valid methods of law creation, and it does not try to exhaustively state all possible types of legal instruments.[121] In lay terms, the normative plurality hypothesis is not concerned with answering the question: What is international law? Instead, it concerns itself with the question: Which norms of international law are applicable to a particular case?

I have already explained the notions that guide the decision-maker in determining the relevant normative information for a case. There is, however, a need to define the raw material from which this information extracted. The main issue here is that not all of the outcomes of international institutions are able to produce instruments relevant to the hypothesis. To discern the relevant information base, as I have already mentioned in the statement of the hypothesis, the decision-maker must research the *acquis* of international law. In this regard, the meaning given by the late ICJ judge Pieter H. Kooijmans to the term '*acquis* of international law' reflects the notion that I wish to express: the "accepted common standard[s]".[122] In the next section I will propose the content of the *acquis* by reference to a broader concept of acceptance, and explain how the acquis relates to the rules of law formally binding in a particular situation.

5.5.3 *Theorising the* Acquis

The acquis of international law refers to the totality of instruments of normative meaning applicable to a given topic. The terminology is not to be taken lightly; I still understand that international law is formed by all those norms that have been agreed upon by its main actors. Having said that, my view of what has been agreed to goes beyond the simple acceptance of customary or conventional norms.

---

[120]Jorg Kammerhofer, "The Benefits of the Pure Theory of Law for International Lawyers, Or: What Use Is Kelsenian Theory" (2006) 12 Int'l L Theory 5 at 25 ("A normative theory does not have such a "given," because here the theory through the creation of the intellectual superstructure determines its object: the Ought. A purported "norm" that does not satisfy the criteria of normative theory simply is not a norm!").

[121]"Leaving ultimates aside, what this shows is not so much that the sources of law are undiscoverables, as that they can never be exhaustively stated…", Gerald G. Fitzmaurice, "Some Problems Regarding the Formal Sources of International Law", in Frederick Mari van Asbek, ed, *Symbolae Verzijl, présentées au professeur J. H. W. Verzijl à l'occasion de son LXX-ième anniversaire* (The Hague: Martinus Nijhoff, 1958) 124 at 161; see also Antônio Augusto Cançado Trindade, "International law for humankind: towards a new jus gentium (I). General course on public international law" (2005) 316 Rec des Cours 9 at 150 [Cançado Trindade, "General course"].

[122]Pieter H. Kooijmans, "Human Rights, Universal Values?", Dies Natalis Address, Institute of Social Studies, 12 October 1993, p. 7 online: Erasmus Universiteit Rotterdam <http://lcms.eur.nl/iss/diesnatalis1993OCR.pdf>.

As international institutions continuously grow in number and complexity, it is often the case today that an authority is empowered by international law and by the consent of the parties to intervene, arbitrate or simply make a determination about the rights and obligations of two subjects of international law. I see agreement in the mere participation of States in the diverse institutional arrangements that they have created to tackle issues within the province of international law. That is, if an international institution makes a pronouncement of normative value, I understand that the States that participate in the institution have consented to this pronouncement as a norm unless their disagreement is clearly established. Therefore, an instrument is part of the *acquis* of international law when a given actor:

- has agreed in the forms prescribed by parliamentary law or the law of treaties to an instrument;
- has participated with peers in the elaboration of an instrument without specifically stating its disagreement with the totality or parts of the preliminary or final content of the instrument;
- has consented to the existence and operation of a collegiate body of its peers or a body of experts which is expected to produce instruments, and has not specifically stated its disagreement with such powers in general or an instrument in particular; or,
- has interacted with a body of experts in the process of elaboration of an instrument, and has not specifically stated its disagreement with the totality or parts of the preliminary or final content of the instrument.

In all of the cases discussed in Chap. 4, the European and Inter-American Court interpreted their respective human rights instruments in such as way as including the standards found in other instruments that are not within their material jurisdiction. While there were clear mentions and even direct quotation of the content of these instruments outside their jurisdiction, the operative part of the judgment always stated that there was a violation of the instruments within their jurisdiction. This is so, because the rules establishing the jurisdiction of both Courts specifically empower them to find violation of a finite number of rights found in a handful of treaties. For example, while on numerous occasions the Inter-American Court expanded the content of Article 19 of the American Convention to include some of the obligations found in the CRC, the State was always found to have violated Article 19 and not the CRC. As the CRC is not an Inter-American treaty within the material jurisdiction of the Court, finding a violation of any of the rights contained therein would have been a grave violation of the American Convention and the Court's own Rules and Regulations.

In a given situation governed by international law, the decision-maker will find a set of norms that it is called to apply by the virtue of its functions and those that are common to the parties. In the normative plurality hypothesis, those norms are called the *set of rules of law applicable to the situation*. Its immediate function is to define the minimum common obligations that the parties owe to each other, while its mediate function is to become the vehicle through which the other instruments containing specific normative information relevant to the situation are incorporated into the system of norms available to the decision-maker. In the example of the decisions of the Inter-American Court concerning the rights of children, Article 19 of the American Convention would be one of the rules of law applicable to the situation. As it is the norm within the limits of the jurisdiction that is applicable to the situation being litigated, the Court is bound by its own rules and regulations to determine the legality of the actions of the State through Article 19. The rules of law applicable to the situation could encompass any type of norm depending on the nature of the institution and the mandate that it has been ordered to perform.

The manner in which other instruments are incorporated into the system of norms available to the decision-maker depends on the level of specificity of the rules of law applicable to the situation with regard to the particular situation. That is, in the improbable case that the rules of law applicable to the situation contain all the normative meaning necessary to deal with the particular situation, the decision-maker can consider that it has already determined extent and scope of the system of norms available to him/her. However, in the more reasonable case that the referential framework lacks the specificity required in a particular situation, the decision-maker must complete the rules of law with instruments of normative meaning that specifically address the particular situation. The hierarchy among instruments or acts of normative meaning can be measured only in relative terms,[123] as the relevance of a norm vis-à-vis another can be established only on a case-by-case basis and strictly depending on specificity. Norms are not to be applied individually, but as a network of normative commitments. That is, actors have an obligation to contemplate all normative commitments that they haven't specifically rejected which are applicable to an issue.

In this regard, a particular situation may require the application of instruments of normative meaning that belong to more than one specialised area of international law. In such cases, when completing the system of norms available to the decision-maker, priority must be given to the instruments of normative meaning that advance the purpose of the institution or the normative environment in which the institution operates.

5.6 Normative Plurality and Systemic Integration

As one of the arguments made in this book is that the phenomena upon which the normative plurality hypothesis is based have been attributed to systemic integration as a means of concealing the creativity of the decision-maker, I feel compelled to explain the differences between such an objective and my hypothesis.

---

[123] See Mireille Delmas-Marty, *Trois défis pour un droit mondial* (Paris: Editions du Seuil, 1998), at 104 ("Le droit a l'horreur du multiple. Sa vocation c'est l'ordre unifié et hierarchisé, unifié parce que hierarchisé. Et l'image qui vient à l'esprit des juristes, c'est la pyramide des normes, construite pour l'éternité, plutôt que celle des nuages, fussent-ils ordonnés").

The rule of interpretation concerning systemic integration is a rule of interpretation of treaties contained in the VCLT, which has been considered as part of customary treaty law. That is, it applies as a matter of treaty law to treaties among its parties and as a matter of customary law to every other treaty. As it is not clear exactly when the rule emerged, it must be assumed here that the rule applies to every treaty susceptible of being interpreted today.[124] As the rules of interpretation applicable to treaties do not necessarily apply to customary law[125] or unilateral declarations,[126] it is unclear whether one can speak of systemic interpretation of norms other than treaties.

The phrase 'any relevant rules of international law applicable' must be interpreted in the framework of the doctrine of sources, thus limiting the rules used for interpretation to those emanating from sources recognised by the doctrine of sources.[127] The normative plurality hypothesis is meant to allow for the determination of applicability of any normative commitments, irrespective of its source.

The rule of systemic integration is a rule of interpretation, while the normative plurality hypothesis deals with the determination of applicable rules in a particular case. Interpretation is not meant to change the meaning of a norm but to clarify such meaning by reference to the operation of 'any relevant rules of international law applicable' to the situation. In the normative plurality hypothesis, a decision-maker is not obliged to apply 'any relevant rules of international law', but to include them in the system of norms applicable to a situation. The operation of the normative plurality hypothesis is anterior to the need to interpret any norm, and therefore methodologically situated before a rule of systemic integration. The outcome of my hypothesis gives the decision-maker authority only the raw material of his/her craft, which may or may not need to be interpreted in accordance with the cannons accepted by international law.

---

[124]*Case concerning the question whether the re-evaluation of the German Mark in 1961 and 1969 constitutes a case for application of the clause in article 2 (e) of Annex I A of the 1953 Agreement on German External Debts between Belgium, France, Switzerland, the United Kingdom of Great Britain and Northern Ireland and the United States of America on the one hand and the Federal Republic of Germany on the other* (1980), XIX RIAA 67 at para 16 (Arbitrators: Erik Castrén, President, Karl Arndt, Marc J. Robinson, Hedwig Maier, Maurice E. Bathurst, Albert D. Monguilan, and Wilhelm A. Kewenig).

[125]*Military and Paramilitary Activities in and against Nicaragua (Nicaragua v. United States of America)*, Merits, [1986] ICJ Rep 14 at para 178 (reprinted in 25 ILM 1023) ("Rules which are identical in treaty law and in customary international law are also distinguishable by reference to the methods of interpretation and application") [*Nicaragua*].

[126]*Fisheries Jurisdiction (Spain v. Canada)*, [1998] ICJ Rep 432 at para 46 ("The régime relating to the interpretation of declarations made under Article 36 of the Statute is not identical with that established for the interpretation of treaties by the Vienna Convention on the Law of Treaties").

[127]Alexander Orakhelashvili, *The Interpretation of Acts and Rules in Public International Law* (Oxford: Oxford University Press, 2009) at 382 (To conclude, in order to affect the content of treaty rules, other 'relevant rules' of international law must be unambiguously established in terms of the sources of law criteria, and be applicable specifically to the dispute as to the interpretation in question.)

5.7 Conclusion

In this chapter I have argued that the use by international courts and tribunals of instruments outside their material jurisdiction can and should be studied by making use of theories other than those relating to interpretation of international norms. My purpose here is not to discourage the operations performed by the Inter-American and European Courts, but rather to argue that the operation of interpretation effected by the Courts goes beyond the meaning of the systemic interpretation rule and extends the effect of binding and non-binding norms within their respective systems. In that sense, none of the cases presented above is radically different from the ICJ's use in *Nicaragua* of UN General Assembly resolution 2625—an indication of the state of certain aspects of the customary law on the use of force.[128] The conclusion is that the operation characterised as systemic integration by the Courts can plausibly be conceptualised as application and therefore as an issue pertaining to the theory of sources of international law. Alf Ross provided the theoretical framework that explains both the use of such instruments and the decision of the judge to 'mask' that use as interpretation.

A greater theoretical aspect must be acknowledged: there is an academic debate concerning the impact that human rights have had on the understanding of international law in general.[129] While to some the impact is hardly deniable, there is still some discussion as to which parts of international law are increasingly affected and to what degree. Some academics participating in the debate argue that international law is going through a process of humanization[130] That said, the broader point of this book is that the model of normative plurality is not exclusive to international human rights law and permeates the whole of public international law. Although Simma has warned about the participation of the ICJ in the human rights discourse,[131] the reality is that the Court has adopted the methods of international human rights institutions.[132]

[128] *Nicaragua*, *supra* note 125 at para 191.

[129] See e.g. Kamminga and Scheinin, *supra* note 99; See also Cançado Trindade, "General course", supra note 121 at 66. ("The accelerated development of contemporary International Law bears eloquent witness of the purpose of reshaping the international legal order in fulfillment of the changing needs and aspirations of the international community as a whole.")

[130] "That is, the increasing importance of human rights discourse, which is starting to transform the whole body of public international law", Meron, "General Course", *supra* note 3 at 21; Meron, *Humanization*, *supra* note 3 at XV.

[131] Bruno Simma "Human Rights before the International Court of Justice: Community Interest Coming to Life?" in Holger Hestermeyer, et al, *Coexistence, cooperation and solidarity: Liber Amicorum Rüdiger Wolfrum* (Leiden: Martinus Nijhoff Publishers, 2012) 577 at 599–600 ("These actors have developed doctrines and rules custom-made for human rights, for instance with regard to the interpretation of human right treaties and other questions of treaty law, which may go too far to more conservative circles of the legal mainstream, This aquis must not be levelled by the participation on the discourse of a generalist court like the ICJ.")

[132] Bruno Simma, "Mainstreaming Human Rights: The Contribution of the International Court of Justice" (2012) 3:1 J Int. Disp. Settlement 7 at 20–21.

As the phenomenon sustained by systemic integration can be conceptualized in terms of sources, I have argued that such conceptualization must have implications for the current understanding of the doctrine of sources in international law. However, my goal is not to do away with the doctrine of sources altogether. I built a conceptual model for the study of normative interactions in the international legal discourse, a model that takes into account that the determination as to what constitutes law depends on choices made by the decision-maker. The doctrine of sources remains a socio-psychological factor in the mind of the decision-maker who still argues his/her decision within the boundaries set by the doctrine, while a plurality of norms shapes his/her understanding of the legal implications of the issues at stake. The model of normative plurality in international law is based on the understanding that decision-makers understand and apply international law as a whole and each of its normative *nucleae*—self-contained regimes—as complete systems with a purpose. Because it stresses the importance of the purpose, the system must be inclusive as it encounters situations that challenge its material completeness.

Chapter 6
General Conclusion

Abstract In the brief concluding chapter, I situate the normative plurality hypothesis within the framework of the current theoretical work in international law. While recalling the major theoretical methods that have had an influence on my work, I express the aspiration for more theoretical work that, instead of trying to explain issues of grand design, focuses more on the answerable questions. I also reaffirm the central focus of the normative plurality hypothesis: modern theory must take into account the psychological process by which the judge arrives at his decision.

For decades, the international community has been acting collectively through a plethora of global and regional fora. Denying the fact that the discussion in these fora deals, more often than not, with the extent and scope of the legal obligations existing among the members of the community, does not serve general purpose of international law or international politics.

The underlying point of this book is that the exercise of public authority by international organization, institutions and bodies has shaped and continues to shape the content of the legal obligations of States. However, theories, trends and methods on or in international law seem unable to grasp the impact of pluralized normativity.[1]

Part of the problem, as Glenn has suggested, is that legal theory in general seems fixated on explaining the grand design of the law instead of focusing on the answerable questions, such as "what do we take as law, normatively and for good reason, in this particular society at this particular time for this particular case?"[2]

New strands of theory are indeed trying to address the changing nature of the disciplines, but through the study of discrete manifestations of the problem. In their interactional account of international law, Brunnee and Toope have developed a theory of the emergence of the legal obligation.[3] Santiago Villapando has explained

[1]The words of Hideaki Anno come to mind: "In this closed, stagnant modern era, I think what is important is not to have a technical discussion, but to state one's aspirations"; Hideaki Anno, "what are we attempting to create by doing this once more?", Blu-ray Disc: *Evangelion: 1.11—You Are (Not) Alone* (Tokio: Khara Studio, 2010).

[2]H. Patrick Glenn, "A Concept of Legal Tradition" (2008–2009) 34 Queen's LJ 427 at 438.

[3]Jutta Brunnée and Stephen J. Toope, Legitimacy and Legality in International Law: An Interactional Account (Cambridge: Cambridge University Press, 2010).

C.I. Fuentes, *Normative Plurality in International Law*,
Ius Gentium: Comparative Perspectives on Law and Justice 57,
DOI 10.1007/978-3-319-43929-7_6

several concrete issues through reliance on a theory of protection of community interests.[4] Also, d'Aspremont has produced an interesting theory of the ascertainment of formal rules.[5]

This contribution follows the same path. By challenging the doctrine of sources of international law and relying on the practice of international human rights institutions, I propose a hypothesis of identification of relevant normative information which focuses on the completeness of international law, the search for specificity of legal obligations in the broader international governance discourse and the paramount importance of the sense of purpose of the regime and institutions, as understood by the decision-maker.

It must be acknowledged that the Danish trend of Scandinavian realism, the natural law of the inter-war period, and the relatively recent school of humanization of international law have heavily influenced my hypothesis. The convergence of these methods leads me to believe that a theory that does not take into account that decision-makers are human beings is destined for failure. I cannot ignore that the diversity of opinion on what is the function and purpose of the law in a specific case accounts for the most important advances in international law during the last 20 years. Judge Lauterpacht was of the view that "although it is not the business of jurisprudence to investigate the details of the psychological process by which the judge arrives at his decision, it may be noted that this aspect of judicial activity is of special interest in the international sphere."[6] I argue that modern theory must take into account that psychological process and elaborate a theory of how relevant norms are chosen and applied on the basis of that process. If this book has successfully defended that point alone, I will consider myself satisfied with the outcome.

In the end the purpose of this project is to present a plausible explanation of a very complex reality that continues to change as human rights discourse and methods become more relevant to the study of general international law. Paraphrasing Professor Hart, if my view of such a reality or the consequences I have drawn from it are clearly wrong, all I can hope for is that I am wrong clearly.[7]

---

[4]Santiago Villalpando, L'émergence de la communauté internationale dans la responsabilité des Etats (Paris: Presses Universitaires de France, 2005).

[5]Jean d'Aspremont, Formalism and the Sources of International Law: A theory of the Ascertainment of Legal Rules (Oxford: Oxford University Press, 2011).

[6]Hersch Lauterpacht, The Function of Law in the International Community (Oxford: Clarendon Press, 1933) at 112.

[7]These were Hart's words to kindly describe the work of Justice Oliver Wendell Holmes, Jr.: "Like our Own Austin, with whom Holmes shared many ideals and thoughts, Holmes was sometimes clearly wrong; but again like Austin, when this was so he was always wrong clearly", H.L.A. Hart, "Positivism and the Separation of Law and Morals" (1958) 71 Harv L Rev 593 at 593.

Bibliography

1 Cases

1.1 Permanent Court of International Justice

Case Concerning the Factory at Chorzów (Germany v. Poland) (1927), PCIJ (Ser. A) No. 9.
Case of the Mavrommatis Palestine Concessions (Greece v. United Kingdom) (1924), PCIJ (Ser. A) No. 2
Customs Regime between Germany and Austria (1931), PCIJ (Ser. A/B) No. 41 at p 47.
Jurisdiction of the European Commission of the Danube (1927), Advisory Opinion, PCIJ (Ser. B) No. 14.
Legal Status of Eastern Greenland (Denmark v. Norway) (1933), PCIJ (Ser. A/B) No. 53.
Rights of Minorities in Upper Silesia (Minority Schools) (Germany v. Poland) (1928), PCIJ (Ser. A) No. 12.
The Case of the S.S. "Lotus" (France v. Turkey) (1927), PCIJ (Ser. A) No. 10.
Treatment of Polish Nationals and Other Persons of Polish Origin or Speech in the Danzig Territory (1932), Advisory Opinion, PCIJ (Ser. A/B) No. 44.

1.2 International Court of Justice

1.2.1 Judgments

Aegean Sea Continental Shelf (Greece v. Turkey), [1978] ICJ Rep 3.
Aerial Incident of 27 July 1955 (Israel v. Bulgaria), [1959] ICJ Rep 127.
Ahmadou Sadio Diallo (Republic of Guinea v. Democratic Republic of the Congo), Merits, Judgment, [2010] ICJ Rep 639 (reprinted in 50 ILM 40).
Ahmadou Sadio Diallo (Republic of Guinea v. Democratic Republic of the Congo), Preliminary Objections, [2007] ICJ Rep 582.
Alleged Violations of Sovereign Rights and Maritime Spaces in the Caribbean Sea (Nicaragua v. Colombia), Preliminary Objections, Judgment of 17 March 20165, online: ICJ <http://www.icj-cij.org/docket/files/155/18948.pdf>.
Anglo-Iranian Oil Co. case (jurisdiction) (United Kingdom v. Iran), [1952] ICJ Rep 93.
Application of the Convention on the Prevention and Punishment of the Crime of Genocide (Bosnia and Herzegovina v. Serbia and Montenegro), Merits, Judgment, [2007] ICJ Rep 43 at para 403 (reprinted in 46 ILM 188).

C.I. Fuentes, *Normative Plurality in International Law*,
Ius Gentium: Comparative Perspectives on Law and Justice 57,
DOI 10.1007/978-3-319-43929-7

Application of the Convention on the Prevention and Punishment of the Crime of Genocide (Croatia v. Serbia), Merits, online: International Court of Justice <http://www.icj-cij.org/docket/files/118/18422.pdf>.

Arbitral Award of 31 July 1989 (Guinea-Bissau v. Senegal), [1991] ICJ Rep 53.

Armed Activities on the Territory of the Congo (Democratic Republic of the Congo v. Uganda), [2005] ICJ Rep 168.

Armed Activities on the Territory of the Congo (New Application: 2002) (Democratic Republic of the Congo v. Rwanda), [2006] ICJ Rep 6.

Arrest Warrant of 11 April 2000 (Democratic Republic of the Congo v. Belgium), [2002] ICJ Rep 3.

Asylum Case (Colombia v. Peru), [1950] ICJ Rep 266.

Avena and other Mexican Nationals (Mexico v. United States of America), Judgment, [2004] ICJ Rep 48.

Barcelona Traction, Light and Power Company, Limited (Belgium v. Spain), Preliminary Objections, [1964] ICJ Rep 6.

Border and Transborder Armed Actions (Nicaragua v. Honduras), Jurisdiction and Admissibility, [1988] ICJ Rep 105.

Case concerning Certain Norwegian Loans (France v. Norway), [1957] ICJ Rep 9.

Case concerning Right of Passage over Indian Territory (Portugal v. India), [1960] ICJ Rep 6.

Case concerning the application of the International Convention on the Elimination of all Forms of Racial Discrimination (Georgia v. Russian Federation), [2011] ICJ Rep 70.

Case Concerning the Barcelona Traction, Light and Power Company, Limited, (Belgium v. Spain), (Second Phase), [1970] ICJ Rep 3.

Case concerning the Land, Island and Maritime Frontier Dispute (El Salvador v. Honduras: Nicaragua intervening), [1992] ICJ Rep 351.

Case concerning the Northern Cameroons (Cameroon v. United Kingdom), [1963] ICJ Rep 15.

Certain Activities Carried Out by Nicaragua in the Border Area (Costa Rica v. Nicaragua) and *Construction of a Road in Costa Rica along The San Juan River (Nicaragua v. Costa Rica)*, Judgment of 16 December 2015, online: ICJ <http://www.icj-cij.org/docket/files/150/18848.pdf>.

Certain Questions of Mutual Assistance in Criminal Matters (Djibouti v. France), [2008] ICJ Rep 177 at para 112.

Continental Shelf (Libyan Arab Jamahiriya v. Malta), [1985] ICJ Rep 13.

Continental Shelf (Tunisia v. Libyan Arab Jamahiriya), [1982] ICJ Rep 18.

Corfu Channel case (United Kingdom v. Albania), Merits [1949] ICJ Rep 4.

Corfu Channel case (United Kingdom v. Albania), Preliminary Objection [1948] ICJ Rep 15 at 27

Delimitation of the Maritime Boundary in the Gulf of Maine Area (Canada v. United States of America), [1984] ICJ Rep 246 (reprinted in 23 ILM 1197).

Dispute regarding Navigational and Related Rights (Costa Rica v. Nicaragua), [2009] ICJ Rep 213.

East Timor (Portugal v. Australia), [1995] ICJ Rep 90.

Fisheries (United Kingdom v. Norway), [1951] ICJ Rep 116.

Fisheries Jurisdiction (Federal Republic of Germany v. Iceland), Jurisdiction of the Court, [1973] ICJ Rep 49

Fisheries Jurisdiction (Federal Republic of Germany v. Iceland), Merits [1974] ICJ Rep 175.

Fisheries Jurisdiction (Spain v. Canada), [1998] ICJ Rep 432.

Fisheries Jurisdiction (United Kingdom v. Iceland), Jurisdiction of the Court, [1973] ICJ Rep 3.

Fisheries Jurisdiction (United Kingdom v. Iceland), Merits [1974] ICJ Rep 3.

Frontier Dispute (Burkina Faso v. Republic of Mali), [1986] ICJ Rep 554.

Gabčíkovo-Nagymaros Project (Hungary/Slovakia), [1997] ICJ Rep 7.

Jurisdictional Immunities of the State (Germany v. Italy: Greece intervening), [2012] ICJ Rep 99.

Kasikilil-Sedudu Island (Botswana v. Namibia), [1999] ICJ Rep 1045.

LaGrand (Germany v. United States of America), [2001] ICJ Rep 466.

Land and Maritime Boundary between Cameroon and Nigeria (Cameroon v. Nigeria: Equatorial Guinea intervening), Merits, [2002] ICJ Rep 303.
Land and Maritime Boundary between Cameroon and Nigeria (Cameroon v. Nigeria), Preliminary Objections, [1998] ICJ Rep 275.
Maritime Delimitation and Territorial Questions between Qatar and Bahrain (Qatar v. Bahrain), Jurisdiction and Admissibility, [1994] ICJ Rep 112 at para 23.
Maritime Delimitation and Territorial Questions between Qatar and Bahrain (Qatar v. Bahrain), Jurisdiction and Admissibility, [1995] ICJ Rep 6 at para 33.
Maritime Dispute (Peru v. Chile), [2014] ICJ Rep 3.
Military and Paramilitary Activities in and against Nicaragua (Nicaragua v. United States of America), Merits, [1986] ICJ Rep 14 (reprinted in 25 ILM 1023).
Military and Paramilitary Activities in and against Nicaragua (Nicaragua v. United States of America), Jurisdiction and Admissibility, [1984] ICJ Rep 392.
Monetary Gold Removed from Rome in 1943 (Italy v. France, United Kingdom of Great Britain and Northern Ireland and United States of America), [1954] ICJ Rep 19.
North Sea Continental Shelf, (Federal Republic of Germany v. Denmark; Federal Republic of Germany v. Netherlands), [1969] ICJ Rep 3.
Nuclear Tests (Australia v. France), [1974] ICJ Rep 253.
Nuclear Tests (New Zealand v. France), [1974] ICJ Rep 457.
Oil Platforms (Islamic Republic of Iran v. United States of America), [2003] ICJ Rep 161.
Oil Platforms (Islamic Republic of Iran v. United States of America), Preliminary Objection, [1996] ICJ Rep 803.
Pulp Mills on the River Uruguay (Argentina v. Uruguay), [2010] ICJ Rep 14.
Question of the Delimitation of the Continental Shelf between Nicaragua and Colombia beyond 200 nautical miles from the Nicaraguan Coast (Nicaragua v. Colombia), Preliminary Objections, Judgment of 17 March 2016, online: ICJ <http://www.icj-cij.org/docket/files/154/18956.pdf>.
Questions relating to the Obligation to Prosecute or Extradite (Belgium v. Senegal), [2012] ICJ Rep 422.
Request for Interpretation of the Judgment of 15 June 1962 in the Case concerning the Temple of Preah Vihear (Cambodia v. Thailand) (Cambodia v. Thailand), [2013] ICJ Rep 281.
South West Africa (Ethiopia v. South Africa; Liberia v. South Africa), [1966] ICJ Rep 6 (reprinted in 5 ILM 932).
Sovereignty over Pulau Ligitan and Pulau Sipadan (Indonesia v. Malaysia), Judgment, [2002] ICJ Rep 625.
Territorial Dispute (Libyan Arab Jamahiriya v. Chad), [1994] ICJ Rep 6.
Territorial and Maritime Dispute (Nicaragua v. Colombia), Merits, [2012] ICJ Rep 624.
United States Diplomatic and Consular Staff in Tehran (United States of America v. Iran), [1980] ICJ Rep 18.

1.2.2 Advisory Opinions

Accordance with International Law of the Unilateral Declaration of Independence in Respect of Kosovo, Advisory Opinion, [2010] ICJ Rep 403.
Application for Review of Judgment No. 158 of the United Nations Administrative Tribunal, Advisory Opinion, [1973] ICJ Rep 166.
Application for Review of Judgment No. 273 of the United Nations Administrative Tribunal, Advisory Opinion, [1982] ICJ Rep 325.
Application for Review of Judgment No 333 of the United Nations Administrative Tribunal, Advisory Opinion, [1987] ICJ Rep 18.
Certain Expenses of the United Nations (Article 17, paragraph 2, of the Charter), Advisory Opinion, [1962] ICJ Rep 151.

Effect of Awards of Compensation Made by the United Nations Administrative Tribunal, Advisory Opinion, [1954] ICJ Rep 47.
Interpretation of Peace Treaties with Bulgaria, Hungary and Romania (second phase), Advisory Opinion, [1950] ICJ Rep 221.
Judgment No.2867 of the Administrative Tribunal of the International Labour Organization upon a Complaint Filed against the International Fund for Agricultural Development, Advisory Opinion, [2012] ICJ Rep 10.
Judgments of the Administrative Tribunal of the I.L.O. upon complaints made against the U.N.E.S.C.O., Advisory Opinion, [1956] ICJ Rep 77.
Legal Consequences for States of the Continued Presence of South Africa in Namibia (South West Africa) notwithstanding Security Council Resolution 276 (1970), Advisory Opinion, [1971] ICJ Rep 16 (reprinted in 10 ILM 677).
Legal Consequences of the Construction of a Wall in the Occupied Palestinian Territory, Advisory Opinion, [2004] ICJ Rep 136.
Legality of the Threat or Use of Nuclear Weapons Case, Advisory Opinion, [1996] ICJ Rep 226 (reprinted in 35 ILM 809).
Reparations for Injuries Suffered in the Service of the United Nations, Advisory Opinion, [1949] ICJ Rep 174.
Reservations to the Convention on the Prevention and Punishment of the Crime of Genocide, Advisory Opinion, [1951] ICJ Rep 14

1.2.3 Orders

Judgment No.2867 of the Administrative Tribunal of the International Labour Organization upon a Complaint Filed against the International Fund for Agricultural Development, Order of 29 April 2010, [2010] ICJ Rep 298.
Pulp Mills on the River Uruguay, Order of 13 July 2006, 45 ILM 1025, online: International Court of Justice <http://www.icj-cij.org/docket/files/135/11235.pdf>.

1.2.4 Pleadings and Documents

Ahmadou Sadio Diallo (Republic of Guinea v. Democratic Republic of the Congo), "Application instituting proceedings", online: International Court of Justice <http://www.icj-cij.org/docket/files/103/7175.pdf>.
Arrest Warrant of 11 April 2000 (Democratic Republic of the Congo v. Belgium), "Application Instituting Proceedings" (17 October 2000), online: International Court of Justice <http://www.icj-cij.org/docket/files/121/7081.pdf>.
Fisheries Jurisdiction (Spain v. Canada), "Memorial of the Kingdom of Spain (Competence)" (28 September 1995) online: International Court of Justice <http://www.icj-cij.org/docket/files/96/8591.pdf>.
Maritime Delimitation and Territorial Questions between Qatar and Bahrain (Qatar v. Bahrain), "Oral argument of H.E. Dr. Husain Mohammed Al-Baharna" (4 March 1994) online: International Court of Justice <http://www.icj-cij.org/docket/files/87/5431.pdf>.
Maritime Delimitation and Territorial Questions between Qatar and Bahrain (Qatar v. Bahrain), "Application Instituting Proceedings" (8 July 1991) online: International Court of Justice <http://www.icj-cij.org/docket/files/87/7021.pdf> [Qatar v. Bahrain, Application].
Maritime Delimitation and Territorial Questions between Qatar and Bahrain (Qatar v. Bahrain), "Oral argument of Professor Elihu Lauterpacht" (11 March 1994) online: International Court of Justice <http://www.icj-cij.org/docket/files/87/5447.pdf>.

Maritime Delimitation and Territorial Questions between Qatar and Bahrain (Qatar v. Bahrain), "Memorial of the Government of the State of Qatar" (10 February 1992) online: International Court of Justice <http://www.icj-cij.org/docket/files/87/7023.pdf>.

Maritime Delimitation and Territorial Questions between Qatar and Bahrain (Qatar v. Bahrain), "Counter-Memorial of the Government of the State of Bahrain" (11 June 1992) online: International Court of Justice <http://www.icj-cij.org/docket/files/87/7025.pdf>.

Military and Paramilitary Activities in and against Nicaragua (Nicaragua v. United States of America), "Memorial of Nicaragua (Questions of Jurisdiction and Admissibility)" (30 June 1984), ICJ Pleadings (vol. 1) 361 at para 119.

Military and Paramilitary Activities in and against Nicaragua (Nicaragua v. United States of America), "Counter-Memorial of the United States of America (Questions of Jurisdiction and Admissibility)" (17 August 1984), ICJ Pleadings (vol. 2).

Military and Paramilitary Activities in and against Nicaragua (Nicaragua v. United States of America), "Oral Arguments on Jurisdiction and Admissibility" (8 to 18 October and 26 November 1984), ICJ Pleadings (vol. 3).

Military and Paramilitary Activities in and against Nicaragua (Nicaragua v. United States of America), "Application instituting proceedings" (9 April 1984), ICJ Pleadings (vol. 3) online: International Court of Justice < http://www.icj-cij.org/docket/files/70/9615.pdf>.

Legality of the Threat or Use of Nuclear Weapons Case, "Verbatim Record of the Public sitting" (30 October 1995) online: International Court of Justice <http://www.icj-cij.org/docket/files/95/5925.pdf>.

Legality of the Threat or Use of Nuclear Weapons Case, "Verbatim Record of the Public sitting" (7 November 1995) online: International Court of Justice <http://www.icj-cij.org/docket/files/95/5935.pdf>.

Pulp Mills on the River Uruguay, "Application Instituting Proceedings" (4 May 2006) online: International Court of Justice <http://www.icj-cij.org/docket/files/135/10779.pdf >.

Pulp Mills on the River Uruguay, "Verbatim Record of the Public sitting" (8 June 2006) online: International Court of Justice <http://www.icj-cij.org/docket/files/135/13128.pdf>;

1.3 Inter-American Court on Human Rights

1.3.1 Judgments

Case of Apitz Barbera et al. ("First Court of Administrative Disputes") (Venezuela) (2008), Inter-Am Ct HR (Ser C) No 182.

Case of Atala Riffo and daughters (Chile) (2012), Inter-Am Ct HR (Ser C) No 239.

Case of Bámaca-Velásquez (Guatemala) (2000), Inter-Am Ct HR (Ser C) No 70.

Case of Blake (Guatemala) (1996), Inter-Am Ct HR (Ser C) No 27.

Case of Blake (Guatemala) (1998), Inter-Am Ct HR (Ser C) No 36.

Case of Bueno-Alves (Argentina) (2007), Inter-Am Ct HR (Ser C) No 164.

Case of Bulacio (Argentina) (2003), Inter-Am Ct HR (Ser C) No 100.

Case of Chitay Nech et al. (Guatemala) (2012), Inter-Am Ct HR (Ser C) No 212.

Case of Contreras et al. (El Salvador) (2011), Inter-Am Ct HR (Ser C) No 232.

Case of De La Cruz-Flores (Peru) (2004), Inter-Am Ct HR (Ser C) No 115.

Case of Gelman (Uruguay) (2011), Inter-Am Ct HR (Ser C) No 221.

Case of Godínez-Cruz (Honduras) (1988), Inter-Am Ct HR (Ser C) No 5.

Case of Goiburú et al. (Paraguay) (2006) Inter-Am Ct HR (Ser C) No 153.

Case of González et al. ("Cotton Field") (Mexico) (2009), Inter-Am Ct HR (Ser C) No 205.

Case of Heliodoro Portugal (Panama) (2008), Inter-Am Ct HR (Ser C) No 186.

Case of Ivcher-Bronstein (Peru) (2001), Inter-Am Cr HR (Ser C) No. 74.

Case of La Cantuta (Peru) (2006) Inter-Am Ct HR (Ser C) No 162.
Case of Las Palmeras (Colombia) (2000), Inter-Am Ct HR (Ser C) No 67.
Case of López-Álvarez (Honduras) (2006) Inter-Am Ct HR (Ser C) No 141.
Case of Manuel Cepeda-Vargas (Colombia) (2010), Inter-Am Ct HR (Ser C) No 213.
Case of Maritza Urrutia (Guatemala) (2003), Inter-Am Ct HR (Ser C) No 103.
Case of Massacre of Santo Domingo (Colombia) (2012), Inter-Am Ct HR (Ser C) No 259.
Case of Perozo et al. (Venezuela) (2009), Inter-Am Ct HR (Ser C) No 195.
Case of Serrano-Cruz Sisters (El Salvador) (2005), Inter-Am Ct HR (Ser C) No 120.
Case of Servellón-García et al. (Honduras) (2006), Inter-Am Ct HR (Ser C) No 152
Case of the "Juvenile Reeducation Institute" (Paraguay) (2004), Inter-Am Ct HR (Ser C) No 112.
Case of the "Las Dos Erres" Massacre (Guatemala) (2009), Inter-Am Ct HR (Ser C) No 211.
Case of the "Street Children" (Villagrán-Morales et al.) (Guatemala) (1999) Inter-Am Ct HR (Ser C) No 63.
Case of the Girls Yean and Bosico (Dominican Republic) (2005) Inter-Am Ct HR (Ser C) No 130.
Case of the Gómez-Paquiyauri Brothers (Peru) (2004), Inter-Am Ct HR (Ser C) No 110.
Case of the Indigenous Community Yakye Axa (Paraguay) (2005) Inter-Am Ct HR (Ser C) No 125.
Case of the Ituango Massacres (Colombia) (2006) Inter-Am Ct HR (Ser C) No 148.
Case of the Mapiripán Massacre (Colombia) (2005), Inter-Am Cr HR (Ser C) No. 134.
Case of the Miguel Castro-Castro Prison (Peru) (2006), Inter-Am Ct HR (Ser C) No 160.
Case of the Moiwana Community (Suriname) (2005), Inter-Am Ct HR (Ser C) No 124.
Case of the Pueblo Bello Massacre (Colombia) (2006), Inter-Am Ct HR (Ser C) No 159.
Case of the Sawhoyamaxa Indigenous Community (Paraguay) (2006) Inter-Am Ct HR (Ser C) No 146,
Case of the Xákmok Kásek Indigenous Community (Paraguay) (2010), Inter-Am Ct HR (Ser C) No 214.
Case of Tibi (Ecuador) (2004) Inter-Am Ct HR (Ser C) No 114.
Case of Velásquez-Rodríguez (Honduras) (1988), Inter-Am Ct HR (Ser C) No 4.
Case of Velásquez-Rodríguez (Honduras) (1987), Inter-Am Ct HR (Ser C) No 1.
Case of Ximenes-Lopes (Brazil) (2006) Inter-Am Ct HR (Ser C) No 149.

1.3.2 Advisory Opinions

"Other treaties" subject to the advisory jurisdiction of the Court (Art. 64 American Convention on Human Rights) (1982), Advisory Opinion OC-01/82, Inter-Am Ct HR (Ser A) No 1.
Exceptions to the Exhaustion of Domestic Remedies (Arts. 46(1), 46(2)(a) and 46 (2)(b) of the American Convention on Human Rights) (1990), Advisory Opinion OC-11/90, Inter-Am Ct HR (Ser A) No 11.
Interpretation of the American Declaration of the Rights and Duties of Man within the Framework of Article 64 of the American Convention on Human Rights (1989), Advisory Opinion OC-10/89, Inter-Am Ct HR (Ser A) No 10.
The Right to Information on Consular Assistance in the framework of the guarantees of the Due Process of Law (1999), Advisory Opinion OC-16/99, Inter-Am Ct HR (Ser A) No 16.

1.4 European Court of Human Rights

Al-Adsani v. United Kingdom [GC], No 35763/97, [2001] 34 EHRR 11.
Al-Jedda v. United Kingdom, No. 27021/08, (2011) 53 EHRR 23.
Al-Skeini v. United Kingdom, No.55721/07, (2011) 53 EHRR 18.
Aydin v. Turkey, No.25660/94, (2006) 42 EHRR 44.

Banković and others v. Belgium and 16 Other Contracting States, No 52207/99, (2001) XII Reports 333.
Belilos v. Switzerland, No 10328/83, (1988) 132 Eur Ct HR.
Bosphorus Hava Yolları Turizm ve Ticaret Anonim Şirketi (Bosphorus Airways) v. Ireland [GC], 45036/98, ECHR 2005-VI.
Case of Hirsi Jamaa and others v. Italy, No 27765/09, (2012) 55 EHRR 21 at paras 170-171.
Clift v. United Kingdom, No 7205/07, 13 July 2003.
Dogan and others v. Turkey, Nos 8803/02 etc., 29 June 2004.
ER v. Turkey, No 23016/04, (2013) 56 EHRR 13.
Ergi v. Turkey, No 23818/94, (2001) 32 EHRR 18.
Georgia v. Russia (dec), No 38263/08, (2012) 54 E.H.R.R. SE10.
Golder v. United Kingdom (1975), 18 Eur Ct HR (Ser A).
Isayeva v. Russia, No 57950/00, (2005) 41 EHRR 38.
Johnston and Others v. Ireland, 112 Eur Ct HR (Ser A).
KT v. Norway, No 26664/03, (2009) 49 EHRR 4.
Lithgow and Others v. United Kingdom, 102 Eur Ct HR (Ser A).
Loizidou v. Turkey, No 15318/89, (1997) 23 EHRR 513.
Maslov v. Austria [GC], No 1638/03, (2008) 47 EHR.R 20.
Opuz v. Turkey, No 33401/02, (2010) 50 EHRR 28.
Osman v. United Kingdom (1998), (2000) 29 EHRR 245.
Saadi v. United Kingdom [GC], No. 13229/03.
Salgueiro Da Silva Mouta v. Portugal, No 33290/96, (2001) 31 EHRR 47.
Silih v. Slovenia, No 71463/01, (2009) 49 EHRR 37.
Soering v. United Kingdom, No. 14038/88, (1989) 161 Eur Ct HR (Ser A).
T. v. United Kingdom, No 24724/94, 16 December 1999.
Tyrer v. United Kingdom, Ser A No 26, (1979-1980) 2 EHRR 1.
Van Anraat v. Netherlands (dec.), no. 65389/09, (2010) 49 ILM 127.
Varnava v. Turkey, Nos 16064/90, 16065/90, 16066/90, 16068/90, 16069/90, 16070/90, 16071/90, 16072/90 and 16073/90, (2010) 50 E.H.R.R. 21.
Waite and Kennedy v. Germany (1999), (2000) 30 EHRR 26.
Witold Litwa v. Poland, No 26629/95, ECHR 2000–III.

1.5 Arbitral Awards

Ambatielos Case (Greece v. United Kingdom) (1956), XII RIAA 83 (arbitrators: Ricardo J. Alfaro, Algot J. F. Bagge, Maurice Bourquin, John Spiropoulos, Gerald Thesiger).
Arbitration between Barbados and the Republic of Trinidad and Tobago, Award of the Tribunal (2006), 45 ILM 800 (Permanent Court of Arbitration, operating under UNCLOS, Annex VII Arbitration) (arbitrators: Judge Stephen Schwebel, Sir Ian Brownlie, Vaughan Lowe, Francisco Orrego Vicuña, Sir Arthur Watts);
Arbitration between the Government of the State of Kuwait and the American Independent Oil Company (AMINOIL), Final Award (1982), 21 ILM 976 (arbitrators: Paul Reuter, Hamed Sultan, Sir Gerald Fitzmaurice);
Award in the Arbitration regarding the Iron Rhine ("Ijzeren Rijn") Railway between the Kingdom of Belgium and the Kingdom of the Netherlands (2005), XXVII RIAA 35 (arbitrators: Judge Rosalyn Higgins, Guy Schrans, Judge Bruno Simma, Alfred H.A. Soons, Judge Peter Tomka).
Case concerning a boundary dispute between Argentina and Chile concerning the delimitaion of the frontier line between boundary post 62 and Mount Fitzroy (1994), XXII RIAA 3 (arbitrators: Mr. Rafael Nieto Navia, Mr. Reynaldo Galindo Pohl, Mr.Santiago Benadava, Mr. Julio A. Barberis and Mr. Pedro Nikken).

Case concerning the question whether the re-evaluation of the German Mark in 1961 and 1969 constitutes a case for application of the clause in article 2 (e) of Annex I A of the 1953 Agreement on German External Debts between Belgium, France, Switzerland, the United Kingdom of Great Britain and Northern Ireland and the United States of America on the one hand and the Federal Republic of Germany on the other (1980), XIX RIAA 67 (arbitrators: Erik Castrén, Karl Arndt, Marc J. Robinson, Hedwig Maier, Maurice E. Bathurst, Albert D. Monguilan, Wilhelm A. Kewenig).

Dispute Concerning Access to Information Under Article 9 of the OSPAR Convention between Ireland and the United Kingdom of Great Britain and Northern Ireland, Final Award (2003), XXIII RIAA 59 (Permanent Court of Arbitration) (arbitrators: W. Michael Reisman, Gavan Griffith, Rt Hon. Lord Mustill).

Eastern Extension, Australasia and China Telegraph Company, Ltd. (Great Britain v. United States) (1923), VI RIAA 112 at 114.

Indus Waters Kishenganga Arbitration (Pakistan v. India), Final Award, 20 December 2013 (Arbitrators: Judge Stephen M. Schwebel, Sir Franklin Berman Howard S. Wheater, Lucius Caflisch, Jan Paulsson, Judge Bruno Simma, Judge Peter Tomka) online: Permanent Court of Arbitration <http://www.pcacases.com>.

Island of Palmas case (Netherlands, USA) (1928), II RIAA 829 at 845 (arbitrator: Max Huber).

Merrill & Ring Forestry LP v. Canada, [2010] IIC 427 at para 190 (ICSID) (arbitrators: Francisco Orrego Vicuña, Kenneth W. Dam, J. William Rowley QC).

North American Dredging Company of Texas (U.S.A.) v. United Mexican States (1926), IV RIAA 26 at 29 (para 12).

Prisoners of War—Ethiopia's Claim 4(Ethiopia v. Eritrea), Partial Award, 1st July 2003 (Eritrea-Ethiopia Claims Commission) at para 22, online: Permanent Court of Arbitration <http://www.pcacases.com>.

RosInvest Company UK Limited v. Russian Federation, [2007] IIC 315 (Arbitration Institute of the Stockholm Chamber of Commerce) (arbitrators: Prof. Dr. Böckstiegel, The Rt. Hon. Lord Steyn, Sir Franklin Berman KCMG, QC).

Southern Bluefin Tuna (New Zealand-Japan, Australia-Japan) (2000), XXIII RIAA 23 (arbitrators: Judge Stephen M. Schwebel, Judge Florentino Feliciano, The Rt. Hon. Justice Sir Kenneth Keith, Judge Per Tresselt, Chusei Yamada).

The Republic of Mauritius v. The United Kingdom of Great Britain and Northern Ireland, Reasoned Decision on Challenge (2011), [2012] 51 ILM (Permanent Court of Arbitration, operating under UNCLOS, Annex VII Arbitration) (arbitrators: Ivan Shearer, Judge Sir Christopher Greenwood, Judge Albert Hoffmann, Judge James Kateka, Judge Rüdiger Wolfrum).

The Arctic Sunrise Arbitration, Award on the Merits at para 227 (Permanent Court of Arbitration, operating under UNCLOS, Annex VII Arbitration) (arbitrators: Thomas A. Mensah, Henry Burmester, Alfred H.A. Soons, Janusz Symonides and Dr. Alberto Székely) online: Permanent Court of Arbitration <http://www.pcacases.com>

1.6 International and Hybrid Criminal Tribunals

Prosecutor v. Anto Furundžija ("Lašva Valley" Case), IT-95-17/1 Judgment (10 December 1998) (International Criminal Tribunal for the former Yugoslavia, Trial Chamber) online: ICTR <http://www.ictr.org>.

Prosecutor v. Duško Tadić (Prijedor Case), IT-94-1, Decision on the Defense Motion for Interlocutory Appeal on Jurisdiction (2 October 1995) (International Tribunal for the Former Yugoslavia, Appeals Chamber).

Prosecutor v. Duško Tadić (Prijedor Case), IT-94-1, Decision on the Defense Motion on Jurisdiction (10 August 1995) (International Tribunal for the Former Yugoslavia, Trial Chamber).

Prosecutor v. Ieng Sary, Ieng Thirith, Khieu Samphan, 002/19-09-2007-ECCC/OCIJ (PTC38), Decision on the appeals against the Co-Investigative Judges Order on joint criminal enterprise (JCE) (20 May 2010) (Extraordinary Chambers in the Courts of Cambodia) (49 ILM 1345).

Prosecutor v. Jean-Paul Akayesu, ICTR-96-4-T, Judgment (2 September 1998) (International Criminal Tribunal for Rwanda, Trial Chamber), online: ICTR <http://www.ictr.org>.

Prosecutor v. Thomas Lubanga Dyilo, Judgment on the appeal of Mr Thomas Lubanga Dyilo against the decision on the defence challenge to the jurisdiction of the court pursuant to Article 19(2)(a) of the Statute of 3 October 2006, Case No ICC-01/04-01/06-772, 14th December 2006 (International Criminal Court, Appeals Chamber) online: International Criminal Court <http://www.icc-cpi.int/iccdocs/doc/doc243774.PDF>.

1.7 International Administrative Tribunals

Andronov v. Secretary-General of the United Nations, Judgment of 20 November 2003, UNAT Judgment No. 1157, [2003] U.N. Jur. Yb. 497, UN Doc. AT/DEC/1157.

Bernstein v. Director-General of the United Nations Educational, Scientific and Cultural Organisation, Judgment of 29 October 1955, ILOAT Judgment No. 21.

Desgranges v. Director-General of the International Labor Organization, Judgment of 12 August 1953, ILOAT Judgment No. 11.

Duberg v. Director-General of the United Nations Educational, Scientific and Cultural Organisation, Judgment of 26 April 1955, ILOAT Judgment No. 17.

Fasla v. Secretary-General of the United Nations, Judgment of 28 April 1972, UNAT Judgment No. 158, [1972] U.N. Jur. Yb. 127, UN Doc. AT/DEC/158.

Leff v. Director-General of the United Nations Educational, Scientific and Cultural Organisation, Judgment of 26 April 1955, ILOAT Judgment No. 18.

Mortished v. Secretary-General of the United Nations, Judgment of 15 May 1981, UNAT Judgment No. 273, [1981] UN Jur Yb 115, UN Doc. AT/DEC/273.

Mrs A.T.S.G. v. President of the International Fund for Agricultural Development, Judgment of 3 February 2010, ILOAT Judgment No.2867.

Wilcox v. Director-General of the United Nations Educational, Scientific and Cultural Organisation, Judgment of 26 April 1955, ILOAT Judgment No. 19.

Yakimetz v. Secretary-General of the United Nations, Judgment of 8 June 1984, UNAT Judgment No. 333, [1984] UN Jur Yb 146, UN Doc. AT/DEC/273.

1.8 Other

Benefinicaries of late Norbert Zongo, Abdoulaye Nikiema alias Ablassé, Ernest Zongo and Blaise Ilboudo & the Bukinabè Human and Peoples' Rights Movement v. Burkina Faso, No. 013/2011, Judgment, online: African Court on Human and People's Rights <http://www.african-court.org/>; Committee of U.S. Citizens Living in Nicaragua v. Reagan, 859 F.2d 929.

Delimitation of the maritime boundary in the Bay of Bengal (Bangladesh/Myanmar), Judgment, [2012] ITLOS Rep 4.

Femi Falana v. the African Union, No 001/2011, Judgment, online: African Court on Human and People's Rights <http://www.african-court.org/>.

Forti v. Suarez-Mason, 672 F.Supp. 1531 (N.D.Cal.1987).

Juan Carlos Abella v. Argentina (La Tablada) (1997), Inter-Am Comm HR No 24/98.

Lohé Issa Konate v. Burkina Faso, No 004/2013, Judgment, at paras 147, 154, 158, online: African Court on Human and People's Rights <http://www.african-court.org/>.

Procedimiento Excepcional de Urgencia solicitado por la República del Paraguay en relación con la suspensión de su participación en los Órganos del Mercado Común del Sur (MERCOSUR) y la incorporación de Venezuela como Miembro Pleno (2012), Award No 01/2012, online: Tribunal Permanente de Revisión <http://www.tprmercosur.org/es/docum/laudos/Laudo_01_2012_es.pdf>.

Responsibility and Obligations of States Sponsoring Persons and Entities with Respect to Activities in the Area, Seabed Dispute Chamber, Advisory Opinion, [2011] ITLOS Rep 10.

Siderman de Blake v. Republic of Argentina, 965 F.2d 699, 60 USLW 2771.

Tanganyika Law Society and. The Legal and Human Rights Centre v. the United Republic of Tanzania; and Reverend Christopher R. Mtikila v. the United Republic of Tanzania, Nos 009/2011 and 011/2011, Judgment, at paras 82.1 and 106.2-106.4, online: African Court on Human and People's Rights <http://www.african-court.org/>.

Tel-Oren v. Libyan Arab Republic, 726 F.2d 774 (D.C.Cir.1984).

The MOX Plant Case (Ireland v. United Kingdom), Provisional Measures, [2001] ITLOS Rep 95.

United States- Sections 301-310 of the Trade Act of 1974 (Complaint by the European Communities) (1999), WTO Doc. WT/DS152/R at para 7.118 (Panel Report), [2000] 39 ILM 452.

2 International Materials

2.1 Treaties

Additional Protocol to the American Convention on Human Rights in the Area of Economic, Social, and Cultural Rights "Protocol of San Salvador", 17 November 1988, OASTS 69 at art 19.6, (1989) 28 ILM 156

Additional Protocol to the Asunción Treaty on the institutional structure of Mercosur (Ouro Preto Protocol), Argentina, Brazil, Paraguay and Uruguay, 17 December 1994, 2145 UNTS 298.

African Charter on Human and Peoples' Rights, 27 June 1981, 1520 UNTS 271 at art 6, (1982) 21 ILM 58.

Agreement Establishing the Caribbean Court of Justice, 14 February 2001, 2255 UNTS 319.

American Convention on Human Rights, 22 November 1969, 36 OASTS 1 at art 29, 1144 UNTS 123.

American Treaty on Pacific Settlement "Pact of Bogota", 13 May 1949, 30 UNTS 83.

Charter of the United Nations, 26 June 1945, Can TS 1945 No.7.

Consolidated Version of the Treaty on the Functioning of the European Union, [2012] O. J. C 326/47.

Convention Against Torture and Other Cruel, Inhuman or Degrading Treatment or Punishment, 1465 UNTS 85, (1984)23 ILM 1027.

Convention for the Establishment of a Central American Court of Justice. 20 December 1907, (1908) 2 AJIL Supp. 231.

Convention for the Pacific Settlement of International Disputes, 29 July 1899, 187 Cons TS 410.

Convention for the Pacific Settlement of International Disputes, 18 October 1907, 205 Cons TS 277.
Convention on Biological Diversity, 5 June 1992, 1760 UNTS 79, 31 ILM 818.
Convention on International Trade in Endangered Species of Wild Fauna and Flora, 3 March 1973, 993 UNTS 243.
Convention on the Rights of the Child, 20 November 1989, 1577 UNTS 3.
Convention on the Settlement of Investment Disputes between States and Nationals of Other States, 18 March 1965, 575 UNTS 159, (1965) 4 ILM 532.
Convention on the Statute of the Central American Court of Justice, 10 December 1992, 1821 UNTS 291, 34 ILM 921.
Convention on Wetlands of International Importance especially as Waterfowl Habitat, 2 February 1971, 996 UNTS 245, (1972) 11 ILM 963.
Convention relative to the Creation of an International Prize Court, 18 October 1907, 205 Cons TS 381.
European Convention for the Peaceful Settlement of Disputes, 29 April 1957, 320 UNTS 243.
European Convention for the Protection of Human Rights and Fundamental Freedoms, Europ TS No 5, 213 UNTS 211.
Geneva Convention for the Amelioration of the Condition of the Wounded and Sick in Armed Forces in the Field (Geneva Convention I), 12 August 1949, 75 UNTS 31.
Geneva Convention for the Amelioration of the Condition of Wounded, Sick and Shipwrecked Members of Armed Forces at Sea (Geneva Convention II), 12 August 1949, 75 UNTS 85.
Geneva Convention relative to the Protection of Civilian Persons in Time of War (Geneva Convention IV), 12 August 1949, 75 UNTS 287.
Geneva Convention relative to the Treatment of Prisoners of War (Geneva Convention III), 12 August 1949, 75 UNTS 135.
Inter-American Convention on Forced Disappearance of Persons, 9 June 1994, 22 ILM 1429.
Inter-American Convention on the Prevention, Punishment and Eradication of Violence Against Women "Convention of Belém do Pará", 9 June 1994, (1994) 33 ILM 1534.
International Covenant on Civil and Political Rights, 16 December 1966, 999 UNTS 171, (1967) 6 ILM 368.
Protocol Additional to the Geneva Conventions of 12 August 1949, and Relating to the Protection of Victims of International Armed Conflicts, 8 June 1977, 1125 UNTS 3, (1977) 16 ILM 1391.
Protocol Additional to the Geneva Conventions of 12 August 1949, and Relating to the Protection of Victims of Non-International Armed Conflicts, 8 June 1977, 1125 UNTS 609, (1977) 16 ILM 1442.
Protocol No. 12 to the Convention for the Protection of Human Rights and Fundamental Freedoms, 4 November 2000, 2465 UNTS 207.
Protocol No. 13 to the Convention for the Protection of Human Rights and Fundamental Freedoms concerning the abolition of the death penalty in all circumstances, 3 May 2002, 2246 UNTS 112.
Protocol No. 4 to the Convention for the Protection of Human Rights and Fundamental Freedoms securing certain rights and freedoms other than those already included in the Convention and in the First Protocol thereto, 16 September 1963, 1496 UNTS 263.
Protocol No. 6 to the Convention for the Protection of Human Rights and Fundamental Freedoms concerning the Abolition of the Death Penalty, 28 April 1983, 1496 UNTS 281.
Protocol No. 7 to the Convention for the Protection of Human Rights and Fundamental Freedoms, 22 November 1984, 1525 UNTS 195.
Protocol of Signature Relating to the Statute for the Permanent Court of International Justice Provided for by Article 14 of the Covenant of the League of Nations, 16 December 1920, [1921] 6 LNTS 379, (1923) 17 AJIL Supp 55.
Protocol on the Community Court of Justice, 6 July 1991, 2375 UNTS 178.

Protocol on the Statute of the African Court of Justice and Human Rights, 1 July 2008, 48 ILM 317 (not in force).
Protocol to the African Charter on Human and Peoples' Rights on the Establishment of an African Court on Human and Peoples' Rights, 10 June 1998, (1997) 9 Afr J Int'l & Comp L 953.
Protocol to the Convention for the Protection of Human Rights and Fundamental Freedoms, 20 March 1952, 213 UNTS 221.
Revised Treaty of the Economic Community of West African States (ECOWAS), 24 July 1993, 2373 UNTS 233.
Rome Statute of the International Criminal Court, 17 July 1998, 2187 UNTS 90, (1998) 37 ILM 1002.
Statute of the River Uruguay, Argentina and Uruguay, 26 February 1975, 1295 UNTS 339.
Stockholm Convention on Persistent Organic Pollutants, 22 May 2001, 2256 UNTS 119, (2001) 40 ILM 532.
Treaty between the Argentine Republic and the Eastern Republic of Uruguay concerning the boundary constituted by the River Uruguay, Argentina and Uruguay, 7 April 1961, 1970 UNTS 332.
Treaty establishing a Constitution for Europe, 29 October 2004, [2004] O.J. C 310/1.
Treaty for the establishment of a Common Market (Asunción Treaty), Argentina, Brazil, Paraguay and Uruguay, 26 March 1991, 2140 UNTS 257, (1991) 30 ILM 1041.
Treaty of Amity, Economic Relations and Consular Rights between the United States and Iran, 15 August 1955, 284 UNTS 93.
Treaty of Lisbon amending the Treaty on European Union and the Treaty establishing the European Community, 13 December 2007, [2007] I.J. C 306/1.
Treaty of Peace with Turkey Signed at Lausanne, 24 July 1923, 28 L.N.T.S. 11, (1924) 18 Am. J. Int'l L. Supp. 4.
Treaty of the Economic Community of West African States, 28 May 1975, 1976 UNTS 17.
United Nations Convention on the Law of the Sea, 10 December 1982, 1833 UNTS 3.
United Nations Convention to Combat Desertification in those Countries Experiencing Serious Drought and/or Desertification, Particularly in Africa, 14 October 1994, 1954 UNTS 3, 33 ILM 1328.
Vienna Convention on Consular Relations, 24 April 1963, 596 UNTS 261.
Vienna Convention on the Law of Treaties, 23 May 1969, 1155 UNTS 331, (1969) 8 ILM 679.

2.2 International Agreements and Other Documents Published in the United Nations Treaty Series

Declaration of the United States of America relating to the above-mentioned Declaration, United States, 6 April 1984, 1354 UNTS 452.
Declaration recognizing as compulsory the jurisdiction of the Court, in conformity with Article 36, paragraph 2, of the Statute of the International Court of Justice, United States, 14 August 1946, 1 UNTS 9.
Maroua Declaration (with chart), Nigeria and United Republic of Cameroon, 1 June 1975, 1236 UNTS 319.
Minutes on settlement of disputes regarding joint boundaries between Qatar, Bahrain and Saudi Arabia, Objection by Bahrain, 9 August 1991,1647 UNTS 422.
Minutes on settlement of disputes regarding joint boundaries, Bahrain, Qatar and Saudi Arabia, 25 December 1990, 1641 UNTS 239.
Termination by the United States of America, United States, 7 October 1985, 1408 UNTS 270.

2.3 *Documents of International Organizations*

2.3.1 League of Nations

Permanent Court of International Justice - Advisory Committee of Jurists, Procès-Verbaux of the Proceedings of the Committee (The Hague: Van Langenhuysen Frères, 1920).

Resolution adopted by the Assembly of the League of Nations, 19 September 1927, 53 OJ Spec Supp 9, (1947) 41 AJIL Supp 106 at 106-107.

2.3.2 United Nations System

2.3.2.1 Resolutions

Administration of justice at the United Nations, GA Res 63/233, UNGAOR, 64th Sess, UN Doc A/RES/63/233 (2009).

Arbitral procedure, GA Res. 989 (X), UN GAOR, 10th Sess., Supp. No. 9, UN Doc A/RES/989 (X) (1955).

Basic Principles for the protection of civilian populations in armed conflicts, GA Res 2675 (XXV), UNGAOR, 25th Sess, UN Doc A/RES/2675 (XXV) (1970).

Declaration of Principles Governing the Sea-Bed and the ocean Floor, and the Subsoil Thereof, beyond the Limits of National Jurisdictions, GA Res 2749 (XXV), UNGAOR, 25th Sess, UN Doc A/RES/2749 (XXV) (1970).

Declaration on the prohibition of the use of nuclear and thermo-nuclear weapons, GA Res 1653 (XVI), UNGAOR, 16th Sess, UN Doc A/RES/1653 (XVI) (1961).

Declaration on the Protection of All Persons from Being Subjected to Torture, GA Res 3452 (XXX), UNGAOR 30th Sess, Supp No 34 at 91, UN Doc A/1034 (1975).

Illegal Israeli actions in Occupied East Jerusalem and the rest of the Occupied Palestinian Territory, GA Res ES-10/14, UN GAOR, 10th Sp. Sess., UN Doc. A/RES/ ES-10/14 (2003).

International Criminal Tribunal for the former Yugoslavia (ICTY), SC Res 827 (1993), UNSCOR, 1992 UN Doc S/RES/827 (1993), reprinted in (1993) 32 ILM 1159.

Maintenance of international peace and security, SC Res 2240 (2015), UNSCOR, 2015, UN Doc S/RES/2240 (2015).

Oceans and the law of the Sea, GA Res 63/111, UNGAOR, 63th Sess, UN Doc A/RES/63/111 (2008).

Oceans and the law of the Sea, GA Res 65/37A, UNGAOR, 65th Sess, UN Doc A/RES/65/37A (2010).

Oceans and the law of the Sea, GA Res 69/245, UNGAOR, 69th Sess, UN Doc A/RES/69/245 (2014).

Request for an advisory opinion from the International Court of Justice on the legality of the threat or use of nuclear weapons, GA Res. 49/75[K], UN GAOR, 49th Sess., Supp. No. 49, UN Doc. A/RES/49/75[K] (1994).

Review of the procedure provided for under article 11 of the statute of the Administrative Tribunal of the United Nations, GA Res 50/54, UNGAOR, 50th Sess, UN Doc A/RES/50/54 (1995).

Somalia, SC Res 1816 (2008), UNSCOR, 2008, UN Doc S/RES/1816 (2008).

United Nations Rules for the Protection of Juveniles Deprived of their Liberty, GA Res 45/113, UNGAOR, 45th Sess, UN Doc A/RES/45/113 (1990).

Universal Declaration of Human Rights, GA Res 217A(III), UNGAOR, 3d Sess, Supp No 13, U. N. Doc. A/810, (1948).
United Nations Standard Minimum Rules for the Administration of Juvenile Justice ("The Beijing Rules"), GA Res 40/33, UNGAOR, 40th Sess, UN Doc A/RES/40/33 (1985).

2.3.2.2 Reports and Parliamentary Documents

"Appeal of Judgment No.2867 of the International Labour Organization Administrative Tribunal to the International Court of Justice", IFAD Doc EB 2010/99/R.43/Rev.1, online: International Fund for Agricultural Development <http://www.ifad.org/gbdocs/eb/99/e/EB-2010-99-R-43-REV-1.pdf>.
CCPR, "General Comment No. 13: Equality before the courts and the right to a fair and public hearing by an independent court established by law (Art. 14)", (13 April 1984) in Compilation Of General Comments and General Recommendations adopted by Human Rights Treaty Bodies, UN Doc HRI/GEN/1/Rev.9 (Vol. I) (2008).
CCPR, "General Comment No. 14: Nuclear weapons and the right to life (Art. 6)", (9 November 1984) in Compilation Of General Comments and General Recommendations adopted by Human Rights Treaty Bodies, UN Doc HRI/GEN/1/Rev.9 (Vol. I) (2008).
CCPR, "General Comment No. 27: Article 12 (Freedom of movement)", (1999) in Compilation Of General Comments and General Recommendations adopted by Human Rights Treaty Bodies, UN Doc HRI/GEN/1/Rev.9 (Vol. I) (2008).
CCPR, "General Comment No. 32: Right to equality before courts and tribunals and to a fair trial (Art. 14)", (23 August 2007) in Compilation Of General Comments and General Recommendations adopted by Human Rights Treaty Bodies, UN Doc HRI/GEN/1/Rev.9 (Vol. I) (2008).
CCPR, "General Comment No. 8: Right to liberty and security of persons (Art. 9)", U.N. Doc. U. N. Doc. HRI/GEN/1/Rev.1 (1994).
CEDAW, "General Recommendation No. 19: Violence against women", (1992) in Compilation Of General Comments and General Recommendations adopted by Human Rights Treaty Bodies, UN Doc HRI/GEN/1/Rev.9 (Vol. I).
CRC, "General Comment No. 11: Indigenous children and their rights under the Convention", (12 February 2009) UN Doc CRC/C/GC/11.
CRC, "General Comment No. 5: General measures of implementation of the Convention on the Rights of the Child (arts. 4, 42 and 44, para. 6)", (27 November 2003) in Compilation Of General Comments and General Recommendations adopted by Human Rights Treaty Bodies, UN Doc HRI/GEN/1/Rev.9 (Vol. I) (2008).
Draft Articles on Responsibility of States for Internationally Wrongful Acts with commentaries, UN Doc A/56/10, UNGAOR, 56th Sess, Supp No 10.
First Report on the Law of Treaties by Sir Humphrey Waldock, Special Rapporteur (UN Doc A/CN.4/144) in *Yearbook of the International Law Commission* 1962, vol 2 (New York: UN, 1964) (UN Doc A/CN.4/SER.A/1962/Add.1).
Fourth Report on the Law of Treaties, by Sir Humphrey Waldock, Special Rapporteur (UN Doc A/CN.4/177) in *Yearbook of the International Law Commission* 1965, vol 2 (New York: UN, 1967) (UN Doc A/CN.4/SER.A/1965/Add.1).
Fifth Report on the Law of Treaties, by Sir Humphrey Waldock, Special Rapporteur" (UN Doc A/CN.4/183 and Add. 1-4) in *Yearbook of the International Law Commission 1966*, vol 2 (New York: UN, 1967) (A/CN.4/SER.A/1966/Add.1).
Fragmentation of International Law: Difficulties arising from the Diversification and Expansion of International Law: Report of the Study Group of the International Law Commission, UNGAOR, 61st Sess, Supp. No. 10, UN Doc. A/CN.4/L.682.

Interoffice memorandum to the Executive Secretary of the United Nations Convention to Combat Desertification Secretariat regarding questions posed by the Joint Inspection Unit, [2009] UN Jur Yb 450.

Law of Treaties: Report by G. G. Fitzmaurice, Special Rapporteur (UN Doc A/CN.4.101) in *Yearbook of the International Law Commission* 1956, vol 2 (New York: UN, 1957) (A/CN.4/SER.A/1956/Add.1).

Letter dated 18 December 2008 from the Permanent Representatives of Argentina, Brazil, Croatia, France, Gabon, Japan, the Netherlands and Norway to the United Nations addressed to the President of the General Assembly, UNGAOR, 63th Sess, UN Doc A/63/635 (2008).

Organization to house the Global Mechanism and agreement on its modalities, ICCD Doc Dec 24/COP.1, para 1. online: United Nations Convention to Combat Desertification <http://www.unccd.int/cop/officialdocs/cop1/pdf/11add1eng.pdf#page=67>.

Report of the Conference of the Parties on its First Session, Held in Rome from 29 September to 10 October 1997, ICCD Doc ICCD/COP(1)/11/Add.1, at 67-69, online: United Nations Convention to Combat Desertification <http://archive.unccd.int/cop/officialdocs/cop1/pdf/11add1eng.pdf>;

Report of the International Law Commission covering its second session, 5 June – 19 July 1950 (UN Doc A/1316) in *Yearbook of the International Law Commission* 1950, vol 2 (A/CN.4/SER.A/1950/Add.1)

Report of the International Law Commission covering the work of its tenth session, 28 April-4July 1958 (UN Doc A/3859) in *Yearbook of the International Law Commission* 1958, vol 2 (New York: UN, 1958) (A/CN.4/SER.A/1958/Add.1).

Report of the International Law Commission covering the work of its fifteenth session, 6 May – 12 July 1963 (UN Doc A/5509) in *Yearbook of the International Law Commission* 1963, vol 2 (New York: UN, 1964).

Report of the International Law Commission covering the work of its fourteenth Session, 24 April - 29 June 1962 (UN Doc A/5209) in *Yearbook of the International Law Commission* 1962, vol 2 (New York: UN, 1964) (UN Doc A/CN.4/SER.A/1962/Add.1).

Report of the International Law Commission covering the work of its fifth session 1 June-14 August 1953 (UN Doc A/2456) in *Yearbook of the International Law Commission* 1953, vol 2 (New York: UN, 1959) at 210 (A/CN.4/SER.A/1953/Add.1).

Report of the International Law Commission on the work of its eighteenth session Ganeve, 4 May-19 July 1966" (UN Doc A/5309/Rev.1) *in Yearbook of the International Law Commission* 1966, vol 2 (New York: UN, 1967) (A/CN.4/SER.A/1966/Add.1).

Report of the International Law Commission on the work of its fifty-second session (1 May–9 June and 10 July–18 August 2000)" (UN Doc A/55/10) in *Yearbook of the International Law Commission* 2000, vol 2, part 2 (New York and Geneva: UN, 2006) (UN Doc A/CN.4/ SER.A/2000/Add. 1 (Part 2)/Rev.1).

Report of the International Law Commission on the work of its sixty-third session, UNGAOR, 66st Sess., Supp. No. 10, UN Doc. A/66/10 (2011).

Report of the International Law Commission on the work of its fifty-eight session, UNGAOR, 61st Sess, Supp. No. 10, UN Doc A/61/10 (2006).

Rules of Procedure of the General Assembly, embodying amendments and additions adopted by the General Assembly up to September 2007, UNGAOR, UN doc A/520/Rev.17.

Selection of a competent international organization to carry out the functions of the Secretariat of the Convention, CBD Doc COP1 Dec I/4, online: Convention on Biological Diversity <http://www.cbd.int/decision/cop/default.shtml?id=7064>.

Statute of the Administrative Tribunal of the International Labour Organization, online: International Labour Organization <http://www.ilo.org/public/english/tribunal/about/statute.htm>.

Statute of the International Law Commission, GA Res. 174 (II), UN GAOR, 2nd Sess., UN Doc. A/RES/174 (II).

Survey of International Law in Relation to the Work of Codification of the International Law Commission, 10 February 1949, UN. Doc A/CN.4/1/Rev/1.
UNC1OR, 20th Sess, 1423 Mtg, UN Doc A/C. 1/SR. 1423 (1965).
UNC1OR, 51st Sess., 8th Mtg., UN Doc. A/C.1/51/PV.8 (1996).
UNCN4OR, 10th Sess., 473th Mtg., UN Doc. A/CN.4/SR473 (1958) in *Yearbook of the International Law Commission* 1958, vol 2 (New York: UN, 1958) (A/CN.4/SER. A/1958/Add.1).
UNGAOR, 63th Sess, 70 Mtg, UN Doc A/63/PV.70 (2008).
UNHRC, "Elimination of violence against women", Res 2003/45, 59th Mtg, 23 April 2004, UN Doc E/CN.4/2003/L.11/Add.4.
UNHRC, "Report of the Representative of the Secretary-General, Mr. Francis M. Deng, submitted pursuant to Commission resolution 1997/39" UN Doc E/CN.4/1998/53/Add.2, 54th Sess, 11 February 1998, reprinted in (1999) 33:2 Int'l Migration Rev 484, 37 ILM 1482.
UNHRC, "Report presented by Mrs. Radhika Coomaraswamy, Special Rapporteur on violence against women, with the inclusion of its causes and consequences, pursuant to resolution 1997/44 of the Commission" UN Doc E/CN.4/1998/54, 54th Sess, 26 January 1998.
United Nations Documents on the Development and Codification of International Law, U.N. Doc. A/AC.10/5 (29 April 1947), (1947) 41:4 AJIL Supp 29.
United Nations Interim Administration Mission in Kosovo, "Regulation 2001/9 on Constitutional Framework on Interim Self-Government in Kosovo", online: UNMIK Official Gazette <http://www.unmikonline.org/regulations/unmikgazette/02english/E2001regs/RE2001_09.pdf>.

2.3 *Organization of American States*

2.3.1 Resolutions

OASGA, "Follow-up Program for Universal Civil Registry and 'Right to Identity,'" GA Res AG/RES. 2602 (XL-O/10) of 8 June 2010.
OASGA, "Inter-American Program for Universal Civil Registry and 'Right to Identity,'" GA Res AG/RES. 2286 (XXXVII O/07) of June 5, 2007.
OASGA, "Inter-American Program for Universal Civil Registry and 'Right to Identity,'" GA Res AG/RES. 2362 (XXXVIII-O/08) of 3 June 2008.

2.3.2 Documents

OASIAJC, "On the scope of the right to identity", CJI/Res. 137 (LXXI-O/07) of 10 August 2007, in Annual Report of the Inter-American Juridical Committee to the General Assembly 2007, OAS Doc OEA/Ser.Q/VII.38.

2.4 *Other*

Elements of Crimes, Official Records of the Review Conference of the Rome Statute of the International Criminal Court, Kampala, 31 May -11 June 2010, ICC-ASP/1/3(part II-B) online: International Criminal Court <http://www.icc-cpi.int/>.

3 Secondary Materials

3.1 Books

Addo, Michael K. *The Legal Nature of International Human Rights* (Leiden: Martinus Nijhoff Publishers, 2010).
Adorno, Theodor W. *Negative dialectics* (London: Taylor & Francis, 2004).
Akehurst, Michael & Peter Malanczuk, *Modern Introduction to International Law*, *7th ed* (New York: Rutledge, 2007).
Aljaghoub, Mahasen M. *The advisory function of the International Court of Justice 1946-2005* (Berlin: Springer, 2006).
Aust, Anthony. *Handbook of International Law* (Cambridge: Cambridge University Press, 2005).
Aust, Anthony.*Modern Treaty Law and Practice*, 2nd ed, (Cambridge: Cambridge University Press, 2007).
Ayala, Balthazar. *De Jure et Officiis Bellicis et Disciplina Militari Libri III, vol. II* (Washington, D. C.: Carnegie Institution, 1912).
Bates, Ed. *The Evolution of the European Convention on Human Rights: From Its Inception to the Creation of a Permanent Court of Human Rights* (Oxford: Oxford University Press, 2010).
Belli, Pierino. *De Re Militari et Bello Tractatus, vol. II, trans. by Herbert C. Nutting* (Oxford: Clarendon Press, 1936).
Beneyto, José María, et al, eds, *New Approaches to International Law: The European and the American Experiences* (The Hague: TMC Asser Press, 2012).
Bernstorff, Jochen von, *The Public International Law Theory of Hans Kelsen: Believing in Universal Law*, trans by Thomas Dunlap (Cambridge: Cambridge University Press, 2010).
Boyle, Alan & Christine Chinkin. *The Making of International Law* (Oxford: Oxford University Press, 2007).
Brown Scott. James, *Law, the state, and the international community* (New York: Columbia University Press, 1939).
Browning, Robert. *Pippa passes* (Cambridge: Chadwyck-Healey, 1994), online: Literature Online <http://lion.chadwyck.com>.
Brownlie, Ian. *Principles of public international law, 6th ed* (Oxford; New York: Oxford University Press, 2003).
Brunnée, Jutta & Stephen J. Toope. *Legitimacy and Legality in International Law: An Interactional Account* (Cambridge: Cambridge University Press, 2010).
Burlamaqui, Jean-Jacques. *The Principles of Natural Law and Politic Law* (Indianapolis: Liberty Fund, 2006).
Bynkershoek, Cornelius van. *Questionum Juris Publici Libri Duo, vol. 2, trans. by Tenney Frank* (Oxford: Clarendon Press, 1930).
Cançado Trindade, Antônio Augusto. *A Humanização do Dereito Internacional* (Belo Horizonte: Del Rey, 2006).
Cançado Trindade, Antonio Augusto. *International Law for Humanklnd. Towards a New Jus Gentium* (Leiden: Martinus Nijhoff, 2010).
Cassese, Antonio. *International Law, 2nd ed,* (Oxford: OUP, 2004).
Cassese, Antonio. *Realizing Utopia: The Future of International Law* (Oxford: OUP, 2012).
Cheng, Bin. *General principles of law as applied by international courts and tribunals* (Cambridge: Grotius Publications Ltd., 1987).
Chinkin, Christine. *Third Parties in International Law* (Oxford: Clarendon Press, 1993).
D'Amato, Anthony A. *The concept of custom in international law* (Ithaca, N.Y.: Cornell University Press, 1971).
d'Aspremont, Jean. *Formalism and the Sources of International Law: A theory of the Ascertainment of Legal Rules* (Oxford: Oxford University Press, 2011).
Delmas-Marty, Mireille. *Trois défis pour un droit mondial* (Paris: Editions du Seuil, 1998).

Dickens, Charles. *A Tale of Two Cities* (Cambridge: Chadwyck-Healey, 2000), online: Literature Online <http://lion.chadwyck.com>.

Elias, O. A. & C. L. Lim, *The paradox of consensualism in international law* (The Hague; Boston: Kluwer Law International, 1998).

Engelen, Frank. *Interpretation of Tax Treaties under International Law* (Amsterdam: IBFD Publications, 2004).

Fiore, Pasquale. *International law codified and its legal sanction, or, The legal organization of the society of states, 5th ed,* trans by Edwin M, Borchard (New York : Baker, Voorhis, 1918).

Forowicz, Magdalena. *The Reception of International Law in the European Court of Human Rights* (Oxford: Oxford University Press, 2010).

Fox, Hazel. *The Law of State Immunity, 2d ed* (Oxfod: OUP, 2008).

Fuller, Lon. *The Morality of Law, rev ed* (New Haven: Yale University Press, 1969).

Gentili, Alberico. *De Iure Belli Libri Tres, vol. 2,* trans. by John C. Rolfe (Oxford: Clarendon Press, 1933).

Grotius, Hugo. *De Jure Belli ac Pacis, vol. 2,* trans. by Francis W. Kelsey (Oxford: Clarendon Press, 1925).

Grotius, Hugo. *De Jure Praedae Commentarius, vol. 1,* trans. by Gwladys L. Williams & Walter H. Zeydel (Oxford: Clarendon Press, 1950).

Grotius, Hugo. *The Rights of War and Peace,* trans. by Jean Barbeyrac (Clark: Lawbook Exchange, 2004).

Guggenheim, Paul. *Traité de droit international public* (Geneve: Librarie Georg, 1967).

Heineccius, Johann Gottlieb. *Elementa Juris Naturae et Gentium* (Indianapolis: Libery Fund, 2008).

Henckaerts, Jean-Marie & Doswald-Beck, Louise, eds, *Customary international humanitarian law* (Cambridge: Cambridge University Press, 2005).

Herczegh, Géza. *General principles of law and the international legal order* (Budapest: Akadémiai Kiadó, 1969).

Hernandez, Gleider I. *The International Court of Justice and the Judicial Function* (Oxford: Oxford University Press, 2014)

Higgins, Rosalyn. *Problems and Process: International Law and How We Use It* (Oxford: Oxford University Press, 1994).

Hudson, Manley O. *International Tribunals: Past and Future* (Washington D.C.: Brookings Institution, 1944).

Hudson, Manley O. *The Permanent court of international justice 1920-1942: A Treatise* (New York: The Macmillan Company).

Janis, Mark W. *An Introduction to International Law* (New York: Aspen Publishers, 2003).

Kamminga, Menno T. & Martin Scheinin, eds, *The Impact of Human Rights Law on General International Law* (Oxford: Oxford University Press, 2009).

Kelsen, Hans. *Law and Peace in International Relations: The Oliver Wendell Holmes Lectures, 1940-41* (Cambridge: Haravard University Press, 1942).

Kelsen, Hans. *Principles of international law* (New York: Rinehart, 1952).

Kennedy, David L. *International legal structures* (Baden-Baden: Nomos, 1987).

Koskenniemi, Martti. *From apology to Utopia: the structure of international legal argument* (Cambridge: Cambridge University Press, 2005).

Lauterpacht, Hersch. *The Development of International Law by the International Court* (New York: Cambridge University Press, 1982).

Lauterpacht, Hersch. *The Function of Law in the International Community* (Oxford: Clarendon Press, 1933).

Legnano, Giovani de. *Tractatus De Bello, De Represaliis et De Duello* (Oxford: Oxford University Press, 1917).

Letsas, George. *A Theory of Interpretation of the European Convention on Human Rights* (Oxford: Oxford University Press, 2007).

McNair, Arnold. *The Law of Treaties* (Oxford: Clarendon Press, 1961).

Meron, Theodor. *Human Rights and Humanitarian Norms as Customary Law* (Oxford: Clarendon Press, 1989).
Meron, Theodor. *The humanization of international* law (Leiden: Martinus Nijhoff, 2006).
Oppenheim, Lassa, Robert Y. Jennings & C. A. H. Watts, *Oppenheim's international law, 9th ed* (London: Longmans, 1993).
Oppenheim, Lassa. *International Law: A Treatise, vol I, 2nd ed* (London: Longmans, 1912).
Oppenheim, Lassa. *International Law: A Treatise, vol I, 3rd ed by Ronald Roxburgh*, (London: Longmans Green, 1920).
Oppenheim, Lassa. *International Law: A Treatise, vol I, 4th ed by Arnold Duncan McNai*r, (London: Longmans Green, 1928).
Oppenheim, Lassa. *International Law: A Treatise, vol I, 7th ed by Hersch Lauterpacht*, (London: Longmans, 1948).
Oppenheim, Lassa. *International Law: A Treatise, vol. I* (London: Longmans, Green & co., 1905).
Orakhelashvili, Alexander. *Peremptory Norms in International Law* (Oxford: OUP, 2006).
Orakhelashvili, Alexander. *The Interpretation of Acts and Rules in Public International Law* (Oxford: Oxford University Press, 2009).
Parry, Clive. *The Sources and Evidences of International Law* (Manchester: Manchester University Press, 1965).
Pauwelyn, Joost. *Conflict of Norms in Public International Law: How WTO Law Relates to other Rules of International Law* (Cambridge: Cambridge University Press, 2003).
Phillimore, Robert. *Commentaries upon international law, vol. 1* (London: W.G. Benning, 1854).
Provost, René. *International Human Rights and Humanitarian Law* (Cambridge: Cambridge University Press, 2002).
Pufendorf, Samuel. *De Jure Naturae et Gentium, vol. 2*, trans. by C. H. Oldfather & W. A. Oldfather (Oxford: Clarendon Press, 1934).
Rachel, Samuel. *De Jure Naturae et Gentium Dissertationes, vol. 2*, trans. by John Pawley Bate (Washington D.C.: The Carnegie Institution, 1916).
Raimondo, Fabián. *General principles of law in the decisions of international criminal courts and tribunals* (Leiden; Boston: M. Nijhoff Pub., 2008).
René-Jean Dupuy, *La Communauté internationale entre le mythe et l'histoire* (Paris: UNESCO, 1986).
Rosenne, Shabtai. *The law and practice of the International Court, 1920-2005, 4th ed* (Leiden: Martinus Nijhoff, 2006).
Rosenne, Shabtai. *The perplexities of modern international law* (Leiden: Martinus Nijhoff, 2004).
Rosenne, Shabtai. *The World Court: what it is and how it works, 5th completely rev ed* (Dordrecht; London: M. Nijhoff, 1995).
Ross, Alf. *A textbook of international law: general part* (London: Longmans & Green, 1947).
Rozakis, Christos L. *The Concept of Jus Cogens in the Law of Treaties* (Amsterdam: North-Holland, 1976).
Shahabuddeen, Mohamed. *Precedent in the world court* (Cambridge; New York: Cambridge University Press, 1996).
Shahabuddeen, Mohamed. *Precedent in the World Court* (New York: Cambridge University Press, 1996).
Shaw, Malcolm N. *International law, 5th ed* (Cambridge: Cambridge University Press, 2003).
Simpson, A. W Brian. *Human Rights and the End of Empire: Britain and the Genesis of the European Convention* (Oxford: Oxford University Press, 2004).
Somos, Mark. *Secularization and the Leiden Circle* (Leiden: Koninklijke Brill, 2011).
Spiermann, Ole. *International legal argument in the Permanent Court of International Justice: the rise of the international judiciary* (Cambridge: Cambridge University Press, 2005).
Suarez, Francisco. *Selections from Three Works, vol. II* (Oxford: Clarendon Press, 1944).
Sztucki, Jerzy. *Jus Cogens and the Vienna Convention on the Laws of Treaties* (New York: Springer-Verlag, 1974).

Textor, Johann Wolfgang. *Synopsis Juris Gentium, vol. 2,* trans. by John Pawley Bate (Washington, D.C.: Carnegie Institution, 1916).
Thirlway, Hugh. *The Sources of International Law* (Oxford: Oxford University Press, 2014).
van Hoof, G.J.H. *Rethinking the Sources of International Law* (Deventer: Kluwer Law and Taxation Publishers, 1983).
Vattel, Emmerich de. *The Law of Nations or The Principles of Natural Law Applied to the Conduct and to the Affairs of Nations and of Sovereigns*, trans. by Charles G. Fenwick (Washington D.C.: The Carnegie Institution, 1926).
Venzke, Ingo. *How Interpretation Makes International Law. On Semantic Change and Normative Twists* (Oxford: Oxford University Press, 2012).
Victoria, Francisci de. *De Indis et de Ivre Belli Relectiones, trans. by Franciscus de Victoria* (Washington D.C.: Carnegie Institution, 1917).
Villalpando, Santiago. *L'émergence de la communauté internationale dans la responsabilité des Etats* (Paris: Presses Universitaires de France, 2005).
Villiger, Mark Eugen. *Commentary on the 1969 Vienna Convention on the Law of Treaties* (Leiden: Martinus Nijhoff Publishers, 2009).
Villiger, Mark Eugen. *Customary International Law and Treaties: A Study of their Interactions and Interrelations, with Special Consideration of the 1969 Vienna Convention on the Law of Treaties* (Dordrecht: Martinus Nijhoff Publishers, 1985).
Vinx, Lars. *Hans Kelsen's Pure Theory of Law: Legality and Legitimacy* (Oxford: Oxfourd University Press, 2007).
Wheaton, Henry. *Elements of international law: with a sketch of the history of the science* (London,: B. Fellowes, 1836).
Wolff, Christian. *Jus Gentium Methodo Scoentifica Pertractatum, vol. 2*, trans. by Joseph H. Drake (Oxford: Clarendon Press, 1934).
Zouche, Richard. *Iuris et Iudicii Fecialis, sive, Iuris Inter Gentes, et Quaestionum de Eodem Explicatio, vol. 2*, trans. by J. L. Brierly (Washington D.C.: Carnegie Institution, 1911).

3.2 Chapters

Boschiero, Nerina. "Jurisdictional Immunities of the State and Exequatur of Foreign Judgments: a private International Law Evaluation of the Recent ICJ Judgment in Germany v. Italy", in Nerina Boschiero, et al. (eds), *International Courts and the Development of International Law, Essays in Honour of Tullio Treves* (T.M.C. Asser Press, The Hague, The Netherlands, 2013) 781.
Boyle, Alan. "Some Reflections on the Relationship of Treaties and Soft Law" in Vera Gowlland-Debbas, ed, *Multilateral Treaty-making* (The Hague: Martinus Nijhoff Publishers, 2000).
Cançado Trindade, Antônio Augusto. "Hacia el nuevo Jus Gentium del siglo XXI: El derecho universal de la humanidad" in Secretaria General de la OEA, *Jornadas de Derecho Internacional 2003* (Washington: OEA, 2005).
Charney, Jonathan I. "International Lawmaking – Article 38 of the ICJ Statute Reconsidered" in Jost Delbrück & Ursula E. Heinz, eds, *New trends in international lawmaking : international "legislation" in the public interest* (Berlin: Duncker & Humblot, 1997).
Christakis, Théodore. "L'Obligation de non-reconnaissence des situations créées par le recours ellicite à la force ou d'autres actes enfreignant des règles fondamentales", in Christian Tomuschat and Jean-Marc Thouvenin eds., *The Fundamental Rules of the International Legal Order: Jus Cogens an Obligations Erga Omnes* (Leiden: Martinus Nijhoff, 2006) 127.
Christoffersen, Jonas. "The Impact of Human Rights Law on General International Law", in Menno T. Kamminga & Martin Scheinin, eds, *The Impact of Human Rights Law on General International Law* (Oxford: Oxford University Press, 2009).

d'Aspremont, Jean. "Herbert Hart in Post-Modern International Legal Scholarship" in Jean d'Aspremont & Jörg Kammerhofer, eds, *International Legal Positivism in a Post-Modern World* (Cambridge: Cambridge University Press, 2014).

D'Amato, Anthony. "International Law as an Autopoietic System", in Rüdiger Wolfrum & Volker Röben, eds, *Developments of international law in treaty making* (Berlin; New York: Springer, 2005).

Dörr, Oliver. "Article 31. General rule of interpretation", in Oliver Dörr & Kirsten Schmalenbach, eds, *Vienna Convention on the Law of Treaties* (Berlin: Springer-Verlag, 2012).

Dupuy, René-Jean. "Conclusions of the Workshop" in René-Jean Dupuy, ed, *L'Avenir du Droit International Dans un Monde Multiculturel: Colloque de la Académie de Droit International de la Haye, 17-19 Novembre 1983* (The Hague : Martinus Nijhoff, 1983).

Falk, Richard A. "The Interplay of Westphalia and Charter Conceptions of the International Legal Order" in Cyril Edwin Black & Richard A. Falk, eds, *The Future of the international legal order* (Princeton: Princeton University Press, 1969).

Favre, Antoine. "Les principes généraux du droit, fonds commun du droit des gens" in Faculté de Droit de L'Université de Genève, ed, *Recueil d'études de droit international : en hommage à Paul Guggenheim* (Genève: La tribune de Genève, 1968).

Fitzmaurice, Gerald G. "Some Problems Regarding the Formal Sources of International Law" in Frederick Mari van Asbek, ed, *Symbolae Verzijl, présentées au professeur J. H. W. Verzijl à l'occasion de son LXX-ième anniversaire* (The Hague: Martinus Nijhoff, 1958).

Fox, Hazel. "Time, History and Sources of Law Peremptory Norms: Is There a Need for New Sources of International Law" in Matthew Craven, Malgosia Fitzmaurice and Maria Vogiatzi, eds, *Time, History and International Law* (Leiden: Martinus Nijhoff, 2007).

Fuentes, Carlos Iván. "Silent Wars in Our Cities: Alternatives to the Inadequacy of International Humanitarian Law to Protect Civilians during Endemic Urban Violence", in Benjamin Perin, ed, *Modern Warfare: Armed Groups, Private Militaries, Humanitarian Organizations and the Law* (Vancouver: UBC Press, 2012).

Fuentes, Carlos Iván, René Provost and Samuel G. Walker, "E Pluribus Unum – Bhinneka Tunggal Ika? Universal Human Rights and the Fragmentation of International Law" in René Provost & Colleen Sheppard, eds, *Dialogues on Human Rights and Legal Pluralism* (Dordrecht: Springer, 2012).

Galicki, Zdzislaw. "Hierarchy in International Law within the Context of its Fragmentation", in I. Buffard, et al, eds, *International Law between Universalism and Fragmentation Festschrift in Honour of Gerhard Hafner* (The Hague: Koninklijke Brill, 2008).

Gautier, Philippe. "Article 1 Convention of 1969" in Olivier Corten & Pierre Klein, eds, *The Vienna Conventions on the Law of Treaties: A Commentary* (Oxford: Oxford University Press, 2011).

Gioia, Andrea. "The Role of the European Court of Human Rights in Monitoring Compliance with Humanitarian Law in Armed Conflict" in Orna Ben-Naftali, ed, *International Humanitarian Law and International Human Rights Law* (Oxford: Oxford University press, 2011).

Gomaa, Mohammed M "Non-Binding Agreements in International Law" in Laurence Boisson de Chazonrnes & Vera Gowlland-Debbas, eds, *The International Legal System in Quest of Equity and Universality: Liber Amicorum Georges Abi-Saab* (The Hague: Martinus Nijhoff, 2001).

Jacob, Marc. "Precedents: Lawmaking Through International Adjudication", in Armin von Bogdandy and Ingo Venzke, eds, *International Judicial Lawmaking: On Public Authority and Democratic Legitimation in Global Governance* (Heidelberg: Springer, 2012).

Janis, Mark W. "Religion and the Literature of International Law: Some Standard Texts" in Mark W. Janis, Carolyn Maree Evan, eds, *Religion and International Law* (The Hague: Martinus Nijhoff, 1999).

Jennings, Robert Y. "General Introduction" in Andreas Zimmermann, Christian Tomuschat & Karin Oellers-Frahm, eds, *The Statute of the International Court of Justice : A Commentary* (Oxford: Oxford University Press, 2006).

Kamminga, Menno T. "Final Report on the Impact of International Human Rights Law on General International Law" in Menno T. Kamminga & Martin Scheinin, eds, *The Impact of Human Rights Law on General International Law* (Oxford: Oxford University Press, 2009).

Kingsbury Benedict & Adam Roberts, "Introduction: Grotian Thought in International Relations", in Hedley Bull, Benedict Kingsbury & Adam Roberts, eds, *Hugo Grotius and International Relations* (Oxford: Clarendon Press, 1990)

Klabbers, Jan. "Reluctant Groundnormen: Articles 31(3)(c) and 42 of the Vienna Convention on the Law of Treaties and the Fragmentation of International Law" in Matthew Craven, Malgosia Fitzmaurice and Maria Vogiatzi, eds, *Time, History and International Law* (Leiden: Mastinus Nijhoff, 2007).

Koskenniemi, Martti. "Introduction" in Martti Koskenniemi, ed, *Sources of International Law* (Aldershot: Ashgate, 2000).

Lagerwall, Anne. "Article 64 Convention of 1969", Olivier Corten & Pierre Klein, eds., *The Vienna Conventions on the Law of Treaties: A Commentary* (Oxford: Oxford University Press, 2011).

Lauterpacht, Hersch "Some Observations on the Prohibition of 'Non Liquet' and the Completeness of the Law" in Frederick Mari van Asbek, ed, *Symbolae Verzijl, présentées au professeur J. H. W. Verzijl à l'occasion de son LXX-ième anniversaire* (The Hague: Martinus Nijhoff, 1958).

McDougal, Myres S. "The Ethics of Applying System of Authority: The Balanced Opposites of a Legal System" in Harold D. Lasswell and Harland Cleveland, eds, *The Ethics of Power: The Interplay of Religion, Philosophy, and Politics* (New York: Harper 1962).

Nieto-Navia, Rafael. "International Peremptory Norms (Jus Cogens) And International Humanitarian Law", in Lal Chand Vohrah, et al. *Man's inhumanity to man: essays on international law in honour of Antonio Cassese* (The Hague: Kluwer Law International, 2003), 595.

Nollkaemper, André"The Court and its Multiple Constituencies: Three Perspectives on the Kosovo Advisory Opinion", in Marko Milanovic and Michael Wood, *The Law and Politics of the Kosovo Advisory Opinion* (Cambridge: Cambridge University Press, 2015) 219 at 219.

Palchetti, Paolo. "Interpreting 'Generic Terms': Between Respect for the Parties' Original Intention and the Identification of the Ordinary Meaning", in Nerina Boschiero, et al., eds, *International Courts and the Development of International Law, Essays In Honour of Tullio Treves* (T.M.C. Asser Press, The Hague, The Netherlands, 2013) 91.

Pellet, Alain. "Article 38" in Andreas Zimmermann, Christian Tomuschat & Karin Oellers-Frahm, eds, *The Statute of the International Court of Justice : A Commentary* (Oxford: Oxford University Press, 2006).

Pellet, Alain. "Complementarity of International Treaty Law, Customary Law, and Non-Contractual Law-Making" in Rüdiger Wolfrum & Volker Röben, eds, *Developments of international law in treaty making* (Berlin; New York: Springer, 2005).

Petersen, Niels "Lawmaking by the International Court of Justice – Factors of Success", in Armin von Bogdandy and Ingo Venzke, eds, *International Judicial Lawmaking: On Public Authority and Democratic Legitimation in Global Governance* (Heidelberg: Springer, 2012).

Pineschi, Laura. "The Duty of Environmental Impact Assessment in the First ITLOS Chamber's Advisory Opinion: Towards the Supremacy of the General Rule to Protect and Preserve the Marine Environment as a Common Value?" in "Jurisdictional Immunities of the State and Exequatur of Foreign Judgments: a private International Law Evaluation of the Recent ICJ Judgment in Germany v. Italy" Nerina Boschiero, et al., eds, *International Courts and the Development of International Law, Essays in Honour of Tullio Treves* (T.M.C. Asser Press, The Hague, The Netherlands, 2013) 425.

Sands, Philippe & Jeffery Commission, "Treaty, Custom and Time: Interpretation/Application?" in Malgosia Fitzmaurice, Olufemi Elias & Panos Merkouris, eds, *Treaty Interpretation and the Vienna Convention on the Law of Treaties: 30 Years on* (Leiden: Koninklijke Brill, 2010).

Santos, Boaventura de Souza. "Toward a Multicultural Conception of human rights" in Berta Esperanza Hernández-Truyol, ed, *Moral imperialism: a critical anthology* (New York City: New York University Press, 2002).

Schachter, Oscar. "Towards a Theory of International Obligation" in Stephen M. Schwebel, ed, *The Effectiveness of international decisions; papers of a conference of the American Society of International Law and the proceedings of the conference* (Leiden: Sijthoff, 1971).

Simma, Bruno. "Human Rights before the International Court of Justice: Community Interest Coming to Life?" in Holger Hestermeyer, et al, eds, *Coexistence, cooperation and solidarity: Liber Amicorum Rüdiger Wolfrum* (Leiden: Martinus Nijhoff Publishers, 2012).

Simma, Bruno. and Theodore Kill, "Harmonizing Investment Protection And International Human Rights: First Steps Towards a Methodology" in Christina Binder, Ursula Kriebaum, August Reinisch, and Stephan Wittich, eds, *International Investment Law for the 21st Century: Essays in Honour of Christoph Schreuer* (Oxford: Oxford University Press, 2009).

Suy, Eric. "Article 53 Convention of 1969", in Olivier Corten & Pierre Klein, eds., *The Vienna Conventions on the Law of Treaties: A Commentary* (Oxford: Oxford University Press, 2011).

Spiermann, Ole. "Historical Introduction" in Andreas Zimmermann, Christian Tomuschat & Karin Oellers-Frahm, eds, *The Statute of the International Court of Justice : A Commentary* (Oxford: Oxford University Press, 2006).

Thirlway, Hugh. 'The Sources of International Law', in M. D. Evans (ed.), I*nternational Law, 3nd ed* (Oxford: Oxford University Press, 2010).

Van Assche, Cedric. "Article 12 Convention of 1969", in Olivier Corten & Pierre Klein, eds., *The Vienna Conventions on the Law of Treaties: A Commentary* (Oxford: Oxford University Press, 2011).

Verdross, Alfred. "Les principes généraux du droit dans le système des sources du droit international public" in Faculté de Droit de L'Université de Genève, ed, *Recueil d'études de droit international : en hommage à Paul Guggenheim* (Genève: La tribune de Genève, 1968).

Virally, Michel. "Le rôle des "principes" dans le développement du droit international" in Faculté de Droit de L'Université de Genève, ed, *Recueil d'études de droit international : en hommage à Paul Guggenheim* (Genève: La tribune de Genève, 1968).

3.3 Articles

Akehurst, Michael. "The Hierarchy of the Sources of International Law" (1975) 47:1 BYIL 274.

Andenas, Mads. "International Court of Justice, Case Concerning Ahmadou Sadio Diallo (Republic Of Guinea v. Democratic Republic Of The Congo) Judgment of 30 November 2010" (2011) 60 ICLQ 810.

Arai, Yutaka "The Margin of Appreciation Doctrine in the Jurisprudence of Article 8 of the European Convention on Human Rights" (1998) 16 Neth Q Hum Rts 41.

Aust, Anthony. "The Theory and Practice of Informal International Instruments" (1986) 35 ICLQ 787.

Baker, Roozbeh B. "Customary International Law in the 21st Century: Old Challenges and New Debates" [2010] 21:1 EJIL 173.

Bassiouni, M. Cherif. "A Functional Approach to General Principles of International Law" (1989-1990) 11 Mich J Int'l L 768.

Bassiouni, M. Cherif. "International Crimes: Jus Cogens and Obligation Erga Omnes" (1996) 59:4 L. & Cont. Probs 63.

Baxter, R.R. "International Law in Her Infinite Variety" (1980) 29 ICLQ 549.

Bederman, David J. "Reception of the Classical Tradition in International Law: Grotius' De Jure Belli ac Pacis" (1996) 10 Emory Int'l L Rev 1.

Bjorge, Eirik. "Ahmadou Sadio Diallo (Republic of Guinea v. Democratic Republic of The Congo" 105 Am. J. Int'l L. 534.

Bleicher, Samuel A. "The Legal Significance of Re-Citation of General Assembly Resolutions" (1969) 63:3 AJIL 444.
Blix, Hans. "The Requirement of Ratification" (1953) 30 Brit YB Int'l L 352.
Borchard, Edwin M. "'Responsibility of States,' at The Hague Codification Conference" (1930) 24 AJIL 517.
Bordin, Fernando Lusa. "Procedural Developments at the International Court of Justice" (2012) 11:2 Law & Prac Int'l Courts & Trib 325.
Boudreault, François, "Identifying Conflicts of Norms: The ICJ Approach in the Case of the Jurisdictional Immunities of the State (Germany v. Italy: Greece Intervening)" (2012) 25 Leiden J Int'l L 1003.
Brandon, Michael. "Analysis of the Terms 'Treaty' and 'International Agreement' for Purposes of Registration Under Article 102 of the United Nations Charter" (1953) 47 AJIL 49.
Brunnée, Jutta & Stephen J. Toope, "International Law and Constructivism: Elements of an Interactional Theory of International Law" (2000-2001) 39 Colum J Transnat'l L 19.
Bruun, Lori. "Beyond the 1948 Convention Emerging Principles of Genocide in Customary International Law" (1993) 17 Md J Int'l L & Trade 193.
Caflisch, Lucius & Antônio Augusto Cançado Trindade, "Les conventions américaine et européenne des droits de l'homme et le droit international general" (2004) 108 RGDP 5.
Caplan, Lee M. "State Immunity, Human Rights, and Jus Cogens: A Critique of the Normative Hierarchy Theory" (2003) 97 AJIL 741.
Charlesworth, H. C. M. "Customary International Law and the Nicaragua Case" (1984-1987) 11 Austl YB Int'l L 1.
Charlesworth, Hilary & Christine Chinkin, "The Gender of Jus Cogens" (1993) 15 Hum Rts Q 64.
Charney, Jonathan I. "Universal International Law" (1993) 87 AJIL 529.
Cheng, Bin. "General principles of law as a subject for international codification" (1951) 4 Curr Legal Probs 35.
Cheng, Bin. "United Nations Resolutions on Outer Space: 'Instant' International Customary law?" (1965) 5 Indian J Int'l L 23.
Ciampi, Annalisa. "The Italian Court of Cassation Asserts Civil Jurisdiction over Germany in a Criminal Case Relating to the Second World War: The Civitella Case" (2009) 7:3 J. Int'l Criminal Just 597.
Chodosh, Hiram E. "Neither Treaty nor Custom: The Emergence of Declarative International Law" (1991) 26 Tex. Int'l L. J. 90.
Christenson, Gordon A. "Jus Cogens. Guarding Interests Fundamental to International Society" (1988) 28 Va J Int'l L 585.
Cohen, Harlan Grant. "Finding International Law: Rethinking the Doctrine of Sources", (2007) 93 Iowa L Rev 65.
Conklin, William E. "The Peremptory Norms of the International Community" (2012) 23:3 EJIL 837.
Conklin, William E. "The Peremptory Norms of the International Community: A Rejoinder to Alexander Orakhelashvili" (2012) 23:3 EJIL 869.
Czapliński, Wladyslaw. "Sources of International Law in the Nicaragua Case" (1989) 38 ICLQ 151.
d'Aspremont, Jean. "Wording in International Law" (2012) 25 Leiden J Int'l L 1.
D'Amato, Anthony. "Nicaragua and International Law: The "Academic" and the 'Real'" (1985) 79 AJIL 657.
D'Amato, Anthony. "Softness in International Law: A Self-Serving Quest for New Legal Materials: A Reply to Jean d'Aspremont" (2009) 20:3 EJIL 897.
D'Amato, Anthony. "Trashing Customary International Law" (1987) 81 AJIL 101.
Danilenko, Gennady M. "International Jus Cogens: Issues of Law-Making" (1991) 2 EJIL 42.
De Brabandere, Eric. "Individuals in Advisory Proceedings Before the International Court of Justice: Equality of the Parties and the Court's Discretionary Authority" (2012) 11:2 Law & Prac Int'l Courts & Trib 253.

De Sena, Pasquale & Francesca De Vittor, "State Immunity and Human Rights: The Italian Supreme Court Decision on the Ferrini Case" (2005) 16 EJIL 89.

De Visscher, Charles. "Contribution a l'etude des sources du droit international" [1933] Rev de Dr int et de Leg Comparee 395.

Dekker, Ige F. & Wouter G. Werner, "The Completeness of International Law and Hamlet's Dilemma - Non Liquet, The Nuclear Weapons Case and Legal Theory" (1999) 68 Nordic J Int'l L 225.

del-Cerro, Maria A. "Paper Battle on The River Uruguay: The International Dispute Surrounding the Construction of Pulp Mills" (2007) 20 Geo Int'l Envtl L Rev 161.

Doswald-Beck, Louise. "International humanitarian law and the Advisory Opinion of the International Court of Justice on the legality of the threat or use of nuclear weapons" (1997) 316 Int'l Rev. Red Cross 35.

Dupuy, Pierre Marie. "Soft Law and the International Law of the Environment" (1990-1991) 12 Mich J Int'l L 420.

Dzehtsiarou, Kanstantsin. "European Consensus and the Evolutive Interpretation of the European Convention on Human Rights", (2011) 12 German LJ 1730.

Elias, Olufemi. "The Nature of the Subjective Element in Customary International Law" [1995] 44:3 ICLQ 501.

Ellis, Jaye "General Principles and Comparative Law" (2011) 22:4 EJIL 949.

Espósito, Carlos. "Jus Cogens and Jurisdictional Immunities of States at the International Court of Justice: A Conflict Does Exist" (2011) 12 Italian Y. Int'l L. (via SSRN) <http://ssrn.com/abstract=2103482>.

Falk, Richard A. "Nuclear Weapons, International Law and the World Court: A Historic Encounter" (1997) 91:1 AJIL 64.

Falk, Richard A. "On the Quasi-Legislative Competence of the General Assembly" (1966) 60:4 AJIL 782.

Falk, Richard A. "On the Quasi-Legislative Competence of the General Assembly" (1966) 60:4 AJIL 782.

Falk, Richard A. "The Adequacy of Contemporary Theories of International Law–Gaps in Legal Thinking" (1964) 50 Va L Rev 231.

Fischer-Lescano, Andreas & Gunther Teubner, "Regime-Collisions: The Vain Search for Legal Unity in the Fragmentation of Global Law" (2004) 25:4 Mich J Int'l L999.

Fitzmaurice, Gerald G. "Do Treaties Need Ratification?" (1934) 15 Brit YB Int'l L 113;

Fitzmaurice, Gerald G. "Law and Procedure of the International Court of Justice: Treaty Interpretation and Certain Other Treaty Points" (1951) 28 Brit YB Int'l L 1;

Fitzmaurice, Malgosia. "The Tale of Two Judges: Sir Hersch Lauterpacht and Sir Gerald Fitzmaurice Human Rights and the Interpretation of Treaties" (2008) 61 Rev Hell D I 125.

Franck, Thomas M. "Some Observations on the ICJ's Procedural and Substantive Innovations" (1987) 81 AJIL 116.

Franck, Thomas M. "The Decision of the ICJ in the Nuclear Test Cases" (1975) 69 AJIL 612.

French, Duncan. "Treaty Interpretation and the Incorporation of Extraneous Legal Rules" (2006) 55 ICLQ 281.

Friedmann, Wolfgang. "The Uses of General Principles in the Development of International Law" (1963) 57 AJIL 279.

Garner, James W. "The International Binding Force of Unilateral Oral Declarations" (1933) 27:3 AJIL 493.

George, William P. "Grotius, Theology, and International Law: Overcoming Textbook Bias" (1999-2000) 14:2 J L & Religion 605.

Ghandhi, Sandy. "Human Rights and the International Court of Justice The Ahmadou Sadio Diallo Case" (2011) 11:3 Hum Rights Law Rev 527.

Glenn, H. Patrick. "A Concept of Legal Tradition" (2008-2009) 34 Queen's L.J. 427.

Goldmann, Matthias. "We Need to Cut Off the Head of the King: Past, Present, and Future Approaches to International Soft Law" (2012) 25:2 Leiden J I L 335.

Gourgourinis, Anastasios. "The Distinction between Interpretation and Application of Norms in International Adjudication" [2011] 2:1 J Int'l Dispute Settlement 31.

Green, L. C. "Book Reviews: A Text-Book of International Law. By Professor Alf Ross", (1948) 2:2 Int'l L Q 275.

Guillaume, Gilbert. "The Use of Precedent by International Judges and Arbitrators" (2011) 2:1 at J. Int. Disp. Settlement 5.

Hall, Stephen. "The Persistent Spectre: Natural Law, International Order and the Limits of Legal Positivism" [2001] 12 EJIL 269.

Hart, H.L.A. "Book Reviews" (1964-1965) 78 Harv L Rev 1281.

Hart, H.L.A. "Positivism and the Separation of Law and Morals" (1958) 71 Harv L Rev 593.

Higgins, Rosalyn. "Policy Considerations and the International Judicial Process" (1968) 17:1 ICLQ 58 .

Hollis, Duncan B. "Why State Consent Still Matters - Non-State Actors, Treaties, and the Changing Sources of International Law" (2005) 23:1 Berkeley J Int'l L 137.

Hoss, Cristina, Santiago Villalpando and Sandesh Sivakumaran, "Nicaragua: 25 Years Late" (2012) 25 Leiden J Int'l L 131.

Hossain, Kamrul. "The Concept of Jus Cogens and the Obligation under the U.N. Charter" (2005) 3 Santa Clara J Int'l L 72.

Hudson, Manley O. "The Succession of the International Court of Justice to the Permanent Court of International Justice" (1957) 51:3 AJIL 569.

Hutchinson, David. "The Significance of the Registration or Non-registration of an International Agreement in determining whether or not it is a Treaty" (1993) 46 Curr Legal Probs 257.

Jacobs, Francis G. "Varieties of Approach to Treaty Interpretation: With Special Reference to the Draft Convention on the Law of Treaties before the Vienna Diplomatic Conference" (1969) 18 ICLQ 318.

Janis, Mark W. "The New Oppenheim and Its Theory of International Law Oppenheim's International Law" (1996) 16:2 Oxford J Leg Stud 329.

Jennings, Robert Y. "What is International Law and How Do We Tell It When We See It?" (1981) 37 Ann suisse dr int 59.

Jia, Bing Bing. "The Immunity of State Officials for International Crimes Revisited" (2012) 10 J Int'l Criminal Just 1303.

Joyner, Christopher C. "U.N. General Assembly Resolutions and International Law: Rethinking the Contemporary Dynamics of Norm-Creation" (1981) 11 Cal W Int'l LJ 445.

Kammerhofer, Jörg & André de Hoogh, "All Things to All People? The International Court of Justice and its Commentators" (2008) 18 EJIL 971.

Kammerhofer, Jörg. "Kelsen – Which Kelsen? A Reapplication of the Pure Theory to International Law" (2009) 22:2 Leiden J Int'l L 225.

Kammerhofer, Jörg. "Systemic Integration, Legal Theory and the International Law Commission" 19 Finnish YB Int'l L 157.

Kammerhofer, Jörg. "The Benefits of the Pure Theory of Law for International Lawyers, Or: What Use Is Kelsenian Theory" (2006) 12 Int'l L Theory 5.

Kammerhofer, Jörg. "Uncertainty in the Formal Sources of International Law: Customary International Law and Some of Its Problems" (2004) 15:3 EJIL 523.

Kelly, Patrick. "The Twilight of Customary International Law" (1999-2000) 40 Va J Int'l L 449.

Kennedy, David. "A new stream of international law scholarship" (1988-1989) 7 Wis Int'l LJ 1.

Kennedy, David. "The Sources of International Law" (1987) 2 Am U J Int'l L & Pol'y 2.

Kennedy, David. "Theses about International Law discourse" (1980) 23 Ger Yb Int'l L 353.

Kahgan, Carin. "Jus Cogens and the Inherent Right to Self-Defense" (1997) 3 ILSA J Int'l & Comp L 767.

Kingsbury, Benedict. "Concept of Compliance as a Function of Competing Conceptions of International Law", (1997-1998) 19 Mich J Int'l L 345.

Kirgis, Jr., Frederic L. "Custom on a Sliding Scale" (1987) 81 AJIL 146.

Klabbers, Jan. 'The Redundancy of Soft Law' (1996) 65 Nordic J Int'l L 167.

Klabbers, Jan. 'The Undesirability of Soft Law' (1998) 67 Nordic J Int'l L 381.
Klabbers, Jan. "Qatar v. Bahrain: the concept of 'treaty' in international law" (1995) 33 Archiv des Völkerrechts 361.
Klein, David F. "A Theory for the Application of the Customary International Law of Human Rights by Domestic Courts" (1988) 13 Yale J Int'l L 332.
Kleinlein, Thomas. "Judicial Lawmaking by Judicial Restraint? The Potential of Balancing in International Economic Law" 12:5 Ger LJ 1141.
Knight, Stephen J & Angus J. O'Brien, "Ahmadou Sadio Diallo-Republic of Guinea v. Democratic Republic of The Congo-Clarifying the Scope of Diplomatic Protection of Corporate and Shareholder Rights" (2008) 9 Melb J Int'l L 151.
Koskenniemi, Martti. "'The Lady Doth Protest Too Much' Kosovo, and the Turn to Ethics in International Law" (2002) 65:2 Modern L Rev 159.
Koskenniemi, Martti. "Case Analysis: Faith, Identity, and the Killing of the Innocent: International Lawyers and Nuclear Weapons" (1997) 10:01 Leiden J Int'l L 137.
Koskenniemi, Martti. "Letter to the Editors of the Symposium" (2004) 36 Stud Transnat'l Legal Pol'y 109.
Kunz, Josef L. "Book Reviews and Notes: A Text-Book of International Law. By Alf Ross" (1949) 43 AJIL 197.
Lasswell, Harold D. & Myres S. McDougal, "Legal Education and Public Policy: Professional Training in the Public Interest" (1943) 52 Yale LJ 203.
Lillich, Richard B. "The Growing Importance of Customary International Human Rights Law" (1995/96) 25 Ga J Int'l & Comp L 1.
Linderfalk, Ulf. "The Effect of Jus Cogens Norms: Whoever Opened Pandora's Box, Did You Ever Think About the Consequences?" (2008) 18:5 EJIL 853.
Linderfalk, Ulf. "The Creation of Jus Cogens – Making Sense of Article 53 of the Vienna Convention" (2011) 71 ZaöRV 359.
Linderfalk, Ulf. "What Is So Special About Jus Cogens? – On the Difference between the Ordinary and the Peremptory International Law" (2012) 14 Int'l Community L. Rev. 3.
Lixinski, Lucas. "Treaty Interpretation by the Inter-American Court of Human Rights: Expansionism at the Service of the Unity of International Law" (2010) 21:3 EJIL 585.
Love, Ben. "Introductory note to the International Court of Justice: Jurisdictional Immunities of the State (Germany v. Italy: Greece Intervening)" (2012) 51 ILM 563.
McDougal, Myres S. & W. Michael Reisman. "The Prescribing Function in World Constitutive Process: How International Law Is Made" (1979) 6 Yale Stud World Pub Ord 249.
McDougal, Myres S. "A Footnote", (1963) 57 AJIL 383.
McDougal, Myres S. "Some Basic Theorethical Concepts About International Law: A Policy-Oriented Framework of Inquiry" 4:3 J Conflict Resolution 337.
McDougal, Myres S., Harold D. Lasswell & W. Michael Reisman. "Theories about International Law: Prologue to a Configurative Jurisprudence" (1967-1968) 8 Va J Int'l L 188.
McGregor, Lorna. "State Immunity and Jus Cogens" (2006) 55 ICLQ 437.
McLachlan, Campbell. "The Principle of Systemic Integration and Article 31(3)(c) of the Vienna Convention" (2005) 54:2 ICLQ 279.
Meron, Theodor. "Editorial Comment: Revival of Customary Humanitarian Law" (2005) 99 AJIL 817.
Meron, Theodor. "The Geneva Conventions as Customary Law" (1987) 81 AJIL 348.
Meron, Theodor. "On a Hierarchy of International Human Rights" (1986) 80 AJIL 1.
Mitchell, David S. "The Prohibition of Rape in International Humanitarian Law as a Norm of Jus Cogens: Clarifying the Doctrine" (2004) 15 Duke J Comp & Int'l L 219.
Morgenthau, Hans J. "Positivism, Functionalism, and International Law", (1940) 34:2 AJIL 260.
Morrison, Fred L. "Legal Issues in the Nicaragua Opinion" (1987) 81 AJIL 160.
Nahlik, S. E. "The Grounds of Invalidity and Termination of Treaties", (1971) 65 AJIL 736.
Neuman, Gerald L. "Import, Export, and Regional Consent in the Inter-American Court of Human Rights" (2008) 19:1 EJIL 101.

Öberg, Marko Divac. "The Legal Effects of Resolutions of the UN Security Council and General Assembly in the Jurisprudence of the ICJ" (2006) 16:5 EJIL 879.
Onuf, N.G. & Richard K. Birney. "Peremptory Norms of International Law: Their Source, Function and Future" (1974) 4 Denv. J. Int'l L. & Pol'y 187.
Oosterveld, Valerie. "The Definition of Gender in the Rome Statute of the International Criminal Court: A Step Forward or Back for International Criminal Justice" (2005) 18 Harv Hum Rts J 1.
Oppenheim, Lassa. "The Science of International Law Its Tasks and Method" (1908) 2 AJIL 313.
Orakhelashvili, Alexander. "Peremptory Norms of the International Community: A Reply to William E. Conklin" (2012) 23 EJIL 863.
Orakhelashvili, Alexander. "Restrictive Interpretation of Human Rights Treaties in the Recent Jurisprudence of the European Court of Human Rights" (2003) 14:3 EJIL 529.
Orakhelashvili, Alexander. "State Immunity and International Public Order Revisited" (2006) 49 GYIL 327.
Parker, Karen & Lyn Beth Neylon. "Jus Cogens: Compelling the Law of Human Rights" (1989) 12 Hastings Int'l & Comp L Rev 411.
Paust, Jordan. "The Reality of Jus Cogens", (1991-1992) 7 Conn J Int'l L 81.
Pauwelyn, Joost. "The Role of Public International Law in the WTO: How far can we go?" (2001) 95:3 AJIL 535.
Payne, Cymie R. "Pulp Mills on the River Uruguay (Argentina v. Uruguay)" (2011) 105:1 AJIL 94.
Perkins, John A. "The Changing Foundations of International Law: From State Consent to State Responsibility" (1997) 15 BU Int'l LJ 433.
Peters, Anne. "Humanity as the A and {Omega} of Sovereignty" (2009) 20:3 EJIL 513.
Petersen, Niels. "Customary Law Without Custom? Rules, Principles, and the Role of State Practice in International Norm Creation" (2008) 23 Am U Int'l L Rev 275.
Petersmann, Ernst-Ulrich. "Human Rights, International Economic Law and 'Constitutional Justice'", (2008) 19:4 EJIL 769.
Randall, Kenneth C. "Universal Jurisdiction under International Law" (1988) 66 Tex L Rev 785.
Reinisch, August. "The Immunity of International Organizations and the Jurisdiction of their Administrative Tribunals" (2008) 7:2 Ch J Int'l L 285.
Reisman, W. Michael. "Soft Law and Law Jobs" (2011) 2:1 J. Int'l Disp Settlement 25.
Reisman, W. Michael. "The View from the New Haven School of International Law" (1992) 86 Am Soc Int'l L Proc 118.
Reisman, W. Michael. "Unratified Treaties and Other Unperfected Acts in International Law: Constitutional Functions" (2002) 35 35 Vand J Transnat'l L 729.
Rietiker, Daniel. "The Principle of 'Effectiveness' in the Recent Jurisprudence of the European Court of Human Rights: Its Different Dimensions and Its Consistency with Public International Law – No Need for the Concept of Treaty *Sui Generis*" (2010) 79 Nordic J Int'l L 245.
Roberts, Anthea Elizabeth. "Traditional and Modern Approaches to Customary International Law: A Reconciliation" (2001) 95:4 AJIL 757.
Ronen, Yaël. "Participation of Non-State Actors in ICJ Proceedings" (2012) 11 L. and Practice of Int'l Courts and Tribunals 77.
Rubin, Alfred P. "The International Legal Effects of Unilateral Declarations" (1977) 71 AJIL 1.
Ruiz Fabri, Hélène. "Enhancing the Rhetoric of Jus Cogens" (2012) 23:4 EJIL 1049.
Sadat, Leila Nadya. "Custom, Codification and Some Thoughts about the Relationship between the Two: Article 10 of the ICC Statute" (1999-2000) 49 DePaul L Rev 909.
Samson, Mélanie. "High Hopes, Scant Resources: A Word of Scepticism about the Anti-Fragmentation Function of Article 31(3)(c) of the Vienna Convention on the Law of Treaties" (2011) 24 Leiden J Int'l L 701.
Sands, Philippe. "Treaty, Custom and the Cross-fertilization of International Law" (1998) 1 Yale Human Rts & Dev LJ 85.
Schachter, Oscar. "The Twilight Existence of Nonbinding International Agreements" (1977) 71 AJIL 296.

Scheuner, Ulrich. "Conflict of Treaty Provisions with a Peremptory Norm of General International Law" (1969) 29 ZaöRV 28.
Schwebel, Stephen M. "The Effect of Resolutions of the U.N. General Assembly on Customary International Law" (1979) 73 Am Soc Int'l L Proc 301.
Scott, James Brown. "The Draft Scheme of the Permanent Court of International Justice" (1920) 7 International Conciliation 507.
Shelton, Dinah. "Normative Hierarchy in International Law" (2006) 100:2 AJIL 291 at 322.
Shelton, Dinah. "Righting Wrongs: Reparations in the Articles on State Responsibility" (2002) 96 AJIL 833.
Sherman, Gordon E. "Jus Gentium and International Law", [1918] 12:1 AJIL 56.
Sherwin, Emily. "Legal Taxonomy" (2009) 15:1 Legal Theory 25.
Shklar, Judith N. "Comment On Avineri" [1973]:1 Political Theory 399.
Simma, Bruno. "Mainstreaming Human Rights: The Contribution of the International Court of Justice" (2012) 3:1 J Int Disp Settlement 7.
Simma, Bruno and Phillip Alston, Sources of Human Rights Law: Custom, Jus Cogens, and General Principles, (1988-1989) 12 Aust. YBIL 82.
Sohn, Louis B. "Generally Accepted International Rules" (1986) 61 Wash L Rev 1073.
Somos, Mark. "Secularization in *De Iure Praedae*: from Bible Criticism to International Law" (2005–2007) 26:1 Grotiana 147.
Spiermann, Ole. "A National Lawyer Takes Stock: Professor Ross' Textbook and Other Forays into International Law", (2003) 14:4 EJIL 675.
Spiermann, Ole. "'Who Attempts Too Much Does Nothing Well': The 1920 Advisory Committee of Jurists and the Statute of the Permanent Court of International Justice" (2002) 73 Brit YB Int'l L 187.
Steinhardt, Ralph G. "The International Court of Justice at Several Crossroads" (2009) 103 Am Soc Int'l L Proc 397.
Stone, Julius. "Non Liquet and the Function of Law in the International Community" (1959) 35 Brit YB Int'l L 124.
Suzuki, Eisuke. "The New Haven School of International Law: An Invitation to a Policy-Oriented Jurisprudence", (1974) 1 Yale Stud World Pub Ord 6.
Talmon, Stefan. "Jus Cogens after Germany v. Italy: Substantive and Procedural Rules Distinguished" (2012) 25 Leiden J Int'l L 979.
Thirlway, Hugh. "The International Court of Justice 1989-2009: at The Heart Of The Dispute Settlement System?" (2010) 57 NILR 347.
Tzevelekos, Vassilis P. "The Use of Article 31(3)(c) of the VCLT in the Case Law of the ECtHR: An Effective Anti-Fragmentation Tool or a Selective Loophole for the Reinforcement of Human Rights Teleology? Between Evolution and Systemic Integration" (2010) 31 Mich J Int'l L 621.
Vermeer-Künzli, Annemarieke. "Diallo and the Draft Articles: The Application of the Draft Articles on Diplomatic Protection in the Ahmadou Sadio Diallo Case" (2007) 20:04 Leiden J Int'l L 941.
Villalpando, Santiago. "Editorial: On the International Court of Justice and the Determination of Rules of Law" (2013) 26:3 Leiden J Int'l L 1.
Viñuales, Jorge E. "The Contribution of the International Court of Justice to the Development of International Environmental Law: A Contemporary Assessment" (2008-2009) 32 Fordham Int'l LJ 232.
Weil, Prosper. "'The Court cannot conclude definitively . . .' non liquet revisited" (1997) 36 Colum J Transnat'l L 109.
Weil, Prosper., "Towards relative normativity in international law?" (1983) 77 AJIL 413.
Weisburd, Arthur A. "Customary International Law: The Problem of Treaties" (1988) 21 Vand J Transnat'l L 1.
Weston, Burns H. "Nuclear weapons and the World Court: ambiguity's consensus" (1997) 7:2 Transnat'l L & Contemp Probs 371.

Wet, Erika de. "The Emergence of International and Regional Value Systems as a Manifestation of the Emerging International Constitutional Order" (2006) Leiden J Int'l L 611.
Wildhaber, Luzius. "European Court of Human Rights", (2002) 40 Can. Y.B. Int'l L. 309.
Xue Yang, Elton Tan. "The Jurisdictional Immunities Case: Between Immunity and Impunity - Jurisdictional Immunities of the States (Germany v. Italy: Greece Intervening) - Judgment of 3 February 2012, International Court of Justice" [2012] Oxford U Undergraduate LJ 32.
Zemanek, Karl. "Was Hugo Grotius Really in Favour of the Freedom of the Seas?", (1999) 1 J Hist Int'l L 48.

3.4 Collected Courses of The Hague Academy of International Law

Abi-Saab, George. "Cours général de droit international public" (1987) 207 Rec des Cours 9 at 155.
Arangio-Ruez, Gaetano. "The normative role of the General Assembly of the United Nations and the Declaration of Principles of Friendly Relations" (1972) Rec des Cours 419 at 470.
Bishop, WM.W. "General course of public international law" (1965) 115 Rec de Cours 147.
Bourquin, Maurice. "Règles générales du droit de la paix" (1931) 35 Rec des Cours 1.
Cançado Trindade, Antônio Augusto. "International law for humankind: towards a new jus gentium (I). General course on public international law" (2005) 316 Rec des Cours 9.
Castberg, Frede. "La méthodologie du droit international public" (1933) 43 Rec des Cours 309.
Charney, Jonathan I. "Is international law threatened by multiple international tribunals?" (1998) 271 Rec des Cours 101.
De Visscher, Charles. "La codification du droit international" (1925) 6 Rec des Cours 325.
Fitzmaurice, Gerald G. "The contribution of the Institute of International Law to the development of international law" (1973) 138 Rec des Cours 203.
Frowein, Jochen A. "Reactions by not directly affected states to breaches of public international law" (1994) 348 Rec des Cours 345.
Gómez Robledo, Antonio. "Le ius cogens international : sa genèse, sa nature, ses fonctions" (1981) 172 Rec des Cours 9.
Gaja, Giorgo. "Jus Cogens Beyond de Vienna Convention" (1981) 172 Rec des Cours 279.
Guggenheim, Paul, "Contribution à l'histoire des sources du droit des gens" (1958) 94 Rec des Cours 5.
Heilborn, Paul. "Les sources du droit international" (1926) 11 Rec des Cours 1.
Jennings, Robert Y. "General course on principles of international law" [1967] 121 Rec des Cours 323.
Kelsen, Hans. "Les rapports de système entre le droit interne et le droit international public" (1926) 14 Rec des Cours 227.
Kelsen, Hans. "Théorie du droit international public" (1953) 84 Rec des Cours 1.
Kelsen, Hans. "Théorie générale du droit international public. Problèmes choisis" (1932) 42 Rec des Cours 117.
Korff, Serge A. "Introduction à l'histoire du droit international" (1923) 1 Rec des Cours 1.
Le Fur, Louis. "La Théorie du Droit Naturel" (1927) 18 Rec des Cours 260.
McDougal, Myres S. "International law, power, and policy: a contemporary conception", (1953) 82 Rec des Cours 133 at 143
Mendelson, Maurice H. "The formation of customary international law" (1998) 272 Rec des Cours 155.
Meron, Theodor. "International law in the age of human rights: general course on public international law" (2003) 301 Rec des Cours 9.
Schachter, Oscar. "International law in theory and practice: general course in public international law" (1982) 178 Rec des Cours 9.

Slaughter, Anne-Marie. "International Law and International Relations" (2000) 285 Rec des Cours 9 at 217
Thirlway, Hugh. "Concepts, principles, rules and analogies: international and municipal legal reasoning" (2002) 294 Rec des Cours 265.
Truyol Y Serra, Antonio. "Théorie du droit international public : cours general" (1981) 173 Rec des Cours 9.
Tunkin, Grigory I. "Co-existence and international law", [1958] 95 Rec des Cours 1 at 26.
Verdross, Alfred. "Les principes généraux du droit dans la jurisprudence internationale" (1935) 52 Rec des Cours 191.
Verhoeven, Joe. "Considérations sur ce qui est commun : Cours général de droit international public" (2008) 334 Rec des Cours 9.
Waldock, Humphrey. "General course on public international law" (1962) 106 Rec des Cours 1.
Weil, Prosper. "Le droit international en quête de son identité : cours général de droit international public" (1992) 237 Rec des Cours 11.
Wolff, Karl. "Les principles généraux du droit applicables dans les rapports internationaux" (1931) 36 Rec des Cours 479.
Zemanek, Karl. "The legal foundations of the international system: general course on public international law" (1997) 266 Rec des Cours 9.

4 Other

Anno, Hideaki. *Evangelion: 1.11 – You Are (Not) Alone*, 2010, Blu-ray Disc (Tokio: Khara Studio, 2010).
"Collaboration of the American Institute of International Law with the Pan American Union" (1926) 20 AJIL Supp. 300.
"Cumbre del MERCOSUR Mendoza 2012: decisión sobre la suspensión del Paraguay en el MERCOSUR en aplicación del protocolo de Ushuaia sobre compromiso democrático", online: Ministerio de Relaciones Exteriores y Culto, Republica Argentina <http://www.mrecic.gov.ar/es/cumbre-del-mercosur-mendoza-2012-decision-sobre-la-suspension-del-paraguay-en-el-mercosur-en>.
"Paraguay's impeachment: Lugo out in the cold" The Economist (30 June 2012) online: The Economist <http://www.economist.com/node/21557802>.
"Report of the Informal Inter-Allied Committee on the Future of the Permanent Court of International Justice: February 10, 1944" (1945) 39:1 AJIL Supp. 1.
"The Core International Human Rights Instruments and their monitoring bodies", online: Office of the High Commissioner on Human Rights <http://www.ohchr.org/EN/ProfessionalInterest/Pages/CoreInstruments.aspx>.
Comunicado de Prensa", 7 December 2012, online: Ministerio de Relaciones Exteriores de Paraguay <http://www.mre.gov.py/v1/Adjuntos/defensadelosprincipiosDIP/Comunicado-sobre-Reunion-del-Mercosur.pdf>.
Dig. 1.2.1-2 (Ulpian)
Eritrea-Ethiopia Claims Commission, "Rules of Procedure" online. Permanent Court of Arbitration <http://www.pcacases.com>.
Fuentes, Carlos Iván. Redefining Canadian Aboriginal title: a critique towards an Inter-American doctrine of indigenous right to land (LL.M. Thesis, McGill University, Faculty of Law, 2006) online: eScholarship@McGill <http://digitool.library.mcgill.ca/R/>.
Holtermann, Jakob v. H. "Getting Real Or Staying Positive Legal Realism(s), Legal Positivism And The Prospects Of Naturalism In Jurisprudence" online: University of Copenhagen <http://curis.ku.dk/ws/files/40358538/HOLTERMANN_Getting_real_or_staying_positive_DRAFT_2012_05_27.pdf>.

Institut de Droit International, "Projet de règlement pour la procédure arbitrale internationale, online: Institut de Droit international", Session of The Hague – 1875, <http://www.idi-iil.org/idiF/resolutionsF/1875_haye_01_fr.pdf>.

Institut de Droit International, "The Distinction Between Military Objectives and Non-Military Objects in General and Particularly the Problems Associated with Weapons of Mass Destruction", Session of Edinburgh – 1969, online: Institut de Droit international <http://www.idi-iil.org/idiE/resolutionsE/1969_edi_01_en.pdf>.

Institut de Droit International, "The Elaboration of General Multilateral Conventions and of Non-contractual Instruments Having a Normative Function or Objective", Session of Cairo – 1987, online: Institut de Droit international <http://www.idi-iil.org/idiE/resolutionsE/1987_caire_02_en.PDF>.

Institut de Droit International, "The Intertemporal Problem in Public International Law", Session of Wiesbaden – 1975, online: Institut de Droit International <http://www.idi-iil.org/idiE/resolutionsE/1975_wies_01_en.pdf>.

Institut de Droit International, "Vingt et Unième Commission, Les principes généraux de droit comme source du droit des gens (1932) 37 Ann Inst Droit Int'l 283 at 297.

International Commission of Jurists, "Public International Law: Projects to be Submitted for the Consideration of the Sixth International Conference of American States" (1928) 22 AJIL Supp 234 at 239.

International Law Association, Committee on Formation of Customary (General) International Law, "Final Report of the Committee: Statement of Principles Applicable to the Formation of General Customary International Law" (2000) 69 Int'l L Ass'n Rep Conf 712.

International Law Association, Committee on International Human Rights Law and Practice, "Final Report on the Impact of International Human Rights Law on General International Law" (2008) 73 Int'l L Ass'n Rep Conf 663.

Jean Bodin's fifth book of the Commonwealth.

Kammerhofer, Jörg. Unearthing structural uncertainty through neo-Kelsenian consistency: Conflicts of norms in international law, online: SSRN <http://ssrn.com/abstract=1535942>.

Kooijmans, Pieter H. "Human Rights, Universal Values?", Dies Natalis Address, Institute of Social Studies, 12 October 1993, p. 7 online: Erasmus Universiteit Rotterdam <http://lcms.eur.nl/iss/diesnatalis1993OCR.pdf>.

Multilateral Treaties Deposited with the Secretary-General, online: United Nations Treaty Collection: <http://treaties.un.org/pages/ParticipationStatus.aspx>.

Shelton, Dinah. "Humanitarian Law in the Jurisprudence of the Inter-American Human Rights System" online: University of Pretoria <http://web.up.ac.za/sitefiles/file/47/15338/Humanitarian_Law_in_the_Jurisprudence.pdf>.

The Cambridge Dictionary of Philosophy, 1999.

The Gospel of John.

United Nations Treaty Series Database, online: United Nations Treaty Collection: <http://treaties.un.org/ > [UNTS online].

CPSIA information can be obtained at www.ICGtesting.com
Printed in the USA
BVOW06*1140110916

461796BV00005B/9/P

9 783319 439273